British Outlaws of
Literature and History

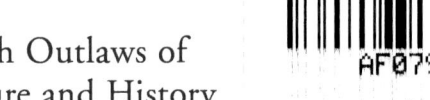

British Outlaws of Literature and History

Essays on Medieval and Early Modern Figures from Robin Hood to Twm Shon Catty

Edited by
Alexander L. Kaufman

McFarland & Company, Inc., Publishers
Jefferson, North Carolina, and London

LIBRARY OF CONGRESS CATALOGUING-IN-PUBLICATION DATA

British outlaws of literature and history : essays on medieval and early modern figures from Robin Hood to Twm Shon Catty / edited by Alexander L. Kaufman.
    p.   cm.

Includes bibliographical references and index.

ISBN 978-0-7864-5877-6
softcover : 50# alkaline paper ∞

1. Outlaws — Great Britain — History. 2. Brigands and robbers — Great Britain — History. 3. Great Britain — History — 1066–1687. 4. Outlaws in literature. 5. English literature — Middle English, 1100–1500 — History and criticism. 6. Literature and society — Great Britain.
I. Kaufman, Alexander L.
HV6453.G7B75   2011
361.1092'241 — dc22   2010046025

BRITISH LIBRARY CATALOGUING DATA ARE AVAILABLE

© 2011 Alexander L. Kaufman. All rights reserved

No part of this book may be reproduced or transmitted in any form or by any means, electronic or mechanical, including photocopying or recording, or by any information storage and retrieval system, without permission in writing from the publisher.

Cover images © 2011 Clipart.com (inset) and Shutterstock.

Manufactured in the United States of America

McFarland & Company, Inc., Publishers
 Box 611, Jefferson, North Carolina 28640
  www.mcfarlandpub.com

For Pauline Freedman

Contents

Acknowledgments ix
Abbreviations xi
Introduction (ALEXANDER L. KAUFMAN) 1

Part I : Outlaws as Outcasts and Outsiders

1. English Jews as Outlaws or Outcasts: The Ritual Murder of Little St. Hugh of Lincoln in Matthew Paris's *Chronica Majora* (KATE MCGRATH) 11
2. Let Her Be Waived: Outlawing Women in Yorkshire, 1293–1294 (JENNIFER BREWER) 28
3. Portraits of Outlaws, Felons, and Rebels in Late Medieval England (BARBARA A. HANAWALT) 45

Part II : Wales and the Marches

4. Fouke le Fitz Waryn and King John: Rebellion and Reconciliation (CATHERINE A. ROCK) 67
5. Fouke le Fitz Waryn: Outlaw or Chivalric Hero? (KATHRYN BEDFORD) 97
6. Social Protest and Narrative Technique in Prichard's *Twm Shon Catty* (MICA DAWN GOULD) 114

Part III : The Robin Hood Tradition

7. Robin Hood: Outlaw or Exile? (ANTHA COTTEN-SPRECKELMEYER) 133
8. Histories of Contexts: Form, Argument, and Ideology in *A Gest of Robyn Hode* (ALEXANDER L. KAUFMAN) 146
9. Popular Devotion and Prosperity Gospel in Early Robin Hood Tales (CRYSTAL KIRGISS) 165

10. The Late Medieval Robin Hood Ballads: Economics Revisited
    (KIMBERLY A. MACUARE THOMPSON) — 179
11. "Where Shall We Rob?": Fantasies of Justice in the Early Robin
    Hood Ballads (MARK LEAHY) — 204
12. "All the yemandry that ys here": *Mankind* and Robin Hood
    (MICHELLE M. BUTLER) — 219

Bibliography — 239
Notes on Contributors — 251
Index — 253

Acknowledgments

My greatest thanks goes to David Hepworth. David was an early champion of this collection; he read a number of these essays and gave helpful and insightful comments on them. The contributors themselves deserve a special amount of praise for their knowledge, scholarly advice, and patience. Several of these essays were presented in different forms at some of the recent International Association for Robin Hood Studies conferences, and a great deal of thanks is given to those who have organized these meetings: Richard Firth Green, Helen Phillips, Lois Potter, Stephen Knight, and Thomas Hahn.

I would also like to thank the greater community of the IARHS for their collegiality and scholarly advice over the years. Thomas H. Ohlgren's support and guidance has been, as usual, second-to-none. Thanks are also due to Edward L. Risden and Kevin J. Harty for their helpful advice on the collection.

At Auburn University at Montgomery, I would like to thank my fellow colleagues in the Department of English and Philosophy, especially my fellow medievalist, Michel Aaij. The faculty and staff at AUM's Library have been instrumental in the completion of this project, especially Karen Williams, the fearless head of Interlibrary Loan. Lastly, I would like to thank my little band for their love and support: Mandy, Cindy, and Abraham.

Abbreviations

Burgess Glyn Burgess, ed. and trans., *Two Medieval Outlaws: Eustace the Monk and Fouke Fitz Waryn* (Cambridge: D. S. Brewer, 2009).

Conlon Denis Joseph Conlon, ed., *Li Romans de Witasse Le Moine: Roman du treizième siècle. Édité daprès le manuscrit, Fonds Français 1553, de la Bibliothèque Nationale, Paris*. University of North Carolina Studies in Romance Languages and Literatures 126 (Chapel Hill: University of North Carolina Press, 1972).

Dobson and Taylor R. B. Dobson and J. Taylor, ed., *Rymes of Robin Hood: An Introduction to the English Outlaw* (London: Alan Sutton, 1989).

EETS Early English Text Society

Hahn Thomas Hahn, ed., *Robin Hood in Popular Culture: Violence, Transgression, and Justice* (Cambridge: D. S. Brewer, 2000).

Hathaway E. J. Hathaway, P. T. Ricketts, C. A. Robson, and A. D. Wilshere, ed., *Fouke le Fitz Waryn*. Anglo-Norman Text Society, 26–28 (Bristol: Basil Blackwell, 1975).

Holt J. C. Holt, *Robin Hood*, rev. ed. (London: Thames and Hudson, 1989).

Keen Maurice Keen, *The Outlaws of Medieval Legend*, rev. ed. (London and New York: Routledge, 2000).

Kew, NA Kew, National Archives

Knight 1994 Stephen Knight, *Robin Hood: A Complete Study of the English Outlaw* (Oxford: Blackwell, 1994).

Knight 1999 Stephen Knight, ed., *Robin Hood: An Anthology of Scholarship and Criticism* (Cambridge: D. S. Brewer 1999).

Knight 2003 Stephen Knight, *Robin Hood: A Mythic Biography* (Ithaca and London: Cornell University Press, 2003).

Knight and Ohlgren Stephen Knight and Thomas Ohlgren, ed., *Robin Hood and Other Outlaw Tales*. TEAMS Middle English Texts (Kalamazoo: Medieval Institute Publications, 2000).

MED *Middle English Dictionary*. Part of the *Middle English Compendium*. Ann Arbor: The University of Michigan, 2001. http://quod.lib.umich.edu/m/med/ (accessed January 17, 2010).

MLN *Modern Language Notes*

n.s. New Series

Ohlgren 2005 Thomas H. Ohlgren, ed., *Medieval Outlaws: Twelve Tales in Modern English Translation*, rev. ed. (West Lafayette: Parlor Press, 2005).

Ohlgren 2007 Thomas H. Ohlgren, *Robin Hood: The Early Poems, 1465–1560: Texts, Contexts, and Ideology* (Newark: University of Delaware Press, 2007).

Phillips 2005 Helen Phillips, ed., *Robin Hood: Medieval and Post-Medieval* (Dublin: Four Courts Press, 2005).

Phillips 2008 Helen Phillips, ed., *Bandit Territories: British Outlaw Traditions* (Cardiff: University of Wales Press, 2008).

PMLA *Publications of the Modern Language Association of America*

o.s. Original Series

Introduction

ALEXANDER L. KAUFMAN

The aim of this collection is to assemble a series of essays on outlaws that contextualize the figures within their literary, historical, and cultural contexts. In doing so, the essays explore the fluid nature of outlawry as a term and a practice, examine the political implications of outlaws on the monarchy and local governments, and discuss how these outlaw narratives fit within the much larger context of early British literature and culture. While many of the outlaws that make up this volume are separated by centuries, this volume examines the many commonalities that exist between the narratives and their main characters, themes, and motifs. Several essays within this volume continue within the tradition of what some scholars might identify as the "new historicism" or "new philology." While I myself am a bit uneasy at placing labels on modes of scholarly criticism, nevertheless, these are two scholarly trajectories that remain central to medieval studies and to the sub-genre that is the focus of this collection of essays: the Matter of the Greenwood. Maurice Keen, in his seminal work on medieval outlaw narratives and their interconnectivity *The Outlaws of Medieval Legend*, argues for a fourth "matter" that is to join the "matters" of Britain, France, and Troy. For Keen, the outlaw narratives of the Middle Ages share certain commonalities; they are in essence "the same stories, merely associated by different authors with the name of a different hero."[1] The forest becomes for the literary outlaws not a place of menace and danger but instead a safe-haven, a sanctuary, and "an asylum from the tyrany of evil lords and a corrupt law."[2] However, it should be underscored that Keen's outlaws were creatures of fiction. And while Hereward and Fouke Fitz Waryn existed, their outlaw narratives tend to minimize the harsh realities of outlaw life in the wild woods.

While forms of popular culture today often portray the life of outlaws through a romantic lens, the life of an outlaw in medieval Britain was one that was nasty and hard. As Keen comments, a sentence of outlawry put the condemned outside the protection of the law of Britain. As an outcast from society, he (and sometimes she) was denied the "ancient inherited privileges at law" and was marked as "civilly dead."³ Moreover, until the thirteenth century, an outlaw could be killed outright without any repercussions. Even if one were inlawed, that individual's property and goods forfeited at the time of outlawry may not necessarily be recovered:

> If anyone has been duly outlawed and later restored to the peace by royal favour, neither he nor his heirs may on that account recover from their lord any inheritance which he had, except by grace and favour of the lord; for the lord king does not wish, when pardoning wrongdoing and outlawry, to infringe thereby on the rights of others.⁴

Thus, even once an outlaw was brought back into the protection of the realm, the stigma of once being outlawed was still very much a presence that was attached to the individual.

As an outlaw, one was certainly a transgressor of the laws of the land. However, there were others in medieval Britain who transgressed (or who were identified as transgressors) who were similar in their actions to outlaws but not necessarily named as such by the courts. Eric Hobsbawm's model of the "social bandit" is one where the scholar identifies a particular type of criminal. For Hobsbawm, social bandits are considered by their people "as heroes, as champions, avengers, fighters for justice, perhaps even leaders of liberation, and in any case as men to be admired, helped, and supported."⁵ Hobsbawm's social bandit is a product of civil unrest within the boundaries of agrarian societies. The medieval period was a time of marginalized individuals, and outlaws were certainly among those who were moved toward the background of the human experience, mostly by their own doing. Like the peasants of Chaucer's *Canterbury Tales*, who are almost always on the periphery of the tales and the pilgrimage, outlaws, too, are some of the more "silent" witnesses to the medieval period.

Part I of this collection examines outlaws and outsiders mainly from historical sources. Kate McGrath's essay brings to fore the question of historical representation of Jews in Matthew Paris's *Chronica Majora* in light of the accusations of ritual murder and the case of Little St. Hugh of Lincoln. The Jews, while expelled in 1290, remained on the minds of the Christian community. While the Jews were vanquished from Britain, they were the subject of numerous anti–Semitic narratives, from Chaucer's *Prioress' Tale* to countless religious texts that expound upon accusations of blood libel, money clipping, usury, the desecration of the Host, and the murder of Christ. McGrath's essay looks at how examples of ritual murder accusations fit into the overall rhetorical strategies of the narrative of Matthew Paris's chronicle. At times, Matthew suggests that the Jews are outlaw-types. As we see, however, Matthew chose to include such anti–Semitic cases in his chronicle because they aided his agenda of representing the Jews as outcasts but not outlaws of Christian society.

Jennifer Brewer's essay is a close study of a court document from late thirteenth-century Yorkshire that records cases of women ordered "exacted and waved"—that is, outlawed—for their crimes. This document, Kew, National Archives JUST 1 1098, presents a number of cases that detail crimes committed by both men and women and the outcome of their sentences. Brewer's essay compares and contrasts the cases of women outlawed by this specific court and examines the types of crimes they committed. While we often think of outlaws as being almost always male, Brewer's piece highlights the very real cases of women outlaws and examines what must have been tense and uncertain times for many who were convicted.

Barbara A. Hanawalt's essay is one that examines the presence of marginal groups in late medieval Britain. Hanawalt proposes three types of portraits to illustrate the varying late medieval perceptions of outlaws, felons, and rebels. Some, like outlaws, are admired and hated. Lower-class political rebels were often intelligent but were disparaged by elite writers. Hanawalt concludes her essay with a study of Eleanor Cobham, who married Duke Humphrey of Gloucester, and who was tried and convicted of sorcery. As Hanawalt demonstrates, these portraits describe how medieval society, at least a portion of it, perceived transgressions in the categories of tolerable, ambiguous, and really heinous.

Part II contains three essays that examine Wales and its border counties as a context for outlaw narratives. The Anglo-Norman ancestral romance *Fouke le Fitz Waryn* dates to around 1330, and the extant prose version appears to be the work of a poet who lived in Ludlow, Shropshire, near the border of Wales. *Fouke le Fitz Waryn* remains an important outlaw narrative that in many ways prefigures the good outlaw stories of the late medieval Robin Hood tradition. Indeed, Keen's "Matter of the Greenwood" is alive and well in *Fouke*, for many scenes of outlawry that are present in *Fouke* reappear in other outlaw texts. The last two-thirds of the romance concern the acts and deeds of Fouke III (d. 1258?) and his period of outlawry. Catherine A. Rock's essay presents a history of the transmission of the manuscript and examines the genre of the text. As Rock examines the structure of other medieval romances, she determines that the romance of *Fouke le Fitz Waryn* blurs traditional genre lines.

Kathryn Bedford's essay examines the characterization of Fouke. *Fouke Fitz Waryn* is one of the Middle Age's most curious overlaps between historical and fictional literature. The duality of Fouke's fictionalized image, as outlaw and as chivalric hero, stands in stark contrast to other contemporary examples, such as Eustace the Monk and Richard I, where events are made to fit a single literary type. Given that *Fouke le Fitz Waryn* places more emphasis on the historical Fouke's period of outlawry, it is the traditional elements of romance, rescuing maidens, single combats and fighting a dragon, that prove particularly interesting. The outlaw motif fits easily onto the historical events as we know them; the chivalric one does not. Bedford's essay explores the process by which historical events an become fiction, for it focuses especially on the extent to which the nature of the fictionalized account was dictated by the events themselves, the circumstances at the time of writing, or the personal interests of individuals with some connection to the events. The conflict that appears within this text between a number of very different literary styles suggests that the demands of each of these influences could not always be met.

The final essay in this section brings us just beyond the traditional ending point of the Middle Ages. Mica Dawn Gould's piece situates the reader in sixteenth-century Wales and the life and times of Twm Siôn Cati (c. 1530–1609), who is often called the Welsh Robin Hood. While there is scant information on his actual outlaw activities, he was pardoned by Elizabeth I in 1559. His legend survives in a number of tales, rhymes, and anecdotes. In 1828, Thomas Jeffrey Llewelyn Prichard wrote *The Comical Adventures of Twm Shon Catty (Thomas Jones, Esq.), Commonly known as the Welsh Robin Hood*. The narrative centers on the titular character who is the natural son of an English nobleman and who is outlawed for his many tricks. After Twm runs, he gradually charms his way up the social ladder by, among other things, rescuing maidens, playing tricks, and eventually becoming the trusted friend and employee of a powerful lord, Sir George Devereux. As in other outlaw tales, such as *Adam Bell* and *The Tale of Gamelyn*, this wily hero not only earns his way back into acceptable society but also eventually becomes a local justice. Gould argues that Prichard's aim was to comment on the condition and cultural life of Wales in the early 19th century. Prichard, Gould believes, is an expert satirist who was determined to create in his readers a sense of Welsh nationalism.

Robin Hood is certainly the most recognizable of all outlaws from the medieval period, or possibly from any historical period in the Western tradition. While some scholars have attempted to find out *who* Robin Hood is (or was), the essays in this collection seek to understand *what* Robin Hood is and what his medieval tales tell us about the contexts in which they were produced. Of late, the field of Robin Hood studies has produced a significant amount of scholarship that has shed light on how Robin Hood and his stories were received in the Middle Ages. Julian Luxford has discovered a brief, pre–Reformation chronicle entry that placed Robin in the reign of Edward I (r. 1272–1307). This note is found on Eton College MS 213, folio 234r, and it paints a rather negative portrait of the outlaw.[6] Chroniclers were not always fond of

Robin; likewise, that he is placed in the thirteenth century supports the growing opinion that the outlaw's literary origins may date from around this time. As Luxford comments, the entry "adds to what is known of medieval perceptions of Robin Hood and his accomplices by representing a voice at once English, monastic (or at least monastic-orientated), and West County in origin. All three contexts are significant."[7]

Thomas Ohlgren has shed new light on the Robin Hood tradition within fifteenth-century mercantile, gentry, and religious contexts. Ohlgren's material philologist approach to the extant Robin Hood manuscripts that contain *Robin Hood and the Monk* (Cambridge University Library, MS Ff.5.48) and *Robin Hood and the Potter* (Cambridge University Library, MS E.e.4.35) has placed the manuscripts, respectively, within the hands of two individuals: Gilbert Pilkington, a Litchfield cleric who was the possible scribe-owner of the manuscript; and Richard Call, the owner of the manuscript, who was the grocer and bailiff of the powerful Paston family and who also secretly married Margery Paston.[8] The textual history of the most significant of the early Robin Hood poems, *A Gest of Robyn Hode*, is still ongoing. Ohlgren and Lister Matheson are in the process of editing all of the extant printed editions of the *Gest* that date from the late medieval and early modern periods. The earliest surviving edition of the *Gest* is made up of fragments from Richard Pynson's *A Lytell Geste of Robyn Hode* (London, 1495?), while the latest is Edward White's from around 1610. White's edition is very similar to William Copland's 1560 printed text. There also exists the "Lettersnijder" edition that was published in Antwerp around 1510–15. York, too, had an edition of the poem, as there is one extant fragment (1506?-9) of the *Gest* that was printed by Hugo Goes.[9] Apart from the variations in spelling in these and other editions, Ohlgren argues that "readers in London, Antwerp, and York responded to [the *Gest*] in different ways and at different times."[10] In the future, when we read the *Gest*, and when scholars write on the poem, which edition of the *Gest* we use may be of some contextual significance.

As Robin Hood's biographer, Stephen Knight sees the potency of Robin Hood: "Robin Hood cannot be constrained by any single view of reality or unreality. Neither solely a myth nor merely biographic, Robin Hood combines both ways of understanding a powerful figure."[11] The essays in this collection that focus on Robin Hood are written within the spirit of Knight's comments. Our contributors are, thus, not concerned with an over-reaching empiricist agenda for the discovery of Robin's origins. Instead, the contributors are interested in the literary Robin Hood of the Middle Ages and his place within the literary and cultural landscape. Antha Cotten-Spreckelmeyer's essay looks at Robin Hood's position within the tradition of exiles from Anglo-Saxon literature. While some may see the two as wholly incongruous, we are, as Cotten-Spreckelmeyer argues, within the world of the greenwood outlaw/exile. This "matter" is one that transcends both time and place. Indeed, one of the earliest of the medieval outlaws was Hereward "the Wake," a Lincolnshire squire who mounted a small and unsuccessful guerrilla-style campaign against William the Conqueror in 1070. Robin's activities in the early poems do indeed remind readers of literary figures from the Anglo-Saxon period, such as Hereward. Cotten-Spreckelmeyer describes how the exiled characters in *Beowulf*, *The Wanderer*, and *The Seafarer* all show notable similarities to the exiled outlaws of the greenwood.

Alexander L. Kaufman's essay focuses on the ways in which *A Gest of Robyn Hode* can be read. The *Gest* remains a decidedly tricky text. While at first glance it may appear as if the *Gest* is a straight-forward narrative with a cast of one-dimensional characters, upon closer inspection the complexity of the narrative's structure and its significant literary, historical, and cultural allusions make the poem anything but a simple read. Kaufman here examines the poem through the use of a historiographical contextualist argument so as to uncover the dominant contextual layers of the *Gest*.

Crystal Kirgiss's essay focuses on one of the dominant themes in the early Robin Hood poems: the role of religion and Robin's attitude toward it. Like many "heroes" of the medieval tradition, Robin is devout, or so he seems. Kirgiss argues here that the forest outlaw is rather choosy about his religious duties and obligations. While Robin is devout, especially to the Virgin Mary, his devotion is ultimately tied to his own financial prosperity.

Kimberly A. Macuare Thompson examines the confluence of medieval economics and Robin Hood's identity. Unlike Robin's later incarnations who "steal from the rich to give to the poor," the medieval outlaw's philosophy seems to be one in which he steals from almost everyone to keep for himself. Robin Hood of the early ballads is not a static figure; indeed, he engages in a remarkable range of often incongruent financial behaviors. Thompson's essay argues that it is in the instability that we should seek the coherence of the medieval ballad texts' economic message. At various times in the ballads, Robin takes on different identities, both through literal disguise and through subtler forms of performance, for the intended purpose of interrogating both the construction and boundaries of the individual subject positions occupied in what Thompson terms the "economic interpellation" of the subject itself. That is, the Robin Hood ballads are interested both in social critique of the various medieval estates — the religious, the mercantile, and the chivalric — and, more broadly, in the process by which all subjects increasingly understood themselves to be constructed by their economic activity.

A number of these essays are concerned with audience's receptions and perceptions of outlaws and their ballads, and Mark Leahy's contribution continues this thread as it relates to aspects of violence and justice in the early Robin Hood poems. In his essay, Leahy first places the ballads within their late medieval audience context. He also reads these texts through the lens of Slavoj Žižek's ideas of fantasies of justice. For Leahy (and perhaps for Žižek), these ballads are not simply expressions of medieval desire for justice in a time when abuse by the upper class was more than rampant, but they are also codified. In essence, these Robin Hood ballads represent how justice could be conceived in such a world.

Violence as a dominant theme is brought forth again in the collection's final essay, which examines the similarities between the characters of Mischief and the Three Worldlings (New Guise, Nowadays, and Nought) of the play *Mankind* with Robin Hood and his band of outlaws. *Mankind* was written most likely in the late 1470s, which would place it within the timeframe of the circulation of a number of the surviving early Robin Hood poems. While these characters are not meant to *be* Robin and his men, they do, nonetheless, resemble the outlaws, replicate many of their actions and behaviors, and evoke the legend. In the late medieval period in England, most people would have known of Robin Hood and his gang through their exposure to Robin Hood play-games, ales, May game and Whitsuntide festivities, and other dramatic performances. The Records of Early English Drama (REED) project has already uncovered numerous Robin Hood references in dramatic records, and scholars such as John Marshall, Alexandra Johnston, and Lois Potter, among others, have demonstrated the centrality of these performances in the continuation (and some might even argue as well the partial creation) of the Robin Hood legend.

In sum, this collection presents a series of essays on outlawry that place us within the context of Britain in the Middle Ages and a bit beyond. They speak of the need for us to consider the historical places in which these outlaws existed, to see these outlaw narratives as texts that speak to one another and are in some cases part of the much larger canon of Western medieval and early modern literature, and to understand the significance of the cultural milieu that produced these figures and their narratives. These essays also allow us a space to see the slipperiness of the term "outlaw." While some of the figures in these essays were indeed officially outlawed by a court, others were not. Yet there exists among outlaws, outsiders, exiles, criminals, renegades, and other transgressors a sense of shared genealogies, personalities, and histories.

NOTES

1. Keen, 65.
2. Ibid., 2.

3. Keen, 9.
4. G. D. G. Hall, ed., and trans., *The Treatise on the Laws and Customs of the Realm of England Commonly Called Glanvill* (Oxford: Clarendon Press, 1993), 91.
5. Eric Hobsbawm, *Bandits* (New York: Delacorte Press, 1969), 11.
6. Julian M. Luxford, "An English Chronicle Entry on Robin Hood," *Journal of Medieval History* 35, no. 1 (2009): 70–76.
7. Ibid., 76.
8. Ohlgren 2007, 35–39, 70–74.
9. Ibid., 97–99.
10. Ibid., 133.
11. Knight 2003, xiii.

PART I

OUTLAWS AS OUTCASTS AND OUTSIDERS

1
English Jews as Outlaws or Outcasts: The Ritual Murder of Little St. Hugh of Lincoln in Matthew Paris's *Chronica Majora*

KATE MCGRATH

As the historian for the Benedictine monastery of St. Albans from 1236–1259, Matthew Paris's work has provided modern scholars with an important resource for understanding thirteenth-century relations between Christian and Jewish communities.[1] In his *Chronica Majora*, Matthew highlights what he considered to be the major political and social events of his times. As is common in historical writings from this period, he does so through a series of interesting anecdotes and narrative descriptions. He, therefore, includes a number of passages that describe either individual Jews or Jewish communities and their interactions with Christians.[2] Modern scholars can learn much from his accounts about medieval mentalities in general and specifically about the transmission of popular opinion about Jewish-Christian relations through Benedictine monastic writing before the expulsion of the Jews in 1290.[3] One of Matthew Paris's focuses in constructing contemporary Jewish-Christian relations is ritual murder accusations for which he includes at least three such cases.[4] Since such charges are clearly not only false but also defamatory and malicious, I am not interested in what might have actually happened in each case as the very nature of the scurrilous charges makes this impossible.[5] Instead, I will examine how ritual murder accusations, and specifically that of Little St. Hugh of Lincoln, fit into the overall rhetorical strategies of Matthew Paris's narrative. Matthew chose to include such cases in his chronicle, because they aided his agenda of representing the Jews as outcasts but not outlaws of Christian society. By charging the Jews with religious deviance but not collective legal transgression, Matthew was able to argue for the eventual conversion and assimilation of English Jews. As a result, Matthew Paris's views on the status of thirteenth-century Jews reflected the contemporary missionary goals of the Church and the new monastic orders and royal policy under Henry III before the important changes in climate reflected in the ultimate expulsion of the Jews in 1290.[6]

While Matthew describes several cases of alleged ritual murder, much of the recent scholarship on his chronicle has focused on the account of Little St. Hugh of Lincoln. These scholars have focused on the historical accuracy of his account in relation to the other sources. This is certainly the result of there being too much textual evidence concerning the incident, a rare problem for most such episodes. In addition to Matthew's text, there are accounts in the annals of Waverley and Burton-on-Trent, an English ballad, the *Prioress' Tale* in Geoffrey Chaucer's *Canterbury Tales*, and various royal records from King Henry III's (1207–1272) patent and close rolls for scholars to consider.[7] Both Joseph Jacobs and Gavin Langmuir in their separate works tried to reconstruct the events surrounding Hugh's demise. When they compared Matthew Paris's account to the other sources, they each emphasized its obvious historical inadequacies.[8] In addition to demonstrating the problems with Matthew's text, their analysis also highlights the difficulties for modern scholars in discussing ritual murder accusations. The texts of these accounts are ultimately irreconcilable, for they furnish different dates, places, and participants for the key events. Instead of attempting to reconstruct Hugh's final moments, then, it is surely more beneficial to analyze Matthew's purpose in including them at all. Matthew's deviation from strict veracity makes it possible to question his narrative agenda. It allows one to question why he chose to modify his account in this fashion and how it functioned in the overall structure of his chronicle. In so doing, it becomes clear that Matthew's discussion of English Jews served a variety of different purposes. At some points in his narrative, they serve as a foil for unjust abuses of royal prerogative and are portrayed in a more sympathetic light. At other times, however, their treatment in his work reflects the growing power of anti–Jewish fantasy and violence.

In Matthew Paris's assessment, ritual murders were intended to be an inverted reenactment of Christ's passion so as to mock, ridicule, and ultimately weaken Christianity. He begins his account by accusing the Jews of Lincoln of kidnapping the eight-year-old Hugh during the festival of Saints Peter and Paul in 1255. He continues to tell how Jews throughout England were summoned to participate in "a sacrifice to occur in Lincoln as an affront and reproach to Jesus Christ; for they had, as they said, a boy hidden to be crucified."[9] Matthew then charges that these Jews theatrically reenacted the Passion, in what Daniel Baraz has termed an inverted "mystery play."[10] Matthew situates one Jew as Pontius Pilate, with others acting as soldiers whose roles were to torment and ridicule Hugh. He alleges that "they beat [Hugh] until he bled and was quite bruised; they crowned him with thorns, spat on him, and harassed him with jeers ... they crucified him, and pierced his heart with a lance."[11] Mathew Paris goes into depth in his description of this scene in order to emphasize to his audience that he believes that the Jews are using Hugh as a proxy for the original Crucifixion of Christ. As Christ was shamed by ridicule and mockery, so too was Hugh. As Christ was crucified and pierced with a lance, so too was Hugh. According to Mathew, Hugh received all of the traditional wounds of Christ. Such a rhetorical strategy is common in all the written accounts of alleged English ritual murder victims. The conflation of the contemporary crucifixion scene with Christ's Crucifixion is essential in these narratives, as it not only proves the sainthood of the victims but also serves to accuse the Jews of working towards the destruction of Christianity.

This narrative agenda is most clearly seen when Matthew relates to his audience what he sees as a possible motive for these actions. He posits that the Jews not only killed Hugh but also disemboweled him so that his entrails could be used for magical purposes. He writes, "After the boy had expired, they took his body down from the cross and disemboweled him. We do not know why they did so, but it was said that it was for practicing the magical arts."[12] While later ritual murder accusations, especially in Germany, would include this charge, it was not yet as common in thirteenth-century English cases.[13] Matthew's allegation, therefore, is important in marking one of the transitions from accusations of ritual murder to blood libel. It also perhaps suggests the increasing pernicious association of Jews with demonic magic in English society.[14]

In fact, this association is also central to Matthew Paris's discussion of another ritual murder case in London. He contends that in August 1244, the citizens of London discovered "the unburied body of a boy in the cemetery of St. Benedict, on whose legs, arms, and under his chest was an inscription written regularly in Hebrew."[15] Concluding that the markings are Hebrew characters, the Christians immediately assume it must be a case of ritual murder. Matthew argues, "For they believed, not without reason, that the Jews had as an insult to Jesus Christ as is frequently said to occur either crucified the little boy or been preparing his crucifixion when he expired from various torments."[16] Moreover, the Christians "sent for some converted Jews who inhabited the house which the king had founded in London, and ordered them, as they regarded their lives and limbs, out of their honor, love and fear of the king, their lord, to reveal the meaning of the writing without any distortion."[17] While these new Christians were obviously unable to read the letters as the community wished, nevertheless, the canons of St. Paul sanctioned it as a ritual murder by burying the boy near the great altar. For the canons and Matthew Paris, the actual crucifixion was not necessary if they could accuse the Jews of torturing the boy, especially if they could associate this torture with demonic rituals or magical incantations, as in this case with the inscribing of Hebrew characters.

Following the crucifixion scene of Hugh, Matthew Paris then relates the discovery of the body by Hugh's mother. After searching for a few days, she is ultimately led to believe that Hugh had last been seen in the yard of one of Lincoln's Jews. She "suddenly went into that house, and she saw that the child's body had been thrown into a well."[18] As Langmuir astutely points out, Matthew's account is the only one in which the boy's corpse is found in a Jewish well. He interprets this as further proof for the inaccuracy of Matthew's account, as "neither Copin nor any other Jew would have left the body of a Christian boy in a well on his property where anyone could enter and see it without being noticed by the household."[19] A question that remains, however, is that if the boy's body was discovered elsewhere, as seems likely, why did Matthew place its discovery in the Jewish well?

I posit that there are two strong possibilities for Matthew's modification of this scene, which are not necessarily mutually exclusive. One is that Matthew wanted to provide concrete proof that the Jews had murdered Hugh. There is no better proof of such a claim than the boy's body being discovered on the property of a Jewish individual. Matthew's claim could be nothing more than an embellishment to provide greater credibility to the Lincoln community's later charges of ritual murder. The other explanation is that Matthew wanted to go further than simply incriminating individual Jews. He chose this location for Hugh's remains because it also allowed him to provide additional theological commentary on the Jewish community's rejection of Christian beliefs. In order to do so, Matthew drew upon contemporary medieval iconography and typology for the relationship between Christianity and Judaism.

Matthew Paris's account of Hugh's body being thrown into the Jewish well is in many ways very similar to a popular medieval legend that Martha Bayless has aptly discussed. Bayless' analysis centers on stories of a Jew who falls into a well, sewer, or latrine.[20] This legend takes the form of a perverse joke in which the fallen Jew initially refuses to be rescued by a Christian, for it is the Jewish Sabbath. Consequently, the Christian then refuses to extract him the next day as it is now the Christian Sabbath. Bayless argues that this story made sense to medieval Christian audiences as the Jew's fall is an allegory for the larger symbolism of the continued presence of Judaism in Christendom. For these medieval Christians, it reflected their beliefs about the refusal of Jews to convert to Christianity and their perceived obstinacy in maintaining their beliefs. Bayless continues to describe how this is most clearly seen in episodes where Jews fall into latrines, as "the association of Jews with excrement is part of a larger iconography of sinners and moral corruption."[21]

Matthew is clearly familiar with this type of iconography, as he provides a variation on it in his 1250 account of Abraham the Jew.[22] In this story, Matthew describes how Abraham had purchased a Marian statue in order to hurl it into his privy.[23] Whereupon, "he, as if in blasphemy of the Virgin Mary, perpetuated a most filthy and unmentioned act upon it day and night, and caused his wife to do the same."[24] His wife, Floria, grew increasingly distressed by this practice until she tried to put an end to it. Matthew then concludes his story by accusing Abraham of smothering his wife to death so that he could continue defiling the Marian statue. Matthew's account is an inversion of the traditional legend of the fallen Jew. Instead of the Jew being immersed in excrement, he attempts to do so to the Virgin Mary and thus to Christianity itself.[25] By having Abraham murder his wife, Matthew Paris is also commenting on the lengths that he believes Jews will go to in order to resist conversion and maintain their hostile relationship to Christianity.

Such motifs were common in thirteenth-century English texts because of the repeated associations of the Jews with earthly and bodily metaphors by Christian authors.[26] During this period, monastic authors associated Christianity with reason and consequently with the mind. Its polar opposite, however, was Judaism, which was related to unbelief and consequently with the body. Anna Sapir Abulafia perhaps put it best when she argued, "the truth, which the mind or spirit was thought capable of perceiving, was essentially Christian. Jews, who continued to refute that 'truth,' were, therefore, increasingly associated with what lay opposite to reason: the senses or appetites of the body."[27] The icon of the fallen Jew, therefore, is a commentary on the Jews' return to the earth and to their sinful and corrupt existence.[28] This iconography is perhaps most apparent in the artistic representations of *ecclesia* and *synagoga* during this period that has been extensively analyzed and discussed by other scholars. *Ecclesia* is personified as a triumphant and regal figure, who is holding the chalice and standard. *Synagoga*, however, is personified as the vanquished foe. She is not only blindfolded but she is looking down as if in shame. The Law tablets are falling from her grasp, and she holds a broken lance.[29] The pairing of the two figures visually marks the triumph of the New Testament over the Old Testament, Christian salvation over Jewish Law, and ultimately, Christianity over Judaism.

In this light, the story of Hugh's demise by Matthew Paris takes on a more explicit moral tone. In Matthew's narrative, the placement of Hugh's body serves to complete the ridicule of Christianity that begun with the ritual murder by returning the defiled body to the site of their own metaphysical immorality. Matthew's extrapolation and modification of Hugh's martyrdom should be read as his attempt to amplify the symbolic vileness of the Jews' crimes and comment on their continued obstinacy towards the Christian faith. In his account, therefore, Matthew sought to emphasize the superiority of Christianity and the very present need for Jewish conversion.

Matthew Paris next describes the exhumation of Hugh's body from the well and the various emotional displays by his mother and the community during this process. At this point in the narrative, John of Lexington stepped in to interrogate Copin, the Jew in whose well Hugh was supposedly discovered. Matthew contends that John offered to spare Copin from execution in exchange for his confession to the ritual murder. As Copin was faced with the certainty of death otherwise, Matthew argues that he told John and the crowd what they wished to hear, which was that he and the Lincoln Jews had murdered Hugh by crucifixion.[30] Langmuir surmises that the confession was the result of John of Lexington's strong ties to royal and ecclesiastical institutions. John was a prominent figure in the royal court, as he often served as King Henry III's steward.[31] Moreover, his family had very strong ecclesiastical ties to Lincoln cathedral, as his brother was Bishop Oliver of Lincoln.[32] Langmuir argues that John was attempting to demonstrate his role in royal justice while also trying to secure a new and popular saint for Lincoln Cathedral.[33] This theory is further supported by the quick reception of Hugh's body by Lincoln Cathedral and its subsequent veneration there.

While John thought that he was executing royal justice, King Henry III apparently did not concur. When he heard that John had granted Copin immunity for his testimony, Matthew describes Henry as outraged. Matthew Paris argues that Henry was infuriated because Copin is "a blasphemer and murderer who ought to be punished by multiple deaths."[34] When Copin heard this, Matthew says that he then confessed to an international conspiracy to kill Christian boys in imitation of Christ's passion. Matthew then remarks, "And after he had said these words and other delusional statements, he was tied to a horse's tail and dragged to the gibbet, where he gave up his body and spirit to the evil spirits in the air."[35] Matthew classifies this testimony as *deliramentis*, suggesting that he is likewise unsure about the veracity of the account of an international conspiracy for ritual murder. By positioning the confession after Henry declares that he deserves to die, Matthew further questions the role of the Jews of Lincoln in Hugh's murder. However, he does conclude that Copin's soul is delivered to demons; it is certainly Matthew's views on the possibility for salvation for unconverted Jews. This passage, then, could be read as Matthew furnishing his audience with another example of the necessity of Jewish conversion as it would eliminate the suspicion of ritual murder and ensure Christian salvation after death.

In Matthew's text, Henry III then proceeds to accuse ninety-one Jews in Lincoln with actively taking part in the murder, and he then has them arrested and imprisoned in the Tower. After this, Henry ordered his justiciaries (who were the chief judicial and political officers during the Norman and early Plantagenet dynasties) to launch an official inquisition into the matter. In his letter to the sheriff of Lincoln impaneling the jury, he argues that it is his right to imprison and punish the Jews because he has the testimony of Lincoln citizens that they crucified Hugh.[36] These justiciaries later concluded that Hugh was kidnapped, tortured, and executed by the Jews. As punishment, therefore, they ordered the execution by hanging of eighteen of the most wealthy and powerful Jews on St. Clement's Day of that year, November 23, 1255. Moreover, they ordered the continued confinement of the remaining Jews until they too should be executed at an unnamed future date.[37]

This is the first case of ritual murder to be actively investigated, adjudicated and punished by the English monarchy. In all previous cases, the king had chosen not to exercise his authority in resolving the accusations. In the case of William of Norwich, King Stephen (c. 1096–1154) refused to deal with the case. In order to delay the matter, he postponed the hearing until the general Council of the Clergy and Barons could be assembled in London. When this day arrived, Stephen again deferred hearing the case.[38] King Stephen never returned his attention to the case. Henry III could have easily pursued a similar strategy and ignored the case entirely. Why, therefore, did Henry act in this case, and why did he act so harshly against the Jewish community in Lincoln?

By examining the close and patent rolls during this period, his possible motives become apparent. The patent roll entry for November 26, 1255, appoints John de Wincle and Simon Passelewe to appraise the houses of the imprisoned Jews and to seize their entire chattel. In addition, it instructs them to examine the chirographers' chests in order to determine any outstanding debts owed to the Jews. It further requires the two men to "take the said houses, chattels, and debts into the king's hands, and [keep] them safe until further order." The document continues by ordering John and Simon to first extract 172li 8s 2d from these assets for the immediate use of the Queen. It finally orders that all the remaining property is to be delivered ultimately to Henry's brother, Robert, Earl of Cornwall, as partial payment for the royal debt owed to him.[39] Henry's enormous debts during this period might explain why he was so readily involved in prosecuting and imprisoning the Lincoln Jews.

According to Matthew's text, such policies were not novel during Henry's reign.[40] Matthew's accounts of Henry's excessive taxation and economic exploitation of the English Jewish communities is documented by other scholars.[41] Henry reinforced the legal serfdom of England's Jews with his statement in 1253 "that no Jew should remain in England unless he does some service to the king and that as soon as possible after birth, whether male or female, every Jew should serve us in some way."[42] It is not surprising then that Henry collected forty-nine tallages during his reign.[43] The effect of this excessive taxation was that Jews often had to call in their debts, forcing the seizure of land and chattel from many barons and other debtors too short on liquid currency to pay up. To compound baronial resentment, the land seized had to be sold to other wealthier nobles, as Jews were not allowed to own the seized property on a permanent basis. The effect of this was that those Christians with enough liquid money to purchase the forfeited property could purchase it at a much-reduced price.[44] W. Johnson argues that the forced collection of debts meant that Jews were often viewed by English barons as "both economic competitors and protected royal property."[45]

Matthew highlights this conflict between Christian and Jewish communities in his description of the almost ritual murder of another boy in Norwich in 1240. Matthew writes, "Around this time, the Jews circumcised a Christian boy in Norwich, and after he was circumcised they renamed him Jurnin. They then held him so that they could crucify him as an affront to the crucifixion of Jesus Christ."[46] Matthew contends that this plot was foiled by the boy's father who discovered him in a Jewish home. In addition to reflecting irrational fears of ritual murder, this story perhaps also reflects contemporary fears that Jewish moneylenders were also "circumcising" (i.e., "clipping") coins, resulting in the debasement of England's coinage.[47] By 1200, English documents refer to coin-clipping with the term *curtus*, which is also the word used to describe a circumcised Jewish man. King Henry reinforced this fear by calling for the recoinage of all monies in 1247.[48] Adding fuel to the barons' hatred of the Jews, Henry imposed an excessive charge of 10d per pound weight of old pennies recoined, claiming the Jews had clipped the coins so much that they needed to be assessed based on weight and not face value.[49]

Matthew Paris endorsed the belief in Jewish coin-clipping in the *Chronica Majora*. He relates that in 1247, Louis IX of France (1214–1270) had decreed that all English coins not of legal weight were to be melted down. Matthew comments on this decree by saying, "It was said and also verified that coins were being circumcised by the circumcised, and that this had come about by the faithlessness of the Jews, who now were forced by the King's very heavy tallage to beg."[50] Given the widespread resentment towards the Jews as a result of Henry's recoinage, it is not surprising that Matthew Paris would relate a story a few years earlier in which the Norwich community was fearful of Jewish circumcision. Unlike the previous case in Norwich of St. William, however, the royal sheriff was unable to stop the bishop from judging the case.

His court ruled that "four of the Jews, therefore, having been declared guilty of the crime, were first dragged by the tails of horses, and then hanged by the gallows, where they exhaled the wretched remains of life."[51]

Despite Matthew's view that the Jews were clipping coins, he nonetheless criticizes Henry's exploitation of Jewish communities to cover his debts. As Sophia Menache points out, traditional scholarship has focused only selectively on episodes hostile to the Jews in the *Chronica Majora*. She argues that "this monolithic stereotyping subsequently justified a selective approach to Matthew Paris and his writing, his manifestations of empathy toward Jews being regarded either as symptoms of a 'lack of coherence' or as a simple oversight."[52] Matthew's at times sympathetic attitude towards the Jews should also be analyzed.[53] In 1250, Matthew writes, "in these days the king became dry with avaricious thirst, and he ordered money to be extorted from all Jews without mercy, so that they appeared to be totally and irreparably impoverished."[54] He goes even further in condemning Henry in his entry for 1252. He laments that Henry "stole away from the Jews everything that those miserable beings seemed to own. He not only cut and skinned them, but disemboweled them as well. Thirstier than a man with dropsy, he eagerly milked talents, gold and valuables from the Christians and the Jews so that it seemed Crassus had risen from the dead."[55] Matthew links Henry's excessive exploitation of the Jews to the seizure of the Lincoln Jews and their assets. In 1255, shortly before the Lincoln incident, Matthew includes a final critique of Henry's expenses and methods of covering debts. In this case, Henry sells the Jews to his brother, earl Richard of Cornwall (1209–72).[56] This might also explain why Matthew later approves of the release of the imprisoned Jews; they were not being held because of the murder but because of the king's greed.

Finally in 1256, Matthew concludes his account of Little St. Hugh. He notes that the seventy-one Jews still imprisoned in the Tower awaiting their execution secretly sent messengers to the Minor Brethren (Franciscans) to beg the monks to assist them in securing their release. The Franciscans agreed to intercede on their behalf with Henry. Matthew comments that most people assumed that the monks were being influenced to aid the Jews by bribes. He, however, argues that the monks were acting out of pity, "for as long as any one is alive in this world he ought to be free from judgment; he can be saved, and hopes ought to be had for him." While the Jews remain alive, Matthew retains hope that they might still achieve salvation through Christian conversion. However, "death and a definitive sentence ensnared these Jews irrevocably."[57] By executing the Jews, there cannot be such hope.

Matthew's emphasis on Jewish conversion to Christianity is part of a larger development in the thirteenth century.[58] As many scholars have noted, Christian theology shifted from the Augustinian view of Jews as "witnesses of the Faith" to a more active justification for Jewish conversion.[59] Augustine believed that the Jews filled a necessary role in Christian society as living testaments to the superiority of Christianity. In fact, the Second Coming of Christ was understood to depend upon the physical presence of the Jews at the Apocalypse, and their ultimate conversion to Christianity.[60] During the thirteenth century, however, this view changed in favor of a greater emphasis on conversion in the present and not the future.[61] This transition is often viewed as the culmination of increasingly hostile attitudes towards medieval Jews and the increasing role of affective piety and Christological devotions in medieval religiosity.[62] It was further influenced by the assumption of conversion as a mission for the friar orders. When the Dominicans arrived in England in 1221, they established their new monasteries near the Jewish section of town in order to facilitate their missionary efforts.[63] By the end of the thirteenth century, these efforts had achieved royal sanction, as Jewish attendance at weekly conversion sermons became mandatory.[64]

Matthew Paris likewise highlights various royal efforts to convert England's Jewish population. For example, he notes that Henry III established a *Domus conversorum* in London in 1233 so that converted Jews would have a refuge from usury for support.[65] M. Adler has discovered documentation that King Henry instructed the Bishop of Carlisle (his treasurer) to pay the *Domus conversorum* seven hundred marks per year for the performance of religious services. Also from this amount, converted Jews were to be paid a weekly allowance in the form of 10½d for men and 8d for women.[66] To further demonstrate that Henry had a personal interest in *conversi*, he encouraged Jewish converts to adopt his baptismal name at their own baptism.[67] The Close Roll relates one such conversion in which Philip of Reading was actually baptized in the King's presence in 1234.[68] In 1247, Henry expanded the *Domus conversorum* program by sending seventeen *conversi* to fourteen different monasteries throughout England, and in 1255, Henry placed 150 *conversi* in 125 different religious houses.[69] As Robert C. Stacey points out, however, the numbers of Jewish converts were minimal until the 1240s and 1250s, when their rise corresponds to increase hostility towards and economic pressure on English Jews.[70] Thirteenth-century English political and religious leaders considered missionizing to the Jews a priority, and Matthew Paris's assessment of the Lincoln Jews reflects these prevailing attitudes.[71]

Matthew's view of English Jews is perhaps best exemplified by his inclusion and illustration of the Wandering Jew legend in his chronicle.[72] His visual and narrative description of this legend reflects common depictions of it in medieval Christian folklore. Matthew was certainly not alone in the use of this motif, as Pope Innocent III (1160 or 1161–1216) argued that it was symbolic of the position of all Jews in Christian society. He commented, "Christian piety accepts the Jews who, by their own guilt, are consigned to perpetual servitude because they crucified the Lord, although their own prophets had predicted that he would come in the flesh to redeem Israel ... and like Cain, they are to be wanderers and fugitives."[73] Matthew retells the legend of Ahasuerus, a Jewish shoemaker, who supposedly taunted and pushed Jesus as he walked towards his crucifixion. Jesus punished Ahasuerus by making him immortal, so that he would have to wander in misery for all time. The illustration in the *Chronica Majora* has Ahasuerus dressed in poor Jewish garb and hunched over as if by suffering and old age.[74] The illustration situates the moment of his punishment with the visual manifestation of that punishment, his eternity of pain and suffering. This depiction is, therefore, a visual manifestation of Matthew's complex attitudes toward the Jews. The Wandering Jew is righteously punished for his transgressions against Christ. And yet, he is a pitiable character, forced to wander the world without refuge or comfort for eternity.[75] Matthew concludes his description of Ahasuerus with the comment that the existence of the Wandering Jew "is one of the wonderful events of the world, and a great proof of the Christian faith."[76] He portrays the Wandering Jew as a pathetic character: dirty, poor, miserable, and perpetually unrepentant. As a result, Ahasuerus represents Jewish moral corruptibility, as he not only denied Jesus but also taunted and assaulted him. For medieval Christians, Ahasuerus's permanence and non-conversion was an important sign of the downfall of the Jews and the passing of God's grace to the Christians. For Matthew, therefore, the Wandering Jew was the physical reminder of the superiority of Christianity and a call for Jewish conversion.

It is easy to oversimplify Matthew's complex and ambivalence characterization of English Jews in his chronicle. He does not have only a sympathetic or antagonistic attitude towards the Jews. Instead, scenes involving the Jews serve to further his own narrative agenda. Matthew portrays the Jews in a favorable light when it serves as proof of royal tyranny, and yet he is equally comfortable showing the Jews as demonic killers of Christian boys when it serves to condemn the failure of Jews to convert to Christianity. By redacting Matthew's narrative to simple emotive attitudes, scholars can lose much of this complexity. Instead, I argue that scholars need to recognize that Matthew employed a variety of typological strategies in his representation of the role of the Jews in Christian society. Instead of focusing on the legality of the Lincoln Jews' supposed crimes, he emphasizes their perceived spiritual and moral deficiencies. Matthew argues that Hugh's murder was horrific, and he fully lauds Henry's execution of those whom he believes actively took part in the crucifixion. However, he maintains hope that those Jews who were only guilty of collective indemnity would eventually be converted and reconciled with the Christian faith. As outlaws, the Jews must be condemned and punished;

as outcasts, the Jews could be eventually restored to the Christian community.

NOTES

1. This paper was first presented at the 2005 Sewanee Medieval Colloquium. I greatly appreciate the comments and suggestions of the participants, especially Dr. Irven Resnik who commented on the panel.
2. Henry Luard counted around seventy-five separate passages that discuss the Jews. Matthew Paris, *Matthæi Parisiensis, Monachi Sancti Albani, Chronica Majora*, ed. Henry Richards Luard, 7 vol. (London: Longman, 1872–1883), 7: 329–30.
3. For other studies on the general status of twelfth- and thirteenth-century English Jews, see Michael Adler, *The Jews of Medieval England* (London: Jewish Historical Society of England, 1939); Paul Hyams, "The Jewish Minority in Medieval England, 1066–1290," *Journal of Jewish Studies* 25, no. 2 (1974): 270–93; Gavin Langmuir, "The Jews and the Archives of Angevin England: Reflections on Medieval Anti-Semitism," *Traditio* 19 (1963): 183–244; Sophia Menache, "Faith, Myth and Politics: The Stereotype of the Jews and Their Expulsion from England and France," *Jewish Quarterly Review* 75, no. 4 (1985): 351–74; Cecil Roth, *A History of the Jews in England*, 3rd ed. (Oxford: Clarendon Press, 1964); Robert C. Stacey, "Jews and Christians in Twelfth-Century England: Some Dynamics of a Changing Relationship," in *Jews and Christians in Twelfth-Century Europe*, ed. Michael Signer and John van Engen (Notre Dame: University of Notre Dame Press, 2001), 340–54; Kenneth Stow, *Alienated Minority: The Jews of Medieval Latin Europe* (Cambridge: Harvard University Press, 1992); J. A. Watt, "The Jews, the Law and the Church: The Concept of Jewish Serfdom in Thirteenth-Century England," in *The Church and Sovereignty c. 590–1918: Essays in Honour of Michael Wilks*, ed. Diana Wood (Oxford: B. Blackwell, 1991), 153–72; Israel Jacob Yuval, *Two Nations in Your Womb: Perceptions of Jews and Christians in Late Antiquity and the Middle Ages* (Berkeley: University of California Press, 2006); Robert Chazan, *The Jews of Medieval Western Christendom, 1000–1500* (Cambridge: Cambridge University Press, 2006), 154–67; and Patricia Skinner, ed., *Jews in Medieval Britain: Historical, Literary and Archaeological Perspectives* (Woodbridge: The Boydell Press, 2003).
4. Matthew Paris's representations of the Jews is more generally discussed by Sophia Menache, "Matthew Paris's Attitudes toward Anglo-Jewry," *Journal of Medieval History* 23, no. 2 (1997): 139–62; and Stephen Benin, "Matthew Paris and the Jews," in *Proceedings of the Tenth World Congress of Jewish Studies, Jerusalem, August 16–24, 1989*, ed. David Assaf, 4 vol. in 7 (Jerusalem: World Union of Jewish Studies 1990), vol. 2, bk. 2, 61–68.
5. For more on English ritual murder accusations, see also Anthony P. Bale, "'House Devil, Town Saint': Anti-Semitism and Hagiography in Medieval Suffolk," in *Chaucer and the Jews: Sources, Contexts, Meanings*, ed. Sheila Delany (New York: Routledge, 2002), 185–210; Jeffrey J. Cohen, "The Flow of Blood in Medieval Norwich," *Speculum* 79, no. 1 (2004): 26–65; Joe Hillaby, "The Ritual Child Murder Accusation: Its Dissemination and Harold of Gloucester," *Jewish Historical Studies* 34 (1996): 69–109; and John McCulloh, "Jewish Ritual Murder: William of Norwich, Thomas of Monmouth and the Early Dissemination of the Myth," *Speculum* 72, no. 3 (1997): 698–740.
6. As Anthony Bale notes, while the new mendicant orders helped to shape rising anti-semitism through active preaching, "the Benedictines sought to develop hagiographic culture with a concomitant emphasis on literacy and the value of book-production." Anthony Bale, "Fictions of Judaism in England before 1290," in Skinner, *Jews in Medieval Britain*, 129–44 at 133.
7. The scholarship on the *Prioress' Tale* is perhaps the most developed. See Philip S. Alexander, "Madam Eglentyne, Geoffrey Chaucer and the Problem of Medieval Anti-Semitism,"

Bulletin of the John Rylands Library of Manchester 74 (1992): 109–20; Merrall Llewelyn Price, "Sadism and Sentimentality: Absorbing Antisemitism in Chaucer's Prioress," *Chaucer Review* 43, no. 2 (2008): 197–214; Roger Dahood, "The Punishment of the Jews, Hugh of Lincoln, and the Question of Satire in the *Prioress' Tale*," *Viator* 36 (2005): 465–491; Roger Dahood, "English Historical Narratives of Jewish Child-Murder, Chaucer's *Prioress's Tale*, and the Date of Chaucer's Unknown Source," *Studies in the Age of Chaucer* 31 (2009): 125–40; Louise O. Fradenburg, "Criticism, Anti-Semitism, and the *Prioress's Tale*," *Exemplaria* 1 (1989): 69–115; and Robert Worth Frank, Jr., "Miracles of the Virgin, Medieval Anti-Semitism, and the 'Prioress's Tale,'" in *The Wisdom of Poetry: Essays in Early English Literature in Honor of Morton W. Bloomfield*, ed. Larry D. Benson and Siegfried Wenzel (Kalamazoo: Medieval Institute Publications, 1982), 177–88.

    8. Joseph Jacobs, "Little St. Hugh of Lincoln," in *Jewish Ideals and Other Essays*, ed. Joseph Jacobs (London: D. Nutt, 1896), 192–224; and Gavin I. Langmuir, *Toward a Definition of Antisemitism* (Berkeley: University of California Press, 1990), 237–62.

    9. Matthew Paris, *Matthew Paris's English History. From the Year 1235 to 1273*, trans. J. A. Giles, 3 vol. (London: H. G. Bohn, 1852–1854), 3: 138. Latin text: "Et cum ipsum in quodam conclavi secretissimo lacte et aliis puerilibus alimentis nutrirent, miserunt ad omnes fere Angliae civitates in quibus Judaei degebant, et convocarunt de unaquaque civitate aliquos Judaeorum, ut in contumeliam et obprobrium Jesu Christi interessent sacrificio suo Lincolniae. Habebant enim, ut dicebant, quondam puerum absconditum ad crucifigendum," Matthew Paris, *Chronica Majora*, 5: 516.

    10. Daniel Baraz, *Medieval Cruelty: Changing Perceptions, Late Antiquity to the Early Modern Period* (Ithaca: Cornell University Press, 2003), 77.

    11. Matthew Paris, *English History*, 3: 138. Latin text: "Verberatus est usque ad crucorem et livorem, spinis coronatus, sputis et cachinnis lacessitus ... crucifixerunt, et lancea ad cor pupugerunt," Matthew Paris, *Chronica Majora*, 5: 516.

    12. Matthew Paris, *English History*, 3: 139. Latin text: "Et cum expirasset puer, deposuerunt corpus de cruce, et nescitur qua ratione eviscerarunt corpusculum; dicitur autem, quod ad magicas artes exercendas," Matthew Paris, *Chronica Majora*, 5: 516.

    13. R. Po-chia Hsia, *The Myth of Ritual Murder: Jews and Magic in Reformation Germany* (New Haven: Yale University Press,1988), 143.

    14. See John G. Gager, *The Origins of Anti-Semitism: Attitudes Toward Judaism in Pagan and Christian Antiquity* (New York: Oxford University Press, 1983); Marcel Mauss, *A General Theory of Magic*, trans. Robert Brain (London: Routledge and K. Paul, 1972); and Joshua Trachtenberg, *Jewish Magic and Superstition: A Study in Folk Religion* (Philadelphia: Behrman's Jewish Book House, 1939). As Gavin Langmuir notes in his review of Hsia's work, such views were very rare before the fifteenth century, as most accusations of ritual murder have more to do with anxieties over the eucharist and resurrection than association with demonic magic. See Gavin Langmuir, "Hsia, *The Myth of Ritual Murder*," Review of *The Myth of Ritual Murder: Jews and Magic in Reformation Germany*, by R. Po-chia Hsia, *Jewish Quarterly Review* 82, no. 3/4 (1992): 538–540.

    15. Matthew Paris, *English History*, 2: 21. Latin text: "Eodem vero anno, kalendis Augusti inventum est corpusculum cujusdam pueri masculi inhumatum in cimiterio Sancti Benedicti, in civitate Londoniarum, cujus cruribus et brachiis et sub mamillis literis Hebraicis regulariter fuit inscriptum," Matthew Paris, *Chronica Majora*, 4: 377.

    16. Matthew Paris, *English History*, 2: 21. Latin text: "Credebant etiam, nee sine causa, quod Judsei ipsum puerulum in Jesu Christi improperium et contumeliam, quod frequenter relatum est accidisse, vel crucifixerant vel crucifigendum variis tormentis exagitaverant, et cum jam exspirasset, eum cruci indignum illuc projecisse. Porro apparuerunt in corpore illo livores et scissurae virgarum, et quorundam aliorum tormentorum signa et vestigia manifesta," Matthew Paris, *Chronica Majora*, 4: 377.

    17. Matthew Paris, *English History*, 2: 21. Latin Lext: "Ad quod spectaculum cum plures convenierent admirantes, et nescirent literas legere, scientes quia literse Hebraicse fuerunt, advocabant converses Judseos, qui domum, quam dominus rex Londoniis fundaverat, inhabitabant

; ut ipsi, sicut vitam aut membra diligebant, pro honore, amore, et timore domini regis, sine figmento falsitatis scripturam illam aperirent," Matthew Paris, *Chronica Majora*, 4: 377.

18. Matthew Paris, *English History*, 3: 139. Latin text: "Mater autem pueri, filium suum absentem per aliquot dies diligenter quaesivit, dictumque ei a vicinis, quod ultimo viderunt puerum, quem quaesivit, ludentem cum pueris Judaeorum sibi coaetaneis, et domum Judaei cujusdam intrantem. Intravit igitur mulier subito domum illam, et vidit corpus pueri in quondam puteum praecipitatum," Matthew Paris, *Chronica Majora*, 5: 517.

19. Langmuir, *Toward a Definition of Antisemitism*, 245.

20. Martha Bayless, "The Story of the Fallen Jew and the Iconography of Jewish Unbelief," *Viator* 34 (2003): 142–56 at 142. For other similar *exempla*, see also Bale, "Fictions of Judaism in England before 1290," 132.

21. Bayless, "The Story of the Fallen Jew," 147.

22. In fact, the exact same legend is found in the continuation of the *Chronica Majora* in the entry for 1260. The continuator writes, "About this same time, at Tewkesbury, a Jew fell into a privy, and out of respect for his Sabbath, on which day the accident happened, would not allow himself to be extricated till the following day, which was Sunday; and in consequence he died, being suffocated by the foul stench." Matthew Paris, *English History*, 3; 333. Moreover, the Anglo-Norman ballad of Hugh of Lincoln and Chaucer's tale place the boy's body in manure. See Bale, "Fictions of Judaism in England before 1290," 136–137.

23. As many scholars have noted, Jews are often represented as opposed to the Virgin Mary in thirteenth-century accounts, and their conversion is often presented as examples of Marian miracles. See Denise L. Despres, "Immaculate Flesh and the Social Body: Mary and the Jews," *Jewish History* 12, no. 1 (1998): 47–69; and Carole Stone, "Anti-Semitism in the Miracle Tales of the Virgin," *Medieval Encounters* 5, no. 3 (1999): 364–374. For a discussion of how this changed before the expulsion, see Harvey J. Hames, "The Limits of Conversion: Ritual Murder and the Virgin Mary in the Account of Adam of Bristol," *Journal of Medieval History* 33 (2007): 43–59.

24. Matthew Paris, *English History*, 2: 340–41.

25. Bale, "Fictions of Judaism in England before 1290," 136–37.

26. Bayless, "The Story of the Fallen Jew," 150.

27. Anna Sapir Abulafia, *Christians and Jews in the Twelfth-Century Renaissance* (London: Routledge, 1995), 107.

28. Bayless, "The Story of the Fallen Jew," 150–51.

29. Suzanne Lewis, "*Tractatus Adversus Judaeos* in the Gulbenkian Apocalypse," *Art Bulletin* 68, no. 4 (1986): 543–66. See also Bale, "Fictions of Judaism in England before 1290," 129–44. Interestingly, David Burr argues that this trend is not present in Apocalypse manuscripts that were not illuminated. Burr, "The Antichrist and the Jews in Four Thirteenth-century Apocalypse Commentaries," in *Friars and Jews in the Middle Ages and Renaissance*, ed. Steven J. McMichael and Susan E. Myers. The Medieval Franciscans 2 (Leiden: Brill, 2004): 23–38.

30. Matthew Paris, *English History*, 2: 114.

31. Ibid., 2: 163–64.

32. Ibid., 2: 138–41.

33. Langmuir, *Toward a Definition of Antisemitism*, 249–53.

34. Matthew Paris, *English History*, 3: 140. Latin text: "Dignus enim erat blasphemus ille et homicida mortis poena multiformi," Matthew Paris, *Chronica Majora*, 5: 518.

35. Matthew Paris, *English History*, 3: 140. Latin text: "Et cum hoc dixisset simul cum aliis deliramentis, ligatus ad caudam equinam et tractus ad patibulum, aeries cacodaemonibus in corpore et anima praesentatur," Matthew Paris, *Chronica Majora*, 5: 519.

36. Walter Waddington Shirley, ed., *Royal and Other Historical Letters Illustrative of the Reign of Henry III*, 2 vol. (London: Longman, Green, Longman, and Roberts, 1862–66), 2: 110.

37. Matthew Paris, *English History*, 3: 141. Latin Text: "Postea vero, per inquisitionem justiciariorum domini Regis perceptum fuit et inventum, quod Judaei Angliae communi consilio puerum innocentem, pluribus diebus flagellatum, interemerunt crucifixum. Sed postea pro iniquitate sua, matre dicti pueri contra ipsos de tali morte appellationem suam coram rege constanter

prosequente, Deus ultionum Dominus dignam pro meritis reddidit retributionem. Nam in die sancti Clementis, octodecim de ditioribus et majoribus civitatis Lincolniensis fuerunt tracti, et ad furcas novas, ad hoc specialiter praeparatas, vento praesentati. Et in turri Londoniarum plus quam ter viginti ad simile judicium in carcere sunt reservati," Matthew Paris, *Chronica Majora*, 5: 519. The execution of the eighteen may have been prompted by a legal dispute over proper jurisdiction. Moreover, eighteen is the number *chai* in Hebrew. Eighteen and multiples of it are traditionally meant to bring good luck, and oftentimes gifts are given in multiples of eighteen. There may be some perverse reason, then, why eighteen Jews were hanged.

    38. Thomas de Monmouth, *The Life and Miracles of St. William of Norwich*, trans. Augustus Jessopp and Montague Rhodes James (Cambridge: Cambridge University Press, 1896), 109.

    39. *Calendar of the Patent Rolls of the Reign of Henry III*, 6 vol. (London: H. M. S. O., 1901–13), 4: 451–52.

    40. For a discussion of the legal position of the Jews under Henry III and Edward I, see Paul Brand, "Jews and the Law in England, 1275–90," *English Historical Review* 115, no. 464 (2000): 1138–58.

    41. For a discussion of Henry's fiscal policies toward English Jews, see Robert C. Stacey, "The English Jews under Henry III," in Skinner, *The Jews in Medieval Britain*, 41–54. Stacey (p. 49) points to Henry's imposition of a 20,000 mark tallage in 1241, another 60,000 mark tallage between 1244 and 1250, and a 44,000 mark tallage between 1250 and 1258.

    42. *Calendar of the Close Rolls of Henry III*, 14 vol. (London: Public Record Office, 1902–38), 7: 312.

    43. Roth, *A History of the Jews in England*, 273.

    44. For a detailed discussion of English Jewish serfdom see Watt, "The Jew, the Law and the Church," in Wood, *The Church and Sovereignty*, 153–72. Robert C. Stacey points out the other choice for Jewish money-lenders. Instead of confiscating the property for a fixed term until the debt was excised, Jews also often accepted a reduced amount for the loan. See Stacey, "The English Jews under Henry III," 50, n. 52.

    45. Willis Johnson, "Textual Sources for the Study of Jewish Currency Crimes in Thirteenth-Century England," *British Numismatic Journal, Including the Proceedings of the British Numismatic Society* 66 (1996–1997): 21–32 at 23.

    46. Matthew Paris, *English History*, 1: 277. Latin text: "Circa illa tempora, apud Norwicum circumciderant Judaei unum puerum Christianum, et eum circumcisum vocaverunt Jurninum. Reservabant autem illum ad crucifigendum in contumeliam Jesu Christi crucifixi," Matthew Paris, *Chronica Majora*, 4: 30.

    47. Zefira Entin Rokeah has provided an exhaustive survey of charges against the Jews for clipping coins in various parts of England. She concludes that the Jews were ten times more likely to be executed for crimes against the currency. Rokeah, "Money and the Hangman in Late Thirteenth-century England: Jews, Christians and Coinage Offences Alleged and Real (Part I)," *Jewish Historical Studies* 31 (1988–1990): 83–109; id., "Part II," *Jewish Historical Studies* 32 (1990–1992): 159–218.

    48. Johnson, "Textual Sources for the Study of Jewish Currency Crimes," 27.

    49. Ibid., 29.

    50. Matthew Paris, *English History*, 1: 277. Latin text: "Dictum est insuper et compertum, quod circumcisis denarii circumcidebantur, et a Judaeorum infidelitate, qui propter regia tallagia nimis gravia mendicare jam cogebantur, hoc et alia scelera dicebantur emanasse," Matthew Paris, *Chronica Majora*, 4: 608–609.

    51. Matthew Paris, *English History*, 1: 277. Latin text: "Judaeorum igitur quatuor super praedicto scelere convicti, prius ad caudas equorum distracti, tandem in patibulo suspensi, vitae reliquias flebiliter exhalarunt," Matthew Paris, *Chronica Majora*, 4: 30–31.

    52. Menache, "Matthew Paris's Attitudes toward Anglo-Jewry," 141.

    53. For a discussion of the following accounts, see also Benin, "Matthew Paris and the Jews," 63.

    54. Matthew Paris, *English History*, 2: 340.

    55. Matthew Paris, *Chronica Majora*, 5: 274.

56. Matthew Paris, *English History*, 3: 114–115.
57. Matthew Paris, *English History*, 2: 114. Latin text: "Ipsi vero, ut perhibet mundus, si mundo in tali casu credendum est, mediante pecunia, ipsos suis precibus et intercessione et a carcere et a morte, quam meruerant, Judaeos liberarunt; ut pie credendum arbitror, spiritu ducti pietatis, quia quamdiu quis in via est in hoc mundo, quia liberum habet arbitrium, salvari potest, et sperandum est de eo…. Ors enim et diffinitiva sententi ipsos semel irrevocabiliter illaqueavit," Matthew Paris, *Chronica Majora*, 5: 546. See also Benin, "Matthew Paris and the Jews," 63.
58. For royal involvement, see Joan Greatrex, "Monastic Charity for Jewish Converts: The Requisition of Corrodies by Henry III," *Studies in Church History* 29 (1992): 133–43. For a discussion of the relationship between Jews and the Church, see John Edwards, "The Church and the Jews in Medieval England," in Skinner, *The Jews of Medieval Britain*, 85–95.
59. Menache, "Matthew Paris's Attitudes toward Anglo-Jewry," 352. See also Robert Chazan, *Daggers of Faith: Thirteenth-Century Christian Missionizing and Jewish Response* (Berkeley: University of California Press, 1989); Jeremy Cohen, *The Friars and the Jews: The Evolution of Medieval Anti-Judaism* (Ithaca: Cornell University Press, 1982), 19–22; Christopher Ocker, "Ritual Murder and the Subjectivity of Christ: A Choice in Medieval Christianity," *Harvard Theological Review* 91, no. 2 (1998): 153–92; and Robert C. Stacey, "The Conversion of the Jews to Christianity in Thirteenth-Century England," *Speculum* 67, no. 2 (1992): 263–83.
60. Adolf F. Leschnitzer, "Reflections on Medieval Anti-Judaism, 5: The Wandering Jew. The Alienation of the Jewish Image in Christian Consciousness," *Viator* 2 (1971): 391–96 at 394.
61. Scholars have posited a variety of explanations for why Christian views changed in the twelfth and thirteenth centuries. For example, Daniel Baraz argues that they were increasingly linked to acts of cruelty, because the revival of affective piety emphasized the Crucifixion and suffering of Christ, in *Medieval Cruelty*, 77–78. See also Robert Chazan, *Fashioning Jewish Identity in Medieval Western Christendom* (Cambridge: Cambridge University Press, 2004); R. I. Moore, *The Formation of a Persecuting Society: Power and Deviance in Western Europe, 950–1250* (New York: B. Blackwell, 1987); Robert C. Stacey, "Crusades, Martyrdoms and the Jews of Norman England, 1096–1190," in *Juden und Christen zur Zeit der Kreuzzüge*, ed. Alfred Haverkemp. Vorträge und Forschungen 47 (Sigmaringen: Jan Thorbecke Verlag, 1999), 233–51; and Israel Jacob Yuval, "Jewish Messianic Expectations toward 1240 and Christian Reactions," in *Toward the Millennium: Messianic Expectations from the Bible to Waco*, ed. Peter Schäfer and Mark R. Cohen (Leiden: Brill, 1998), 105–21.
62. Stow, *Alienated Minority*, 235. Stow argues that this trend reflects contemporary changes in the depiction of Satan. As Satan was visualized less as a fallen angel and more as a demonic devil, the Jews are also increasingly visualized as his agents on Earth. See also Anna Sapir Abulafia, "The Intellectual and Spiritual Quest for Christ and Central Medieval Persecution of Jews," in *Religious Violence Between Christians and Jews: Medieval Roots, Modern Perspectives*, ed. Anna Sapir Abulafia (New York: Palgrave, 2002), 61–85.
63. Stacey, "The Conversion of the Jews to Christianity in Thirteenth-Century England," 267.
64. Ibid., 267–68.
65. Matthew Paris, *Chronica Majora*, 3: 262.
66. Adler, *The Jews of Medieval England*, 279–379. Adler, however, argues that the impetus for the establishment of this *domus* was Henry's personal piety. The evidence from Matthew Paris also suggests fiscal reasons for its foundation.
67. Menache, "Matthew Paris's Attitudes toward Anglo-Jewry," 145.
68. *Close Rolls of the Reign of Henry III*, 2: 415.
69. *Close Rolls of the Reign of Henry III*, 6: 100. For further discussion see Adler, *The Jews of Medieval England*, 279–379; Greatrex, "Monastic Charity for Jewish Converts," 133–43; Stacey, "The Conversion of the Jews to Christianity in Thirteenth-Century England," 266–67.
70. Stacey, "The English Jews under Henry III," 51.
71. Cohen, *The Friars and the Jews*, 77–89.

72. For a discussion of the legend in medieval Europe, see George Kumler Anderson, *The Legend of the Wandering Jew* (Providence: Brown University Press, 1965); Galit Hasan-Rokem and Alan Dundes, eds., *The Wandering Jew: Essays in the Interpretation of a Christian Legend* (Bloomington: Indiana University Press, 1986); and Diane Wolfthal, "The Wandering Jew: Some Medieval and Renaissance Depictions," in *A Tribute to Lotte Brand Philip*, ed. William W. Clark, et al. (New York: Abaris Press, 1985), 217–27.

73. Letter to the archbishop of Sens and the bishop of Paris, dated July 15, 1205, as cited in Lewis, "*Tractatus Adversus Judaeos* in the Gulbenkian Apocalypse," 544.

74. Many art historians contend that Matthew Paris illustrated his own chronicle. For more on the relationship between author and image in medieval manuscripts, see Madeline H. Caviness, "Artistic Integration in Gothic Buildings: A Post-Modern Construct?" in *Artistic Integration in Gothic Buildings*, ed. Chieffo Raguin, Kathryn Brush, and Peter Draper (Toronto: University of Toronto Press, 1995), 248–61.

75. Leschnitzer, "The Wandering Jew," 394.

76. Matthew Paris, *English History*, 2: 532; and Matthew Paris, *Chronica Majora*, 5: 340–41.

2

Let Her Be Waived: Outlawing Women in Yorkshire, 1293–1294

JENNIFER BREWER

In the year 1293, the justices presiding over the wapentake (hundred court) of Skyrack in the West Riding of Yorkshire[1] heard the following account of a burglary:

> Jordan Grunne of Seacroft and his son William at night burgled the sheepfold of William of Ryther in Shadewell and Simon of Eastwick, a shepherd of the same William of Ryther living in the same sheepfold ... hearing [them] got up and taunted the aforesaid Jordan and ... killed that robber. And the aforesaid William, son of the aforesaid Jordan, fled at once after the deed and is suspected. Let him be exacted and outlawed. He had no chattels.[2]

Since the criminal charges against William Grunne cannot be laid against him in absentia,[3] the justices attempt to compel him to return to stand trial by ordering him to be "exacted and outlawed" (*exigatur et utlegatur*); that is, he is to be summoned to appear at five successive court sittings to answer the charges against him. If he does not make an appearance within the time allowed, he will be placed outside the law and denied its protection and all his civil rights.

This was the standard method of dealing with absentee defendants in the medieval English courts, and when viewed within the corpus of the hundreds of outlawry sentences passed by the court in this session, the story of William Grunne is unremarkable. However, the Grunne family's case has one feature that makes it stand apart from many of the rest. After the entry records a lengthy list of chattels and land that belong to the late Jordan Grunne (which will now be forfeit to the king), the scribe adds a short notation at the end stating that Juliana Grunne, daughter of Jordan, is to be "exacted and waived" (*exigatur et waivietur*) for her part in her family's crime.[4]

Although Juliana is mentioned only briefly and the extent of her involvement in her family's crime is never made clear, her story contains many elements common to many of the waiving sentences that form the basis of my paper.[5] In the first place, just the fact that it is considered noteworthy to have been waived suggests something of the general rarity of this occurrence. My research reveals that, in late thirteenth-century Yorkshire, those individuals who were placed outside the law were overwhelmingly male. Also, Juliana is accused of involvement in a property crime and, rather than act independently, she commits this crime with associates (in her case, a family unit) who are either outlawed or otherwise punished at the same time. Although there are some exceptions, an examination of the cases of the women ordered exacted and waived in this court record, which is preserved in the National Archives in Kew as JUST 1 1098, shows many of these similarities between them.

The purpose of this paper is to compare and contrast the cases of the women ordered waived by this court, to examine and discuss the types of crimes they committed, and to identify with whom (if anyone) they acted. In conclusion, I will speculate on possible reasons why these women may have chosen to flee the law and why, in general, it may have been particularly difficult for women to do so.

It should be said, at the outset, that the record I use has certain limitations. Although it is generally well-preserved, there are places where the roll is damaged, faded, or simply illegible, making it difficult to make out individual words. Unfortunately, a few of the entries involving waiving sentences did not escape unscathed. Whenever I encountered this situation, I suggested logical possibilities for the missing words, but there is, of course, always the possibility of error.

There are also some limitations as to how far the waiving cases in this record can be considered the norm in the general picture of medieval female criminality. JUST 1 1098 is only one record that survives from the 1293–1294 Yorkshire circuit and, as we shall see, represents only a small group of individuals. Therefore, I am hesitant to claim that the experience of the women who will be discussed was typical of all women who were ordered exacted and waived. However, when compared to the findings of other studies,[6] the behaviour and associations of these Yorkshire women seem to follow similar patterns to those of other medieval female felons in other locations around the country.

Before going into more detail about the cases of waived women that will be discussed in this paper, it seems best to begin with a brief explanation of what "waiving" actually involved. It must be said, at the outset, that the title of this work is somewhat inexact because, strictly speaking, a woman could not actually be "outlawed." This is stated by the English jurist Henry de Bracton, who argued in his mid-thirteenth century work *Legibus et Consuetudinibus Angliae* that, because a woman could not belong to a frankpledge or a tithing, as did all males over the age of twelve, she could not be considered "in law" and therefore could not be "outlawed." However, Bracton does go on to make it quite clear that this technicality is of small concern should an accused woman not make an appearance before the judges. He also writes that, if such a woman flees justice, "she may well be waived and regarded as one abandoned, for waif is that which no-one claims." Once this happens, Bracton reveals that a woman who has been waived is considered no different from a man who has been outlawed. Both will be denied full legal protection, both deserve to die "without law" if they resist arrest and both will be at the mercy of the king should they be captured. Both will, in short, "bear the wolf's head,"[7] which is a common saying for those English who are marked as outlaws; it comes from the tradition that the monetary reward for capturing an outlaw and handing him/her over to the authorities was the same as that given for killing a wolf (which was five shillings at the time of Richard I).[8] The women sentenced to be exacted and waived in this record, it seems, can expect no special favours or treatment, for the difference between "outlawed" and "waived" is one of mere terminology.

Who, then, were these women, and what brought them to the attention of the courts? Waiving a woman was a relatively rare occurrence, for even the most cursory examination of JUST 1 1098 reveals that the overwhelming majority of those sentenced to be placed outside the law were male. Out of the 252 outlawry sentences that are recorded in this court roll, only twenty-seven deal with cases of waiving; in total, forty-two women are identified.[9] This puts the number of waiving cases at only 10.7 percent of the total number of outlawry cases passed. This figure puts these women almost exactly within the range of the findings of Barbara Hanawalt in her 1979 work *Crime and Conflict in English Communities 1300–1348*, which says that only 10 percent of indictments had a female suspect.[10] Also, an analysis of the individual cases reveals that these women were involved in a wide variety of crimes, from property felonies to murder to prison breaking. In this paper, I will group the individual cases by the types of crimes the accused committed, starting with the most common crimes, those involving illegally obtained property.

Out of the forty-two women mentioned, a staggering thirty-one (74 percent) of them are charged with burglary, theft, or larceny, or a combination of two or more of these. In JUST 1 1098, there is a noticeable difference between the way in which property crimes are recorded and how the entries dealing with more serious crimes such as murder and assault are set down. While the latter tend to be dealt with individually, property crimes are often crammed into one long indictment at the beginning of that wapentake's business, thereby ordering exacting and outlawing/waiving for dozens of people at once and perhaps freeing up the court to hear graver charges. This can, unfortunately, put us at something of a disadvantage: these cases are dealt with very quickly and often do not go into two much detail. Occasionally, it can be difficult to ascertain exactly what the crime was, and for a full fourteen of the women I cannot determine if they were charged with burglary, theft, or larceny, although their charges do clearly involve property crimes.

Fortunately, however, the remaining seventeen cases are much better preserved and can allow us to ascertain the actions which led up to the accused's flight and the passing of the waiving sentence. It appears that, in this record at least, there is an even split between the three crimes of burglary, theft, and larceny, with six women involved in each crime.[11] We have already heard the case of Juliana Grunne, ordered exacted and waived for her participation in a burglary committed by her father and brother, but her story is not unique. The justices in the wapentake of Boulmer, located in the North Riding, heard the following case:

> Aylmer of Ferlington and his wife Agnes fled [*subtraxerunt*] for the burglary of the grange of John of Ferlington ... [let the said Aylmer be exacted and outlawed and the said Agnes waived].[12]

Like Juliana Grunne, Agnes commits her crime with members of a family unit, as do two other women accused of burglary in this court roll. However, in the two remaining burglary cases, the women do not appear to have had accomplices. One Matilda of Brite is condemned to be exacted and waived in the wapentake of Morley for burgling the house of a certain John Bocerthur,[13] and the wapentake of Gilling passed the same fate on Emma Trenekyrtle, who was indicted for both burglary and larceny.[14] Unfortunately, the entries do not mention if any goods were taken from the victim's home, and so we can only speculate as to what these women hoped to gain from these burglaries or what drove them to this crime in the first place.

We do acquire more details when we read the cases of the six women who were accused of theft. Again, these cases are seen to follow a particular, established pattern. Fourteenth-century jurists in England argued that theft, unlike the more open robbery, was a crime done in secret and included, among other things, the taking of fish and livestock from others.[15] The theft cases discussed in this record appear to be textbook examples of the above definition, for all of them seem to have involved stealing food, livestock, and grain. One Margery Stoke is indicted at the wapentake of Pontefract for the theft of fish.[16] The wapentake of Strafforth deals with a Sybil Denning who, while staying in Trunfield, is accused and ordered exacted and waived for the theft of grain.[17] The indictment of one Matilda de la Grene of Middleton for two thefts is handled in the northern wapentake of Gilling.[18] Significantly, a case that leads to interesting speculation about the woman's social status was heard at the wapentake of Osgoldcross:

> Cecilia, who was the wife of Richard of Kirk Bramwith, fled for the theft of two sheep from John of Nemle ... and for the theft of grain and for other larcenies and is suspected. Let her be exacted and waived.[19]

Out of all the cases in this roll, Cecilia's is the only one in which the woman's marital status is described in the past tense. This is interesting, because it may suggest that Cecilia, who was either widowed or abandoned by her husband, may have been driven to steal by economic necessity. Indeed, the fact that *all* of the women waived for theft in this court roll acted alone while committing their crimes and that the goods they stole seem to have been quite small and had a practical, immediate use, leads to conjecture that they were forced to become thieves because of a lack of support and economic stability. As these women would then be the main providers for their families, it would make sense that they would steal animals that could be turned into food, as Hanawalt argues when she reveals that sheep and poultry were items stolen more often by fourteenth-century women than men.[20] If these women were so lacking in support and standing, it may have been the reason why they did not stay to face trial. This possibility will be discussed more fully later in the paper.

Cecilia is useful to us for another reason, because she is also accused of committing "many larcenies" [*pluribus latrociniis*]. Charges of larceny make up the remainder of the property crimes committed by these women, and this felony is the most likely to be combined with another offence. Out of the seven women who were accused of this crime, only three of them, who were apparently working together in the wapentake of Gilling, appear to have been charged with larceny alone. In the other cases, the women are accused of other crimes at the same time. The aforementioned Cecilia is a clear example of this. Another instance is that of Agnes Rasur, exacted and waived in the wapentake of Boroughbridge for *pluribus latrociniis*, as well for giving shelter to a certain Robert of Ergmur, a thief who was later caught and beheaded.[21] Emma Trenekyrtle, mentioned above, is ordered exacted and waived for larcenies and burglary.[22]

Unfortunately, the use of the formula *pluribus latroniciis* means that we are denied some potentially crucial evidence. We cannot tell if these women are accused of committing "grand larceny" (theft of goods greater than the value of a shilling and a capital offence) or of the lesser charge of "petty larceny."[23] But the fact that the phrase is in the plural gives the impression that some of these women may have been taking part in these illegal activities for some time and had, perhaps, built up a certain reputation. If, in fact, these women were suspected of several crimes, they may have felt that it was more prudent to avoid trial by fleeing the locale, though of course we have no way of knowing this for certain.

Perhaps surprisingly, cases of murder account for 14.28 percent of the charges against these women, making it the second most common crime. When compared to the statistics of the men who were outlawed on suspicion of murder in this record (77 percent of all indictments), this does not appear to be too large of a number, but given that we are working with a much smaller pool of people, the six women who are accused of participation in murder take on a new significance. It is to these women that we now turn.

While women involved in property crimes seem to have been more likely to work alone, most of the women involved in murder do not appear to have acted independently, for analysis reveals that in four of these six homicide cases, the woman's role is that of an accessory to the homicide, thus helping a male accomplice. Among these four cases, only one seems to involve the killing of a person with no clear relationship to the woman or her accomplice. This is found in an entry among the records for the wapentake of Upper Claro:

> Robert, the farm bailiff of Leathley and Agnes, daughter of Searle from the same place at night wounded Thomas Steybain so that he died the next day and the aforesaid Robert and Agnes fled at once after the deed and are suspected. Let them be exacted and outlawed.[24]

As one can see in this entry, there is nothing to indicate whether the unfortunate Thomas Steybain had any personal relationship with either Robert or Agnes. However, the other three cases mentioned in JUST 1 1098 are clearly family affairs, with the woman's husband being the victim in two of the cases. The wapentake of Skyrack recorded the following case when the justices sat in session:

> William Pikehead, once farm bailiff of [roll un-clear] at night killed Radulf Rudde in his house in Harewood. And Agnes, wife of the said Radulf aided and abetted together with the said William in the killing of Radulf her husband. And they fled at once after the deed and are suspected. Let them be exacted and let the aforesaid William be outlawed and Agnes waived.[25]

Similarly, Cristancia, wife of murder victim William del Ferry, is ordered exacted and waived in the wapentake of Ainsty for her role in the said William's death. Her accomplice, Robert son of Inette, is ordered outlawed for the same crime. Rather ironically, the same entry also records that William himself had been outlawed earlier for committing a murder of his own![26] The possibilities for the motivations and exact nature of the relationships between the killers will be discussed further on in the paper.

The next case is also a family affair, a rather disturbing story of one Henry son of Matilda, from the village of Bashall Eaves and of his daughter Isabella, who are accused in the wapentake of Staincliffe of killing Henry's wife, Alice, with a shovel. After the deed, Henry is captured and sentenced to hang, but Isabella makes good her escape and is duly ordered exacted and waived.[27] Although we have no way of knowing what it was that led Isabella to help her father dispose of his wife, this story does leave us with the unappetizing possibility that this murder was something that parent and child planned together. It was not unusual for children to be drawn into violent conflicts between a parent and stepparent, and this may have been the situation here.[28]

The lone female killer seems to have been a rarity in the Middle Ages,[29] but in the remaining two murder cases in this roll, the woman apparently did do the killing herself. The case of Emma, daughter of Matilda of Salfordthure, indicted in the wapentake of Strafforth, leaves no doubt about who struck the fatal blow:

> Emma, daughter of Matilda de Salfordthure, killed Alice daughter of Radulf Galt in the village of Brunesford with a hatchet and at once after the deed fled and is suspected. Let her be exacted and waived.[30]

Emma's case has an aspect to it that makes it stand apart from the other cases mentioned, in that the weapon she used to kill her victim is noted, making it the only women's murder case in this record where this is so. The fact that she used a hatchet to commit her bloody deed is noteworthy, as this puts her case within the findings of other historians on medieval female criminality. Although women tended to use fewer weapons than men when committing murder,[31] and while they did not generally receive any weapons training,[32] it does not mean that women did not have access to weapons. They had ready access to a steady supply of household items, such as knives and hatchets, which could be used with deadly force.[33] It is likely that Emma would have had experience with hatchet use in her day-to-day duties, and it may have been easy for her to use the when committing her crime.

The remaining murder case does not give us any such detail. It is a short, rather offhand notation written among a long list of indictments from the wapentake of Upper Claro, and it states that one Alice of Demild killed the local shoemaker from the village of Bramham and is ordered to be exacted and waived.[34] Sadly, the record does not tell us what provoked this attack.

Although the women mentioned in this roll clearly take an active role in murder and property crimes, the fact remains that these were offences that were dominated by males, and so and the question needs to be asked: were there any crimes in this record in which women took the leading role? A study of the cases in JUST 1 1098 show that, in one criminal area at least, female involvement outnumbers that of the men. Giving shelter to wanted felons and outlaws (or *receiving*) was one area that was almost exclusively a female domain. The abovementioned Agnes Rasur was accused of opening her home to the thief Robert Ergmur,[35] but the court roll reveals that she was not unique in doing this. In fact, the number of women accused of receiving wanted fugitives makes up 9.52 percent of the indictments against them. In comparison, less than 2 percent of the men are accused of the same crime.

In theory, once a person was outlawed, one was denied the right to live among one's community. Bracton refers to the outlaw as a "friendless man" who, by his actions, has forfeited the right to have friends.[36] In practice, of course, one's ties to the community and to one's family did not automatically dissipate once a sentence had been passed. However, giving shelter to known felons was a felony in itself,[37] and Bracton continues on to say that one who knowingly harbours a recognized outlaw is therefore an "outlaw's friend" (*cuthutlaghe*) and "is to be punished with a like punishment."[38] This was clearly the fate of one Agnes Kiggelay, who was waived in the Northern Riding of Boulmer for receiving William of Barton, a thief who was later captured and hanged.[39] The justices in the wapentake of Strafforth order Idonea of Malebures to be exacted and waived for taking in one John Rider, another known thief.[40] Idonea is accused of committing several robberies on her own.

Considering that men's rate of receiving felons is less than a third of that of women, why then was giving refuge to criminals and fugitives primarily a woman's crime? It could be that the answer lies in societal norms. Given that women have the traditional role of wife, mother, daughter, and nurturer, it may have been inevitable that they take on the role of receiver.[41] A receiving case that appears in the entries from the wapentake of Pontefract might have been a tragic result of this situation. A certain Agnes Boberon is ordered to be exacted and waived for giving shelter to one Thomas Boberon, a fugitive thief.[42] Although the actual nature of the relationship between them is not specified, their shared surname makes it likely that there was a family connection. But however tempting it might be to see these cases as simply abiding love and family loyalty, there are other, more unpleasant factors that may explain why women were placed in the role of receiver. As some of the other cases previously discussed indicate, it was not uncommon for family members to commit crimes together. A little over a third of known fourteenth-century criminal gangs had family connections; therefore, it was common to take the role of receiver in such families.[43] Perhaps, therefore, these women were merely fulfilling their familial duties when they sheltered these wanted felons or were doing it for personal gain. There is also, of course, the unsettling possibility that these women were forced or intimidating into receiving criminals.

The last waiving case mentioned in JUST 1 1098 involves a prison escape. Although prison breaking is not a peculiarly female activity, this particular case has a uniquely feminine twist that makes it worthy of mention. Agnes, daughter of William Federles, is captured while in the company of thieves and is taken to a prison in York. Apparently, she put her time behind bars to go use, for the record states that the sheriff "lay with her" and then allowed her to leave the prison unchallenged, even though he knew of her reputation.[44] After her escape, Agnes is thus ordered exacted and waived. Unfortunately, the eventual fate of her lover is not recorded, although it appears that he was ordered to explain himself to the authorities. Agnes Federles presumably worked on her own, but how does her experience fare when compared to that of the other women mentioned in JUST 1 1098? Did these women act alone or in groups? If it were the latter, then with whom did these women associate? As discussed earlier, the practice of outlawing and waiving large numbers of individuals at once can make it difficult to determine with whom those named acted (if anyone). For sixteen of the forty-two women listed, it is close to impossible to determine whether these women worked alone or with accomplices. However, the remaining cases can be studied in this regard, and they can yield some interesting finds on the company that many of these women kept. My research indicates that, while a majority of these women did work alone, a sizeable portion of them acted with accomplices, often members of their own families.

For the twenty-six women for whom it is possible to determine their entourage, it seems that fifteen acted on their own. We have seen this in the murder cases of Emma of Salfordthure[45] and Alice Demild,[46] as well as in the prison escape of Agnes Federles.[47] However, the remaining twelve women are indicted for receiving, burglary, larceny, and theft. There is no indication that the receivers Agnes Rasur,[48] Agnes Boberon,[49] and Agnes Kiggelay[50] had accomplices who helped them shelter the thieves that they knew. Also, the accused thieves Margery Stoke,[51] Cecilia of Kirk Bramwith,[52] and Sybil Denning[53] also appear to have been working unaccompanied. That it should be so in these cases is not surprising, for women were the natural receivers and the goods stolen were relatively small and easy to carry away. Indeed, these crimes offered an anonymity that more aggressive crimes did not,[54] and while committing them, solitude was probably necessary and preferred.

In the other eleven cases, the women acted with accomplices who are usually either ordered exacted and outlawed or otherwise punished. When women acted with accomplices, these associates were usually drawn from a close (at times familial) vicinity,[55] and this is borne out in the instances mentioned here. The most easily recognized grouping was husband and wife teams (sometimes with children or other associates in tow). This was such a common occurrence that Bracton makes mention of the treatment of wives found to be aiding and abetting their husbands in crime, arguing that they should both be held liable, for as "partners in crime," they should also be "partners in punishment."[56] In three of the burglary cases listed in JUST 1 1098, the woman's accomplice was her husband. When discussing burglary charges, I mentioned the case of Aylmer and Agnes of Ferlington, who were indicted for burgling a barn in the wapentake of Boulmer,[57] and two more cases, taken from the wapentakes of Morley and Doncaster respectively, also follow much the same pattern:

> William le Fullar of Halifax and his wife Annabella and John, son of the same William, fled for the burglary of the mill of Halifax and of the house of Richard le Barker of Halifax...[58]
>
> ...John Wale, his wife Matilda and Richard le Cupere fled for the burglary of the house of Richard son of Gervase of Ansterford.[59]

Given the normally close relationship between spouses, it may have been inevitable that some husbands and wives would band together to commit crimes.

In his study of thirteenth-century homicide patterns, James Buchanan Given argues that over 30 percent of criminals turned to their parents and children when looking for accomplices.[60] None of the women involved turned to their children for help, but we have seen the cases of Juliana Grunne[61] and Isabella of Bashall Eaves[62] who helped their fathers commit burglary and murder respectively.

In the above cases, the exact nature of the relationship between the woman and her accomplice(s) is easily determined, but in another three cases, the bond between the woman and her male accomplice is open to speculation. Revisiting the case of Agnes, daughter of Searle, who was ordered exacted and waived in the wapentake of Upper Claro for helping Robert of Lethley wound and kill one Thomas Steybain,[63] we can see nothing in the wording of the entry to give us a clue as to what relationship (if any) that they may have had. The fact that the victim also does not have a clear link to either of the perpetrators does not clarify the situation.

The cases of Agnes Rudde[64] and Cristancia del Ferry,[65] who were both suspected of helping male accomplices kill their husbands, lead us to wonder if those involved may have had a personal reason for wanting Radulf Rudde and William del Ferry off the scene. It is tempting to see the relationship between Agnes and William Pikehead and Cristancia and Robert as examples of the "classic criminal combinations" of lovers banding together to remove the inconvenience of the woman's husband.[66] However, we must be careful not to read too much into these cases, since we have no way of knowing the truth.

The women mentioned so far worked with male family members, male companions, and on their own, but did the women in this record ever work with other women? At least one case in this record leaves us with the impression that, occasionally at least, they did. A lengthy case from the wapentake of Gillling makes mention of Juliana, wife of Robert of Donham, Alice daughter of Bylla, and Alice daughter of Tassard, who are all accused of *"pluribus latrociniis."*[67] This trio stands out from the other fifty-five felons who are mentioned in this case because the wording seems to imply that Juliana and the two Alices were involved in these crimes as a group. Although the scribe does not specifically say that these women actually worked together, the fact that their names are listed together in an unbroken sentence (and that there is only one charge between them) leads me to think that this might indicate criminal activity of a group on their part. Those who took part in larceny often did not seem to have trouble finding accomplices,[68] and if these women were indeed working together, then it would show that women sometimes did band together in criminal organizations without male associates.

Up to this point, I have done some speculation as to why the women in this record may have chosen to flee the law and, inevitably, become waived. However, as it has been seen, the vast majority of the people who were ordered exacted and placed outside the law in this record were male. Fleeing the law dies not seem to have been an option that many women chose or were able to take. I would like to conclude this paper with some tentative theories on why this might have been so. Since these women did not leave behind evidence of their thoughts and feelings for us to study, many of my remarks will, inevitably, be speculation and conjecture. However, I do believe that it is possible to make a few suggestions as to why outlawing may have been such an overwhelmingly male experience.

So few outlawry sentences involve women; as mentioned earlier, the number of 10.7 percent of the total is almost identical to the 10 percent that Hanawalt suggests as the approximate number of female defendants one finds in other criminal cases of the time.[69] But why, if supposedly "ten men were outlawed for every one hanged,"[70] were so few women meeting the same fate? I am not going to argue that women are naturally less inclined to commit criminal acts, or that they are just caught less frequently, because I do not have sufficient evidence to make such statements. However, I believe that there are several very practical reasons for why women are so seldom found to be placed outside the law.

It is possible that one reason so few waived women are found is that they were not ordered to trial in the first place. It has been argued that justices may have been more lenient with female defendants who came to court less frequently and were more likely to be acquitted.[71] This may explain why there is such a small number of women being ordered exacted and waived in general, but since our focus is those women who *did* get charged, this argument has a rather limited usefulness.

For the more severe charges, the opportunity to flee trial may have been the preferred option. This may be particularly true in the murder cases that were discussed. Considering that murder was, technically at any rate, a capital offence, it is certainly not surprising that many accused of this crime should choose to flee the area. In the cases of Isabella of Bashall Eaves, Agnes Rudde, and Cristancia del Ferry, flight might have been the only sensible option, since courts tended to deal harshly with those who had killed their relatives.[72] Agnes and Cristancia, in particular, would have faced a much more severe punishment if they had been found guilty of killing their husbands. The murder of one's husband was thought to be "more heinous, more sinful and more treacherous" than many other crimes.[73] It was more than mere murder. It was, in fact, a form of treason, as the woman was thought to be killing not just her partner, but also her lord and master.[74] Burning punished such a criminal. The case of Cristancia del Ferry is particularly intriguing because, as mentioned above, one could actually receive a reward for killing an outlaw. It is tempting to wonder why she did not try to claim this reward. Perhaps she feared that the justices would be unsympathetic towards her because the outlawed man was still her husband, regardless of his status before the law. The fact that another man was involved in the killing might also have turned the authorities against her. This is, of course, only speculation, but it is still an interesting mystery.

Women's traditional place in society as "kin keeper" may have had a role in their becoming involved in receiving and other family-based crimes, but it may also explain why women were so seldom waived. As discussed above, being outlawed for a flight from justice meant being denied the right to live in one's community, and it became a crime for the outlaw's family to associate with them. Therefore, being outlawed or waived would mean leaving one's family and home. Considering that women were then, as now, primarily responsible for the well-being of the children and the family, it may have been next to impossible for many women to flee the locale as it would have meant leaving behind spouses and children. Several of the cases discussed in this paper, I believe, touch on this point. In the instances where spouses and children are mentioned at all, it is usually in connection with the crime for which the woman herself has been waived. This is seen in the stories of Agnes of Ferlington and Annabella le Fullar. Since Annabelle's husband and Agnes' husband and stepson are indicted and outlawed at the same time as the women, presumably the family did not face an automatic break up. As for the other women working alone, the wording of the cases leaves us with the impression that they may have had no family ties keeping them in one particular place. We cannot rule out the possibility that this was the situation of Cecilia, who was the onetime wife of Richard of Kirk Bramwith. While it is possible that Cecilia may merely have been widowed, the fact that the words "was the wife..." are used, rather than the more normal "widow," may suggest that Cecilia had been abandoned by her husband. Abandoned or widowed, and possibly without children, she may have had no reason to remain in the area after her theft was discovered. Her shaky social status may have been the reason she was forced to turn to crime in the first place.

It is also possible that the women were aware of the risks they would face if they were placed outside the law, and this may be another reason for the small number of waiving sentences. The world is a violent place for women, even at the best of times, but a woman in medieval England who was within the pale of society could at least bring her case to the courts for possible redress if she were raped or otherwise harmed. If she were waived, she lost this protection, perhaps leaving herself more vulnerable to abuse or harm. Moreover, where was she to go if she were cast out of her community? To be exacted and ordered outlawed or waived often meant that one's reputation became widely known, because all who attended court sessions were made aware of the indictments and crimes, and this publicity gave the entire shire the means and incentive to prevent these people from joining their communities.[75] Given such circumstances, it may have been very difficult for a woman to survive once she was outside the law's protection.

Male outlaws often banded together in criminal gangs after sentence was passed. Could women have joined these groups? The statistics gleaned from such sources as jail delivery rolls and other indictments suggest that most women did not. Hanawalt has uncovered that only 4.6 percent of known criminal bands were made up of women; these women were usually the wives and female relatives of the men and not necessarily outlaws in their own right.[76] Since outlawry was so primarily a man's world, it is possible that women may not have been welcome in the company of other, male outlaws for whom survival was a struggle.

I hope that I have suggested some reasonable possibilities as to why outlawry was mostly a man's experience and that I have shed some light in the experience of some of the women who were unfortunate enough to find themselves thrust into this world. However, I confess to a vague sense that the story is not yet finished. Occasionally, in JUST 1 1098 and other similar records, a postscript will be found at the end of some of the court entries. These are later additions to the document that record the return of the accused before the allotted time has expired and at times the explanations the accused gives as to why he or she committed the crime and fled the law in the first place. In almost all of these cases, the accused is acquitted, and his outlawry sentence is declared null and void.⁷⁷ When I began this study, I hoped that some of the women's entries would have similar additions, and they would have revealed to us what happened to these unfortunate women. However, none of the women in this roll appear to have come back to tell their side of the story. Therefore, their explanations, and their eventual fates, remain a mystery.

NOTES

1. At this time Yorkshire was divided up into three administrative ridings roughly corresponding to modern day South Yorkshire (West Riding), Humberside (East Riding) and North Yorkshire (North Riding). Unless otherwise stated, the cases in this court record are from the West Riding, which appears to have been more populated than the other two. For more information see A. H. Smith, ed., *The Place Names of the North Riding of Yorkshire*. English Place-Name Society 5 (Cambridge: Cambridge University Press, 1928); A. H. Smith, ed., *The Place Names of the East Riding of Yorkshire*. English Place-Name Society 14 (Cambridge: Cambridge University Press, 1937); and A. H. Smith, ed., *The Place Names of the West Riding of Yorkshire*, 8 vol. English Place-Name Society 30–37 (Cambridge: Cambridge University Press, 1961–63).

2. Kew, NA JUST 1 1098: wapentake of Skyrack, p. 13a: "Jordannus Grunne de Secroft & William filius eius noctante burgaverunt bertariam Williami de Rythere in Shadewell et Simon de Esthewick bertarius eiusdem Williami existens in eadem bertaria ... audiebat surrexit & predictum Jordanum insultavit et ipsum [tangit?] latronem occidit. Et predictus William predicti Jordanni statim post factum fugit & malecreditur. Exigatur & utlegatur. Nulla habet catalla." All transcriptions and translations are my own. The numbers in brackets refer to the numbers placed on the record by modern archivists. I have tried to reproduce the original Latin record written as accurately as impossible.

3. J. G. Bellamy, *Crime and Public Order in England in the Later Middle Ages* (London: Routledge & Kegan Paul, 1973), 104

4. Kew, NA JUST 1 1098: wapentake of Skyrack, p. 13a: "Et Juliana filia Jordanni Grunne subtraxit se per burgariam predictam & malecreditur. Exigatur & wayvietur."

5. She may not have been physically present at the failed robbery, but her role might have been as an intended receiver of stolen goods or of any fugitive family members.

6. I refer primarily to the work of Barbara A. Hanawalt on medieval English crime.

7. Henry de Bracton, *On the Laws and Customs of England*, ed. George E. Woodbine, trans. Samuel E. Thorne, 4 vol. (Cambridge: Harvard University Press, 1968–77), 2: 353–354.

8. Andrew McCall. *The Medieval Underworld*, 2nd ed. (Stroud: Sutton Publishing, 2004), 71.

9. The numbers deserve some explanation. The twenty-seven refers to the actual number of *entries* in which the formula "*exigatur et waivietur*" appears in the records. However, it was not unusual to pass sentence on large numbers of people at once, using the formula only one time. The forty-two indicates the number of *individual* women involved, as several of the indictments waive several women at once. I have chosen to discuss women as individuals, rather than as case numbers.

10. Barbara A. Hanawalt, *Crime and Conflict in English Communities, 1300–1348*. Cambridge: Harvard University Press, 1979), 115

11. Although in one case, one woman is involved in both burglary and larceny.

12. Kew, NA JUST 1 1098: wapentake of Boulmer, p. 64a: "Et Aylmer de Ferlington & Agnes uxor eius subtraxerunt se per burgariam grangae Johnnis de Ferlington ..." The word *subtraxit* is found in several of these cases. I have found it best to translate it as "fled" because there

is a connotation of flight. My theory is that this word was used, instead of the usual *fugit*, in cases where the crime had been committed some time previously and whose perpetrators had not fled immediately after the fact.

13. Kew, NA JUST 1 1098: wapentake of Morley, p. 26b: "Et Matilda de Brite subtraxit se per burgaris domi Johannis Bocerthur ... [exigatur et waivietur]."

14. Kew, NA JUST 1 1098: wapentake of Gilling, p. 67a: "Et Emma Trenekyrtle similiter subtraxit se per burgariam domorum & pluribus latrociniis ... et Emma [exigatur] et wayvietur."

15. J. G. Bellamy, *The Criminal Trial in Later Medieval England: Felony Before the Courts from Edward I to the Sixteenth Century* (Toronto: University of Toronto Press, 1998), 71

16. Kew, NA JUST 1 1098: wapentake of Pontefract, p. 10b: "Et Margeria Stok [subtraxit] se per [roll unreadable] & furationis pisce."

17. Kew, NA JUST 1 1098: wapentake of Strafforth, p. 43a: "Et Sybilla Denning manens quondam in Trunfeld subtraxit se per blado furationem..." She does not seem to have been a local resident of Trunfield.

18. Kew, NA JUST 1 1098: wapentake of Gilling, p. 68a: "[E]t Matilda de la Grene de Midelton similiter subtraxit se per duabus [roll unclear] furationes ... & Matilda wayvietur."

19. Kew, NA JUST 1 1098: wapentake of Osgoldcross, p. 56b: "Cecilia qui fuit uxor Ricardi de Bramwyth subtraxit se per II ovibus furtionem de Johannes de Nemle ... & per bladu furationem & aliis latronibus & malecreditur. Exigatur & waivietur."

20. Barbara A. Hanawalt, "Women Before the Law: Females as Felons and Prey in Fourteenth-Century England," in *Women and the Law: The Social Historical Perspective*, ed. D. Kelly Weisberg, 2 vol. (Cambridge, MA: Schenkman, 1982), 1: 165–195 at 169.

21. Kew, NA JUST 1 1098: wapentake of Boroughbridge, p. 24a: "[E]t Agnes Rasur de eadem [Boroughbridge] subtraxit se per pluribus latrociniis & receptione Roberti de Ergmur latroni decollate."

22. See note 14 above.

23. Frederick Pollack and Frederick William Maitland, ed., *The History of English Law Before the Time of Edward I*, 2nd ed. 2 vol. (Cambridge: Cambridge University Press, 1968), 2: 495–96.

24. Kew, NA JUST 1 1098: wapentake of Upper Claro, p. 17a: "Robertus le messarius de Letheley et Agnes filia Serloni de eadem noctante vulneravit Thomas Steybayn ita quod in crastino inde obiit. Et predicti Robertus & Agnes statim post factum fugierunt & malecrediuntur. Exigantur et utlagentur." Interestingly, the word "waived" is not actually used here. It is worth speculating whether Agnes, had she challenged the ruling, would have had grounds to argue that the sentence was invalid.

25. Kew, NA JUST 1 1098: wapentake of Skyrack, p. 12b: "William Pykehed quoddam messarius de [roll unclear] noctante occidit Radulfum Rudde in doma sua in Harewood. Et Agnes uxor predicti Radulfi in vi & auxilia simul cum predicto William ad occidendum predictum Radulfum virum suum. Et statim post factum fugierunt et malecrediuntur. Exigantur et predictus William utlegatur et Agnes wayvietur."

26. Kew, NA JUST 1 1098: wapentake of Anisty, p. 58a: "Robertus filius Inette & Cristancia uxor predicti William del Ferry similiter se subtraxerunt per morte predicti Williami & malecrediuntur. Exigantur & predictus Robertus utlegatur & Cristancia waivietur."

27. Kew, NA JUST 1 1098: wapentake of Staincliff, p. 5a: "Henricus filius Matildae de Bacshelf et Isabella filia eius occiderunt Aliciam uxorem predicti Henrici cum quodam vanga in villa de Bacshelf. Et predictus Henricus statim captus fuit & coram justices ad gaolem deliberandus assignus suspensus fuit ... Et predicta Isabella statim post factum fugit & malecreditur. Exigatur & waivietur."

28. James Buchanan Given, *Society and Homicide in Thirteenth-Century England* (Stanford: Stanford University Press, 1977), 63.

29. Richard J. Sims, "Secondary Offenders? English Women and Crime, c. 1220–1348," in *Victims or Viragos?*, ed. Christine Meek and Catherine Lawless. Studies in Medieval and Early Modern Women 4 (Dublin: Four Courts Press, 2005), 69–88. Sims states that "by and large, it is fair to say women throughout the land preferred to commit homicide with somebody else, be it a husband, a lover, a brother or another woman," 75.

30. Kew, NA JUST 1 1098: wapentake of Strafforth, p. 40b: "Emma filia Matildae de Salfordthure occidit Aliciam filiam Radulfi Galt in villa de Brunesford cum quadam hachia. Et statim post factum fugit & malecreditur. Exigatur & waivietur."
31. Garthine Walker, *Crime, Gender, and Social Order in Early Modern England* (Cambridge: Cambridge University Press, 2003), 78.
32. Given, *Society and Homicide*, 136.
33. Hanawalt. "Women Before the Law," 174.
34. Kew, NA JUST 1 1098: wapentake of Upper Claro, p. 20a: "Et Alicia Demyld subtraxit se per morte cuiusdem sutoris de Bramham occisi [roll unreadable]."
35. See note 21 above.
36. Bracton, *On the Laws and Customs of England*, 2: 361.
37. Bellamy, *The Criminal Trial*, 79.
38. Bracton, *On the Laws and Customs of England*, 2: 362.
39. Kew, NA JUST 1 1098: wapentake of Boulmer, p. 64a: "Et Agnes Kiggelay de Stylon subtraxit se per receptamento William de Barton latronem suspensum."
40. Kew, NA JUST 1 1098: wapentake of Stafforth, p. 41a: "Idonea de Maleburès subtraxit se pro receptando Johannis le Ryder latronem decollatum & pro pluribus latrociniis & malecreditur. Exigatur & utlegatur."
41. Hanawalt, *Crime and Conflict*, 123.
42. Kew, NA JUST 1 1098: wapentake of Pontefract, p. 10b: "Et Agnes Boboeron subtraxit se per receptando Thomas Boberon latronem fugitem."
43. Barbara Hanawalt (Weston), "The Peasant Family and Crime in England," *The Journal of British Studies* 13, no. 2 (1974): 1–18 at 13–14.
44. Kew, NA JUST 1 1098: wapentake of Barkston Ash, p. 52a: "Agnes filia Williami Federles capta fuit apud Aberford in societate Williami de Misterton probatoris suspensi & aliorum latronum decollatorum & ducta apud Eboracum & ibidem imprisonata tempe Johannis de Melsa tenet vicecomes ... et idem Johannes cubuit cum ipsa & ea de causa eam permisit abire sciens ipsam esse latronisse. Et predicta Agnes modo so subtraxit & malecreditur. Exigatur & waivietur."
45. See note 30 above.
46. See note 34 above.
47. See note 44 above.
48. See note 21 above.
49. See note 42 above
50. See note 39 above.
51. See note 16 above.
52. See note 19 above.
53. See note 17 above.
54. Sims, "Secondary Offenders," 88.
55. See J. M. Beattie, "The Royal Pardon and Criminal Procedure in Early Modern England," *Historical Papers* 22, no. 1 (1987): 9–22 at 15 for a brother and sister who, in eighteenth-century London, were condemned for robbery.
56. Bracton, *On the Laws and Customs of England*, 2: 428. However, there is some debate on how strictly this was followed in practice.
57. See note 12 above.
58. Kew, NA JUST 1 1098: wapentake of Morley, p. 28a: "Et William le Fullar de Halyfax & Annabella uxor eius & Johannes filius eiusdem Williami Subtraxerunt se per burgaria molendarii de Halyfax et domus Ricardi le Braker de Halyfax..."
59. Kew, NA JUST 1 1098: Doncaster, p. 45b: "Et Johannes Wale, Matilda uxor eius & Ricardus le Cupere subtraxerunt se per burgariam domi Ricardi filii Gervase de Ansterford."
60. Given, *Society and Homicide*, 46.
61. See note 4 above.
62. See note 27 above.
63. See note 25 above.

64. See note 25 above.
65. See note 26 above.
66. Hanawalt, "Women Before the Law," 174.
67. Kew, NA JUST 1 1098: wapentake of Gilling, p. 68b: "Et Juliana uxor Roberti de Donham & Alicia filia Byllae & Alicia filia Tassard subtraxerunt se de pro pluribus latrociniis."
68. Given, *Society and Homicide*, 111.
69. Hanawalt. *Crime and Conflict*, 115.
70. Pollack and Maitland, *The History of English Law*, 1: 478.
71. Hanawalt, "Women Before the Law," 186–91.
72. Given, *Society and Homicide*, 102.
73. Walker, *Crime, Gender, and Social Order*, 138.
74. Thomas Andrew Green, *Verdict According to Conscience: Perspectives on the English Criminal Trial Jury, 1200–1800* (Chicago: University of Chicago Press, 1985), 57–58.
75. H. R. T. Summerson, "The Structure of Law Enforcement in Thirteenth Century England," *The American Journal of Legal History* 23, no. 4 (1979): 313–27 at 325.
76. Hanawalt, "Women Before the Law," 178.
77. Most of these cases involve charges of murder. The accused inevitably claims self-defense and is usually acquitted.

3

Portraits of Outlaws, Felons, and Rebels in Late Medieval England

BARBARA A. HANAWALT

We have so many portraits of those who rebelled against laws, cultural mores, royal and religious authorities, and civil officials that it is hard to pick and choose among the possible pictures of these offenders. Picking out rebels in medieval society reminds us that the vast majority of people chose to live within the boundaries. Some, it is true, recanted or fled when it became dangerous to live outside the law and some simply escaped with a reprimand or a fine. Those on the margins of legal behavior stand out. Sometimes they are notorious, sometimes they are ordinary, and sometimes they are simply a matter of legend, poetry, and the inspired imagination of chroniclers. Three types of medieval social constructs of marginals appear in this essay: felons and outlaws, rebels against political authority, and transgressors of social barriers. People have a range of reactions to the real and mythical rebels. Their stories provide a vicarious thrill of actions that a normal, law-abiding person would not do. They are a type of medieval fantasy folklore or literature. Some appear to right wrongs that are a common complaint of the society. Some of those portrayed are pitied, but some are truly evil. The figures, real or mythical, teach lessons of behavior. In this respect they have much in kin with courtesy books. But they are also like sermon exemplars in that their eventual punishment makes a moral story out of their tales.

Medieval opinion differs little from our own perceptions since current attitudes toward those living outside the law provoke so many mixed emotions. Robin Hood is an appealing figure in myth. He lived in the greenwood, behaved like a gentleman, and robbed from the rich and gave to the poor. But real outlaws were felons who were very much dreaded by the population at large.[1] The perceptions of different social classes can make either a villain or a hero out of rebels, depending on who is telling their story. A wealthy landlord takes a very different view of a peasant rebel than the rebel's fellow villagers. The prevailing misogyny in the Middle Ages could put women at risk of being labeled as deviant, but women were seldom indicted for crimes. Our modern categories are as slippery as those of the Middle Ages, and we owe a great deal to our medieval forbearers for giving us strong traditions to express our own ambivalent thinking about these people who moved outside the laws and social mores of society.

I am proposing three types of portraits that illustrate the varying late medieval perceptions of outlaws, felons, and rebels. The first is the outlaw, a figure both loathed and admired. The outlaw in the thirteenth century was a felon who was said to have the price of a wolf's head. That is, he could be hunted like a wolf and the person bringing in his head would get a reward. By the fourteenth and fifteenth centuries, outlawry was extended to those who fled from some sort of personal action. Some of the outlaws were very benign folk who simply chose not to appear in court or did not pay their debts, but others were real oppressors of the countryside. We need to know what local jurors thought of robbers and outlaws and to speculate on why the Robin Hood legends enjoyed such popularity when real outlaws could prove to be dangerous. The second group portrait is of political rebels of the lower classes who expressed the views of many in towns and countryside, but who were very much feared by those in positions of power. To diminish their appeal, elite writers described them as barnyard animals. Many of the rebels were articulate and able to express their goals in both words and actions. The final example is that of the gentry-class woman, Eleanor Cobham, who married a king's son, Duke Humphrey of Gloucester, but was tried for sorcery and punished with a public, penitential march through London. Was she a sorceress or did she simply move above her social rank in marrying a Duke? What did people think of this social climber? The portraits are instructive about how medieval society, at least portions of them, perceived transgressions that fell into the categories of tolerable, ambiguous, and really heinous.

The sources are various so that they are useful as a check, one upon another. Literary sources are vivid in their descriptions, but they need to be counter balanced with historical records. Trial and indictment records are a valuable framing device for the literary works. What images and ideals did judges, ecclesiastical officials, and juries appeal to when they labeled people as law breakers or sorcerers? Knowledge of the person accused certainly was part of their framework for decisions, since they wanted to know if the person was of good or ill repute or if their governance was good. Gender and class was of paramount importance. Officials and communities worked with a wide range of cultural assumptions about correct and incorrect behavior that are hard to tease out of literature and court cases, but their prejudices had an enormous impact on the interpretation of law and the labeling of deviants.

Norbert Elias in *The Civilizing Process: The History of Manners* provides a useful framework for investigating the labeling of deviants.[2] Elias explored the transition from the medieval assumptions of polite behavior to those of the early modern period, drawing extensively on the increasing popularity in the fifteenth and sixteenth centuries of advice manuals, courtesy books, and mirror of princes' literature. His thesis was that in the medieval period only the elite could be expected to participate in civilized culture, but in the early modern period the concept of civilization spread to all classes. Elias's juxtaposition of courtesy books of acceptable, elite manners to those of the lower orders suggests a challenging agenda in historical analysis. Although Elias defines civilized with frequent references to its opposite, the uncivilized, he does not explore this obverse extensively. This paper analyses those who fell into disfavor with society and the reasons that they did so. What sets apart those of good repute from those of ill repute and who, other than legal authorities, offered judgments on their behavior? What words, analogies, and metaphors did the society use to call people's actions and words unacceptable? Was there any consensus of what behavior was labeled "beyond the pale?" Medieval society was a hierarchical one, and those who did the labeling had considerable power over those who were marginalized. A study of these portraits, therefore, is also a study of the flow of power in late medieval society.

Felons, Outlaws, and Robin Hood

My first exploration of the power of labeling is of social attitudes toward robbers and outlaws. A contrast between the heroic medieval versions of "Robin Hood" and the conviction of robbers in court provides a striking contrast. By the late fourteenth and fifteenth centuries, the population had come to know and enjoy the ballads, but in reality the population had a great fear and loathing of robbery and outlaw bands. The ballad makes him a courteous outlaw who robbed from the rich and gave to the poor. A student of Elias and the courtesy literature that he relied on might find elements in the fifteenth-century Robin Hood stories for a book of manners, but the poems themselves are full of violence to the innocent.[3] I will not use this occasion for a detailed comparison of real bandits to Robin Hood, because I have already done that in "Ballads and Bandits: Fourteenth-Century Outlaws and the Robin Hood Poems."[4]

Real outlaws and bandits inspired considerable consternation in the English countryside. If one looks at the statistics on indictments and convictions for various felonies (larceny, burglary, robbery, rape, homicide, and receiving known felons and stolen goods) for the first half of the fourteenth century, it is clear that robbery was among the most threatening crimes. The figures come from the first half of the fourteenth century rather than from the latter half when the first mention of Robin Hood appears in *Piers Plowman* or from the fifteenth century when the first versions of a Robin Hood poem are preserved, but changes in administration of justice makes this material unreliable.

The figures come from the jail delivery rolls, which reflect the attitudes of juries towards various felonies and the people they acquitted or convicted. Members of the jury who made the criminal indictments and convicted those whom they deemed guilty came from the peasant communities. In their deliberations and sentencing, they were expressing their own sense of who was dangerous and what felonies were most heinous. Their judgments were not imposed by the king, his justices, nobles, or ecclesiastical authorities. They represent decisions of peasant and urban jurors who found the actions of some people punishable by hanging and others excusable by acquittal. The power flowed through juries of local people. In the period between 1300–1348, in a five county survey including 16,365 criminal indictments, the mean number of convictions was 25 percent.

The jurors had a hierarchy of crimes that they punished with hanging. Those indicted for simple larceny, picking up and absconding with goods not their own, were convicted in only 22 percent of the cases. Larceny is a loose category in medieval law because it was so easy to call it a matter of self help in getting back goods perceived as belonging to the perpetrator or as trespass rather than a felony. Furthermore, the value of the goods was often low. Burglary with 38 percent convictions and robbery with 31 percent seemed to have been more offensive to jurors. In both these felonies, the secrecy and violence of the offense lent a sinister quality. People who should have been secure in their homes or travelers going about legitimate business suffered sudden and unexpected violence in burglary and robbery. Both these felonies also involved weapons of war, such as bows and arrows, battle axes, and swords. Jurors added to the official records such off hand statements as "broke a wall [or window] and entered," or "broke into the house at night," or "under the cover of darkness," or "lay await in ambush," indicating a sense of the helplessness and defenselessness on the part of the victims and cowardice on the part of the accused. Although the law provided for no additional punishment, other than hanging, the jurors and clerks recording their testimony expressed heightened disapprobation. Thus the property crimes committed in stealth, under the cover of darkness, and with violence or the threat thereof were more likely to end in a conviction than were those involving simple theft.

When one considers that crimes against the person — homicide and rape — did not result in wide spread convictions (12 percent and 10 percent, respectively), the community intolerance of burglary and robbery is all the more striking. Rape, then as now, was a hard felony in which to secure a conviction, and homicide usually occurred between people in the community and arose from arguments that the jurors knew about and understood. These people were unlikely to commit homicide again.[5]

The figures do not represent actual guilt. Some people were guilty, but the community and the jurors chose to excuse them or accept them with the understanding that they would not commit further crimes. Long-time residents of the community were more likely to be excused, than were transients or complete strangers. Women were indicted and convicted less frequently than men. Robbers and violent burglars, however, had a different profile.

Robbers were considered sinister and with good reason. They were strangers to their communities — only 10 percent of the accused robbers lived in the same village as their victims. Most came from fifteen miles away from the scene of their crime and almost 50 percent came from a different county. Although only 11 percent of all indictments were robberies, the jurors convicted over a third of those accused. Robbers were impatient thieves and did not wait for goods to be left unguarded. They set up ambushes for their victims. Their weapons were not those of the ordinary peasant, the knife or staff, but bows and arrows, swords, and other weapons of war. While many crimes were seasonal, occurring in warmer months, robbers struck at all times and usually at twilight. They worked as gangs and were well organized with defined leadership and plans for division of the spoils. While their victims were sometimes spectacularly wealthy merchants, bishops, and royal officials, most of their victims were among the peasants themselves. Peasant households could provide bread, clothing, meat, blankets, as well as some valuables.[6]

While Robin Hood presumably did not rob and brutalize husbandmen and did not harm women, the record gives a different picture.

> Towards vespers at twilight on 1 September 1267 six thieves came to Honeydon in the parish of Eton Socon and found a boy Philip son of Roger Golde, who was coming from his father's fold, beat, ill treated and wounded him, and forced him to lead them to Ralph son of Geoffrey of Honeydon's house and called to Ralph to let them in. Ralph recognized Philip and opened the door. The thieves entered, assaulted, wounded and then bound Ralph, killed his mother Denise and his servant William of Roxton and then robbed the whole house and took away all its goods. From there they went to William Courtepie's house and broke it, assaulted and badly wounded William with swords, axes [and] lances and stole the goods of the house.

By the end of their rampage in the village, they had killed a widow in her house, gravely wounded another couple, chased another family out of their house and stole their goods, bound another man, and wounded another and burnt his house. Eventually, Philip managed to get away and raise the hue and cry.[7]

We know something of popular fear of robbery from a medieval charm poem. After calling on the Father, the Son, and the Holy Ghost, the charm goes on to talk about the stealth of robbers who find cover in herb, grass, stone and tree:

> yf here come eny fon   *foes*
> me to robbe, other me to sclon;   *or to kill me*
> they stond as stylle as eny ston,
> they haue no powere away to gon,
> By the vertu of the holy trinite...[8]

The charm talks of people hiding and threatening to do bodily damage to extract goods, as does William Langland, in *Piers Plowman*:

> Outlaws in the Wode, and under banke lotyeth,
> And many uch man se, and good merk take,
> Who is bihynde and who before, and who ben on horse,
> For he halt hym hardyer on horse, than he that is a fote.[9]

Much earlier the Statute of Winchester (1285) stated this: "It is commanded that the highways leading from one market town to another shall be broadened, wherever there is a ditch or underwood, or bushes, so that there be neither dyke, tree, nor bush where a man may lurk to do hurt."[10]

In 1439 a petition was made in Parliament about a gang that went around terrorizing "and, in manere of Insurrection, went into the wodes and in that Contre, like as it hadde be Robynhode and his meyne."[11] Even the 1381 rebel, John Ball, is purported to have written a letter: "chastise wel Hobbe the Robbere."[12]

At the same time that peasants and the country as a whole expressed fear of outlaw and robber gangs, positive myths and poems grew in circulation, popularity, and sophistication. Bandits did sometimes attack common oppressors of the populace and these acts brought public approval.[13] The Robin Hood verses of the fifteenth century give Robin Hood the civilized virtues of courtesy, generosity, knowledge of woodcraft, skill in weaponry, and a taste for good food and ale. While the tales include the killing of innocent victims, such as a young page, Robin Hood could be expected to behave well at a dinner table and serve the king in style with table linens and serving dishes (probably stolen from peasants). The outlaw of the poems knew etiquette.[14]

The attractive image of life in the outdoors figures in one of the most literate fifteenth-century courtesy books, the *Boke of Nurture*. The author, John Russell, was usher to the Duke of Gloucester (the husband of Eleanor

Cobham, who is the last portrait). In his prologue, he describes himself as being in the forest in May, enjoying the freshness of spring, when he sees three deer grazing in the sunshine. Close by is a "seemly young man that slender was and lean" with a bow and arrow in his hand. The young man is a poacher. He invites the youth to walk with him and asks him who he serves. The youth replies that he serves no other than himself. Upon being asked if his "gou*er*naunce is good," he replies that he is "wantou*n* & nyce, recheles & and lewd*e* / as Iangelyng*e* as a Iay."[15] This attractive, noble savage is barred from civilized society because he does not know the behavior that would make him acceptable at court, but Russell sees in him the makings of a civilized servant and writes the book for him explaining how to rise through the ranks to serve a duke. Russell expressed the possibility of moving from the forest to an elite dinner table. Robin Hood is part of an assumption that elite behavior is a learned skill in the fifteenth century. With the proper advice book and teaching, elite manners permitted an individual to ascend into the ranks of a major household servant to the Duke of Gloucester.

By the fifteenth century, the matter of individual governance had gained considerable currency. The term "good governance" also comes up in the ballad of Eleanor Cobham, who rose from the ranks of gentry to marry the Duke. If we again think of the suggestive model of Elias, we can see the presumption of a move from forest, felony, and robbery to a more civilized form of behavior and one that is an internalized individual achievement of upward mobility. By the fifteenth century, polite society presumed that the well-trained person would have made etiquette and a sense of social hierarchy part of their internal sensibilities.

Peasant and Urban Rebels: The Animals Among Us

Elias observes in *The History of Manners* that in books of hours and art works that were commissioned by elites the texts show the pleasant diversions of their lives, including their castles, their hunting parties, and picnicking. Peasants are represented in these scenes as part of a backdrop landscape. They may be laborers in rags, participants in rustic merriment, beggars, and even felons hanging from trees. They are in the picture, but they are controlled and subservient to the foreground that emphasizes the pleasures and activities of the elites.[16] The elite of England and London shared this view of peasants-in-their-place or suffering due punishment should they deviate from the controlled environment. The urban centers of Europe, including London, assimilated large numbers of peasants into their ranks, but as much as possible they did so through apprenticeship and service contracts, marketing arrangements, and other explicit means that kept the new comers and country bumpkins in the city's control. The city authorities' desire for control came from their fear of potential rebellions, either in small groups of workers or in mass uprisings.

Revolts of the lower orders in the late thirteenth and fourteenth centuries changed the manageable landscape that urban dwellers and elites had created in their economic dealings with the countryside. The popular revolts brought images to their minds that were best expressed in terms of domestic animals gone wild. The degraded lower orders forced themselves into the foreground of the picture and into the landscape that the elite occupied.

The elites — urban, official, and noble — regarded the rebels as uncivilized. The terms that they used to describe them were animalistic. The characterization was consistent throughout the chronicle accounts from the thirteenth century through the revolt of 1381 and thereafter. Scholars have investigated the use of these denigrating descriptive terms about the rebels of 1381, but insults were already part of the literature in describing the revolt of London merchants, craftsmen, and laborers against Henry III and the London oligarchs who sought to temporize with them. In the Barons' Revolt of the late thirteenth century, the majority of Londoners, including craftsmen and some of the oligarchs, sided with the barons and their leader, Simon de Montfort. Henry III did not have an easy relationship with London because of his expensive wars and his promotion of foreign interests. Some of the merchant elite saw the revolt of the barons as a time to express their dislike of Henry III's policies. They found ready allies in the craftsmen of London.[17]

Unrest among the London craftsmen and commoners broke out against the Henry III and the urban elite who remained loyal to him. By the late thirteenth century (1263–70), the London crafts has grown in importance as producers of leather and other goods, and their numbers increased substantially. The old merchant elite, who dealt in wool, luxury items, and other pan-English and continental trade, had dominated the government, but they were losing control over London because of Henry III's favoritism toward foreign merchants, particularly those from the Hanse, Italy, and the English possessions in France. The whole reign of Henry III had proved a traumatic period for London. The elite had been part of the revolt against John I that had led to the Magna Carta, but London suffered from the political unrest in the years following. When the revolt of the barons broke out, London was the major target of control. While many of the elite were royalists, the craftsmen and laborers sided with Simon de Montfort and the barons. Some of the elite, seeing an opportunity to gain offices such as sheriffs, aldermen, and mayor, sided with the populists. What the craftsmen wanted were charters that would guarantee them a monopoly over their trades and forbid foreign workers from taking away their customers or invading their crafts with experts from the continent. The ambitious rebel elites exploited the situation and offered charters to the crafts. In some respects, it was Henry III himself who had brought about the trouble by reviving the popular folkmoot to check the patricians. Once having overpowered the old rulers, the populists took power into their own hands.[18] Henry III could not have foreseen the mistake of appealing to the population.

Under the leadership of the radical new leaders, the *populares* sided with Simon de Montfort. While there was considerable mob action, the leaders organized some of the Londoners into an orderly militia. But what remained in the minds of chroniclers describing the event was crowd mentality of the Londoners.

In 1263 the chronicler Thomas Wykes of Osney described the outrages of the London rabble. In his vivid words, a "furious crowd" from London, led by Hugh le Despenser, a supporter of Simon de Montfort, participated in an assault on the estates of the king and his supporters outside London. They went "in the evening, by a straight route, with a few banners to the manor" of the king.[19] Burning the manor and destroying a surrounding fence and ditch as well as out buildings, "they seized for their own use all the movables they found there, with wretched daring."[20] Next, they went to the mansion of Richard de Cornwall at Westminster and "not leaving one stone upon another which they thought he needed, ripping out bushes, tiles and thatch, and taking all the stone they could from the towers," they departed to attack the homes of other royal supporters.[21] These were not the actions of a "furious crowd" but of an organized assault on particular targets. Their pursuit of the objects of their hatred look very much like the pattern that the rebels of 1381 would take in destroying the buildings of their oppressors.

To Wykes the worst offense was when they stopped the queen, who was of better mettle than her husband, Henry III. She had taken a barge from their refuge in the Tower up the Thames toward Westminster to secure the government. When the queen reached London Bridge, "an infinite number of Londoners" stopped her barge and called her a whore and an adulteress and pelted her "with stones, filthy mud, broken eggs and all sorts of disgusting projectiles."[22] She took refuge in St. Paul's Cathedral.[23]

Wykes described the rebels as a "vast multitude of ribalds, who call themselves bachelors" (laborers who were organized into potential guilds); he also condemned the attack on Jews, which occurred at the same period.[24] Other chroniclers described riots in which the commoners "roaring abuse" used "all sorts of disgusting projectiles" against "the senior and wisest men of the city." The chroniclers used barn-yard imagery with ease calling the commons "fools of the vulgar herd."[25] These people were not articulate in language as were their betters, but were capable only of confused, loud sounds. The protests of the London craftsmen and laborers broke out repeatedly in individual actions and in riots that centered on mayoral elections, taxation, and administration of justice. One disgruntled rebel was described as standing at the roadside and neighing like a horse every time an alderman rode by.[26]

These were not, however, a group of uncivilized, unorganized "*rustici Londonienses.*" Their leaders were men with strong oligarchic ties themselves, many of whom had formerly held positions in the city or royal government. Respectable craftsmen made up the rank and file. In addition to attacking royal manors outside London and the property of royalists in London, they took a major role in the campaigns and pitched battles on the side of Montfort and the barons. Although they had insulted the queen, laid waste to the lands and homes of their enemies near London, and threatened the king, they had an articulate agenda to take control of the city government and to support the reforms of Simon de Montfort. They endorsed limits on royal authority and spending and agreed to the plan of a government directed by a council inclusive of middle class representatives. It was a middle class uprising, not one of the rustics.[27]

During and after the Peasants' Revolt of 1381, the literary characterization of rebels as mere animals who lacked speech had become, once again, a major theme among chroniclers. Added to the negative, inarticulate image of the peasantry and urban commons is the great divide of literate as opposed to the illiterate. Commons "roar" rather than talk; they attack literacy by destroying court records that are written by their oppressors (anyone with an ink pot at his arm is attacked). They are barn-yard animals let loose to destroy the culture of the literate. As Susan Crane has shown, when one of the chroniclers describes the scene in which Richard II repudiated the charters that he had given out to the peasants to disperse them, he gives the king the speech: "Rustics you were and rustics you remain ... For as long as we live ... we will strive to trample you so that your slavery may be an example to posterity, and so that those like you may now and in future have always before their eyes as if in a book of your misery and reasons for cursing you."[28] The rebellion against the literate, by the illiterate, therefore, is presented in terms of oppression and torture by a book. To the chronicler this irony meant that the beasts and monsters of the peasants and commoners would have before them an icon they could not decipher, but which would torment them.

But were these rebels really universally illiterate and *rustici*? Stephen Justice in *Writing and Rebellion: England in 1381* has argued that writing and practical literacy played a large role in the revolt and that an understanding of writing may have been much wider spread than we think.[29] The peasants' knew the importance of writing, and it was not lost upon those who sought upward mobility; they were quite as good at playing the game as those who tried to impose writing and laws upon them. One route that peasants had to open their way to upward mobility was to acquire an education and move into various manorial positions or even that of parish priests. For my example, let us examine the movement of the Cellarer family from the abbey of Meaux.

In the late fourteenth century, three cousins, John, Richard, and Thomas Cellarer, made such an impression on the abbey of Meaux with their joint strategy to change their status from villeins of the abbey and serfs of the royal demesne, that their case was recorded in the abbey chronicle thirty years later. To be villeins of the royal demesne guaranteed them more freedoms than did that of the abbey. The royal demesnes were listed in the *Domesday Book*, and many peasants knew about the benefits of being "people of the book," which included fewer service obligations.[30] The Cellarers, as their name implied, had risen to prominence because their grandfather, Adam, had been an abbey official. He was in charge of the abbey stores. Perhaps he was literate or at least kept a record of the stores with a tally sticks. In 1356 the monastic administration had lapsed because of an argument over the selection of a new abbot. Richard Cellarer was one of the ringleaders of the revolt but managed to avoid punishment by going to the royal escheator of Holderness and claiming that he and his family were really villeins of the king and fell under the rules of the *Domesday Book*. He claimed that they had mistakenly gone over to the abbot sometime before and taken their land with them. The escheator called an inquest of villeins, and they agreed with Richard's claim. With his neighbor's collusion he had his lands transferred to the royal demesne of Holderness. The abbots were not going to let the Cellarers escape so easily, and in 1357 and 1358 the monks' request for another inquisition was granted. This time it was property holders who served on the inquest, not fellow villeins and Richard lost his case.

This ambitious family was not discouraged. In 1359 John and his cousin Thomas, along with two other kinsmen, made a clever legal maneuver. They claimed that, in violation of the Statute of Laborers of 1351, the abbot had taken by force and detained a plowman whom they had hired. The Cellarers claimed £5 each in damages. At the time of the plea the abbot was in London negotiating with the royal auditors about Richard's claims. Since charges had been brought against him for violation of the Statute of Laborers, the auditors kept the abbot's horses. He was forced to rent horses to return Meaux. The plea was quashed when the cousins, examined singly, admitted that they were villeins of the abbot. Being the abbot's villeins, they could not bring charges against him.

Richard then appealed to the king on behalf of the family for a judgment on their status. Edward III himself ordered the sheriff to have the Cellarers and their property returned to the royal manor. The abbot made a hasty trip to London with two lawyers and gifts for the king. Edward allowed him to retain the Cellarers and their property until he returned from a campaign in France.

Yet another infraction of manorial rules landed John in the abbey's prison, but he crawled out at night through a shaft in the latrine system. He and William, another cousin, then tried to get their freedom declared. When Edward III returned from France, he set up a new series of commissions to investigate their plea. The family was returned to the abbot with the provision that the Cellarers were not to be punished in any way for their actions. Throughout these legal maneuvers, the members always acted in the interest of the whole family, worked together, and assumed the legal costs jointly. They were highly cognizant of the law in its intricate, written form and they used it in a most sophisticated manner.[31] These men were very well versed in the civilized laws of the court.

According to the elites, the rebels of 1263 and those of 1381 are animals. But the urban craftsmen finally got their guild charters from the king in the early fourteenth century and serfdom demised in the fifteenth century. The Cellarers used their education and knowledge of the law to advance their own fortunes. The attempt to use labels referring to barnyard animals to curb the ascent of the "uncivilized" did not work in the long run.

Perhaps the "truth," as Richard Firth Green puts it, lies in the problem that late medieval English society was caught up in anxieties of social distinctions and social climbing. In his analysis of John Ball's letters and a Wycliffite poem about peasantry, he concludes that the issue for conservative writers was not just the attempt to put people in their place and in their hierarchical order, but to defend these borders of the hierarchy.[32] In other words, elite society was very concerned about the transgressions of the lower classes into the polite society. To learn law and to manipulate the system as did the mythic Robin Hood or upstart peasants (such as the Cellarers) was a warning. While courtesy manuals could move a noble savage into the polite world of service to an aristocrat, and while Robin Hood might be portrayed as a potential dinner guest at a good table, the fear that an outlaw might ascend to this status or that the rebels might take over the government of London or the realm was terrifying.

But this observation about the threat of crossing boundaries moves us on to our third case history, that of Eleanor Cobham, married to Duke Humphrey of Gloucester, fourth son of Henry IV. Here we have a more complicated issue of social transgression, labeling, threat to the elite, and the intricate drama of appropriate punishment for an upstart duchess.

Disputed Social Status and Gender Issues

Eleanor Cobham's marriage to Duke Humphrey of Gloucester was a matter of scandal. With the victory of his older brother, Henry V, at Agincourt, Humphrey had hoped to extend his own fortunes by marrying Jacqueline, countess of Hainault and Holland, but she was already married to the Duke of Brabant. She was heiress to her title and her liege lord, Duke Philip of Burgundy, wanted to insure his control over her by marrying her to someone who would be loyal to him. An alliance with the brother of the king of England was out of the question. With the dominant position that England enjoyed on the continent after Agincourt and the Treaty of Troyes in 1429, Humphrey negotiated marriage with her and secured an annulment of her first marriage. But Henry V's early death changed the balance of power in England and on the continent. While Humphrey had hoped to carve out a lucrative possession in Hainault and Holland, the administrators of Henry V's triumphs had other ideas. His marriage to Jacqueline would have required troops to secure her inheritance, but his brother, the Duke of Bedford, and Cardinal Beaufort manipulated Parliament into refusing funds to raise troops. Duke Philip of Burgundy was an ally of the English against the French, and Humphrey's plans would jeopardize a valuable alliance. Furthermore, with Henry V's early death, Humphrey became deeply immersed in English politics as heir apparent to the throne should the infant Henry VI die. The marriage with Jacqueline was brief, lasting from 1424 to 1426, when it was annulled. Jacqueline defended her territory as best she could under the watchful eye of Duke Philip, but without any help from England. Humphrey, however, was not without female companionship. Opinion at the time held that Eleanor Cobham, an English lady-in-waiting to the Countess, was Humphrey's paramour.[33]

Eleanor came from a knightly family in Kent, but its relationship to power came through her father's cousin. Perhaps it was he who used his influence to place Eleanor in Humphrey's and Jacqueline's court. It was not unusual for a lady-in-waiting to become the mistress of the husband, but Humphrey married Eleanor in 1328, soon after he signed a peace treaty with Duke Philip of Burgundy. The relationship received much negative comment in the chronicles. The general opinion was that she had moved above her status in society and should not have married a prince and especially one who was next in line to the throne. Eleanor was a rebel against the perceived social hierarchy.

Londoners took an active role against Eleanor from the beginning. On March 8, 1428 a deputation of London women appeared before Parliament with a letter of complaint about Gloucester's desertion of his wife and her subsequent imprisonment by Duke Philip of Burgundy. Preserving their own ideas of marriage and appropriate behavior, they rallied against Eleanor in favor of Jacqueline. Perhaps they did not know that the marriage was already dissolved. London officials also complained to Parliament about "the lamentable state to which the lady" had fallen.[34] They claimed that their trade with the continent had suffered because of Gloucester's treatment of her. The men of London were willing to pay for some assistance for her.[35]

Married to Humphrey in 1428, her triumphant rise to power, riches, and social prominence ended abruptly in 1441 when she was charged with witchcraft, sorcery, and treason. Chronicles that were written after her trial and a ballad, "The Lament of the Duchess of Gloucester," have elements of the truth about her case, but their portrayal of this social and perhaps political rebel tells us about the mores of the period. The true story of Eleanor and her trial is not easy to establish. No trial transcript remains, and the chronicle accounts are biased and appeared long after the trial. There are few references to her in the Patent Rolls, Close Rolls, and the Privy Council.[36] Eleanor seems to have been a convenient target in the struggle between Duke Humphrey and Cardinal Beaufort for control over Henry VI.[37] Humphrey was a popular figure, but his power was not as great as that of the Cardinal. Eleanor, along with members of his household, was accused of necromancy, witchcraft, sorcery, and treason. Eleanor's high-handed manner and obvious enjoyment of her elevated status brought condemnation from Londoners.

Duke Humphrey had built a residence called La Plesaunce in Greenwich that included a large library that would eventually form the basis of the Bodleian Library. He patronized a variety of learned people including the poet John Lydgate, musicians, and scholars. Among those writers that the duke supported was Roger Bolingbroke, an Oxford priest, and a scholar of astronomy (astrology), who was his chaplain. Eleanor had access to and perhaps owned a book translated from Arabic that contained both medical and astrological texts. This kind of book, however, was common in noble women's libraries, and astrology was routinely used to predict the future. Humphrey and Eleanor both knew Queen Joan of Navarre, who had been accused of witchcraft in 1419 but was never tried. Humphrey had offered a haven for her confessor. The patronage of people such Bolingbroke added to the suspicions of Eleanor's own behavior.

The charge against Eleanor, coming in 1440–1441 when Humphrey and Cardinal Beaufort were at political loggerheads, was that she had formed a conspiracy with Roger Bolingbroke and three other people: a priest and canon of Westminster, a priest named John Home (or Hunne), and Margery Jourdain, otherwise known as the "Witch of Eye." The men all held distinguished positions in the church, and Home was secretary to both the Duke and Eleanor. On 28 or 29 June 1441 Eleanor was, according to the sources, in London dining in luxury at the King's Head, a hotel that Edward III had built for royalty to watch London pageants. According to the London chroniclers, who were fascinated by her downfall, she received a message there that her co-conspirators had been arrested.[38]

The charges of necromancy and heresy were for the church to judge, rather than a secular court. But Bolingbroke was charged with treason as well so that he was tried before the most prestigious members of the church hierarchy, as well as members of the king's council.[39] If one can trust the chroniclers, it was a dramatic ceremony in which he was placed on a painted chair in St. Paul's churchyard. He clasped a sword with images in one hand and a scepter in the other. He had a paper crown on his head and was surrounded by the instruments of necromancy. He must have looked very much like the king that often appeared in illustrations of the wheel of fortune. He renounced heresy, but was still convicted of treason. The whole effect was publicly to expose the treason and to imply the complicity of Eleanor of Cobham.[40] She seems to have gotten the message and fled to Westminster Abbey for sanctuary. She pleaded innocent and returned to sanctuary on 24 July 1441.

The potent political rivals of Duke Humphrey, who combined the might of both the royal council and the powers of the ecclesiastical court, pursued charges against her. Duke Humphrey, out of favor, was unable to defend her. Her accusers brought her face to face with Bolingbroke, and she admitted the charges against her: treason for plotting the king's death and possible necromancy. With the charge of treason Eleanor and her "accomplices" fell into the hands of the royal authority, which meant a death penalty: burning for women and drawing and quartering for men. Ecclesiastical authorities could only impose a penance.

Many claims appeared in the chronicles. It was said that she had her co-conspirators fashioned a figure of the king to predict when he would die of melancholia (he certainly suffered from it — but they seemed to want to hasten it). The chroniclers suggested that she had consulted with Margery Jourdain, the "Witch of Eye," for potions to become pregnant by Humphrey.[41] She was kept in Leeds Castle while the investigation proceeded.

Eleanor was tried in London before leading ecclesiastical authorities, including Cardinal Beaufort. Presumably, Henry VI was also present. London's city officials and perhaps the justices of the king's courts and a number of nobles were also present. She admitted to part of the charges, but not all. Bolingbroke was convicted of treason and was drawn and quartered (another clerk died in prison). Home was pardoned. Margery Jourdain was burned at the stake as a witch.[42] Eleanor was not condemned for treason. Instead, she was given an ecclesiastical penance, which suggests that the treason charges were dropped and that only the charge of sorcery remained. Her marriage to Humphrey was dissolved.

Eleanor was to proceed in her chemise with burning taper in her hand from Westminster to designated London churches (St. Paul, Christ's Church, and St. Michael in Cornhill) on three market days, which she did on November 13, 15, and 17. It was not an easy penance. She went barefoot along the street, as a true penitent. It was a difficult walk, for the streets were dirty and rough, and she was not used to walking barefoot. She was scantily clothed for November. Her punishment was an extreme version of ecclesiastical penance for sin. It was typical to condemn adulteresses to parade around their parish churches on successive Sundays in similar attire. Perhaps there was a hint of an earlier sin of adultery in the punishment. Because she was ultimately considered a political threat, she ended her life in exile on the Isle of Man where she died in 1457, seven years after her husband's death.[43]

Chronicles were rife with comment and condemnation of Eleanor, and some of the fifteenth-century chronicles of London may have represented opinion of the time. Certainly, the Londoners had shown no early sympathy for her and the officials of London were present at her trial. The London poem written after her trial in 1441 on suspicion of treason and sorcery tells a moral tale purportedly in her own words. "The Lament of the Duchess of Gloucester" is a portrayal of her social climbing as well as a warning to other women not to follow in her footsteps.[44] In many ways it is the negative side of the advice poem for women, "How the Good Wijf Tauȝte Hir Douȝtir."[45] In that poem, the narrator tells her daughter about all the bad things she should avoid because they might endanger her marriage and all of the good behavior she should acquire so that she can manage a household. The writer of "The Lament" points to all the negative things that Eleanor did to make her so disliked and that ultimately led to her downfall. The poems are the opposite sides of the same coin. Both fall into the category of advice poetry or courtesy literature, but the "The Lament" is tied to a historical figure. If the poem does not tell us the true history of Eleanor of Cobham, it does provide a cultural reference for the behavior that a woman of her social class should have pursued.

The clear message of the "The Lament" was that those who rose too high on the "wheel of fortune" were sure to fall off. Of the wheels of fortune, Catherine's wheel was important in fifteenth-century illustrations in which Fortuna turns the wheel and some rise to the top and are there for a space of time and then they fall off. Sometimes the person on the top of the wheel appears as a monarch with a crown, and it is possible that Bolingbroke's comic appearance was supposed to represent this figure who was about to fall off the wheel. The author of the "The Lament" was certainly aware of the wheel: "I was so high upon my whele, / Myne owne estate I cowld not know..."[46]

The author has Eleanor lament how she presumed a higher estate than she was born to and the poem is a warning to other women not to do the same:

> Alle women that in this world be wrowght,   *angry*
> By me they may insaumpulle take,   *example*
> As I that was browght up of nowght,
> A prince had chosyn me to his make;
> My soffern lorde so to forsake,
> Yt is dulfulle destenye.
> Alas! For to sorow how shuld I slake;
> Alle women may be ware by me.⁴⁷

She gives the usual warning from advice literature that she has risen above her class and that she has suffered punishment for presumption.

The poem does not speak of the charges of witchcraft and necromancy against her, but it does speak to her confessions of breaking the class boundaries and hints that she may have committed treason. She speaks of being the Duchess of Gloucester and how this was a great honor, but through the temptations of the devil she succumbed to pride. All of London was at her beck and call. As usual, the poem cites a plea for mercy and for other women to remember her plight and to avoid the sin of pride. The trial and penance is also played out in the poem with full sympathy.

> Before the counselle of this londe,
> At Westmynster, upon a day,
> Ffulle rewfully ther dide I stonde;
> A worde for me durst no many say...
>
> Hys grace to me was evermore gayne,
> Thowgh I had done so gret offence;
> The lawe wolde I hade bene slayn,
> And sum men dyde there delygence.
> That worthy prynce of high prudence
> Of my sorow hade gret petye.⁴⁸

Having appeared before the king and council, she escaped the charge of treason, thanks to the mercy of the king.

The sorcery charge still remained, and she was turned over to the ecclesiastical authorities for trial.

> I come before the spiritualité;
> Two cardynals, and byshoppis fyve,
> And oder men of gret degré,
> Examened me of alle my lyffe.
> And openly I dyde me shryffe   *give confession*
> Of alle thyng that they asked me.
> Than was I putt in penaunce belyffe;
> Alle women may be ware by me.⁴⁹

The poem speaks of her punishment and her remorse. She says that she "went bare fote on my fette..."⁵⁰

The poem suggests that she even had to "ride raille" or at least follow the traditional route that this civic ritual of humiliation took. Riding the hurdle (or rail) was a common punishment in London for people who committed fraud and even prostitution. Bolingbroke rode to his execution on a rail. The guilty person rode through the streets on a hurdle drawn by a horse with the offending product or a written message about their misdemeanor around their necks. Bakers who sold bad bread, fishmongers who sold stale fish, and bawds were driven through the main streets of London in this way until they got to the pillory on Cornhill. It was a very public, degrading ceremony, done with rough music rather than minstrels that Eleanor used to dance to. If this had happened, it would have called attention to her lapses of social station. It branded her as a person who would be excluded from the city after her public humiliation. In the end, she went into exile. The rest of the poem is her farewell to London, to her house in Greenwich, to her "damask and clothes of gold" and velvet, to her minstrels, and to her husband. She calls this last farewell a painful one. The poem concludes with a confession of wrong doing and her "mysgovernaunce."[51]

We return to the cultural play between the categories of civilized and uncivilized and its use as a powerful tool of social regulation. Those in a position to label the offenders as "uncivilized" used their authority with a sense of their power to preserve social boundaries. Peasants, as jurors, indicted and condemned robbers and outlaws. Both ecclesiastical and lay chroniclers condemned the behavior of rural and urban rebels as barnyard animals. They likewise condemned the social-climbing Eleanor of Cobham, as did London men and women did. Kings and justices punished those who egregiously stepped over the boundaries. But lurking in the condemnations, hangings, and penances was a grudging admiration and titillation about those who crossed the boundaries, whether they were historical figures such as Eleanor Cobham and the Cellarers or ballad bandits. Perhaps as we consider Elias's *The History of Manners* we should not be surprised that the transition to "civilization" also brought strong revulsion to the idea that the lower classes, the outlaws, rebels and social climbers should be so easily admitted across the boundaries to the "civilized" despite the advice literature and poems that helped them to do so.

Notes

1. Barbara A. Hanawalt, "The Female Felon in Fourteenth-Century England," *Viator* 5 (1974): 253–268.
2. Norbert Elias, *The Civilizing Process: The History of Manners*, trans. Edmund Jephcott (Oxford: Blackwell, 1978).

3. Richard Firth Green, "Violence in the Early Robin Hood Poems," in *"A Great Effusion of Blood?" Interpreting Medieval Violence*, ed. Mark D. Meyerson, Daniel Thiery, and Oren Falk (Toronto: University of Toronto Press, 2004), 268–286.

4. Barbara A. Hanawalt, "Ballads and Bandits: Fourteenth-Century Outlaws and the Robin Hood Poems," in *Chaucer's England: Literature in Historical Context*, ed. Barbara A. Hanawalt. Medieval Studies at Minnesota 4 (Minneapolis: University of Minnesota Press, 1992), 154–175.

5. Barbara A. Hanawalt, "'Of Good and Ill Repute': The Limits of Community Tolerance," in *'Of Good and Ill Repute': Gender and Social Control in Medieval England* (New York: Oxford University Press, 1998), 1–17 at 4–6. For more information on criminal statistics, see Barbara A. Hanawalt, *Crime and Conflict in English Communities, 1300–1348* (Cambridge: Harvard University Press 1979).

6. Hanawalt, *Crime and Conflict*, 83–90; and "Ballads and Bandits," 156–168.

7. R. F. Hunnisett, ed., *Bedfordshire Coroners' Rolls*. Publications of the Bedfordshire Historical Society 41 (Streatly, UK: Bedfordshire Historical Record Society, 1960), 7. Similar cases appear on 12, 22, and 101.

8. Rossell Hope Robbins, ed., *Secular Lyrics of the XIVth and XVth Centuries*, 2nd ed. (Oxford: Clarendon Press, 1954), 58–59, lines 11–15.

9. Dorothy Chadwick, *Social Life in the Days of Piers Plowman* (Cambridge: Cambridge University Press 1922), 77–78.

10. William Stubbs and H. W. Carless Davis, ed., *Select Charters and Other Illustrations of English Constitutional History*, 9th ed. (Oxford, Clarendon Press: 1913), 467–468.

11. J. C. Holt, "The Origins and Audience of the Ballads of Robin Hood," *Past and Present* 18 (1960): 89–110 at 93.

12. Richard Firth Green, "John Ball's Letters: Literary History and Historical Literature," in Hanawalt, *Chaucer's England*, 176–200 at 181–83.

13. R. H. Bowers, "'Foleuyles Lawes' (*Piers Plowman*, C.XXII. 247)." *Notes and Queries*, n.s., 8 (1961): 327–28 at 327.

14. J.C. Holt, "Origins and Audience," 89–110, argues that the audiences were mostly for the gentry and upper classes, but it is obvious that they were well known to all classes and that the "plays of Robin Hood" were performed locally.

15. John Russell, *The Boke of Nurture Folowyng Englondis Gise*, in *The Babees Book*, ed. F. J. Furnivall, EETS, o.s., 32 (London: N. Trübner & Co., 1868), 118–19, lines 27 and 36.

16. Elias, *History of Manners*, 206–217.

17. Gwyn A. Williams, *Medieval London: From Commune to Capital* (London: Athlone Press, 1963), 106–110, 129, 219–242.

18. For a complete discussion of the political and constitutional crises in London for the period of 1216–1263 see Williams, *Medieval London*, Chapters 7 and 8.

19. Antonia Gransden, *Historical Writing in England: C. 550 to C. 1307* (Ithaca: Cornell University Press, 1974; repr. London: Routledge, 1996), 465.

20. Ibid.

21. Ibid.

22. Ibid., 466.

23. Williams, *Medieval London*, 219.

24. Gransden, *Historical Writing*, 466-67.

25. Ibid., 515.

26. Williams, *Medieval London*, 201.

27. Ibid., 223–242.

28. Susan Crane, "The Writing Lesson of 1381," in Hanawalt, *Chaucer's England*, 201–221 at 207.

29. Stephen Justice, *Writing and Rebellion: England in 1381* (Berkeley: University of California Press, 1994).

30. Barbara A. Hanawalt, "Peasant Resistance to Royal and Seignorial Impositions," in *Social Unrest in the Late Middle Ages*, ed. Francis X. Newman. Medieval and Renaissance Texts

and Studies 39 (Binghamton, NY: Center for Medieval and Early Renaissance Texts and Studies, 1986), 23–47 at 32–33.

31. Marjorie J. O. Kennedy, "Resourceful Villeins: The Cellarer Family of Wawne in Holderness," *Yorkshire Archaeological Journal* 48 (1976): 107–117.

32. Richard Firth Green, "John Ball's Letters," 192–193.

33. K. H. Vickers, *Humphrey, Duke of Gloucester: A Biography* (London: Archibald Constable and Company, 1907), 164–205.

34. Reginald R. Sharpe, ed. and trans., *Calendar of Letter-Books of the City of London: Letter Book K* (London: John Edward Francis, 1911), 68.

35. Ibid., 68.

36. Ralph A. Griffiths, "The Trial of Eleanor Cobham: An Episode in the Fall of Duke Humphrey of Gloucester," *Bulletin of the John Rylands Library*, 51 (1968): 381–399. I have used his broad outline of events, but he has taken the accounts of the chroniclers as an accurate description of the allegations against her and of her trial. He supplemented these with record sources so that it is as reliable an account as can be made. Julia Geiger, "The Trial of a Duchess: Heresy in Fifteenth-Century England and the Case of Eleanor Cobham," Masters Paper, Ohio State University, February 2007, has tried to trace the evidence of changes against her. She concludes that she was charged with witchcraft.

37. Vickers, *Humphrey, Duke of Gloucester*, discusses the duke's political career. For the political struggle and the reign of Henry VI, see Bertram Wolffe, *Henry VI*, 2nd ed. (New Haven: Yale University Press, 2001).

38. For two of the more detailed fifteenth-century London chronicle accounts, see A. H. Thomas and I. D. Thornley, eds., *The Great Chronicle of London* (London: George W. Jones, 1939; repr. Gloucester: Alan Sutton, 1983), 175–76; and Friedrich W. D. Brie, ed., *The Brut or The Chronicles of England*. EETS, o.s., 131 and 136 (London: Kegan Paul and Oxford University Press, 1906, 1908; repr., Woodbridge and Rochester: Boydell and Brewer, 2000), 478–79.

39. John G. Bellamy, *The Law of Treason in England in the Later Middle Ages* (London: Cambridge University Press, 1970), 126. The charge against Bolingbroke was for "treasonable necromancy" in that he was using necromancy to overthrow the king.

40. Griffiths, "The Trial of Eleanor Cobham," 388.

41. Wolffe, *Henry VI*, 127.

42. Griffiths, "The Trial of Eleanor of Cobham," 386–393.

43. Ibid., 395–399.

44. "The Lament of the Duchess of Gloucester," in *Political Poems and Songs Relating to English History Composed During the Period From the Accession of Edward III to that of Richard III*, ed. Thomas Wright, 2 vol. Rolls Series 14 (Longman: London, 1859-61), 2: 205–208.

45. Furnivall, "How the Good Wijf Tau3te Hir Dou3tir," in *The Babees Book*, 36–47.

46. Wright, "Lament," 2: 206.

47. Ibid., 2: 205–206.

48. Ibid., 2: 206–207.

49. Ibid., 2: 207.

50. Ibid., 2: 207.

51. Ibid., 2: 208.

PART II

WALES AND THE MARCHES

4

Fouke le Fitz Waryn and King John: Rebellion and Reconciliation

CATHERINE A. ROCK

Fouke le Fitz Waryn is one of the most highly regarded of the Anglo-Norman prose romances. It was copied by the Ludlow scribe of Harley 2253, and was quite likely created by him from an Anglo-Norman metrical source.[1] Containing a rich mixture of historical fact and marvelous adventures, the story concerns the historical Fouke III (d. 1258?), who became an outlaw for a time during the reign of King John (r. 1199–1216). Central to the story is the legal issue concerning John's responsibility to his vassals; when he breaks this feudal contract, Fouke, in turn, breaks with him. The copyist, as we know, was for many years a legal scribe, so the subject matter of this romance might have attracted him, both for its legal ramifications and also for its local setting in Ludlow, Shropshire. The tale has aspects of both Christian and ancestral romance, but it is, in the main, a legalistic romance of the outlaw type. Some scholars, in fact, suspect the historical Fouke III to have been the original Robin Hood.[2] The romance shows, with occasional humor and plenty of action, that one man on the side of right can, in the end, obtain justice, and that no man, not even the king, is above the law.

Transmission History

The Anglo-Norman prose romance *Fouke le Fitz Waryn* exists today in only one manuscript, British Library MS Royal 12.C.XII, folios 33–61, although at one time there existed at least two other versions of the narrative that were summarized by the sixteenth-century antiquarian John Leland. The earliest of these was an Anglo-Norman verse version of the romance in octosyllabic couplets. Presumably, the extant Anglo-Norman prose version came next. An incomplete English version in what may be alliterative verse, perhaps contemporaneous with the extant version, also existed. Although at least three versions of the romance existed, the sparse evidence available indicates that they were essentially very similar.

An unknown author most likely composed the missing original romance shortly after 1250. According to Thomas Wright, the work was written sometime after the death of the historical Fouke III (the title character of the romance) in 1256 and before the death of Fouke IV (his son) in 1264, since the latter's death is not mentioned in the tale.[3] Other scholars generally accept this timeframe, although some believe that the romance might date to the latter part of the century.[4] The romance was evidently written in octosyllabic couplets, as Louis Brandin deduced by his examination of the underlying rhyme patterns.[5] The editors of the Anglo-Norman Text Society (ANTS) edition of the Anglo-Norman prose romance, E. J. Hathaway, P. T. Ricketts, C. A. Robson, and A. D. Wilshere, assert that "the verse romance appears to have been the work of a Ludlow poet, who may have been chaplain or tutor in a great household."[6]

The prose romance evidently originated in Shropshire, in the vicinity of Ludlow (the "Dynan" of the romance), for this is the locale in which the scribe who redacted the extant copy routinely operated.[7] Over the years, a number of scholars have attempted to date the extant Anglo-Norman prose version of *Fouke le Fitz Waryn* largely by examining the scribal hand in the sole surviving manuscript and concluded that it was written during the period of about 1310–40.[8] The Ludlow scribe who copied much of British Library MS Harley 2253 very likely composed the prose version of the romance, as well as copying it into the Royal manuscript.[9]

At one time there also existed an English verse version of *Fouke le Fitz Waryn*. John Leland summarized the partial version of this romance to which he had access, appending to it his translation and summary of the French verse version.[10] Approximately 80 percent of Leland's summary is taken from the English verse narrative, and the remaining 20 percent from the French verse version.[11] The English metrical version of the romance was quite likely written in alliterative verse, as Wright has shown, perhaps at about the same time as the Anglo-Norman prose version.[12]

Most critics agree that the three versions of the romance are very similar. The editors of the ANTS edition state that both Leland's summary of the English verse beginning of the romance and his summary and translation of the French verse concluding section "agree closely and sometimes verbally, even in Leland's abridged paraphrase, with the extant *FFW*."[13] Wright noted that the extant Anglo-Norman prose version and summary of the lost Anglo-

Norman poem agree so closely that he was certain that this same metrical version was the precursor of the prose.[14] The ANTS editors find this resemblance so close as to "suggest that [Leland] had access to the same copy of the couplet romance as the prose *remanieur* two centuries earlier."[15]

Today, we have only the Anglo-Norman prose version of *Fouke le Fitz Waryn*, although at one time Leland apparently had access to two different versions: one in Anglo-Norman verse, which is possibly the original version of the story; and one in English verse, which was composed at approximately the same time as the extant version. All that we know of the Anglo-Norman verse version comes from Leland's translation and summary, as well as from a close examination of the rhyme underlying the Anglo-Norman prose version of the romance. The little that we know of the English verse version comes entirely from Leland.

Structure and Argument

Fouke le Fitz Waryn is a three-part romance divided into chronological periods. It is built upon an underlying double structure with numerous parallels and reversals that occur throughout the romance, during the course of which the protagonist seeks the return of the lands of which he has been unjustly deprived. This combination tripartite-double structure supports the movement of the plot: one notes the "out and back" movement as Fouke leaves his native region, travels several times to foreign shores and into the realm of fantasy, and finally returns to claim his inheritance in England.

Medieval romances, both in Middle English and in Anglo-Norman, often have complex structures that serve a definite purpose. These structures can range from the simple diptych model of *The Awntyrs off Arthure* to those of much more intricate romances, such as *Sir Gawain and the Green Knight* or Chaucer's *Knight's Tale*. These works are often divided into two, three, or four parts, frequently chronological, with a number of "characteristic repetitions and parallels [which] not only serve a ritual function, but at the same time also build suspense, denote the passing of time, or indicate the relative weight or proportion of certain elements."[16] *The Awntyrs off Arthure*, for instance, has a very clear two-part structure wherein the juxtaposition of the halves gives meaning to the whole. The two halves, in fact, are so different that some critics argue that they were originally two separate poems and that they might have been written by two different poets.[17] In the first part of the poem, Guenevere is warned by the ghost of her mother that Arthur and the Round Table will fall because of Arthur's covetousness. Guenevere and her mother represent, respectively, Guenevere as she is now and as she will be in the future: like her mother, an unhappy ghost. The second part reveals a repudiation of the prediction concerning the king: Arthur demonstrates largesse by giving land generously to Gawain to recompense him for having given up land to Sir Galeron. Guenevere remains as she herself was in the first episode, ever beautiful and still the queen in full possession of her powers. As A. C. Spearing explains, "The two episodes, like the two leaves of a diptych, are indeed separate and self-contained, but there are numerous links between them, and when put together they incite the reader to participate in the creation of a meaning that is larger than either possesses in isolation."[18] Arthur is generous, so he and the Round Table will not fall, and Guenevere will not age and die, at least not yet.

Chaucer's *Knight's Tale*, from the *Canterbury Tales*, has a more complex chronological four-part structure. The two protagonists, cousins Palamon and Arcite, are virtually identical. In the first part, both are found together lying in a pile of bodies after a battle. Both are imprisoned, and both fall in love with Emily. It is their love of Emily that drives them apart. When Arcite breaks their oath of brotherhood, the stories of Palamon and of Arcite diverge, becoming parallel and juxtapose to each other. At first, the knights are imprisoned together, but they are psychologically no longer integrated; they have become enemies of each other in the prison of their mutual enemy. Indeed, the two figuratively become prisoners of Emily and literally prisoners of Theseus. Eventually, Arcite is released from prison and told never to return to the country, while Palamon remains incarcerated. Each thinks the other has the advantage: Arcite is free, but exiled; Palamon in imprisoned, but he is where he can distantly see Emily. In the second part of the story, Arcite returns in disguise to serve Emily and Duke Theseus. Palamon escapes, and the two knights happen to meet in the woods. At this point, every time the two former brothers come together, they fight over Emily: like magnets, they both attract and repel one other. Duke Theseus arrives and stops their fight. Although they both deserve death, Theseus will allow them to return a year later with one hundred knights each to fight formally for the hand of Emily. The enmity is still in place, but it will be subjected to Theseus's authority and his insistence on the structure of the battle; Theseus will also maintain the absolute equivalence of both sides. The third part of the romance consists of the description of the protagonists' and of Emily's visits to the temples of their chosen gods, as well as of the opposing armies. The three temples are equivalent, representing the three people most concerned in the outcome of the impending battle. The opposing armies are alike in number of combatants, and each is commanded by an illustrious king. Here, not only are Palamon and Arcite equal, but their supporters are as well. The spectators cannot decide which side has the better chance of winning. Theseus has seen to it that the battle of the two armies in the specially-constructed arena will exactly parallel the single combat that he found taking place in the woods the prior year. He intends to assure that the outcome will be absolutely fair. The final section of the story contains the climax, wherein Palamon is vanquished, and then Arcite is thrown from his horse when the gods send "a furie infernal" that arises from the ground.[19] After a long and painful decline, roughly mirroring and juxtaposing his short and glorious victory, Arcite dies, asking Emily to think of the worthy Palamon. Eventually, Palamon and Emily are married. Numerous juxtapositions throughout the story serve to show that, although the two knights may be in different locations, working with different people, and praying to different gods, there is essentially no difference between them.[20] It is the love each man has for Emily that breaks apart their brotherhood pact and their friendship; in the end, however, Arcite reconciles himself to his death and once again befriends Palamon, restoring balance to their relationship just before he dies.

Similar in ways to both *The Awntyrs off Arthure* and the *Knight's Tale* is *Sir Gawain and the Green Knight*. Like *The Awntyrs*, the plot of *Sir Gawain and the Green Knight* "is made up of two originally independent stories."[21] Like the *Knight's Tale*, it is made up of four chronological segments. Elizabeth Scala has called it "the most structurally perfect of medieval English narratives" and "a richly ornate and structurally complex artifact."[22] In the first part, which takes place in Arthur's court, the Green Knight issues his beheading challenge that is in the guise of a game, and which is eventually accepted by Gawain. In the second, Gawain travels through the wilderness, finally arriving at a castle in proximity to his final destination. His host proposes a game (yet another game) wherein he and Gawain every evening exchange what they have acquired that day, he while hunting and Gawain while at the castle. Again, Gawain accepts. In the third part, over the course of three days, the host goes hunting three times. Gawain is tempted three times by the host's wife, and three times there is an exchange of the day's winnings. On the third day, Gawain fails to give the host the green girdle given him to protect his life by the host's wife. In the final part, Gawain reaches the Green Chapel and undergoes the second part of the beheading challenge. The Green Knight swings thrice, feints twice, and then barely nicks him the third time in order to reprimand Gawain for having failed to exchange the girdle. Gawain, suitably chastened, returns to Camelot thoughtful and much humbled by his experience. Throughout the romance, there are often contrasts between civilization and wilderness. Gawain, the courtly knight, is at home in the civilized court of Camelot (and the apparently civilized world of the other castle), but he is uncomfortable when he discovers that the Green Chapel is in reality simply a rude mound in the countryside. He also suffers in the wilderness from wild animals, wild men, and the harsh winter as he finds his way to the Chapel. The Green Knight is obviously identified with nature and the wilderness that threatens Gawain throughout his quest. While the Green Knight, as the host, is out hunting in the wilderness, his wife is hunting in Gawain's bedchamber. We see the juxtaposition of the two kinds of the three hunting scenes — his and hers — and after these, the dead animals are cut up and dressed. Here, the juxtaposing scenes are delayed and combined into one where Gawain is threatened with beheading after all the hunts are concluded. The scenes of animal slaughter foreshadow the possibility of Gawain's dismemberment. Gawain, however, does not realize that he is undergoing a double trial: the beheading test of his courage and the temptation test of his ethical principles. Both Gawain and the reader are shown eventually that these two tests are in fact closely linked to each other, providing a satisfying and superlatively logical conclusion to this highly complex romance.

The Anglo-Norman verse romance *Gui de Warewic* has a similar structure to that of *Fouke le Fitz Waryn*, but it is not as tightly constructed. In the lengthy first part of the romance, Gui falls in love with his lord's daughter Felice, but he has to prove himself before she will have him. Most of his time is spent traveling and fighting, usually with his master Heralt. In the lengthy second part, Gui and Felice are married and spend fifty days together before Gui repents of his having served Felice rather than God. He says farewell to his new wife, becomes an anonymous pilgrim, and spends most of his time traveling and fighting, this time in the name of God. He finally returns to England, where Felice sees him again briefly before he dies in a hermitage. In the very brief third part of the romance, Gui's son Reinbrun, Heralt, and Heralt's son are united after separate adventures, and they all return to England to take up their positions within society.

Like Fouke, Gui goes abroad for extensive periods of time, but Gui's purposes seem rather contrived. William Calin sees it this way: "I cannot help wondering if the hero's sudden conversion, like his sudden falling in love, does not function primarily as a device to (re)launch the narrative and force the protagonist to set out on further adventures."[23] The first and second parts of the romance are very similar to each other in a general way. Calin asserts that in both halves, good conquers evil, in the first half by means of battle, and in the second by means of single combat. In addition, each contains the same pattern: Gui fights for "the crusade, [then] the comrade, and [finally] the homeland."[24] In the first part of the story, Felice tells Gui that she can only love a knight; after he is knighted, she says that he must be a proven knight, so he goes abroad to earn a reputation. When he returns, Felice tells him that he must also be the best knight in the world. Once again, Gui goes abroad to prove his valor and earn a name for himself. In the second half of

Gui's adventures (his third fighting trip abroad), even though he presents himself as a pilgrim and uses a pseudonym, his true name and reputation pursue him. In Antioch, he meets Count Jonas, a pilgrim who is in search of either Gui or Heralt, the only two men who could possibly win an upcoming battle.[25] In Germany, he meets his old companion Terri, who is searching for Gui to fight in his defense, or for Heralt.[26] In England, he finds King Athelstan, who is badly in need of a champion to fight the giant Colebrant in single combat in order to free England forever of the Danes. Athelstan fervently hopes for the return of either Gui or of Heralt.[27] In all three cases, Gui fights as the pilgrim; after each battle he reveals his identity when asked, on condition of secrecy and just before he departs for his next adventure. Gui's arch-enemy in the first part is Duke Otun de Pavie, whom he bests in his very first tournament and who tries repeatedly to kill or dishonor him, until Gui kills him near the end of his quest for fame. In the second part, Duke Otun's treacherous nephew Berard seeks revenge for his uncle's death until Gui kills him, too. While he is supposedly fighting for the love of Felice, Gui forgets himself to such an extent that he agrees to marry the daughter of the emperor of Constantinople. It is not until the morning of the wedding that he finally remembers Felice. The abortive first marriage is paralleled by the later true, but abbreviated one.

Gui de Warewic is often regarded by critics as being far too long and having too much repetition.[28] The problem is perhaps not so much in the amount of repetition as in its style: it is not cleverly done, as it is in *Fouke le Fitz Waryn* and *Sir Gawain and the Green Knight*, for instance. The repetition in *Gui de Warewic* is fairly obvious and requires little of the reader. The same can be said for the instances of juxtaposition in the romance. When the characters are separated, the poet tells, for example, what Gui is doing, then he moves to Heralt's situation, and often to that of a third person, perhaps Felice. The purpose of this technique is simply to tell the reader what is happening in several places at once; there is no deeper meaning in these juxtaposed events. The events themselves tend to be unimaginative as well. Rosalind Field writes, "Here we have all the characteristics of a series, stock responses to recurrent situations, each reaching a favorable conclusion without bringing the whole to a close, each episode connected by character but self-sufficient and self-explanatory, set against a different background, quick-moving, dramatic and making few demands on an audience's attention." She goes on to say, however, that even though we may view the action as formulaic, "the discovery of the formula may start here[;] the narrative has a purposeful structure consistent with the nature of its audience and reception."[29] *Gui de Warewic* was in fact immensely popular despite its shortcomings. According to M. Dominica Legge, *Gui* "became one of the most widely known and influential of texts written in England," having "an enthusiastic reception all over Europe."[30] Ironically, *Fouke le Fitz Waryn*, a much more structurally complex romance, survives in only one manuscript.

The three-part chronological division of *Fouke le Fitz Waryn* is fairly obvious for first-time readers to identify. In the first part, which comprises about one-third of the story, the reader is given the background of the Fitz Waryn family dating back to the time of the Conquest and including the loss of Blauncheville (Whittington) and Dynan (Ludlow). The second and longest part of the romance concerns the outlawry of Fouke le Fitz Waryn (Fouke III), which occurs historically about 1200 to 1203.[31] This includes the heart of the story: the many realistic and fantastic adventures of Fouke and his companions (both in England and abroad) as he tries to regain his lost land from King John. Having recovered his inheritance and reconciled with the King, all that remains in the very brief third part (historically comprising about fifty years) is for Fouke to retire, regret his killing of many men, gain the forgiveness of God, and die peacefully after devoting his last years to the service of mankind and, by extension, to God.

Fouke le Fitz Waryn, a man of honor, is forced to rebel against the actions of an unjust monarch, King John. John dislikes Fouke and his brothers because of a grudge that he bears against the eldest of the Fitz Waryn siblings that dates back to their childhood: John is punished by his father the king after hitting Fouke with a chessboard, and the prince then complains when Fouke knocks him senseless. When John in turn becomes king, he uses his new power to confirm Fouke's enemies in their possession of some of the Fitz Waryns' property. In a dramatic scene, Fouke confronts the King, telling him that he has been his man, but since John has now failed to live up to his part of the bargain, Fouke renounces his fealty:

> "Sire roy, vous estes mon lige seignour, e a vous su je lié par fealté tant come je su en vostre service, e tan come je tienke terres de vous; e vous me dussez meyntenir en resoun, e vous me faylez de resoun e commun[e] ley, e unqe ne fust bon rey qe deneya a ces franke tenauntz ley en sa court; pur quoi je vous renke vos homages."[32]

> ["Sir king, you are my liege lord, and to you was I bound by fealty, as long as I was in your service, and as long as I held lands of you; and you ought to maintain me in right, and you fail me in right and common law; and never was he a good king who denied his frank tenants law in his courts; wherefore I return you your homages."][33]

Very early in the romance, William Bastard "e si estably pees e leys" [established peace and law] in England.[34] Later, Henry II promises Joce de Dynan "ley e resoun" [law and justice].[35] In contrast, King John fails to give his vassal law and justice.[36] The importance of the law and the duty of the king to uphold it are shown twice in order to demonstrate how very wrong John is to refuse it to Fouke in this third case. King John then confiscates the rest of Fouke's lands and sends men to hunt him down. Fouke thus becomes an outlaw. Similarly, William Bastard had given land to his vassals, and King Richard gave Fouke his inheritance when his father died.[37] John, however, knowingly and wrongfully confirms possession of Blauncheville (Whittington) to Morys de Powys, effectively depriving Fouke of a portion of his birthright. When Fouke leaves the country, John takes the opportunity to seize the rest of his lands.[38] Again, two positive cases are presented to show that what John does is contrary to the practices of effective kingship. Glyn Burgess argues that "The Norman kings are ... presented as strong, energetic and just; they are very sensitive to the issues of land and the need to reward those knights who have given good service."[39] In the case of King John, however, this is not true: "[T]he romance shows King John to be the source of social disruption and not the upholder of peace, order and justice."[40] Ingrid Benecke argues that Fouke's "actions [in renouncing his fealty to John] are perfectly legitimate, that is, in accordance with a vassal's right of insurrection against an unjust feudal lord, as laid down in feudal laws and contracts and [later] in Magna Carta."[41] He is an "excellent vassal whose example is worth following for any knight in feudal society. Disinherited, wrongfully outlawed, and pursued by a corrupt monarch, the good outlaw manages nevertheless to reestablish moral order in feudal society through his victory over an unjust lord and king."[42] Even though Fouke owes him fealty, when King John acts unjustly, the knight, bound by his principles, has no choice but to revolt. Although this event (both in the romance and in life) predates the signing of Magna Carta by about fifteen years, the growing independent spirit of the English barons is clearly shown in the person of Fouke le Fitz Waryn.[43] He eventually succeeds, as the later barons did, in forcing the hand of King John, thus making him acknowledge his duty and the limitations on his power under the law.

Just as Fouke le Fitz Waryn manages to bring a corrupt government back into balance to serve his own interests, the double structure of the romance reflects the protagonist's loss of balance or harmony (via the loss of his property and his place in society) and the regaining of that balance as the story progresses. Balance is shown at both the beginning and the end of the romance by means of two prophecies concerning the deeds of the Fitz Waryns and especially of Fouke's victory over King John. Although the double prophecies are written as prose in the manuscript, the underlying rhyme is obvious, and they are traditionally printed as verse in modern editions. The first of these prophecies is given by Geomagog, a dead giant whose body is possessed by a demon and who is definitively vanquished by Payn Peverel, Fouke's ancestor.[44] Geomagog is apparently a reference to the biblical Gog and Magog, found in

Ezekiel 38 and 39 as well as Apocalypse. Gog, the enemy of Israel, is the ruler of the kingdom of Magog. Some scholars argue that Gog was Gyges, king of Lydia, while others suggest that Magog was Scythia.[45] The second prediction is said to be a prophecy of Merlin.[46] Delving further, one notes that both prophecies are ultimately of demonic origin: Geomagog's body is animated by and possesses the intelligence of a spirit or demon, while Merlin, according to Geoffrey of Monmouth, is the offspring of a mortal woman and an incubus; Merlin's powers, then, like Geomagog's, are derived from a demonic being.[47] Geomagog, however, is an evil demon, while Merlin is generally considered to be benign. This double pattern of bad (influence, action, etc.) followed by good is often repeated in the romance. There are, for example, two fights with giants: in the very first adventure, Payn Peverel, Fouke's ancestor, defeats Geomagog.[48] The king, William Bastard, retains the giant's mace as a trophy.[49] In the story's very last adventure that concerns the action of Fouke le Fitz Waryn after his reconciliation with King John and just before his retirement, Fouke takes on and defeats a giant in Ireland at the behest of Rondulf of Cestre.[50] This time, however, the hero himself keeps the giant's weapon, an axe that he takes to Blauncheville.[51] In both adventures, the heroes fight on behalf of a third party. The heroes win both battles, but in the first, the king keeps the trophy, and by extension, part of the glory of the deed; while in the second battle, Fouke himself retains the trophy and all the glory of his accomplishment. Fouke's possession of the trophy in the second case demonstrates how not just he but also the Fitz Waryn family as a whole has grown in power and prestige over the years. Fouke is now, at the end of the romance, his own man; he fights his giant not as a vassal, but as a free man as a favor to a friend.

Another example of the romance's double structure involves two chess games, each one leading to violence. In the first, we observe the origin of King John's grudge against Fouke. The boy Prince John is playing chess when he becomes angry and hits Fouke over the head with the board. Fouke kicks him so hard that John loses consciousness. John later runs to his father the king, hoping for revenge. Instead, the king tells him that he must have deserved this treatment and calls John's master to beat him as punishment for complaining.[52] John is too young and, as he discovers, too powerless to take his revenge immediately. He saves his anger for the much later time when he becomes king and Fouke becomes his pawn. In the second chess-playing episode, which happens in the midst of their fantastic adventures abroad, several of Fouke's companions are challenged to games of chess by seven shepherds, who arrive in unkempt clothing and immediately and inexplicably change into sumptuous attire. The shepherds defeat all of Fouke's men. Fouke then is given the choice of either playing chess or taking part in a wrestling match. Since this "choice" is really a veiled threat, he refuses both. Instead, he draws his sword and quickly strikes the heads off of three of his opponents before his companions join in, and Fouke quickly dispatches the others. This violence may seem unduly harsh; however, the reader learns right soon after how Fouke enters another room and discovers that the youths and the youths' mother had taken seven maidens captive.[53] The women are rescued; the evil-doers are punished. In the first case, young Fouke knocks the villainous child John unconscious, foreshadowing adult victories over John and perhaps the seven evil shepherds. The second episode, which both balances and recalls the first, results in much greater good: the rescue of a maiden and her ladies from imprisonment and the killing of the villains who had held them captive.

There are, in addition, two interesting episodes of reversal involving deceitful men who climb in and out of castle windows. In the first, Dynan is treacherously taken after careful planning when Ernalt de Lyls, and later his men climb up a ladder and into a window. They then put the garrison to the sword and burn much of the town.[54] In the second episode, Johan de Rampaigne, one of Fouke's men, gains admittance to King John's household disguised as a minstrel. He drugs the inhabitants (killing none), rescues Audulf de Bracy, and escapes out the castle window by means of towels and sheets that are tied into an improvised rope.[55] Again, we see the double structure: evil followed by good. The evil-doer climbs in a window to kill the inhabitants of the castle, while the good man climbs out with a rescued compatriot, slaying none.

The use of pseudonyms provides us with a clever double structure within another double structure. Pieres de Brubyle, a noble ruffian, steals Fouke's name for an evil purpose: gathering a band of noble scoundrels and performing wicked deeds under the name of Fouke le Fitz Waryn. The genuine Fouke hears of it, discovers the man and his band, has Pieres bind and behead his own men, and then he himself beheads their leader.[56] Roger Pensom remarks on the parallel between the episodes with King John and Pieres de Brubyle: Pieres robs under Fouke's name, which is "an act of robbery, in a march [i.e. borderland], with Fouke as the victim — his name has been stolen"; moreover, John "deprives Fouke of the due inheritance of his father's fiefs (an act of robbery, in a march, in which Fouke is the victim!)."[57] Fouke regains his name, perhaps suggesting he will later regain his lands. Fouke turns the situation around, saving both his reputation and Pieres's innocent victims. In this case, there are not one, but two opposite events to provide balance. There are perhaps two because in these situations the second and third events are rather more simply benign than positively good. On two occasions, Fouke himself takes a pseudonym, both in cases where he unexpectedly arrives at a court asking for the monarch's hospitality: first, in the court of King Philip of

France, where he calls himself "Amys del Boys"; and second, in that of Messobryn of Barbary, where he calls himself "Maryn le Perdu de Fraunce."[58] His intention in the court of Philip, as becomes obvious, is to protect the King from the absolute knowledge that he is harboring the famous outlaw. The intention in Barbary might be to protect himself from the possibility of being ransomed by the pagan inhabitants, had they known that he was desperately wanted by King John.

During his period of outlawry (the chronological second, or middle, part of the romance), Fouke's adventures take place both in England and also on foreign shores. The adventures in England are often colorful, but they are such that a reasonable person could imagine them actually happening: there are exciting chases and disguises, for example. It is here, however, that the normal situation of justice is reversed in another example of the double structure: the court and the "civilized" world of King John are corrupt, while the wilderness — the woods that Fouke and his men use as their base of operations and call their home — is actually the seat of justice. During this time, Fouke and his men twice capture King John, who says that he will return Fouke's lands. The first time, John, with evil intention, perjures himself, breaking his promise.[59] The second time, John keeps his word, and Fouke is once again integrated into society, yielding the good outcome to counterbalance the prior evil on the part of the king.[60] While living in the forest, Fouke and his companions maintain their own system of justice by, for example, punishing Pieres de Brubyle (the one who stole Fouke's identity) and by stealing from King John and from no one else:

> Fouke ne nul dé suens, de tot le tens qu'il fust exilee, unqe ne voleint damage fere a nully si noun al roy e a ces chevalers.[61]
>
> [Neither Fulk, nor any of his, during the whole time that he was outlawed, would ever do hurt to any one, except to the king and to his knights.][62]

When things become too hot for them in England, or when they need to recuperate from their skirmishes with John's soldiers, the band of companions takes to the sea and to foreign shores. In France, Fouke and his men fight in tournaments and win honor, a common practice of English knights at the time. Fouke gains renown:

> "... e fust amee e honoree de le roy e la roigne e totes bone gentz ... e partot fust preysé, amee e honoree pur sa proesse e sa largesse."[63]
>
> [... and was loved and honoured by the king and the queen and all good people ... and everywhere he was prized, loved, and honoured for his prowess and his liberality.][64]

Here we have yet another example of doubling: the French honor Fouke, while, perversely, he is an outlaw for a time in his native England.

Later in the second part, when Fouke and his men take to the sea again and venture to unknown lands, they enter the realm of the fantastic before again returning to England. Here, Fouke takes a pair of bad situations and turns them around, yielding good results. Fouke and his men rescue the daughter of King Aunflor of Orkanye and her six ladies from an old woman and her seven shepherd sons on an island completely inhabited by robbers and thieves.[65] Fouke then kills a dragon in "la Graunde Eschanye," which is a land of "serpentz e autres lede bestes" ["serpents and other foul beasts"].[66] Almost immediately, he encounters and defeats a second dragon and rescues another maiden; this time, the girl is the daughter of the Duke of Carthage, who has been held captive by the dragon for seven years and forced to serve him by washing the blood from his muzzle.[67] In the brief third, or final, section of the romance, Fouke himself goes blind for his final seven years, during which time he willingly serves mankind at the behest of God as penance for his previous life as a knight and an outlaw. Although Fouke is constrained for seven years by his blindness, much as the maiden had been constrained physically by the dragon, Fouke regards this as a period of freedom and happiness in the service of others. In other words, he sees this as a blissful penance, rather than as a period of forced labor and continual fear, as was the case for the girl. It will be noted that the number seven appears repeatedly, particularly in these paired episodes. In Scripture, the number seven generally is symbolic of "completeness" or "perfection." In the Old Testament, particularly, seven years was the term commonly used for periods of time, for example in Genesis, "Jacob's 7 years' service for Rachel" and "7 years of plenty and 7 years of famine."[68] Thus, after seven years, Fouke's penance and the maiden's service to the dragon are complete.

This complex double structure of the romance underscores the plot movement, demonstrating how Fouke learns from experience and works to improve his life by ameliorating bad situations and ultimately restoring balance in his world. The story begins and ends with prophecies concerning how King John will be defeated by Fouke le Fitz Waryn, symbolically showing that the tale has come full circle and that the world of the protagonist and of King John is once again functioning politically as it should be. Throughout the tale, doubled episodes are frequent and are often widely separated in the text. In most of these parallel situations, the first episode represents the evil or hopeless side of a situation, whereas the second represents a return to the side of good; for instance, enemies climbing in the window to take Dynan castle, killing many / Fouke's companion climbing out a window after liberating another, killing none; and the maiden's service of seven years to the dragon / Fouke's service of seven years to God and to mankind. King John's unbalanced view of kingship — his essential unfairness — is shown in the two related sets of tripartite examples in which two earlier kings establish law and justice and give land, while King John fails to uphold law and justice and wrongfully takes Fouke's land. The world itself is often reversed, in a sense, for Fouke: "society" is neither civilized nor just, while he finds justice and normalcy only in the wilderness; he is praised abroad but pursued as an outlaw in his native land. King John attempts to impose his perverse "justice" on Fouke, but it is John who is finally brought to justice. At the end of his outlawry, after reversing his normal role in life and conquering his own king (foreshadowing Magna Carta), Fouke le Fitz Waryn resumes his role as John's vassal. At that point all that remains for him to do in the brief third part of the romance is to make his peace with God, restoring balance in his spiritual as well as his political life. His penance completed, the world of the romance is again in equilibrium, and Fouke le Fitz Waryn dies serenely.

Genre and Fouke le Fitz Waryn

Fouke le Fitz Waryn is an eclectic Anglo-Norman romance. Although it has characteristics of the epic or *chanson de geste*, the narrative is actually more of a romance. Moreover, it does not fall neatly into any of the traditional romance classifications, but rather it combines a number of them into a unified whole. Brandin writes that the consensus of the scholars of his day was that *Fouke le Fitz Waryn* was "an historical romance containing much romance and little history."[69] Sidney Painter colorfully called it "a weird combination of accurate information, plausible stories that lack confirmation, and magnificent flights of pure imagination."[70] There are fantastic elements, but in the main, particularly when it takes place in England, the action is realistic: Fouke and his men live in the forest and are pursued by the king's men; they escape in creative, but credible, fashion. The tale contains aspects of love, but not of French courtly love. There are also aspects of Christian romance: several important characters perform deeds as Christians, but this is only incidental to the story. The tale does contain many of the characteristics of the ancestral or baronial romance, without falling entirely into that category. The best fit is the legalistic romance and its subsidiary, the outlaw romance.

According to Stephen Knight, all romances concern both a knight and "the ethic of chivalry."[71] To this, Natalia Breizmann adds that romances have a narrator or various narrative voices, and that the protagonist "tries to assert his narrative authority over the other storytellers"[72] Fouke is a knight who practices chivalry, rescues maidens, comes to the aid of friends, and fights for good causes. He also strives to make his version of the story the one that is heard and remembered. In Pieres de Brubyle, we have another narrator who presents himself as Fouke; he assumes his name, his voice, and in a sense hijacks story of the romance from him. Fouke, however, steps in and forces Pieres to take back his version of both the knight Fouke and the story by killing him.[73] Later, it is King John who tries to take the narrative from Fouke. The first time Fouke captures John, the king willingly says that he will restore Fouke's land and will let him live in peace and security from that time on. When John is freed and returns to court, he changes the story, telling everyone that he had been forced to make those promises. When Fouke captures him the second time, John makes the same promises, but keeps his word.[74] By forcing King John to keep his word, Fouke has regained his narrative authority and control of the story.

Romances also commonly include a number of fantastic incidents. During the period of Fouke's outlawry, the protagonist undertakes several marvelous digressive adventures in strange lands: slaying dragons, rescuing maidens and other ladies, and taking vengeance on a family of robber/shepherds on an island of robbers and thieves. Marijane Osborn suggests that these episodes were added to the story "to make this romance conform to the exotic and chivalric (princess-rescuing) adventure story demanded of the genre by the age, and also ... to give the hero something to do in an unfilled story-space during a period when Fulk may actually have been at sea."[75] The historical Fouke did indeed have "a reputation as a sea-captain."[76] Josephus Stevenson located evidence in the Close Rolls of the Chancery Records indicating that Fouke had "a grant made to him of the rigging and fittings of an old Norwegian galley," and Burgess notes that one of Fouke's ships was seized in 1202 or 1203, either during or near the time of the historical Fouke's period of outlawry.[77] The fantastic episodes may indeed have been added in order to fill in some unknown time in the storyline. These marvelous adventures abroad do add color to the tale, but they are not by any means central to the plot.

Although the romance contains a number of women, there is nothing that could be called courtly love. None of the Fitz Waryn family engages in dalliance. Susan Dannenbaum Crane notes that the English heroes of Anglo-Norman romances take marriage and family very seriously indeed; they do not make a game of love as do the heroes of French romances.[78] Fouke, in fact, never appears to fall in love, nor does love prompt him to perform great deeds. True, he marries Mahaud de Caus, sister-in-law of the Archbishop of Canterbury, but this is a marriage to "the sort of beautiful heiress who was highly sought after by knights, whether they were real individuals or the heroes of a courtly romance."[79] Any thought of courtly love on the part of the reader is quickly dashed when Fouke returns to his companions in the woods, leaving his new wife in Canterbury:

> Yl ly escharnyerent e rierent e le apelerent hosebaunde, e ly demanderent ou il amerreit la bele dame, lequel al chastel ou a le boys, e s'entresolaserent.⁸⁰
>
> [They made game of him and laughed, and called him *husband*; and asked him where he should take the fair lady, whether to castle or to wood; and made merry together.]⁸¹

Later, after Fouke returns a rescued maiden to her father, the Duke of Carthage, the Duke offers his daughter in marriage to Fouke:

> Fouke ly mercia finement de cuer pur son bel profre, e dit qe volenters prendreit sa file, si sa cristieneté le poeit soffryr, quar femme avoit esposee.⁸²
>
> [Fulk thanked him finely and heartily for his fair offer, and said that he would willingly take his daughter, if his Christianity would suffer it; for he had already a married wife]."⁸³

Each time Fouke might be tempted to love, the romance is deflected instead to humor.

However, the author also uses love to darker ends in the story. When the injured Fouke, who is alone in a boat, arrives on the shore of Barbary and is taken into the care of Isorie, the sister of King Messobryn, he invents a tale wherein he unluckily loved a treacherous maid. The maid loved another, and this other man one day attacked Fouke with a sword and set him adrift in a boat to die.⁸⁴ The reason for this fabrication is never explained, but it is plausible that Fouke wishes to ward off any possible advances from Isorie and so creates a story in which he suffers because of his love for the maid. He, presumably, could not possibly love another.⁸⁵ Finally, there is the case of Marioun de la Bruere. In the most poignant and pathetic episode of the romance, the maiden falls in love with Ernalt de Lyls, one of the enemy, and by his trickery Dynan is lost; then, Marioun kills Ernalt and leaps to her death from the castle window.⁸⁶ This is a tragic and touching story of a girl who is so much in love that she is blind to her lover's treachery. The author clearly suggests that love is often disastrous. Burgess tartly sums up the cumulative opinion shown by these episodes: "Evidently, love lays an individual open to deception and it puts lives at risk. It is not something to be trusted."⁸⁷ Although Marioun de la Bruere is sensitively and deftly portrayed, this is very rarely the case in such stories. Legge remarks, in fact, that the uncourtly treatment of women by the authors of these ancestral romances is characteristic: "All the writers seem to take a curiously detached view of girls and women, almost as if they had never met any outside a book."⁸⁸ This is not, then, a romance of love.

Fouke le Fitz Waryn and his predecessors are Christian knights, but religion plays a relatively small role in the story as a whole, so *Fouke le Fitz Waryn* cannot be called a Christian romance. At the beginning of the tale, we read that many years previously, Corineus defeated the giant Geomagog in a wrestling match. A demon enters into the dead giant's body and terrorizes the countryside. Fouke's ancestor Payn Peverel definitively defeats the possessed Geomagog, relying on his faith:

> "Chevaler," fet yl, "vous m'avez vencu ne mie par force de vous meismes, eynz avez par vertue de la croys qe vous portez."[89]
>
> ["Knight," said he, "you have conquered me, not by your own strength, but by virtue of the cross which you carry."][90]

Later, when he is asked to fight as the champion of Barbary against the champion of Carthage, Fouke declares himself a Christian knight:

> "... mes jamés bataille ne prendrei pur Sarazyn countre cristien pur perdre la vie. Mes, si le roy vueille reneyer sa ley, e devenyr cristien, e estre baptizé, je prendroy la bataille..."[91]
>
> ["... I will never take battle for Saracen against Christian, though I should lose my life. But if the king will relinquish his faith, and become a Christian, and be baptized, I will take the battle..."][92]

In the course of the battle, Fouke discovers that the opposite champion is his own brother. The fight ends, all the members of the king's household are baptized, the King of Barbary marries the Duchesse of Carthage, and everyone is content.[93] This outcome is not viewed, however, as a great victory for Christianity, but rather as a happy ending to a difficult situation. The protagonist does not seek to fight Saracens, and, as we see in this episode, he has no particular animosity toward them. Finally, at the very end of the romance, Fouke turns to religion, repents of his many killings, and God accepts his penance. He dies a Christian knight.[94]

Although the romance contains characteristics of the types of romances discussed previously, a much stronger case can be made for *Fouke le Fitz Waryn* as an ancestral romance. Legge writes that Anglo-Norman romances like this one were "written to lend prestige to a family which, for one reason or another, could be regarded as parvenu."[95] She regards *Fouke le Fitz Waryn* not just as one of these, but as "the truest of them all."[96] Ancestral romances were written either at the behest of a family, or at least with that family's cooperation, in the hope of some recompense for the author. One would assume that, if this were so, most of the information given in the romance would be historical, but it is not. Although at least part of the story appears to have come from the family or its documents, a great number of errors exist in the chronology and in the facts of the story.[97] Of the many blatant errors in the romance, perhaps the greatest is that Fouke in real life never captured King John: the king "was in Normandy, instead of Windsor or Westminster, during the greater part of the outlawry, and ... he was never at that time in Gloucester, as he is here represented."[98] Urban T. Holmes accepts the ancestral romance theory and tries to explain the errors: "Surely the Fitz Warins must have cooperated. They probably cared very little for historical accuracy and gloried in a tale that was so lively in the telling," and he adds that such "fictitious biography" was popular in the thirteenth century when the romance was written.[99] W. F. Prideaux agrees: "The record of [Fouke's] doings in England was doubtless based on family tradition, and is as authentic as such contemporary accounts usually are," which is to say, not very true at all.[100] One of the strongest advocates of *Fouke le Fitz Waryn* as an ancestral romance was Thomas Wright, one of the text's earliest translators, who suggested that someone in the family's service wrote the tale. He declared that the reason for the many historical errors in the romance was that there were several historical Foukes in the family and that the stories of these individuals naturally became confused.[101] Painter was one of the scholars who asserted that the author had no connection to the family at all since many of the errors are of "facts that must have been well known to [the most likely patrons, Fouke IV and Fouke V] and to their retainers."[102] He argued, on the contrary, that the public wanted the story, and that the author responded to this demand, rather than to any instigation on the part of the family.[103]

Although it has characteristics of the ancestral romance, *Fouke le Fitz Waryn* can best be described as a legalistic romance of the outlaw type. Crane refers to the general category (what I call the legalistic romance) as "Anglo-Norman romances of English heroes":

> These romances are centrally concerned with the workings of the English feudal and legal systems, and ... their heroes exemplify in idealized form the qualities important to the Anglo-Norman barony. Their narratives typically trace the hero's protection or recovery of his seigneurial rights; he struggles primarily for the honor and security of his family, and only secondarily, if at all, for the rights of his countrymen.[104]

This is a distinctly English type of romance such as tends not to exist on the Continent.[105] Other examples include the Anglo-Norman *Lai d'Havelok le Danois* and its English version *Havelok the Dane*, and *Boeve de Haumtone/ Bevis of Hampton*. Since the time of Henry II (r. 1154–1189), feudal power in England no longer depended on military might, but "depended upon the control and administration of land"; as a result, the "Anglo-Norman barony was uniquely peaceful ... and its domesticity was well-served by the Angevin moves toward legal systematization."[106] It was because of this "smooth-running landed baronial hierarchy" that members of the nobility were "[ready] to work within bureaucratic structures."[107] When Fouke le Fitz Waryn believes that King John has broken the social contract, he does not gather an army with which to overthrow the king, but instead he withdraws his fealty and departs. Eventually, he forces John to accept and to follow the contract, which means that Fouke regains his lands and that the king will henceforth protect his right to them.

The central part of *Fouke le Fitz Waryn* is an outlaw romance, a form of legalistic romance. Again, this is characteristically English. Some argue that the French *geste des révoltés* is the same type of romance, but, as Crane argues, this is not true: the Anglo-Norman romances end in the protagonists' success while "the *gestes des révoltés* move toward destruction in an atmosphere of chaos, violence, misfortune, and disillusion."[108] Although there are bad outlaws (for example, the one described in the *Song of Trailbaston* found in another of the Ludlow scribe's books, British Library MS Harley 2253), tales of good outlaws generally enjoy wider popularity.[109] These medieval outlaw tales "emphasize their heroes' moral integrity in various ways."[110] As we have seen, the Fouke of literature is a noble and a moral man. He fights for his rights, rescues maidens, dispatches evil-doers, and dies in bed, forgiven by God for past misdeeds. He does not become an outlaw by choice (as does Pieres de Brubyle in the romance), but because he, as an honorable man, has no other ethical option. He is one of those "crown vassals who comply with their feudal duty by opposing the royal tyrant."[111] The real Fouke III was pardoned by King John on November 15, 1203, with "more than forty other men who had been associated with him in his outlawry."[112] One may well wonder why King John forgave the historical Fouke. According to Painter, the king may have seen him as a successful fighter with a good sense of strategy and wit for survival: "John may have felt that any one capable of defying the government for three years was too good a man to lose," and, Painter adds dryly, [s]lightly reformed outlaws made excellent servants."[113] John's pardon was apparently a wise choice. From the time of Fouke's pardon until about 1210, he and King John appear to have had no contact, but from 1210 to 1215, the knight sometimes accompanied the king on his travels and several times received gifts from him. Fouke III was among the barons who rebelled against John in 1215, perhaps because he owed the crown a great deal of money. However, he soon made peace with the next king, Henry III, by February 1218, and served him faithfully for the rest of his life, as did his son and grandson (Fouke IV and V), respectively.[114]

The outlaw tales, like much of the narrative of *Fouke le Fitz Waryn*, often take place in the forest. As Maurice Keen notes, "For Arthur and his knights the Greenwood was a dangerous no-man's land," while for outlaws, "it was sanctuary."[115] Gawain, it will be remembered, feared the forest with good reason in *Sir Gawain and the Green Knight*. In contrast, Fouke, like many other outlaws, found it to be "an asylum from the tyranny of evil lords and a corrupt law."[116] The fantastic usually had no place in these narratives; the actual forest was dangerous enough without invented threats.[117]

Compared to other outlaw narratives, *Fouke le Fitz Waryn* is more of a romance. One of the earliest of outlaw narratives, the *Gesta Herewardi*, is a Latin text dating possibly to the early twelfth century.[118] The story of the Anglo-Saxon knight is neatly divided into two halves:

> The first half records the romantic adventures of a young exile, but with Hereward's return from banishment to his native land, to combat William the Conqueror and his Normans and to claim the English inheritance which the slaughter of his kindred has left him, this warrior ... is forgotten and the outlaw appears on the scene. We hear no more of the life of kings and courts or of the pageantry of pitched battle; we are introduced to the wild life of fugitives among the fens and to a new war of tricks and disguises and ambushes laid in waste places.[119]

This emphasis on "tricks and disguises and ambushes" continues for several centuries in outlaw narratives as the aspects of romance diminish. *The Tale of Gamelyn*, a mid-fourteenth century narrative in English, has been called a ballad epic, a ballad romance, or a metrical romance.[120] Maurice Keen argues, however, that "there is nothing romantic about its tone or style," and he declares that "we have turned our backs once and for all upon the world of chivalry and the courts of Kings. We shall have no more of necromancers and dragons; there is nothing enchanted about the forest in which Gamelyn took refuge from justice and joined the outlaws."[121] The action of *Gamelyn* is far less elegant than that of *Fouke le Fitz Waryn*. Whereas Fouke refuses to either wrestle or play chess with one of the seven shepherds,[122] Gamelyn bests a wrestling champion, then breaks the neck of a porter and throws his body down a well.[123] Later, Gamelyn brutally takes justice into his own hands in court: he condemns the justice, the sheriff, and jury to hang; and then he see to it that the sentences are summarily carried out.[124] The classic outlaw text *A Gest of Robyn Hode*, an English ballad probably dating to the mid-to-late fifteenth century, sharply contrasts with *Gamelyn*. In this work, although the protagonist is a yeoman, he behaves much as a knight would: he kneels and shows courtesy to guests, and like Arthur in *Sir Gawain and the Green Knight*, he will not sit down to his meal until something happens—in both cases, the event is the arrival of a dinner guest.[125] The noble, brave, and daring knight of romance has now become the noble, brave, and daring middle-class champion of ballads: a new type of hero for a new middle-class readership.[126]

One might think that an Anglo-Norman outlaw narrative contemporary with *Fouke le Fitz Waryn* might be more of a romance than the English narratives, but this is definitely not the case with *Eustache the Monk*. *Li Romans de Witasse le Moine* was composed between 1223 and 1285; more probably

1223–1235.[127] Like Fouke, Eustace was real person, in this case, a Benedictine monk and eventually knight who entered the service of the Count of Boulogne as his seneschal by 1203. He broke with the Count, and by 1205 he had entered the service of the English King John. He died in a naval battle where he was acting as admiral in 1217.[128] The tone and style of *Eustace* is very different from the courtliness of *Fouke*. While *Fouke* occasionally has amusing episodes, *Eustace* is full of exuberant and exaggerated scenes. Keen writes that the first part of the narrative, where Eustace makes full use of his knowledge of necromancy, "is pure burlesque savoring of the horseplay scenes in *Dr. Faustus* rather than of chivalrous romance."[129] He sees Eustace's outlaw period as one that "continues the burlesque mood of the opening passages of the story."[130] *Eustace* is not, then, an elegant Anglo-Norman romance, but is actually much closer in tone and style to a fabliau, particularly when the monk uses his powers to make people perform lewd acts in public and in the cloister.

A number of critics have pointed to similarities in the romance of *Fouke le Fitz Waryn* to the tales of Robin Hood. Some suspect that Fouke may in fact have been the inspiration for Robin. As evidence, Brandin cites this well-known line from the B-Text of William Langland's *Piers Plowman*: "But I can rymes of Robyn Hood and Randolf Erle of Chester," noting that Randolf of Chester plays an important role in *Fouke le Fitz Waryn* and that both Fouke and Robin rob King John.[131] In fact, the historical Randolf of Chester could not have attempted to capture Fouke in real life because he, like King John, was abroad at the time.[132] Burgess suggests that Randolf may have been included in the romance simply because he was already famous in other outlaw tales and it seemed appropriate to add him here.[133] Some critics suggest that Marioun de la Bruere was the inspiration for Maid Marian despite the fact that Marioun would have been a contemporary of the outlaw Fouke's grandmother.[134] Hathaway et al. point out the similarity between the romance and the legends of Robin Hood and other outlaws: "The life of the outlaw is idealized, with the joy of companionship in the struggle against government and society quite overshadowing the real-life hardships."[135] Thomas E. Kelly gives specific examples of the similarities in our romance and the most famous of the Robin Hood tales:

> Some of the incidents in *Fouke fitz Waryn* and *A Gest of Robyn Hode* are ... too close to be accounted for by 'common tradition' or coincidence — the game of truth or consequences by which those who lie are robbed, while those who tell the truth keep their money; the trick of enticing the enemy into a forest trap by promising him a long-horned stag; the captured king or sheriff swearing an oath not to harm the outlaw and then breaking it; and the wounded side-kick begging the hero to kill him by cutting off his head.[136]

Even those who know nothing of the Fitz Waryn family can appreciate the lively outlaw story. Indeed, after his death Fouke III went on to become "a popular romantic figure."[137] Prideaux sums up the popularity of the outlaw romance as follows: "The sturdy common sense ... which distinguishes the [English] tells them that if society is to be maintained[,] law must be obeyed; but their independent spirit is quick to feel injustice, and it is almost a logical inference from the law-abiding principles that if a man does revolt against authority it is because the laws have been strained against him."[138] This is certainly the case in *Fouke le Fitz Waryn*.

Analysis of This Text's Uniqueness

Only one manuscript of the romance concerning the historical Fouke III survives — British Library MS Royal 12.C.XII, folios 33–61. The Anglo-Norman metrical version was the first written; the Ludlow scribe created the Anglo-Norman prose adaptation of it. At about the time of this second version, an English verse translation was made. Anything that may be said comparing the Royal text to the other two, now missing, texts that Leland used for his sixteenth-century summary of the romance is highly suspect since our knowledge is secondhand at best. Leland was not the most precise or conscientious of researchers; in places he might also have misunderstood the text he translated and/or summarized, or he might have relied on his memory. At one point in his summary, in fact, while translating from the French metrical version concerning Fouke II (actually III), he noted this statement: "As I remember the Englisch Historie of the Fizwarines attributith this to Fulco the firste."[139] Also, where facts appear in the extant version but not in Leland's summary (such as most of the fantastic elements), Leland could have decided to omit these items, no matter how crucial they appear to the plot of the romance. That said, we may note that the extant text is the only one known ever to have existed in Anglo-Norman prose, and is the only one to survive of at least three versions in two languages.

In terms of content, the two French versions appear to be virtually identical, while there are a number of differences between the missing English metrical version and the present text. Brandin made a careful comparison of facts found in these two versions. He noted seven that are found in the English version but not in the extant text.[140] The most significant of these is the mention of several characters, in particular Garin, a brother of Fouke. The extant version names Fouke as one of five sons; the English version lists him as one of six.[141] Brandin also listed twenty-two divergences between the texts, often in the order of events.[142] Notable among these divergences is the following example: in the extant version, after Marioun de la Bruere discovers the treachery of Ernalt de Lyls, she kills him, then leaps to her own death; in the English version, upon discovery of the treachery she leaps to her death, and Ernalt afterwards kills many in the town.[143] Hathaway et al. point out the intriguing fact that in the romance William Peverel has two nieces, while Leland's English source gives him two daughters, and in real life he had four sisters.[144] After considering the differences between the texts, Brandin concluded:

> [Q]uelque obscur qu'ait pu être [le poème en anglais], quelque incompétent qu'ait pu être Leland pour en déchiffrer les arcanes, on ne peut imputer à de simples contresens les différences présentées par [le poème en anglais et le remaniement anglo-normand en prose.[145]
>
> [However difficult the English poem may have been, however incompetent Leland might have been at deciphering the obscure points, one cannot ascribe to simple mistranslation the differences represented by the English poem and the Anglo-Norman prose reworking.][146]

The differences between the lost English version of the romance and the present French prose are such that the broad outline of the plot remains the same. There is no question that this is the same story, and as we have seen, most of the critics judge the differences to be relatively minor. Just as the romance is at odds with many of the historical facts, the English metrical version is sometimes in disagreement with the extant romance.

We can discern items that seem to have been added by the *remanieur* (presumably the Ludlow scribe) who rewrote the Anglo-Norman poem as a prose romance. Hathaway et al. assert that he very likely "corrected" what he believed to be errors in his source text. Indeed, the scribe did the same in the *Short Metrical Chronicle*, a work that is found in the same manuscript as *Fouke le Fitz Waryn*. The editors suggest, for example, that "the suppression of an early mention of Alveston, and of Roger and Jonas of Powys, may be due to the *remanieur*, who knew that the grant of Alveston and the Welsh vassals of the English crown belonged to the reign of Henry II."[147] The editors also note that the details concerning the dedication date of the chapel at Ludlow castle show evidence of local knowledge, as does the addition of the words "a Wormeslow" inserted above the line of text to give a more precise location to the site of a battle near Hereford.[148] In addition, the scribe left a blank after the name of the Hereford bishop, "Robert de..."; here, the editors tell us that "No doubt, the scribe intended to fill in the correct name after research in the archives."[149] In an unpublished B. Litt. Thesis, G. Stephenson writes that if the *remanieur* "did add or subtract from his source made no major alterations."[150] Elizabeth A. Francis paraphrases Stephenson's work, writing that "the long description of Fulk III's adventures in and around Spain ... seems to have been inspired by events after 1267, in the life of Fulk VI (ca. 1276–1336), for an analysis of the Royal manuscript suggests that [Fulk VI], or a member of his family, owned the manuscript."[151] Stephenson notes similarities in the lives of Fouke III and Fouke VI: "Both were rebels, both went into exile at the court of a French king called Philip and both seem to have been esteemed by their contemporaries as men of outstanding character."[152] Perhaps the *remanieur* was influenced in his work by Fouke VI or by the story of his life. Further inquiry into the life of Fouke VI and the ownership of the manuscript might prove rewarding for an enterprising student of *Fouke le Fitz Waryn*.

The spirit and style of the prose *remaniement* deserve some attention here, since these literary elements, in many ways, make this romance such a fascinating piece of work. Brandin, in his introduction to Alice Kemp-Welch's 1904 translation of the romance, commented wryly: "The Manuscript is written in rather poor French. All the faults committed by Anglo-Norman writers are to be found in it."[153] In the years since Brandin made his memorable remarks, we have come to see Anglo-Norman not as mangled French, but as a distinct insular dialect of the language. Legge has mixed praise for the *remanieur*: "The writer who turned the poem into prose worked clumsily, but the result, with its traces of rhythm and rhyme-words, has a sparkling attraction of its own. Nobody could ever use the words 'dull' or 'tedious' about *Fouke FitzWarin*."[154] Although the first part of the romance — the background and history of the family — sometimes reads like a chronicle, the remaining two-thirds of the romance moves rapidly and is full of colorful details and action. Francis praises "the spirit and tone of the narrative, the effective dialogue, [and] the ingenious, sometimes elegant, treatment of material."[155]

The story contains deeds of chivalry, but also a good deal of comic relief that sometimes undercuts the high moral tone of the tale. One instance of this is when Fouke's companions tease him mercilessly, calling him "hosebaunde" after his marriage to the high-born Mahaud de Caus and asking him whether he will take the lady to the castle or to the forest.[156] Some of these episodes, at least, may be the work of the Ludlow scribe since they are absent in Leland's summary, since the details given are such that they could very easily have been added after the fact as embroidery on the basic story, and since the Ludlow scribe apparently enjoyed humorous literature.[157] In one instance not dissimilar from the twelfth-century *Aliscans* and the much later *Don Quixote*, the eighteen-year-old Fouke flies to the rescue of Joce de Dynan wearing an old hauberk, carrying a rusty axe, and riding a packhorse.[158] Although his appearance is comical, Fouke proves himself the superior knight in the confrontation that follows.[159] Leland described this episode thus: "And he ... toke his Horse and Spere to rescow Joos ... as one Godarde was aboute to streke of his hede; so that Godarde was slayne of hym, and Gualter Lacy driven away."[160] There is nothing even faintly comical in Leland's version of the episode. Later, as we have already seen, Fouke refuses the offer of the hand of the Duke of Carthage's daughter in marriage because, alas, his Christianity will not allow him to have more than the one wife he already has.[161] Leland totally omitted the girl's rescue and the subsequent meeting with her father. It is possible that he chose not to summarize this episode because of his aversion to fantasy and his reluctance to summarize anything not related strictly to the Fitz Waryn family history as he saw it. However, the episode might not have been in his version of the story at all, or it might have appeared in a very different form than that we know today. Finally, during Fouke's battle as champion fighting in disguise for Barbary, he makes a serious miscalculation: instead of striking his opponent, he strikes the opponent's horse, an exceedingly unchivalrous act. The opposing knight, thrown to the ground, is beside himself in his frustration and anger, hardly knowing what to say. Outraged, he splutters:

> "Maveis payen, maveis Sarazyn de male foy, Dieu de ciel vous maldie! Purquoy avez ocis mon chival?"[162]
>
> ["Wicked pagan, wicked Saracen of ill faith, God of heaven curse you! Why have you slain my horse?"][163]

Although Leland mentioned Fouke's stay in Barbary, he omitted all reference to this crucial battle.[164] This seems incomprehensible. One would think that the battle would certainly qualify as a major event in the history of the Fitz Waryn family, yet Leland omitted these, like some of the other details discussed previously. If not to engage in battle, what is the purpose of Fouke's sojourn in the pagan country? We will probably never know whether the humorous descriptions were added by the scribe or simply omitted by the antiquarian.

The author-function of the Ludlow scribe in this romance is rather complex. First, there was the scribe's now-lost exemplar: the original Anglo-Norman verse romance. The original story, about whose author some scholars have conjectured, appears to have been well-written and entertaining. The Ludlow scribe took this work and adapted it, rewriting it as a prose romance while adding and clarifying details of local geography and of history. Although we cannot know for certain how much of the surviving version's excellence is attributable to the author and how much to the Ludlow scribe, we do know that the scribe here did much more than simply copy the text and make a few changes. His role in relation to this text is very close to that of author.

Fouke le Fitz Waryn is a fascinating, morally uplifting, and often very funny romance. The action is interesting and frequently fast-moving. The geographical details are generally accurate, although the historical "facts" fall disappointingly short of the mark. Fouke's outlaw period is full of narrow escapes, disguises, and good-natured trickery. There is enough violence and knightly fighting to please those who like violent romances, and there are marvelous adventures that include battles against dragons and the rescue of fair damsels from cruel and evil men. The passage of six centuries has not hurt this romance one whit. Although we live in a different world than did Fouke and his companions, human nature is ever the same. The romance of *Fouke le Fitz Waryn* still has the power to fascinate and to make readers and listeners alike laugh aloud.

NOTES

1. Timothy Jones, "Geoffrey of Monmouth, Fouke le Fitz Waryn, and National Mythology," *Studies in Philology* 91, no. 3 (1994): 233–49 at 233–34.
2. See especially Keen, 45–48, 50–52, 209–11, and 213–14 for comparisons of *Fouke le Fitz Waryn* to the Robin Hood tradition.
3. Thomas Wright, *The History of Fulk Fitz Warne, an Outlawed Baron in the Reign of King John, Edited from a Manuscript Preserved in the British Museum, with an English Translation and Explanatory and Illustrative Notes* (London: Printed for the Warton, Club, 1855), x; M. Dominica Legge, *Anglo-Norman Literature and Its Background* (Oxford: Clarendon Press, 1963), 171, agrees with these dates.
4. Louis Brandin, ed., *Fouke Fitz Warin, Roman du XIVe Siècle*. Les Classimques Français du Moyen Âge 63 (Paris: H. Champion, 1930), vi–vii; Louis Brandin, "Nouvelles Recherches sur *Fouke Fitz Waryn*," *Romania* 55 (1929): 17–44 at 37; Burgess, 127–29; Hathaway, ix.
5. Brandin, "Nouvelles Recherches," 43.
6. Hathaway, ix. Timothy Jones, "Geoffrey," 233, also asserts that the verse romance's author was a Ludlow cleric. Derek A. Renn, "'Chastel de Dynan': The First Phases of Ludlow," in *Castles in Wales and the Marches: Essays in Honour of D. J. Cathcaret King*, ed. John R. Kenyon and Richard Avent (Cardiff: University of Wales Press, 1987), 55–73 at 56, draws attention to the author's minute knowledge of Ludlow Castle.
7. For evidence of the scribe's work other than his manuscripts, see Carter Revard, "Scribe and Provenance," in *Studies in the Harley Manuscript: The Scribes, Contents, and Social Contexts of British Library MS Harley 2253*, ed. Susanna Fein (Kalamazoo: Medieval Institute Publications, 2000), 21–109.
8. Wright, *History*, v; Brandin, *Fouke*, iv; Legge, *Anglo-Norman*, 171; Hathaway, et al., *Fouke*, xxxv; Burgess, *Two*, ix; and Revard, "Scribe," 60–61.
9. Hathaway, xl; Glyn S. Burgess, "'I kan rymes of Robyn Hood, and Randolf Erl of Chestre,'" in *"De sens rassis": Essays in Honor of Rupert T. Pickens*, ed. Keith Busby, Bernard Guidot, and Logan E. Whalen (Amsterdam: Rodopi, 2005), 51–84 at 64; Thomas E. Kelly, ed. and trans., *Fouke fitz Waryn*, in Ohlgren 2005, 165–247 at 165; and Jones, "Geoffrey," 233–49, agree. Stephen Knight and Thomas Ohlgren write that *Fouke le Fitz Waryn* "influenced the Robin Hood tradition," in Knight and Ohlgren, 3–4.
10. John Leland, *Joannis Lelandi Antiquarii De Rebus Britannicis Collectanea*, ed. Thomas Hearne, 6 vol. (London: Benjamin White, 1774; repr. Farnborough: Gregg International Publishers, 1970), 1: 230 and 236.
11. Ibid., 1: 230–37.
12. Wright, *History*, xi–xii.
13. Hathaway, xxi–xxii.
14. Wright, *History*, viii.
15. Hathaway, xxiii, xxvi; Jones, "Geoffrey," 234, agrees.
16. Bart Veldhoen, "Psychology and the Middle English Romances: Preliminaries to Readings of *Sir Gawain and the Green Knight, Sir Orfeo*, and *Sir Launfal*," in *Companion to Middle English Romance*, ed. Henk Aertsen and Alasdair A. MacDonald. (Amsterdam: VU University Press, 1990), 101–28 at 113.

17. Ralph Hanna III, *The Awntyrs off Arthure at the Terne Wathelyn: An Edition Based on Bodleian Library MS. Douce 324* (Manchester: Manchester University Press, 1974), 17 and 24.

18. A. C. Spearing, "Central and Displaced Sovereignty in Three Medieval Poems," *The Review of English Studies*, n.s., 33, no. 131 (1982): 247–61 at 249.

19. Geoffrey Chaucer, *The Knight's Tale* in *The Riverside Chaucer*, ed. Larry D. Benson, 3rd ed. (Boston: Houghton, 1987), I(A), line 2684.

20. In my article, "Forsworn and Foredone: Arcite as Oath-Breaker in the *Knight's Tale*," *Chaucer Review* 40, no. 4 (2006): 417–33, I have argued that Arcite loses the battle because he broke the brotherhood oath.

21. A. C. Cawley and J. J. Anderson, ed., *Sir Gawain and the Green Knight, Pearl, Cleanness, Patience* (London: Everyman-Dent, 1996), xxi.

22. Elizabeth Scala, *Absent Narratives, Manuscript Textuality, and Literary Structure in Late Medieval England* (New York: Palgrave Macmillan, 2002), 38.

23. William Calin, *The French Tradition and the Literature of Medieval England* (Toronto: University of Toronto Press, 1994), 83.

24. Ibid., 84 and 86.

25. Alfred Ewert, ed., *Gui de Warewic: Roman du XIIIe Siècle*, 2 vol. Les Classiques Français du Moyen Âge, 74–75 (Paris: É. Champion, 1932–33), 2: 42, lines 8,097–8,106.

26. Ibid., 2: 88–89, lines 9621–47.

27. Ibid., 2: 127, lines 10,893–10,900.

28. Paul Price, "Confessions of a Godless Killer: Guy of Warwick and Comprehensive Entertainment," in *Medieval Insular Romance: Translation and Innovation,* ed. Judith Weiss, Jennifer Fellows, and Morgan Dickson (Cambridge: D. S. Brewer, 2000), 93–110 at 94–95.

29. Rosalind Field, "From *Gui* to *Guy*: The Fashioning of a Popular Romance," in *Guy of Warwick: Icon and Ancestor*, ed. Alison Wiggins and Rosalind Field. Studies in Medieval Romance 4 (Cambridge: D. S. Brewer, 2007), 44–60 at 52.

30. Legge, *Anglo-Norman*, 162 and 167.

31. Hathaway, ix.

32. Ibid., 24, lines 26–32.

33. Translation: Wright, *History*, 68–69.

34. Hathaway, 3, lines 12–13.

35. Ibid., 21, line 23.

36. Ibid., 24.

37. Ibid., 3 and 23.

38. Ibid., 23–25.

39. Glyn S. Burgess, "Fouke Fitz Waryn III and King John: Good Outlaw and Bad King," in Phillips 2008, 73–98 at 75.

40. Ibid., 74.

41. Ingrid Benecke, *Der gute Outlaw. Studien zu einem literarischen Typus im 13. Und 14. Jahrhundert. Studien zur englischen Philologie* ,n.s., 17 (Tübingen: Niemeyer, 1973), 157.

42. Ibid., 159.

43. Regarding the historical events, Janet Meisel writes, "Precisely how much of a threat Fulk's rebellion posed to King John is difficult to determine ... It would seem, however, that Fulk and his followers were, if not a direct threat to the throne, at least a considerable nuisance to the king," in *Barons of the Welsh Frontier: The Corbet, Pantulf, and Fitz Warin Families, 1066–1272* (Lincoln: University of Nebraska Press, 1980), 36.

44. Hathaway, 6.

45. James F. Driscoll, s.v. "Gog and Magog," in *The Catholic Encyclopedia*, vol. 6 (New York: Robert Appleton Co., 1909).

46. Hathaway, 60–61.

47. Ibid., 167–68.

48. Ibid., 5–6.

49. Ibid., 7.

50. Ibid., 58–59.

51. Ibid., 58.
52. Ibid., 22–23.
53. Ibid., 43–45.
54. Ibid., 16–18.
55. Ibid., 37–38.
56. Ibid., 30–32.
57. Roger Pensom, "Inside and Outside: Fact and Fiction in *Fouke le Fitz Waryn*," *Medium Aevum* 63, no. 1 (1994): 53–60 at 55.
58. Hathaway, 41, 53–54.
59. Ibid., 49–50.
60. Ibid., 57–58.
61. Ibid., 27, lines 26–27.
62. Wright, *History*, 77–78.
63. Hathaway, 41, lines 3–4, 12–13.
64. Wright, *History*, 119–20.
65. Hathaway, 44.
66. Hathaway, 45, line 20. Translation: Wright, *History*, 133–34.
67. Hathaway, 46–48.
68. John J. Davis, *Biblical Numerology* (Grand Rapids: Baker Book House, 1977), 118–19.
69. Alice Kemp-Welch, trans., *The History of Fulk Fitz-Warine Englished by Alice Kemp-Welch with an Introduction by L. Brandin Ph.D.* (London: Moring, 1904), x.
70. Sidney Painter, *The Reign of King John* (Baltimore: Johns Hopkins University Press, 1949), 50.
71. Stephen Knight, "The Social Function of the Middle English Romances," in *Medieval Literature: Criticism, Ideology, & History*, ed. David Aers (New York: St. Martin's Press, 1986), 99–122 at 99.
72. Natalia Breizmann, "*Beowulf* as Romance: Literary Interpretation as Quest," *MLN* 113, no. 5 (1998): 1022–35 at 1025 and 1029.
73. Hathaway, 31–32.
74. Ibid., 50 and 57.
75. Marijane Osborn, "The Real Fulk Fitzwarine's Mythical Monster Fights," *Words and Works: Studies in Medieval English Language and Literature in Honour of Fred C. Robinson*, ed. Peter S. Baker and Nicholas Howe (Toronto: University of Toronto Press, 1998), 271–92 at 286.
76. Painter, *Reign*, 51.
77. Ralph of Coggeshall, *Radulphi de Coggeshall Chronicon Anglicanum, De Expugnatione Terrae Sanctae Libellus, Thomas Agnellus De Morte et Sepultra Henrici Regis Angliae Junioris, Gesta Fulconis Filii Warini, Excerpta ex Otiis Inperialibus Gervasii Tileburiensis*, ed. Josephus Stevenson. Rolls Series 66 (London: Longman, 1875), xxii–xxiii; Burgess, 101.
78. Susan Dannenbaum [Crane], "Anglo-Norman Romances of English Heroes: 'Ancestral Romance'?" *Romance Philology* 35, no. 4 (1982): 601–8 at 605.
79. Glyn S. Burgess, "Women in the *Fouke le Fitz Waryn*," in *Por le soie amisté*, ed. Keith Busby and Catherine M. Jones. Etudes de Langue et Litterature Francaises 183 (Amsterdam: Rodopi, 2000), 75–93 at 83. In actuality, Fouke III married heiress Matilda (Maud or Mahaud) de Vavasur within four years after his period of outlawry, according to Meisel, *Barons*, 38.
80. Hathaway, 30, lines 27–29.
81. Wright, *History*, 87.
82. Hathaway, 48, lines 17–19.
83. Wright, *History*, 143.
84. Hathaway, 54.
85. Leland, in fact, writes that Isorie—he calls her "Idonie," misreading the manuscript's letters *s* and *r*—loves Fouke. Leland, *Joannis*, 1: 236.
86. Hathaway, 14–17.
87. Burgess, "Women," 81.
88. Legge, *Anglo-Norman*, 175.

89. Hathaway, 5, lines 27–29.
90. Wright, *History*, 9. Timothy Jones argues that this episode parallels that of St. Margaret's defeat of the demon in the guise of a dragon in her legend: Jones, "Geoffrey," 241–46.
91. Hathaway, 54, lines 35–37.
92. Wright, *History*, 163.
93. Hathaway, 55–56.
94. Ibid., 59 and 61.
95. Legge, *Anglo-Norman*, 174.
96. Ibid., 171.
97. Brandin, "Nouvelles Recherches," 23–24. For more information on Fouke III as a historical figure, see Burgess, 92–107; and Frederick C. Suppe, *Military Institutions on the Welsh Marches: Shropshire, A. D. 1066–1300*. Studies in Celtic History 14 (Woodbridge: Boydell Press, 1994).
98. H. L. D. Ward and J. A. Herbert, *Catalogue of Romances in the Department of Manuscripts in the British Museum*, 3 vol. (London: Trustees of the British Museum, 1883), 1: 504. For more examples of historical errors found in the romance, see Brandin, "Nouvelles Recherches," 23–24; Hathaway, xxvii–xxix; Ward, *Catalogue*, 1: 503–4; and Wright, *History*, xiii.
99. Urban T. Holmes, "The Adventures of Fouke Fitz Warin," in *Medium Aevum Romanicum: Festschrift für Hans Rheinfelder*, ed. Heinrich Bihler and Alfred Noyer-Weidner (Munich: Max Hueber, 1963), 176–85 at 179.
100. W. F. Prideaux, "Who Was Robin Hood?" *Notes and Queries*, 7th Series, 2 (1886): 421–24 at 422.
101. Wright, *History*, xiii–xiv.
102. Sidney Painter, "The Sources of *Fouke Fitz Warin*," *MLN* 50, no. 1 (1935): 13–15 at 14.
103. Painter, "Sources," 15.
104. [Crane], "Anglo-Norman," 602.
105. There is, however, a twelfth-century French *chanson de geste*, *Raoul de Cambrai*, which also concerns the issue of inheritance. In the story, "the emperor grants the county of Cambrai to someone other than the late count's infant son," Raoul, then later tries to "make it up to Raoul by giving him someone else's fief!" Although Raoul grows into a cruel lord, the character Bernier remains loyal to him, but eventually returns his homage after Raoul murders Bernier's mother. Constance Brittain Bouchard, *"Strong of Body, Brave and Noble": Chivalry and Society in Medieval France* (Ithaca: Cornell University Press, 1998), 46 and 44.
106. [Crane], "Anglo-Norman," 607.
107. Ibid., 606–7.
108. Ibid., 606.
109. Carter Revard, ed. and trans., *The Outlaw's Song of Trailbaston*, in Ohlgren 2005, 151–64.
110. Benecke, "Der gute Outlaw," 157.
111. Ibid., 158.
112. Hathaway, xxvii.
113. Painter, *Reign*, 52.
114. Fouke IV fought for Henry against Simon de Montfort at Lewes in 1264 and died there, ignobly drowning in a stream under the weight of his armor. Fouke V died in 1315. See Meisel, *Barons*, 40–42, 52–53.
115. Keen, 2.
116. Ibid., 2.
117. Ibid., 6.
118. Michael Swanton, ed. and trans., *The Deeds of Hereward*, in Ohlgren 2005, 28–99 at 30.
119. Keen, 11.
120. Stephen Knight, ed. and trans., *The Tale of Gamelyn*, in Ohlgren 2005, 264–89 at 265; Keen, 79.

121. Keen, 79.
122. Hathaway, 44.
123. Knight, *Gamelyn*, 175–77.
124. Ibid., 185; Keen, 82 and 87.
125. Thomas H. Ohlgren, ed. and trans., *A Gest of Robyn Hode*, in Ohlgren 2005, 356–96 at 357 and 366.
126. Ohlgren, *Gest*, 361.
127. Burgess, viii.
128. Keen, 54 and 60.
129. Ibid., 55.
130. Ibid., 56.
131. Kemp-Welch, *History*, xvii.
132. Burgess, "I kan," 61.
133. Ibid., 62. For information on the actual Randolf III of Chester and for later links between Randolf and Robin Hood, see respectively Burgess, "I kan," 53–54 and 77–81.
134. Prideaux, "Who Was Robin Hood?," 423.
135. Hathaway, xxxiii.
136. Kelly, *Fouke*, 171.
137. Painter, "Sources," 15.
138. Prideaux, "Who Was Robin Hood?" 424.
139. Leland, *Joannis*, 1: 237.
140. Brandin, "Nouvelles Recherches," 34–35.
141. Ibid., 35.
142. Ibid., 35–37.
143. Ibid., 35.
144. Hathaway, 70, n. 8. 4–6.
145. Brandin, "Nouvelles Recherches," 37
146. Ibid., 37. My translation.
147. Hathaway, xxvi.
148. Ibid., 76, n. 13. 30–31; and 83, n. 21. 36. My thanks to Carter Revard for clarifying my understanding of the latter point.
149. Ibid., 77, n. 14. 27.
150. Quoted in Elizabeth A. Francis, "The Background *to Fulk FitzWarin*," in *Studies in Medieval French, Presented to Alfred Ewert in Honour of His Seventieth Birthday* (Oxford: Clarendon Press, 1961), 322–27 at 323.
151. Ibid., 323.
152. Quoted in Francis, "The Background," 323.
153. Kemp-Welch, *History*, xviii.
154. Legge, *Anglo-Norman*, 174.
155. Francis, "The Background," 323.
156. Hathaway, 30, lines 27–28.
157. See, for example, the fabliaux of British Library MS Harley 2253.
158. Joan M. Ferrante, trans., *Guillaume d'Orange: Four Twelfth-Century Epics* (New York: Columbia University Press, 1974), 218.
159. Hathaway, 12.
160. Leland, *Joannis*, 1: 232.
161. Hathaway. 48.
162. Ibid., 55, lines 16–18.
163. Wright, *History*, 165.
164. Leland, *Joannis*, 1: 236.

5
Fouke le Fitz Waryn: Outlaw or Chivalric Hero?[1]

Kathryn Bedford

The thirteenth-century romance of *Fouke le Fitz Waryn* is a literary description of the life and family of a Shropshire nobleman of the late twelfth and early thirteenth centuries. As such, it provides an interesting window onto popular memory of the past. A mix of history, chivalry, and farce, the romance's hero is represented as at once a knight errant, a trickster, a political freedom fighter, and an important member of the feudal nobility. This variety of characterizations is unusual for a medieval literary account of historical events. Texts from the *History of William Marshal* to saintly *vita* tended to select anecdotes about their subjects in order to conform to a single literary typos. In the case of Fouke, the historical fact of outlawry allowed easy access to the motif of the literary outlaw, but the author moved outside that narrative style to one far more reminiscent of romance. The duality of Fouke's fictionalized image, as both outlaw and chivalric hero, raises questions about how and why certain archetypes become attached to certain individuals. This essay will explore how the author characterized his subject, compare the romance to the historical events, and provide a comparison with the romance *Eustache the Monk*, a near contemporary historical outlaw tale, in order to demonstrate the coherent historical arguments that emerge from the initially confusing jumble of narrative styles.

The historical Fouke was a baron of the Welsh Marches born around the 1160s. He was extraordinarily long lived, not dying until 1258, but it appears that he had handed over control of his property to his sons several years earlier.[2] There are no doubts about his existence and it is possible to establish a rough family history as well as his biography. The text of *Fouke le Fitz Waryn* broadly corresponds to the verifiable facts but focuses primarily on Fouke's period of outlawry between 1200 and 1203 when he was at odds with King John over his right to an area of land named Whittington. This three-year period occupies approximately sixty percent of the text, the other forty percent being taken up with a fairly detailed but not entirely accurate account of the hero's family from the time of the conquest up until his own childhood, and a very brief account of his later years and death.

Fouke's story has been extensively studied. The traditional approach has been to attempt to establish which sections of the text are historically accurate.[3] This method has led scholars to judge it on its merits as a historical source. For example the Anglo-Norman Text Society editors comment that "[t]he historian is bound to criticize [*Fouke le Fitz Waryn*], both for its distortions of twelfth-century history, and for its almost complete suppression of the later years of Fouke's life," while the most recent translator maintains that "although it can be condemned for its occasional inaccuracies, the *Romance* is an important source not only for the history of the Fitz Waryns as a family but for the history of the Welsh Marches in the twelfth and early thirteenth centuries."[4] Although in recent decades the *Fouke le Fitz Waryn*'s literary aspects have also been increasingly acknowledged and analysed, its historical accuracy remains at the heart of the discussion.

However, as long ago as 1935, Painter suggested an alternative approach. The genres of history and fiction had considerable overlap in the medieval period: both were primarily composed by the same set of clerical authors, and there was an expectation that history conform to literary conventions. That is not to say that there was no understanding of their difference; it was simply that facts were subordinate to a higher moral truth, which meant that history was that which was willingly believed rather than what was authentically factual.[5] When attempting to classify *Fouke le Fitz Waryn*, Painter came to the conclusion that, in spite of the many inaccuracies and imaginative interludes, there is so much historical content that it must be "a compilation of legends rather than a work of pure imagination."[6] He argued that, as a consequence, the legends must not only have been current in Fouke's native area but that there must also have existed some public demand for the story; therefore, "one may in the pages of *Fouke Fitz Warin* study the nature and accuracy of popular historical tradition in the late thirteenth century."[7] For Painter, the imaginative material was as much part of the popular understanding of *Fouke*, just as the "historical tradition" was part of the text's factual content. The nature of the fantastic elements of Fouke's story can reveal as much as those elements that can be verified as accurate.

If we are to explore the text in this way, the first issue to be considered is whose memory the *Fouke le Fitz Waryn* preserves. Its date, provenance, and textual history are a good place to start. The text survives in a single Anglo-Norman prose redaction of the early fourteenth century, which is heavily based on a late thirteenth century Anglo-Norman verse original.[8] The dating of the original verse is problematic, the attempts at identifying a specific date have created much debate. Thomas Wright suggested that it was written sometime between 1256 and 1264, and Louis Brandin cited philological reasons to accept a date c.1260, but more recent commentators like Glyn Burgess believe this to be too early and prefer a late thirteenth century date of composition.[9] The surviving manuscript dates from between 1325 and 1340, but the earlier end is more likely, and it has been suggested that the prose was composed before 1314.[10] No firm consensus has been reached between scholars, but it is clear that Fouke's fictionalization took place within only three or four decades of his death, not within living memory but probably only a generation later.

The fictionalization also took place within Fouke's own locality, where the audience could be expected to be already familiar with the locations and individuals being described. Brandin confirmed the suspicion that the text was composed in England in the area of the South-West Midlands and especially Shropshire.[11] However, his conclusions have been narrowed even further by Meisel, who suggests that the author had a personal connection with Ludlow, a prominent location in the early part of the story and the home of Fouke's mother, but was not necessarily a native of the place.[12] The copyist of the extant manuscript also had connections to Ludlow, probably having lived there at some point; he has been identified as a canon of Hereford who accompanied Adam de Orleton, bishop of Hereford, when he became bishop of Worcester in 1327.[13]

What is particularly interesting is that although only the one, derivative, version of the story survives, two prophecies at the beginning and end of the manuscript preserve the original verse and it is possible to reconstruct further sections which were included more or less unchanged in the prose.[14] Consequently, it is possible to discuss the textual history of the work in far more detail than would initially be expected. Combined with a sixteenth century synopsis by John Leland of a Middle English version, which contains excerpts from another French verse text, it is possible to draw comparisons between four different redactions of the story.[15] Composition in French suggests a noble, educated, and therefore specialized audience, which could have been broadened to become more popular by the move to English, but that cannot be assumed. Since Leland gives no information about the date of the manuscript he was using, it is impossible to tell whether the English or French version was the earliest. In fact the level of similarity between the different versions demonstrates that, although they had different sources, they do not illustrate distinct traditions.[16] Details change, but the audience did not receive a substantially different fictionalized image of Fouke depending on which language they heard it in.

A brief summary of the text's account of Fouke's life and its narrative style will be helpful at this point. As a youth Fouke, is described as universally popular; he grew up at court alongside the future kings Richard I and John, and he was successful in the knightly pastime of the tournament.[17] Problems only emerged on John's accession when Fouke was refused rights to the castle of Whittington that he had a claim to through his father, and as a result of the king's failure to act in his subject's interests, Fouke renounced his homage and became an outlaw.[18] Fouke's actions here are presented as entirely justified. The family history section that takes up the opening third of the *Romance* is a defense of the Fitz Waryn's right to Whittington, utilizing prophecy, royal grant, and inheritance to prove unambiguously that Fouke has the superior claim. In addition, John is presented as knowing the truth but deciding to favor the other claimant, Morys de Powys, as a result of greed and revenge for a childhood squabble.[19] Fouke elects to move outside the law because the law is demonstrably unjust; although he is technically a criminal, the romance is entirely favorable towards him and presents him as having a superior moral authority to any other character in the text. As such, he appears to be being placed within the standard remits of the literary "good outlaw" topos.[20]

However, the situation is immediately complicated. As an outlaw, Fouke's first act is to defeat twenty-five of Morys' men with the assistance of his retinue. They move into the forests of Shropshire and continue to battle Morys, who asks John for help. John sends one hundred knights to attempt to capture them.[21] In these stories, Fouke is still operating to some extent within a knightly remit; he still has the same followers that he did as a baron, and leads he them in chivalric battles. Although they live in a forest, which is the traditional local of the outlaw, the trickery and isolation that characterizes the outlaw tale are absent at the start.[22]

A number of short, outlaw-style, episodes follow, including stealing from John's merchants and punishing a group in Scotland who had been using Fouke's name to cover for their own crimes. Finally, Fouke was able to kill Morys by having his companion John de Rampaigne convince Morys that Fouke had been killed so that he would let his guard down.[23] It is here that we begin to see the kind of stories that we would expect of the medieval outlaw. Trickery and disguise come to the fore, and the hero's opponents are kept abreast of events by messages delivered by those who have been robbed. However, it is noticeable even here that the character who tricks Morys is John de Rampaigne. Fouke is the general, planning the attack and waiting on horseback with his knights for Morys to appear for another knightly style battle.

The characterization of Fouke as one who continues to operate as a baron in spite of his outlaw status persists with his marriage to Matilda de Caus, a rich widow whose brother-in-law the Archbishop feared John's intentions towards her. Fouke was asked to marry her in order to protect her. After Morys' death, the family moved to Wales under the protection of the prince, Llywelyn, where Fouke took an active part in ending conflict between Llywelyn and his subject, Gwenwynwyn.[24] Although, ultimately King John was able to put sufficient pressure on Llywelyn to make it necessary for Fouke to leave, Fouke simply made his way to France and the court of another king, Philip Augustus.[25] He was welcomed in France under an assumed name, having taken part anonymously in a tournament and gained the king's attention, but soon John heard of his presence there and asked Philip to remove him. Instead, Philip offered Fouke a permanent place at court and rich lands to support himself.[26] These episodes demonstrate that Fouke was still moving in the same circles as he did before he was an outlaw and was still seen as being of similar status by his peers and superiors.

Although these early outlaw episodes retain considerable aristocratic elements, rather than shift to traditional outlaw motifs, they maintain a historic and folkloric narrative style. From the French episode onwards, the narrative style shifts for a time towards that of full-blown romance, with Fouke being presented as the chivalric hero. Fouke takes to the sea with the mariner Mador de Monte de Russie. They are blown off course to an island beyond Orkney, where they are challenged to play chess by a group of peasants and end up rescuing the princess of Orkney; they then journey to Sweden and face vicious and fantastic beasts, before finding themselves in Spain by the deserted castle of the Duke of Carthage.[27] Fouke rescues the duke's daughter and kills the dragon that has been terrorizing the area, but he has to decline the princess's hand in marriage because he already has a wife.

The company return to England, causing another shift in narrative style, and Fouke is able to capture John by disguising himself as a charcoal burner in typical outlaw fashion. Although John promises to return Whittington, he goes back on his word and instead sends first a knight and then an army after the band. The battle here returns the narrative to the aristocratic tone that characterized many of the earlier English episodes. The king's general even speaks to Fouke as an equal and has to be persuaded by Fouke to follow his lord's orders.[28] During the battle, one of Fouke's brothers is captured, and Fouke himself is wounded before they are able to escape back to sea and another romance section begins.

When they arrive at a deserted island, everyone goes ashore except the wounded Fouke. A storm causes the ship to float until it arrives, unharmed, in the land of Barbary. Fouke comports himself well in arms and is made welcome by the king, who is at war with the princess, whom Fouke had rescued from the dragon. The Saracen King wants to marry the princess, and Fouke agrees to be the King's champion in a single combat to decide the outcome of the war on the condition that the King and court will convert to Christianity if he wins. It turns out that he is fighting one of his brothers, and the king and princess agree to a Christian marriage.[29] Finally, Fouke returns home again, rescues his other brother, and captures John again in another forest; this time John keeps his promise, and they are pardoned and their lands returned.[30]

To analyze the characterization of Fouke, it is important to know how much of the way he is represented is based on fact. Unlike in a purely fictional narrative, the author of *Fouke le Fitz Waryn* was restricted to some extent by his material. Historical elements were combined with the addition of entirely new stories, and it is only when we know which are which that we can truly understand their place within the overall text. There are a number of details from the summary given above that can be confirmed as accurate from other sources. A reference in a continuation to William of Newburgh's chronicle refers to Fouke and his band taking refuge in Stanley Abbey, which is probably the basis of one of the short stories near the beginning of the outlawry. We also know that Fouke had some contact with sea travel, because in 1202–3 a ship owned by him was captured by royal officials, though this does not prove that Fouke himself went abroad.[31] Painter suggested that the romance may be correct in having Fouke kill Morys. Specifically, Morys' sons inherited Whittington only shortly after he had been confirmed in possession of it and were mentioned in 1201 in connection with hunting outlaws.[32] The account of events in Wales coincides with other sources, except that there is no evidence that Fouke was there.[33] It is also possible that the hundred knights sent after Fouke are a memory of the hundred knights given to Hubert de Burgh as custodian of the Welsh Marches since Fouke was the main threat in the area.[34] In addition, this short list may not be exhaustive; there are very few alternative sources of evidence for Fouke's activities at this time, so it is possible that other elements are based in fact. However, we have no evidence for the historical Fouke doing anything that is not reflected in the romance. It does not appear that the author deliberately left anything out of his account.

Given that there are so few sources, assessing the level of historicity in some stories becomes dependent on plausibility rather than fact. A particularly suitable example is that of the Scottish group who uses Fouke's name as a cover. In the story, they are said to be noblemen in league with robbers, and it is plausible that such an alliance could have developed. In 1331, at around the time the surviving manuscript was written, the Folville gang were in operation, and it was comprised of members of the gentry.[35] This is not one of the episodes that can be reconstructed in verse, so it may have been added by the manuscript's compiler in response to his own time. However, the idea of using an outlaw's name to cover other misdeeds can be seen to have happened to

Fouke. One Richard Wigun used the accusation of sheltering Fouke as a means of attempting to pressure William of High Ercall into accepting his claim to some land.[36] So although the story itself cannot be shown to have been based on historical circumstances, it should not be seen as necessarily fictional.

There are also a number of incidents of truncating widely-spaced events into the time span of the outlawry that appear to be focussed on Fouke's family, namely the death of Fouke's mother Hawyse and his marriage. In *Fouke le Fitz Waryn*, Fouke learns of his mother's death very shortly after becoming an outlaw, however in fact she lived for at least twenty years longer than this and last appears in the historical record in 1226.[37] In addition his marriage is placed very early. Matilda, widow of Theobald Walter, was granted to Fouke in 1207 in exchange for 1200 marks and 2 palfreys, which is five or six years later than the romance suggests. Since there is a fairly lengthy section detailing her sufferings and hardships during her husband's outlawry, this cannot simply be a mistake. By placing important elements of his life, especially ones that the audience might be expected to have heard about, within the area of narrative that is of most interest, that narrative is tied more firmly to reality. Additionally, this change in the timeline allows Fouke to be presented as a protector of endangered women.

Changes made to Fouke's interactions with other historical figures serve a similar fictive purpose. One very prominent and wide-ranging result of the changes is to emphasize the outlawry as a personal conflict between Fouke and John, two well-matched foes. The text's account of Fouke's pardon after capturing John in a forest is widely acknowledged to be inaccurate because John was not in the country at the time, but Meisel also points out that the same is true for almost the whole period between 1200 and 1203.[38] The opening of the thirteenth century was difficult for the English crown, which was facing considerable opposition in its French territories from Philip Augustus, and John spent most of his time there until the loss of Normandy in 1204. Consequently, the regular interactions between king and outlaw cannot have taken place as described.

In part, this personal connection is simply a traditional element of outlaw narratives. John is the equivalent of the Sheriff of Nottingham in the Robin Hood legends; his constant tricking and increasing frustration characterize him as the figure of fun from comedy or farce.[39] It is important that the hero has a villain to overcome in order to measure his success, so John's presence in the country could simply be a form of artistic license in order to aid the narrative flow. However, a number of the alterations to historical events earlier in the story serve to mark Fouke "a very minor personage" and as a suitable opponent for a King.[40] At the very beginning of the romance, the family's founder, Payne Peverel, is stated to be a cousin of William I, and this family connection is reasserted when Fouke's father, Fouke the elder, goes to Henry II for help.[41] In fact, Henry II mentions the relationship at once while Fouke appears to be unaware, implying that the royal family is more interested in their relationship than the Fitz Waryns are.

The significance of the two children being brought up together can hardly be underestimated. It implies that they had the same education and training, another form of equality. In contrast, however, are the comments on their childhood actions, which show that Fouke was superior by talent if not by birth.[42] When Fouke and John argue, the king assumes that it is Fouke who is in the right. The relationship between the two characters is that of equals in birth and education, rather than lord and subject, allowing them to be judged by the same criteria. As such, an important theme of the text that plays out through this relationship is the proper use of authority.

John is the quintessential bad ruler. He is vindictive, greedy, violent, and lecherous; he thinks of himself rather than the welfare of those over which he rules. This is repeatedly stated throughout *Fouke le Fitz Waryn*, starting with Fouke's formal renunciation of fealty:

> "Sire roy, vous estes mon lige seignour, e a vous su je lïé par fealté tant come je su en vostre service, e tan come je tienke terres de vous; e vous me dussez meyntenir en resoun, e vous me faylez de resoun e commun[e] ley, e unque ne fust bon rey qe deneya a ces franke tenauntz ley en sa court; pur quoi je vous renke vos hommages."[43]

> ["Lord King, you are my liege lord, and I am bound by fealty to you whilst I am in your service and as long as I hold lands from you. You ought to maintain my rights, and yet you fail me both in rights and in common law. He was never a good king who denied justice to his free-born tenants in his court."][44]

John's fellow ruler Lywelyn states that "I am unable to gain peace under any circumstances"[45] from John. And the narrator has even harsher words:

> Le roy Johan fust home santz conscience, mavois, contrarious e hay de tote bone gent e lecherous, e, s'yl poeit oyr de nulle bele dame ou damoisele, femme ou fyle de counte ou de baron e d'autre, yl la voleyt a sa volenté aver, ou par promesse ou par don engyner, ou par force ravyr, e pur ce fust le plus hay. E pur cele encheson plousours grantz seignours d'Engleterre aveyent rendu al roy lur homages; dont le roy fust le meynz doté d'assez.[46]

> [King Kohn was a man without a conscience, wicked, quarrelsome, hated by all good people and lecherous. If he ever heard of any beautiful maiden or lady, wife or daughter of an earl or a baron or anyone else, he wanted to have his way with her, either by tricking her with promises or gifts or by taking her by force. For this he was hated the most, and this is why many great English lords had renounced their homage to the king. As a result, the king was far less feared.][47]

This is not a singular view of John, for the chroniclers Ralph of Coggeshall and Roger of Wendover made similar negative comments about him during the 1212–15 Baronial Revolt against him.[48] By contrast, Fouke represents good rulership. He treats women honorably; he seeks council from the wise men around him, especially Mador the sailor and John de Rampaigne; he aids any and all of his men who need help; and he resolves conflicts. In Wales especially, Fouke is the law bringer, even though he is outside of the law and focuses his violence only on those who have done him wrong. Indeed, Fouke and his men have a strict code of conduct, and we learn whom Fouke and his men will and will not harm:

> Fouke ne nul dé suens, de tot le tens qu'il fust exilee, unqe ne voleint damage fere a nully si noun al roy e a ces chevalers.[49]
>
> [During the whole period of his exile, neither Fouke nor any of his men ever attempted to harm anyone other than the king and his knights.][50]

The inaccurately early marriage to Matilda shows the contrast especially well; her brother-in-law chooses the righteous outlaw to protect her from the lecherous king.

From what we have seen so far, *Fouke le Fitz Waryn* fits comfortably within the medieval "genre" of historical fiction by taking a framework of historical events and embroidering them with a number of common story types that present the hero in a suitably favorable light, for example, disguise to lead an enemy into an ambush, winning an anonymously entered tournament, and saving a princess from a dragon.[51] True, there is a greater aristocratic tone than might be initially expected in the outlaw sections, but that can easily be explained by the limitations of Fouke's historicity. Maurice Keen saw Fouke's noble lineage as preventing his legend moving away from knightly concerns towards those of the "real outlaw" narrative.[52] Although it was his time as an outlaw that was being fictionalized, an author and audience from his own locality would have been more familiar with his role as a noble landholder, and so one would want to retain elements of that characterization.

It is when we compare the story of Fouke Fitz Waryn with another, similar, contemporary example that essential examples of characterization begin to stand out. Eustache the Monk was another outlaw of noble birth. He became a pirate in the employment of both England and France and died in 1217. Eustache had a French verse romance, *Eustache the Monk*, written about him at some point in the early-to-mid-thirteenth century in his home area that, similar to Fouke's romance, focused very strongly on the time he spent as an outlaw.[53] So we have two romances of historical outlaws, each being composed in the area in which its hero lived within only a few decades of that hero's death and approximately contemporary with each other. As would be expected, there are large numbers of similarities, but there are equally dramatic differences in both style and content.

Both characters and their respective narratives are imbued with outlaw motifs, like spending large sections of their stories in the forest and undertaking trickster activities. There is also considerable overlap in the content of these stories between the two romances; for example, both escape their enemies by reversing their horses' shoes.[54] The theme of disguise appears repeatedly; Eustache appears, among other things, as a monk, a charcoal burner, a potter, a pilgrim, and a leper.[55] Although Fouke was more restrained, he still dressed as a monk, a charcoal burner, merchant, and a female prostitute; moreover, Fouke had other members of his band, especially John de Rampaigne, disguise themselves at various points.[56]

However, already differences begin to emerge. Even within the outlaw conventions of forest living, trickery, and disguise, Fouke has noticeably more moral and political aims for his activities; he does not want simply to humiliate his enemy but to achieve a particular set of law- and land-based objectives. While Eustache uses his disguises to steal horses and small amounts of money, or to play tricks like having pies at a feast filled with tar so the guest's teeth get stuck together, Fouke uses trickery to try to force a settlement with John.[57] This difference points to a fundamental distinction between the two works. Both Fouke and Eustache were outlaws and it was that aspect of their lives which was fictionalized but the resultant characters have few similarities beyond their surroundings.

In spite of the variety of story types in Fouke's romance, Eustache is presented as having a much wider variety of skills. He is a magician, can imitate the calls of birds, construct elaborate disguises, bake, and sail, among other talents. He is the central character in every story in which he appears; any companions are reduced to ciphers who simply follow orders and have no initiative of their own. By comparison, Fouke's brothers, and especially the duo of John de Rampaigne and Mador de Monte de Russie, have a considerable degree of autonomy; they are able to emerge as characters in their own right. It is John, not Fouke, who wears the more complex disguises to infiltrate their opponents' homes, and it is Mador who controls the voyages at sea.[58] Fouke is still being presented as a lord; he has the ability to delegate rather than having to do everything himself, whereas Eustache, even when he is in favor and well off, is never seen in a commanding position.

Eustache's inability to become an authority figure parallels his inability to associate with them. Unlike Fouke, Eustache was not a model youth. He studied with the devil abroad and caused uproar in the monastery he entered.[59] In later years, even though he worked for the kings of both France and England, he is not operating out of fealty but for money or revenge, and with his family as hostages for his good behavior.⁶⁰ At no point during his life is he presented in an unambiguously positive light. Fouke on the other hand is portrayed positively at all times and maintains good relationships with all authority figures except John. During his outlawry he is made welcome in five royal courts where he is honored and rewarded.⁶¹ One gains the impression that it is only as a result of extreme circumstances that Fouke has become an outlaw, whereas for Eustache it is his natural way of life.

Moving on to stories about the fantastic, one is made even more aware that very different things are being done in the two texts. In the *Fouke Fitz Waryn*, for large sections of Fouke's period of outlawry, he is portrayed as leaving the forest to take part in adventures that are reminiscent of romance rather than folktale. In these romance sections, Fouke is a knight errant bringing justice to distant lands through deeds of arms. He overthrows tyrannical lords, such as the richly dressed peasant thieves and the dragon, who oppress their lands so that none can safely live there. Also, via single combat with another knight, Fouke persuades a Saracen king to convert to Christianity so that he can marry an heiress rather than force himself on her and take her lands through war. All of these stories are entirely fictional and compare far more readily to works such as those of Chrétien de Troyes or Marie de France than to any outlaw narrative. This is a narrative style that has no parallel in Eustache's tale.

Within the romance of *Eustache the Monk*, the fantastic is still present, but its place is easy to identify, though less well integrated. Eustache himself is a magician who learned his craft from the Devil but is very rarely seen to use it. Only in the first few hundred lines to we see any evidence of his magic; for example, Eustache takes revenge for petty wrongs done to him by a landlady and a carter. The style remains folkloric and burlesque. Eustache is definitely not a knight in these stories: he has no horse and has to hire passage with the carter, and we see none of the typical romance motifs like single combats or princesses.⁶² In fact, the magic elements are probably the most low-brow and least romance like parts of the text.

Overall, although both texts focus on their hero's time as an outlaw and spend a similar proportion of their time upon it, the balance of narrative elements is very different. While Eustache's fantastic tales seem to be incidental, the outlaw elements in Fouke's story are overwhelmed by the long foreign digressions into romance. Although for sixty percent of his romance Fouke is an outlaw, for only about half of that space sees him acting in an outlaw style context. The fact that Fouke's story contains so many romantic incidents was not simply an automatic consequence of fictionalization but particular to Fouke's characterization. As was done by the author of the *Eustache the Monk*, it would have been easy to remain within the historical framework of Fouke's life, thereby tell an entertaining story, and produce a very different kind of hero.

Although the *Fouke le Fitz Waryn* is unusual in its variety of styles, it is not as unusual a structure as might be supposed; family history followed by a longer and more fantastic central story is a typical form of Old Norse–Old Icelandic Sagas, for example.[63] The variety of styles has caused problems for a number of commentators, such as Maurice Keen, who was unable to reconcile his ideas of the place of fantastic tales within Fouke's overall story. He claimed both that "his outlawry and his long struggle with John are only the background theme lending its unconnected incidents some shadow of continuity," and that the "voyages to distant lands were no more, really than colourful interludes in the tale of Fouke's long battle with the tyrant who was reigning in his native land."[64] But there is no reason to assume that a medieval audience would have been similarly confused.

Although we cannot be sure exactly how closely the surviving text corresponds to the original verse, it is worth remembering that all four versions that we have evidence for are extremely similar. There are a number of differences, and we can be less certain about the most fantastic episodes since Leland summarized them considerably, but it seems that all the versions in circulation had essentially the same basic pattern and balance of historical to fantastic episodes.[65] This suggests that the original version was consciously constructed by a single author rather than being simply a group of legends told one after the other. The chivalric and political side to Fouke's story was a conscious decision on the part of the author.

Particularly valuable here is the methodology of Roger Pensom who rejects the common image of the story as chaotic.[66] While David Ross describes the text as "a curious mixture of frequently misrepresented fact with elements of folklore and episodes of conventional adventure romance," Pensom instead sees these three initially disparate elements as forming part of an organized structure.[67] He describes the story as taking place within three shells, each with its own style and subject matter, whose boundaries correspond with geographical areas: the centre is around Shropshire and contains historical, political and geographical information; moving outwards Fouke then comes to the forest where the story takes on the characteristics of outlaw folktale; then finally at the furthest extreme, travel overseas brings the fantastic stories of high romance.[68] Each of these shells emphasizes the same themes using different techniques.

Pensom argued, for example, that the lords whom Fouke overcomes while abroad in the romance sections symbolize King John and the tyranny and injustice he is bringing to England, thereby allowing Fouke to continue seeking the same political objectives as he did as an outlaw.[69] In Spain, the dragon represents John. He has forced the rightful lord from the land, leaving the castle deserted, and consequently harming all who lived there. He has also stolen away the princess to serve him, an act that reminds us of the behavior that has been criticized in John. At the end of the episode, the rescued princess is offered to Fouke as a bride; Fouke refuses because he already has a wife.[70] The narratival reminder to readers at this point in the story of Fouke's marriage reminds us also of the circumstances in which it took place: Matilda was rescued from John just as the princess was rescued from the dragon. This appears to suggest that the inclusion of such episodes was an attempt to strengthen a theme that could not be brought out as forcefully as the author desired within the outlaw typos alone.

Fouke le Fitz Waryn is often seen as a ancestral romance of a similar type to *Bevis of Hampton* or *Guy of Warwick*, so scholarly attention naturally falls on the Fitz Waryn family as a possible influence on, or even patron of, the story.[71] If this were the case, then the presentation of Fouke as a chivalric knight could be easily explained as a way of glorifying his descendants, and the political message may have been connected with their own aims. However, it is impossible to demonstrate that there was any direct influence by the family, and Fouke's son actually died fighting for Henry III at Lewes.[72] The best possible source of inside information that has been suggested is Fouke's mother; however, her death in the romance is over two decades before she is last heard of in the historical record makes that unlikely, and the very large number of other inaccuracies in the family history, especially the missing out of an entire generation, supports the view that the work was not intended for the family.[73]

This does not of course mean that Fouke's family had no impact at all. As has already been mentioned, according to Keen, since Fouke was from a knightly family, remnants of chivalric ideals were attached to him; moreover, since "historical reputation acted as a natural magnet to myth," some of the stories had a chivalric bent.[74] The same applies to Eustache, but it is possible that since he remained a problematic character for the rest of his life (whereas Fouke rejoined the nobility), Fouke's knighthood was a more important part of his image. Even if Fouke's family did not directly influence the story, it is unlikely that an author writing in the area in which they held power would want to present him in a less that entirely favorable light. However, Fouke's romantic presentation had wider implications than just to benefit his descendants.

The theme that comes out of all sections of *Fouke le Fitz Warin* most strongly is authority, especially royal authority, and its limitations. John is not a bad king because he denies his vassal lands in favor of a non–Norman but because he does so unlawfully. The argument of the romance is that the abuse of royal authority by John has damaged the kingdom to the extent that the only way to stay within the law is to reject that authority and become an outlaw. As Timothy Jones has argued, "our author has drawn for us an exemplum of loyalty, not to kings, but to family, God, and a national myth."[75] The peasants and the dragon are similarly bad because they have taken authority from those who should rightfully have it, the peasants by making demands of men with a higher social standing and the dragon by driving the Duke from his castle.

The question of the crown's position in regards to the law was still under debate in the thirteenth century. A thirteenth-century law book claimed that the barons felt a duty to "put a bridle, that is the law, on the king."[76] The events of the Baron's War demonstrate that, for many of the nobility at least, the King was not the final arbiter; if he failed his people, then they had the right to correct him.[77] Therefore, by discussing the relationship between a lord and an unlawful king, the romance of *Fouke le Fitz Waryn* was speaking directly to the concerns of the (largely noble) audience for whom it was intended.

Exactly which elements of the romance reflect a particular time is impossible to discover with any degree of certainty. It is unfortunately difficult to analyse how far the fantastic sections that survive are the product of revisions or interpolations by the fourteenth-century prose author. Based on the survival of the original verse within the surviving prose, it is the family history and outlaw episodes that are closest to the original, but comparison with Leland's sixteenth-century summary demonstrates that there were far more similarities than the verse fragments indicate.[78] However, Leland was relatively uninterested in the fantastic parts of the story and gave only very brief notes on that section, making it impossible to say with any certainty what the fourteenth-century scribe altered.

In spite of this, the circumstances surrounding the writing of the surviving manuscript deserve greater consideration. As previously stated, the scribe was probably a canon of Hereford who accompanied Adam de Orleton, bishop of Hereford, when he became bishop of Worcester in 1327, writing at around that time. It has been suggested, by both the Hathaway et al. and Burgess, that he rewrote the story he inherited with that specific bishop in mind, since Adam de Orleton was a very political bishop.[79] Adam de Orleton had a history of conflict with the king and some connection with Roger Mortimer who, along side Queen Isabella, overthrew Edward II in 1327.[80] So regardless of whether the scribe changed his text significantly, it is interesting that both the original text and the surviving manuscript were written in circumstances when there was considerable conflict between the king and the higher nobility.

If we return to the comparison with Eustache, no similar political context can be seen surrounding his story. Boulogne around the 1230s was largely stable, and its Count, Renaud de Dammartin, focused on events happening elsewhere. Although there had been questions over the rights of the French kings to authority in this area, these had ceased to be of immediate importance and were anyway less pervasive in the lives of ordinary people than were the continuing problems in England. Eustache's outlawry would not have had the same associations for the people in his area as Fouke's did since they did not share his objectives and his later life serving the kings of England and France at sea made him geographically, as well as ideologically, separate.

The romance of *Fouke le Fitz Waryn* draws together strands of historical, folkloric, and romantic narratives to present a consistent argument about the limitations on lordship with regards to the landholding rights of tenants. Although, naturally, no single factor can explain the puzzling and unusually prominent inclusion of such a range of narrative styles; however, the fact that this was an important issue within the wider events surrounding the time of authorship must have played a part in the author's decision to go beyond the types of narrative that easily fitted the facts at his disposal. Fouke's position as an important member of the feudal nobility eased the transition into romance, but is not sufficient on its own to explain why such a large proportion of the text is in that style. The typos of outlaw as bringer of justice could not provide the same kind of authoritative precedent to an audience as could the chivalric hero, so Fouke's image was manipulated into a more useful shape in the interests of later political concerns.

NOTES

1. Thanks are due to my funding body, the AHRC, and my supervisor, Dr. Giles Gasper.
2. Janet Meisel, *Barons of the Welsh Frontier: The Corbet, Pantulf, and Fitz Warin Families, 1066–1272* (Lincoln: University of Nebraska Press, 1980), 138.
3. For example, Meisel, *Barons of the Welsh Frontier*; and Sidney Painter, "The Sources of *Fouke Fitz Warin*," *MLN* 50, no. 1 (1935): 13–15.
4. Hathaway, xxviii; Burgess, 91–2.
5. Suzanne Fleischman, "On the Representation of History and Fiction in the Middle Ages," *History and Theory* 22, no. 2 (1983): 278–310 at 289 and 305.
6. Painter, "Sources of *Fouke Fitz Warin*," 13.
7. Ibid., 15.
8. Burgess, 91.
9. Thomas Wright, ed. and trans., *The History of Fulk Fitz Warine, an Outlawed Baron in the Reign of King John, Edited from a Manuscript Preserved in the British Museum, with an English Translation and Explanatory and Illustrative Notes* (London: Printed for the Warton, Club, 1855), x; Louis Brandin, "Nouvelles Recherches sur *Fouke Fitz Waryn*," *Romania* 55 (1929): 17–44 at 32–3 and 38–9; Burgess, 127.
10. Burgess, 129.
11. Brandin, "Nouvelles Recherches," 40–3.
12. Meisel, *Barons of the Welsh Frontier*, 134.

13. Burgess, 129–30. For evidence of the scribe's work other than his manuscripts, see Carter Revard, "Scribe and Provenance," in *Studies in the Harley Manuscript: The Scribes, Contents, and Social Contexts of British Library MS Harley 2253*, ed. Susanna Fein (Kalamazoo: Medieval Institute Publications, 2000), 21–109.

14. Hathaway, xix–xx.

15. John Leland, *Joannis Lelandi Antiquarii De Rebus Britannicis Collectanea*, ed. Thomas Hearne, 6 vol. (London: Benjamin White, 1774; repr. Farnborough: Gregg International Publishers, 1970), 1: 230–7; Brandin, "Nouvelles Recherches," 34–8, convincingly demonstrates that none of these versions was identical with each other.

16. Brandin, "Nouvelles Recherches," 37.

17. Hathaway, 22–3.

18. Ibid., 24.

19. Ibid., 24. The squabble is detailed on 22.

20. Thomas H. Ohlgren, in Ohlgren 2005, xxviii–xxix. Fouke was actually one of the examples used by Ingrid Benecke when proposing the scholarly model of the "good outlaw." See Ingrid Benecke, *Der gute Outlaw. Studien zu einem literarischen Typus im 13. Und 14. Jahrhundert. Studien zur englischen Philologie*, n.s., 17 (Tübingen: Niemeyer, 1973).

21. Hathaway, 25–6.

22. While it is true that literary outlaws usually have some kind of band of followers, these tend to be gathered after the outlaw is already active, and many of the tales will involve him acting alone or with only one or two close associates.

23. Hathaway, 32–3.

24. Hathaway, 34

25. Ibid., 40.

26. Ibid., 41.

27. Ibid., 43–6.

28. Ibid., 51–2.

29. Ibid., 55–6.

30. Ibid., 57.

31. William of Newburgh, *Historia Reum Anglicarum*, in *Chronicles of the Reigns of Stephen, Henry II and Richard I*, ed. Richard Howlett, 4 vol. Rolls Series 82 (London: Longman, 1884–89), 2: 506–7.

32. Sidney Painter, *The Reign of King John* (Baltimore: Johns Hopkins University Press, 1949), 50; Thomas Duffus Hardy, ed., *Rotuli chartarum in Turri Londinensi* (London: Public Record Commission, 1837), 74.

33. Burgess, 189 n. 31.

34. Meisel, *Barons of the Welsh Frontier*, 38.

35. Burgess, 189.

36. Doris Mary Parsons Stenton, ed., *Pleas Before the King or His Justices, 1198–1202*, 4 vol. Publications of the Selden Society, 67–68, 83–84 (London: Quaritch, 1952–67), 3: 82.

37. Hathaway, xxxii.

38. Burgess, 103; Meisel, *Barons of the Welsh Frontier*, 36.

39. Burgess, 123.

40. Painter, *The Reign of King John*, 49.

41. Hathaway, 21.

42. Hathaway, 23.

43. Hathaway, 24, lines 26–32.

44. Burgess, 151.

45. Burgess, 159.

46. Hathaway, 35–36, lines 34–38 and 1–3.

47. Burgess, 161.

48. Hathaway, xxix.

49. Ibid., 27, lines 26–27.

50. Burgess, 153.

51. Hathaway, 32–3, 40, 46–7.
52. Keen, 174. The concept of the "real outlaw" as representing popular concerns against noble authority has been rejected, not least by Keen himself, xii–xiv. But the connection drawn between historical reality and the consequent narrative remains relevant.
53. Burgess, 41–3, 48.
54. Conlon, 78–81, lines 1494–1607; Hathaway, 32; Burgess, 68, 157–58.
55. Conlon, 65–73, lines 996–1283; Burgess, 62–64, 67–68.
56. Hathaway, 29, 32; Burgess, 155–58.
57. Conlon, 87–88, lines 1820–81; Hathaway, 49; Burgess, 172–73.
58. For example, compare the disguises of John as a black minstrel, Fouke as a charcoal burner and Eustache as a one-legged man. We are told about the complexity of the first and last, both of which also require some considerable acting talent, whereas all Fouke does is switch clothes. See Hathaway, 37, 49; Conlon, 76–78, lines 1423–65; Burgess, 162–63, 172–73, 67–68.
59. Conlon, 39–40 and 45–46, lines 1–38 and 220–79; Burgess, 50, 52–53.
60. Conlon, 89 and 95–98, lines 1882–910 and 2136–250; Burgess, 73, 76–77.
61. The five are Wales, France, Orkney, Carthage and Barbary.
62. Conlon, 43–45, lines 160–219; Burgess, 52.
63. *Njál's Saga* is commonly sighted in this context; but others, such as the *Laxdæla Saga*, follow a similar pattern, Hathaway, xxxvii. The possibility of the *Fouke le Fitz Waryn* having been influence by Scandinavian literature has been considered, for example, by Marijane Osborn, "The Real Fulk Fitzwarine's Mythical Monster Fights," *Words and Works: Studies in Medieval English Language and Literature in Honour of Fred C. Robinson*, ed. Peter S. Baker and Nicholas Howe (Toronto: University of Toronto Press, 1998), 271–92.
64. Keen, 39, 43.
65. Brandin, "Nouvelles Recherches," 33–7; Hathaway, xx–xxiii.
66. Roger Pensom, "Inside and Outside: Fact and Fiction in *Fouke le Fitz Waryn*," *Medium Aevum* 63, no. 1 (1994): 53–60.
67. David J. A. Ross, "Where did Payn Peverell defeat the Devil?," in *Studies in Medieval French Language and Literature: Presented to Brian Woledge in Honour of His 80th Birthday*, ed. Sally Burch North. Publications Romanes et Françaises 180 (Geneva: Droz, 1988), 135–44 at 135.
68. Pensom, "Inside and Outside," 54.
69. Ibid., 56.
70. Hathaway, 48; Burgess, 171–72.
71. M. Dominica Legge, *Anglo-Norman Literature and Its Background* (Oxford: Clarendon Press, 1963), 171–4.
72. Burgess, 107.
73. Hathaway, xxxii; Painter, "The Sources of *Fouke Fitz Warin*," 13.
74. Keen, 132.
75. Timothy Jones, "Geoffrey of Monmouth, Fouke le Fitz Waryn, and National Mythology," *Studies in Philology* 91, no. 3 (1994): 233–49 at 249.
76. Ralph V. Turner, *Magna Carta: Through the Ages* (Harlow: Longman, 2003), 2.
77. For example, the settlement after the battle of Lewes put a council in charge of court appointments and included the statement that it would outlive the person of the king and be binding to his heirs. See Alan Harding, *England in the Thirteenth Century* (Cambridge: Cambridge University Press, 1993), 292.
78. Hathaway, xix–xxiii.
79. Ibid., xliii; Burgess, 130.
80. Burgess, 131.

6
Social Protest and Narrative Technique in Prichard's *Twm Shon Catty*

MICA DAWN GOULD

Since its first publication in 1828, Thomas Jeffrey Llewelyn Prichard's novel, *The Comical Adventures of Twm Shon Catty, (Thomas Jones, Esq.) Commonly Known as the Welsh Robin Hood*, has had a turbulent reception. Despite both the author's claim that it was the first Welsh novel and its numerous reprints, *Twm Shon Catty* has remained virtually ignored by critics.[1] Often described as the Welsh Robin Hood, Twm Siôn Cati (ca. 1530–1609) has a life that is more legendary than historical. We know that he was pardoned in 1559 under the Great Seal by Queen Elizabeth I, and that his official names were Thomas Jones or John or Thomas Siôn Dafydd.[2] The story of *Twm Shon Catty* centers on a Welsh peasant and natural son of an English nobleman, who because of his tricks and foolery was outlawed. After Twm runs, he gradually charms his way up the social ladder by, among other things, rescuing maidens, playing tricks, and eventually becoming the trusted friend and employee of a powerful lord, Sir George Devereux. As in other outlaw tales, such as *Adam Bell, Clim of the Clough, and William of Cloudesley* and *The Tale of Gamelyn*, this wily hero not only earns his way back into acceptable society but also eventually becomes a local justice.[3]

Prichard's book has been both cited as historical fact and condemned as libelous rubbish. *The Oxford Companion to the Literature of Wales* calls *Twm Shon Catty* "a crudely shaped narrative" and "stylistically coarse and turgid."[4] The most vehement of the detractors is J. Kyrle Fletcher, Esq., a well-known antiquary, who writes in *Western Mail*:

> Why should the story (by Llewelyn Pritchard) be still considered as the true life of Twm Shon Catti? He has made him a wild Robin Hood and a comic Dick Turpin all in one, and I am surprised that Welsh people have accepted this for so long as a real life story...
> In serious history where we find the real Twm Shon Catti, he is not even

styled by that name, for there he is styled 'Thomas Jones of Fountain Gate' in Tregaron. His home was a charming old house built out of the ruins of an old Hafod which had belonged to the Gwaethfod family, and here in his study he had collected a vast store of Welsh MSS and rolls of arms ... the recognized best heraldic scholar in Wales. We find the scholar in his study hard at work, piecing together the records of old Wales. Instead of the tavern and the smell of the beer-can, we find only the pleasant odour of old vellum rolls mixed with the keener smell of the midnight oil.

After all, it is only fair to rescue the reputation of this scholar from the reproach — well, if not the reproach at least the buffoonery — of a silly clown. He probably did some foolish things when he was young. Well! haven't we all done the same? But few of us have found our good name put in the pillory for our youthful follies as this man has been. We need more light on our old Welsh worthies: this is only a feeble spark to light up the name and fame of Master Thomas Jones of Fountain Gate, mis-called Twm Shon Catti.[5]

Yet these scholars and critics, I argue, have misunderstood Prichard's purpose, which was to comment on the condition and cultural life of Wales in the early nineteenth century. For this purpose, it would not have been necessary for Prichard to retain the historical aspects of Thomas Jones; still, his story maintains much of both the history known in his time and the oral tradition. A close examination of the text reveals that Prichard used satire — and altered both the history and the oral tradition — to create in his readers a sense of Welsh nationalism. Therefore, to understand the way in which Prichard altered the story to his own ends, it is first necessary to understand the tradition from which he was writing.

The Development of the Legend

Historically, Thomas Jones was born in 1530 to Catherine in Tregaron.[6] A pedigree that he gave to Lewys Dwnn in 1588 states that his natural father was not Sir John Wynn of Gwydir, as has been believed and as Prichard asserted, but was John the son of David ap Madog ap Howel Moethau.[7] Joan, who is believed to be Jones' second wife, was the daughter of Sir John Price. The Rev. D. C. Rees explains that Joan was actually the "widow of Thomas Rhys Williams, Esq., of Ystrad-ffin, a large landowner, and High Sheriff of Cardigan, 1579 and 1596; Brecon, 1582; and Carmarthen, 1587 and 1592. From these dates, it would be seen that Thomas Jones must have been over 70 years of age, before he married Mrs. Williams."[8] Rees continues: "[T]he fact that he [Thomas Jones] married the widow of such a respectable man, was proof of the high esteem in which he was held."[9]

Traditionally, it was Jones' writing ability that earned him such respect.

When Prichard describes Twm singing poems of his own making at fairs, he was more correct than the history established by Prichard's time indicated. Jones was both a genealogist and a poet. When the Act of Union was passed by Henry VIII in 1536, Wales was compelled to adopt English laws, including the law of primogeniture, which made the skills of genealogists such as Thomas Jones essential. As Jones' skills and services grew, so did his fame in both genealogy and poetry. He was a prolific writer; the Tonn manuscript at the Cardiff City Library, a small tome, contains at least 171 folios that are in Jones own handwriting.[10] Referring to Jones' research abilities, Sion Dafydd Rhys wrote that a Herald Bard must be acquainted with the

> real descendants, armorial bearings, dignities, and illustrious actions of the nobility of gentry of Wales, the most celebrated, accomplished, and accurate (and that beyond doubt) [of the genealogists] is reckoned *Thomas Sion*, alias *Moethau*, of Porth y Ffynnon, near Trev Garon (Thomas Jones of Fountain Gate), and when he is gone, it will be very doubtful chance that there will be able for a long time to leave behind him an equal, nor indeed any Genealogist, (with regard to being so conversant as he in that science) that can even come near him.[11]

Sion Dafydd Rhys also wrote in his famous *Grammar* (1592) that Jones was "y godidocaf a phennaf a pherffeithiaf ... yng nghelfyddyd arwyddfarddoniaeth (the most excellent, most impressive and most perfect in the art of genealogical poetry)."[12]

Despite his fame as a genealogist, it is the first reference to Thomas Jones when he was among hundreds who obtained a pardon in the great amnesty extended by Elizabeth I in the first year of her reign on January 1, 1559, that has attracted such attention. Although the pardon lists Jones' given name and aliases, the nature of his offence is not known.[13] Some time after this pardon and Jones' marriage, Jones became a local magistrate in Brecon, where he stayed until he died at over ninety years of age.[14]

The questions that remain, then, are why these tales would have progressed and what purpose Prichard had when he modified them. It is not difficult to imagine the development of the story from this point. A local magistrate, a mysterious pardon, and Thomas Jones' eminent position afterward, all provided a seed for an oral history to grow.

Prichard and the Oral Tradition

In order to fill in the historical gaps for his own tale, Prichard draws his information from a variety of sources. Gerald Morgan writes that Prichard, in his second edition, gives some indication of his sources, which include

Theophilus Jones, a historian of Breconshire; Meyrick's *History of Cardiganshire*; and "Tomshone Catty's Tricks," a pamphlet printed by John Ross of Carmarthen in 1763. However, much of the story was based on oral tradition. Morgan states, "In his [Prichard's] preface he also alludes to a great quantity of traditional material gathered on his travels — travels which gave the book much of its value."[15] What Fletcher called into question in his tirade was the truth behind Prichard's book, but did Prichard intend for his story to be historically accurate? Both George Borrow and Meyrick, one of Prichard's direct sources, mention the myth behind the oral tradition of Thomas Jones. George Borrow expands upon this notion: "Concerning the actions attributed to him, it is necessary to say that the greater part consist of myths, which are told of particular individuals of every country, from the Indian Ocean to the Atlantic."[16]

Prichard himself plays on the myth behind his story in the first chapter, which consists of a quasi-historical summary of history of the Thomas Jones, who, according to Prichard, was born in 1570 and was the natural son of Sir John Wynn of Gwydir. Although Prichard cites previous plays and publications purporting to portray the life of Tom Jones, such as *The Inkeepers Album* and W.F. Deacon's "The Welsh Rob Roy," he condemns them by saying that they claim Twm as a national hero of Wales, thus "conveying the villainous inference that Wales was barren of real heroes."[17] Prichard implies the truth of his own tale by criticizing the historical inaccuracies of "Welsh Rob Roy," saying that: "This may do for London, but in Wales, where 'Gwir yn erbyn y byd' is our motto, we know better."[18] Although Prichard implies that his version will remain true to history, he reverses this inference at the end of the chapter. After briefly explaining Jones' known history, Prichard continues: "And now, having given our hero's birth and the parentage with the fidelity of a true historian, who has a most virtuous scorn of the spurious embellishments of fiction, a more excursive pen shall flourish on our future chapters."[19] From these remarks, it is clear that it was not Prichard's purpose to remain faithful to either the history or the oral tradition. Therefore, he must have had a different purpose in mind.

Prichard's Audience

Prichard's real purpose, which was to write a social commentary, becomes clear when we realize his intended audience. *The Oxford Companion to the Literature of Wales* says that *Twm Shon Catty* "was presumably intended to appeal to Welshmen, as Prichard is openly critical of the English Tourists and there is in it an element of blatant anti-English feeling."[20] However, there are several indications that Prichard was in fact writing to a different audience as well: the English themselves. The first and most obvious indication is Prichard's direct address to the English readers, which appears sporadically throughout the book.[21] Second, as Gerald Morgan has noted, is the anglicized spelling of Welsh names in the second edition and afterward; for example, Ystrad Ffin, which is spelled Ystrad Fîn in the first edition, becomes Ystrad Feen in the second.[22] Third, Prichard goes into elaborate detail in describing Welsh customs, such as relating traditional Welsh dress,[23] recounting bidding and marriage ceremonies,[24] and translating several popular ballads for Twm to sing at fairs.[25] These descriptions would not be necessary for a Welsh audience, and can therefore be assumed to be explanations for the English readers that Prichard addresses so frequently.

In addition to these, Prichard explains the writing of the novel in terms of English taste. Prichard's gifts of satire and understatement come through when he, in humble guise, ridicules English lack of interest in its principality and complains about England's treatment of Welsh history and literature. He criticizes the English:

> Although neither the legends, the poetry, nor the history of the principality, seem to interest, or accord with the taste of our English brethren, the name of Twm Shon Catty, curiously enough, not only made its way among them, but had the unexpected honour of being woven into a tale, and exhibited on the stage, as a Welsh national dramatic spectacle, under the title, and the imposing second title, of Twm John Catty, or, the Welsh Rob Roy.[26]

Prichard has been referred to as "a clever defender of Welsh customs and nationality by manoeuvering his readers into hostility towards certain characters before revealing their anti–Welsh feelings."[27] It is only logical that the readers whom Prichard would be maneuvering would be the English, the very group of people who he sees in his own time as destroying the Welsh.

Prichard's time, like so many other times in the history of Wales and its people, was tumultuous. Since 1793, land enclosures were granting property to the already wealthy and driving increasing numbers of farmers to the cities. The establishment of the Calvinist Methodist Denomination in 1811 was a mixed blessing. Although the Methodists taught reading and writing to the public through their Sunday Schools, secular literature and music suffered. The advent of peace after the long wars with Napoleon obliterated the Welsh iron industry, brought along depression, and soon after rioting. The riots continued until the Merthyr Rising in 1831, which was only three short years after the first publication of *Twm Shon Catty*. The rising called for rebellion against and freedom from England. During this time, the problems in Wales were virtually ignored in England; Wales, although affiliated to England, remained separate from its prosperity. The riots were hardly mentioned in English newspapers.

When school reform came to England, its effects did not reach Wales until the late 1850s.[28] The English were absentee landlords, taking into consideration neither their lands nor their tenants except to raise rents. This was the world that Prichard was born into, and the world he was writing against.

The Welsh Robin Hood

What Prichard did was to modify both the history and also the oral tradition through the characterization and satire of Thomas Jones in order urge his readers, including his English readers, into a sense of Welsh nationality. In the eighteenth and nineteenth centuries, after the American and French revolutions, the Robin Hood legends became a popular means of commentary on liberty and social justice in England. Joseph Ritson wrote that Robin Hood was "a man who, in a barbarous age, and under a complicated tyranny, displayed a spirit of freedom and independence, which has endeared him to the common people, whose cause he maintained."[29] Around the time of Prichard's publication, there appeared in England several works which reinterpreted Robin Hood for the modern age: John Keats's poem "Robin Hood: To a Friend," Thomas Love Peacock's *Maid Marian* and Sir Walter Scott's *Ivanhoe* are just a few.[30] What these works and Ritson's collection did was to create a national history through England's legends. As Stephen Knight explains, "At such a time, when overt political dissent was highly dangerous, a story from the past like that of Robin Hood was a suitable medium to convey feelings of a more or less critical character."[31] Stephane Barczewski, writing of the importance of the Robin Hood legends in the 19th century, continues,

> By pointing to ancestral heroes from whom the nation's present inhabitants are purportedly descended, it suggested a degree of continuity between generations. By reminding the members of a community of its first greatness, it instills them with a sense of inner worth and collective dignity. And finally, by displaying the past as a mirror of the future, it points the community toward a glorious destiny. An invented history is therefore crucial to the development of nationalism."[32]

In the same vein as his English counterparts, Prichard takes a historic figure and transforms both him and his story into a vehicle for social protest and nationalism. Prichard restyles Twm Shon Catty, the only Welsh character to whom the English would listen, not as The Welsh Rob Roy or freedom fighter, but as the Welsh Robin Hood. Prichard does this in order to accord with the libertarian sympathies of the English. Like for the authors of the Robin Hood stories of the eighteenth and nineteenth centuries, liberty and social justice did not mean for Prichard independence or disloyalty to the crown, but it did mean equality and respect for the Welsh customs. Welsh culture, through the venue of Twm Shon Catty, becomes something authentic because of the long history of the Welsh customs.

Prichard's goal for Twm's character is paradoxical. In order to induce English readers to pay heed to the Welsh plight and therefore to incite sympathy, Prichard must create an outlaw that would parallel England's Robin Hood; moreover, Prichard's literary creation would have to be more worthy of respect than Robin Hood was. At the same time, in order to justify Wales, he must make sure that his character is not assumed to be a real national hero, since he would then, as "The Welsh Rob Roy" did, imply that Wales was devoid of authentic heroes.

In order to accomplish this, Prichard at first de-emphasizes Twm's importance as a national character. Prichard's Twm was simply a thief. By making Twm a thief, Prichard is perhaps criticizing England's valorization of Robin Hood, another thief. Once Twm's antics are condemned, the reader is ready for the deconstruction of the other characters in the book, who are oftentimes either English or individuals who maintain a considerable amount of power. Twm can, despite his relative unimportance to Welsh history, reemerge as a moral character to be positioned against the amoral Robin Hood. It is only then that through Prichard's satire of Twm and other characters that a sense of Welsh nationalism can emerge.

Burgeoning of a Hero

At first, Prichard ironically speaks of Twm as a hero. In chapter one, he explicitly states that Twm does not belong in the ranks of Welsh national heroes, yet Twm is called a hero nonetheless.[33] The exaggeration, and therefore depreciation, of Twm's heroic nature is exemplified in the first two chapters of Prichard's book. Prichard compares Twm to Homer[34] and explains that like eminent men such as Pope, Sir Joseph Banks, and Sir Isaac Newton, who all "exemplified the motto that 'Coming events cast their shadows before them' ... it will not appear strange to those already acquainted with his fame, that we have to add to these eminent names that of our long neglected hero."[35] Prichard sets Twm up to be a man of great worth only to retract the statement in the next line: "It is true he became neither a poet, a painter, nor a natural historian, but, according to the unbiased opinions of geniuses of the same caste with himself, who could not be suspected of either egotism or partiality, a superior character of either — an eminent antiquary — to which may be added, though perhaps it ought to take the lead — a no less eminent thief."[36] The reduction of Twm continues into Prichard's descriptions of Twm's early years. Prichard makes use of an oral tradition of the stories of Twm, which says that Twm had a normal childhood "but always showed a disposition to roguery and mischief" in order to deflate his hero.[37] Like the geniuses named previously, Twm shows his natural ability at an early age by his "intense affection for street rubbish," the "close affection he had for mother earth," and by his early abilities of thievery that "showed his filial piety, in saving his mother the expense of his victuals."[38] Twm is set up as a buffoon in order to contrast him with the real heroes, whom Twm meets in the book; men who during the seventeenth century kept the Welsh language and the politics of nationalism alive. For example, Sion Dafydd Rhys, who was Twm's teacher, wrote a grammar of Welsh.[39] Both Rhys Prichard, whom Twm meets while traveling, and Sir John Wynn, Twm's natural father, were both historically patrons of literature and authors. Therefore, Prichard uses the historical heroes to contrast with his fictional one. The effect is to create a sense of true national pride, one that is based upon tradition rather than on fiction. Despite this opening, Twm was not to remain the object of Prichard's satire throughout the book. After the first two chapters where Twm is de-emphasized, Prichard's satire switches to other, historically more sinister, characters.

Catty and the Welsh Educational System

Although the prominent Welsh characters of the story are treated sardonically, the satire is more jovial, and the aim of the satirical lash is not the characters themselves but instead the English. For example, after Sir John gives Catty's farm to Joan, her new position gains her enough respect that she is able to open a school for the neighborhood children who pay the modest expense of a penny a week for her services. This section of the tale is based on both oral tradition and history. George Borrow writes of the oral tradition: "His mother, who was a person of some little education, brought him up, and taught him to read and write."[40] Catty's school is also based on historical schools. In 1731, Welsh circuit schools were established which continued until 1854. These schools served as a rival for the English system, which was far too expensive for the lower classes to afford. The circuit schools were taught in Welsh; however, were too few to make any noticeable difference in the education of the lower classes. Schools such as Catty's supplemented these. Poor students could pay a pence a week for an education at a "private adventure" school. As Sir Reginald Coupland describes, these schools were "wretchedly inadequate — a small bare room, no proper equipment, few books, and, worst of all, a teacher who, often as not, was only half-educated himself."[41] Similar to the students at the "private adventure" schools, Catty's students benefit more from their fellow classmates' education than her own. However, Prichard defends her:

> [B]e it recollected that tastes differ, and that many wealthy plebeians, who are considered the great, the mighty, and the respectable of the land, deprecate with becoming vehemence the prevailing mania for educating the poor. We have heard ladies, and great ones too, attired in silks and velvets, pall and purple, and "faring sumptuously every day," declare the most positively that they never knew a servant good for anything that could read and write. No sooner are they capable of wielding a goose quill, than the impudent hussies presumed to have a will of their own, and their opinions mounted a step nearer to the altitude of their mistresses. And on men, they said, education had a worse effect, as thereby they became the idle readers of books and newspapers, which made them saucy to their superiors, and sometimes the most villainous cut-throat radicals.[42]

Prichard here makes use of an unreliable narrator whose focus is too narrow for the logical reader to agree. What is important here is that the reader keeps separate the various manifestations of author and narrator in the satire in order to understand the satire's object. The author, Prichard, must not be confused with the narrator or narrating agent, whose point of view and tone shifts depending on the focalizer (the person's whose eyes we are looking through) and the focalized (the object being depicted). Prichard's narrator will both narrate history (in which he combines the narrating agent and the focalizer in order to portray events), and he will separate the two in order to create a more dialogic narration. Rather than create an objective view in another section of the story, Prichard's form of satire, which depends on exaggeration and the narrow point of view of the narrating agent at the time, relies at times on the reader to take on the role of the historian. It is the reader's charge and challenge, therefore, to be see through the satire and find its true object, the English.

Although Catty's school is described through the eyes of an unreliable narrator, the satire is not against Catty herself. Instead, it is aimed against the ladies who are attired in silks and who believe that the poor masses should remain subjugated. The satire comes through in single, ambiguous words: the "prevailing *mania*," and "*presumed* to have a will of their own." These words are the same that the ladies themselves would have used. The narrating agent combines with the focalizer so that the logical reader sees the discrepancy of standards between the rich, who are educated, and the poor. The irony here is that Prichard himself would have been one of these educated radicals who would have presumed to tell his social superiors that their policy was wrong. Catty's school, then, is representative of the educational system in Wales, which allowed for unqualified individuals to teach the lower classes, the very class that the anglicized nobles and English did not care to instruct.

Squire Graspacre and the English Landlords

But England's role in the Welsh education system was not the only scheme to be ridiculed in the novel. After the Act of Union, the Welsh nobles continued their reign over Wales. Gwynfor Evans elucidates: "It was these who betrayed the nation. In contrast with the Irish aristocracy who were in exile or were decimated by death in battle for Ireland, the Welsh aristocracy faded into rootless, anglicized landlords in whom, strive as one may, one can discern little that is admirable."[43] Yet although there were English and anglicized landowners in Wales for centuries, Gerald Morgan is correct when he describes Squire Graspacre, Twm's landlord, as "obviously an eighteenth or early nineteenth century figure, typical of the enclosing landlords of Prichard's own time."[44] Therefore, Graspacre is not meant to be historically accurate, for his only role that of a social commentary on Prichard's time.

The first time we are introduced to the character of Squire Graspacre, he is in the process of taking over Welsh lands. In the description of Squire Graspacre, Prichard uses satire to reach his English audience. He again makes use of an unreliable narrator who takes on some of the characteristics of Graspacre himself, providing a discourse between Graspacre's thoughts and justifications and the historical narration. With the focalizer of the satire as Graspacre, the satire again comes through the description in single, ambiguous words. For example, Twm's grandfather's farm was "provokingly" located in the middle of the Squire's land. And the squire, an Englishman, takes up the "laudable" cause of "civilizing" the Welsh.[45] The narrator continues:

> The most feasible mode of accomplishing so grand an undertaking, that appeared to him, was, to dispossess them of their property, and to take as much as possible of their country into his own paternal care. The rude Welsh, to be sure, he found so blind to their own interests as to prefer living on their farms to either selling or giving them away, to profit by his superior management.[46]

The narrating agent's reasoning and language is that which the squire himself would have used, yet the tone remains distant, indicating that the squire's reasoning is unreasonable. The overall impression is that, despite the narrator's misdirection, Prichard believes that the Welsh people were already civilized, in fact more civilized than their English subjugators, who, more often than not, destroyed the cultures of those they ruled.

Indeed, Graspacre is later described as uncivilized. However, the argument can be made that Squire Graspacre is not an unlikable character. He argues against his wife in favor of courting in bed and for the maids keeping their Welsh dress,[47] he attends Catty and Carmarthen Jack's wedding in disguise,[48] and he employs Twm in his own household after Twm's almost fatal dealings with Morris Greeg (in other versions "Grug," meaning "heather"), the farmer to whom he was an apprentice.[49] However, Graspacre's negative aspects by far outweigh his positive ones. For instance, after the death of his wife, the narrator says that Graspacre was forever "Wench-hunting."[50] Gerald Morgan sees the influence of Henry Fielding in the characterization of Graspacre here, writing that "the first important character we meet, Squire Graspacre, obviously derives in part from Squire Western, being for much of the time an amiable bully with a taste for country wenches."[51]

However, his tenants do not later see Graspacre as amiable. When Graspacre sets his eyes on Gwenny Cadwgan, the new love of Twm, her father sees no choice but to hand her over to the squire: "[F]or what small farmer would dare deny his landlord such a favor, though his heart might tremble with apprehensions?"[52] Gwenny's rescue is left to Twm, for when Squire Graspacre tells him to bring the farmer's lass, Twm brings instead Cadwgan's ass, tied to the saddle of a horse. The bedroom scene that follows is filled with some fantastic carnivalesque moments. The ass is tied to the Squire's bed so that when Graspacre enters in the dark and tries to kiss the young Gwenny, he is met with a loud bray and a hoof to the forehead. Thinking that he has been tricked by the devil himself for his lust, Graspacre falls to the ground, and Twm escapes into the night. But his tenants do not forgive the squire, and the impression is that the reader should not forget his misdeeds either. Not only are we reminded that Graspacre helped Sir John Wynn bestow his "delicate attention"[53] on Catty at the beginning of the book, but we are reminded several times of the reaction of his tenants, and that "The respect in which he was formerly held by the country people gradually declined."[54] Therefore, not only is Graspacre represented as a typical enclosing landlord, as his name makes clear, but the fairness of his absolute power over his tenants is also questioned. It is evident from his commentary that Prichard is criticizing the moral and judicial rights of the English landlords in Wales in his own time.

Twm Shon Catty as the Good Outlaw

Once Graspacre is deconstructed as a good judge of character, he is no longer seen as qualified to judge right from wrong. Therefore, when Graspacre later outlaws Twm, his judgment is in question, and the reader, even the English reader, is forced into the position of scoffing at the English landlord and cheering for the Welsh peasant, Twm.

In the oral tradition of Twm, it is unknown what Twm's first crime was, only that he became a thief between the ages of eighteen and nineteen in order to rid himself of poverty.[55] However, we do know that Twm was guilty of several crimes. Prichard, however, softens Twm's misdeeds. In the book, the crime for which Twm is outlawed is not serious, if it can be called a crime at all. Technically, Twm is outlawed for assaulting Squire Graspacre's son, Marmaduke. Yet when Marmaduke relates the event to his father, he exaggerates: "such as the trifling mis-statement that the blows inflicted on him were by the butt-end of the [gun] piece, instead of the fist."[56] The narrator points out that it was the exaggeration of the deed and not the deed itself that caused the authorities to go after Twm. The reader's response, that Twm has been accused unjustly, is supplemented by the fact that although Prichard says that Twm is wanted, he is careful not to refer to him as an "outlaw." Prichard applies historical narration to say that a "hue and cry instantly was raised and spread abroad,"[57] he but finishes the sentence with a discursive comment of satirical narration, saying that the cry "excited as great a commotion throughout the country as if a convicted murderer were chased through the land."[58] Because this reaction is exaggerated, much as Marmaduke inflated Twm's actions, and because this reaction is contrasted with the actual deed, the reader's response (as well as the response of those who knew Twm) is sympathetic.

When Inco Evans searches the county for Twm, the events and reactions are again exaggerated. Now, Prichard plays upon the phrase "as if a convicted murderer." Evans then must play the role of the dutiful protector of the people, a role that the Welsh feel is neither necessary nor desired. When the people of the county hear of Parson Evans' search for Twm, they bemoan Twm's misfortunes. Evans reveals his ignorance and self-importance by mistaking, whether intentionally or accidentally, the people's laments for their own fear. Prichard writes that he "*took care* to *assure* them, that when caught, all the world could not save him from the gallows, as he had *attempted to murder* the young squire of Graspacre–Hall."[59] As such, not only is the reaction to Twm's crime exaggerated, but also the crime of assault itself is embellished again and again: from a simple fistfight, to attack with the butt of a gun, to attempted murder. The need for Twm's enemies to aggrandize his crimes diminishes Twm's actual deed and in turn elicits the sympathy of the reader, even the English reader.

Despite Prichard's comments in the first two chapters that imply that Twm is not a hero, the sympathy of the reader from this point on remains with Twm. Although Twm is depicted as being mischievous in his youth, in later years he is shown to be a just and moral person. For example, when Twm later returns to Tregaron and faces Inco Evans, Prichard takes another oral tradition and softens it. In Prichard, Twm poses as Evan's man and takes money from Evans' wife. Oral tradition says that as a local man was coming to apprehend Twm, the outlaw dressed as an old woman, directed him into his home. George Borrow continues:

No sooner was he inside than the beggar, or rather Tom Shone Catti, for it was he, jumped on the horse's back, and rode away to the farmer's house which was some ten miles distant, altering his dress and appearance as he rode along, having various articles of disguise in his wallet. Arriving at the house he told the farmer's wife that her husband was in the greatest trouble, and wanted fifty pounds, which she was to send by him, and that he came mounted on her husband's horse, and brought his whip, that she might know he was authorized to receive the money. The wife, seeing the horse and the whip, delivered the money to Tom without hesitation, who forthwith made the best of his way to London, where he sold the horse, and made himself merry with the price, and with what he got from the farmer's wife, not returning to Wales for several months."[60]

This scene parallels the one in chapter nineteen in the novel in which Twm tricks Inco Evans at the house of Watt. Yet Prichard changes the story so that Twm maintains his moral character. Once Twm has escaped the parson, he feels a pang of conscience. Prichard writes: "On the impulse of the moment, he determined to leave the parson's nag behind him, and then return his cash and coat as early as possible."[61]

After Twm is outlawed, it is not long before, through his heroism, he returns to honest society in a different county. Unlike his enemies, Twm is actually an honest and just man, for he was trusted enough to carry payment from Sir George Devereux to London. During this trip, Twm is contrasted with true villainy through the character of Watt. When Twm encounters him, Watt tells how he is pursued for theft and murder. Prichard writes: "Twm was but a poor comforter; for his strict ideas of justice and retribution made him look upon Watt's terrible agony as part of the punishment which he was called upon to pay for the awful crime of murder."[62] Throughout this scene, satire is conspicuously absent. The seriousness of Watt's crimes does not allow the author's usual bantering tone. Although it may seem, out of context, that Twm's "strict ideas of justice" would be satirical, the narration remains historical, not discursive, and the tone that surrounds the scene, as well as Twm's just and honorable actions elsewhere in the story, dictates the direct reading of Twm's reaction.

It is strange, then, that Twm is later described, albeit briefly, in a negative manner. When Lady Devereux spurns him, Twm turns to childish tricks and thievery. Yet compared to the enduring and dire misdeeds of his enemies and Watt, even Twm's darker moments appear trifling. The narrator assures us that these ostensibly random acts are not his typical ways. After Twm steals Inco Evans' gray horse, the narrator continues: "This last transaction sat uneasily on Twm's conscience."[63] The narrator is also careful to assure the reader that Twm's deeds were unselfish: "Our hero never used the money acquired by his art for his own requirements, and we must not forget to say here that the cash our hero received for the parson's horse, was cast into the parish poorbox."⁶⁴ Therefore, Twm, like the English Robin Hood, commits unselfish acts. But Twm is also contrasted with Robin Hood, who, unlike his Welsh counterpart, does not always feel the pang of guilt that is a result of from his thievery.

By the time of the Llandovery Fair, the narrator no longer approves of Twm, yet he is still not spoken of through satire. Although it is direct narration, the tone of this section is undeniably disparaging. Twm, who denies his conscience for the sake of fun, acts in a dissolute and impulsive manner. Here is the first instance that Twm is referred to as "the desperate outlaw."⁶⁵ Here also the narrator takes on a paternal tone, indicating Twm's recklessness and need for guidance. When Twm is about to enter the hall and confront his enemies, the narrator, for the first and only time, addresses Twm directly: "Softly, Twm, softly, my boy!"⁶⁶ Twm listens to the narrator's advice; this elicits a change in his overall disposition, and is initiates of the return of his former self. Instead of hastening into the hall, Twm disguises himself. It is then, when his wit is exhibited, that his life begins to return to its previous order. By the next chapter, Justice Powell, who had pursued him, now invites Twm to a ball and gives him the very gray horse that Twm had previously stolen. All is not only forgiven, but Twm's transgressions are scarcely mentioned. This quick turnabout in events comes from the oral tradition. George Borrow writes that Twm, while an outlaw, maintained the goodwill of his countrymen: "The poor he conciliated by being very free of the money which he acquired by theft and robbery, and with the rich he ingratiated himself by humorous jesting, at which he was proficient, and by being able to sing a good song."⁶⁷ The lack of a grand pardon from the king or any official gives the impression that Twm, unlike the English Robin Hood, did not behave as corruptly as it would at first seem. Twm therefore maintains his moral character, despite the occurrences at Llandovery Fair.

That Twm never finds fault in himself has not affected all readers in the same way. George Borrow opposes Prichard's book and how he characterized Twm in a footnote:

> Its grand fault is endeavoring to invest Twm Shone with a character of honesty, and to make his exploits appear rather those of a wild young waggish fellow than of a robber. This is committing a great mistake. When people take up the lives of bad characters the more rogueries and villainies they find, the better are they pleased, and they are very much disappointed and consider themselves defrauded by any attempt to apologize for the actions of heroes. If the thieves should chance to have reformed, the respectable readers wish to hear nothing of their reformation till just at the close of the book, when they are very happy to have done with them forever.⁶⁸

It is ironic, then, that Prichard's interpretation of Twm Shon Catty is probably in truth closer to the historical Thomas Jones, whom Fletcher defended so vehemently, than the Twm of the oral tradition. Yet once we understand Prichard's characterization and use of satire, it becomes clear that he, far from merely keeping a Welsh tradition alive, used it to criticize the condition of Wales and its relations to the English in the nineteenth century. Jan Morris summarizes the Welsh resistance: "But really perhaps, prince and people alike, they were all fighting for something not so easy to articulate — a return to that half-imaginary Golden Age, that lost age of dignity, which survived deep within the Welsh consciousness ... yearning sometimes for a more magnificent past, sometimes for a future more rewarding. It is the nature of the people: very likely the genius too."[69] What Prichard's genius was, then, was to take an old story of an outlaw and restyle it after Robin Hood, the character most likely to inspire his English readers. Through his satire and characterization, Prichard was able to manipulate his readers to see both the longevity of Wales and its subsequent decline in the hands of its English managers. The result is a novel of social protest, intended to inspire its readers, even its English readers, toward a sense of Welsh nationalism.

Notes

1. A second, expanded edition appeared in 1839, followed by a third edition published posthumously at Llanidloes, and a Welsh translation by John Evans "Eilonydd" was printed at Llanidloes in the following year. Several pirated editions appeared later, including one from Western Mail. See Gerald Morgan, "The First Anglo-Welsh Novel," *The Anglo-Welsh Review* 17, no. 39 (1968): 114–22 at 115; and Meic Stephens, comp. and ed., *The New Companion to the Literature of Wales* (Cardiff: University of Wales Press, 1998), s.v. "*Twm Shon Catti*" for more details. All quotations and references are extracted from one such pirated edition published some time after Prichard's death: Thomas Jeffrey Llewelyn Prichard, *The Comical Adventures of Twm Shon Catty, (Thomas Jones, Esq.) Commonly Known as the Welsh Robin Hood* (Wakefield: William Nicholson and Sons, 1886).

2. Adrian Price, "Welsh Bandits," in Phillips 2008, 58–72 at 67.

3. For a more complete summary of *Twm Shon Catty* as well as a discussion of Prichard's style, see Morgan, "First Anglo-Welsh Novel," 114–122.

4. Stephens, *New Companion*, s.v. "*Twm Shon Catti*."

5. J. Kyrle Fletcher, "*Western Mail*, August 22, 1921," in *Tregaron: Historical and Antiquarian*, ed. D. C. Rees (Llandyssul: J. D. Lewis & Sons, Gomerian Press, 1936), 104–5. Fletcher is mistaken here on only one point: historically, Thomas Jones was referred to as Catty in a pardon quoted later in this article.

6. Stephens, *New Companion*, s.v. "Jones, or Johns, Thomas or Thomas Siôn Dafydd Madoc (Twm Siôn Cati, c. 1530–1609)." For clarity's sake from this point forward in the essay, Jones will be called "Thomas Jones" when I refer to the historical person and "Twm Shon Catty" when I refer to the character of either legendary tradition or Prichard's book.

7. Rees, *Tregaron*, 99.

8. Ibid.. 100.

9. Ibid., 100.

10. Ibid., 102.
11. Robert Williams, *Enwogion Cymru: A Biographical Dictionary of Eminent Welshmen* (Llandovery: William Rees, 1852), s.v. "Jones, Thomas."
12. Stephens, *New Companion*, s.v. "Jones, or Johns, Thomas or Thomas Siôn Dafydd Madoc (Twm Siôn Cati, c. 1530–1609)."
13. Rees, *Tregaron*, 105.
14. Ibid., 105.
15. Morgan, "First Anglo-Welsh Novel," 115. Morgan cites the reference to the pamphlet in Prichard's Preface but does not name it.
16. George Henry Borrow, *Wild Wales*, vol. 13 of *Works of George Borrow*, ed. Clement King Shorter (New York: AMS Press, 1967), 315.
17. Prichard, *Twm*, 9. The phrase "Gwir yn erbyn y byd" is translated by the original editor as "Truth against the world."
18. Ibid., 9.
19. Ibid., 11.
20. Stephens, *New Companion*, s.v. "*Twm Shon Catti.*"
21. A few examples of which are: "The English reader will not be offended..." and "To our English readers it may be a piece of information...," Prichard, *Twm*, 28 and 32.
22. Morgan, "First Anglo-Welsh Novel," 121.
23. Prichard, *Twm*, 46–48.
24. Ibid., 53–65.
25. Ibid., 152–56.
26. Ibid., 8.
27. Morgan, "First Anglo-Welsh Novel," 122.
28. For the purposes of this paper, these references are necessarily brief. For a more detailed discussion of the various risings and for the conditions of education in Wales see Gwynfor Evans, *Wales: A History* (New York: Barnes and Noble Books, 1996), and Reginald Coupland *Welsh and Scottish Nationalism; a Study* (London: Collins, 1954).
29. Joseph Ritson, *Robin Hood: A Collection of all the Ancient Poems, Songs and Ballads, Now Extant, Relative to that Celebrated English Outlaw* (London: John C. Nimmo, 1885), ix.
30. Stephanie L. Barczewski, *Myth and National Identity in Nineteenth-Century Britain: The Legends of King Arthur and Robin Hood* (New York: Oxford University Press, 2000), 44. See also John Barnard, "Keats's 'Robin Hood,' John Hamilton Reynolds, and the 'Old Poets,'" and Marilyn Butler, "The Good Old Times: *Maid Marian*, in Knight 1999, 123–140 and 141–153, respectively; Knight 1994, 158–92; and Helen Phillips, "Scott and the Outlaws," in Phillips 2008, 119–42.
31. Knight 1994, 154.
32. Barczewski, *Myth and National Identity*, 46.
33. Prichard, *Twm*, 9.
34. Ibid., 10.
35. Ibid., 13.
36. Ibid., 14.
37. Borrow, *Wild Wales*, 312.
38. Prichard, *Twm*, 14.
39. Evans, *Wales: A History*, 304.
40. Ibid., 312.
41. Coupland, *Welsh and Scottish Nationalism*, 187–188.
42. Prichard, *Twm*, 18–19.
43. Evans, *Wales: A History*, 304.
44. Morgan, "First Anglo-Welsh Novel," 116.
45. Prichard, *Twm*, 11.
46. Ibid., 11.
47. Ibid., 43–52.
48. Ibid., 64–65.

49. Ibid., 113.
50. Ibid., 114.
51. Morgan, "First Anglo-Welsh Novel," 116.
52. Prichard, *Twm*, 116.
53. Ibid., 116.
54. Ibid., 123.
55. Borrow, *Wild Wales*, 312.
56. Prichard, *Twm*, 135.
57. Ibid., 135.
58. Ibid., 135–36.
59. Ibid., 136, italics mine.
60. Borrow, *Wild Wales*, 313–14.
61. Prichard, *Twm*, 147.
62. Ibid., 223.
63. Ibid., 268.
64. Ibid., 271.
65. Ibid., 286.
66. Ibid., 286.
67. Borrow, *Wild Wales*, 314.
68. Ibid., 311.
69. Jan Morris, *The Matter of Wales: Epic Views of a Small Country* (New York: Oxford University Press, 1984), 385.

Part III

The Robin Hood Tradition

7

Robin Hood: Outlaw or Exile?

ANTHA COTTEN-SPRECKELMEYER

In recent years, historians and literary scholars have searched for a factual basis of Robin Hood as he appears in medieval English literature. But, historical sources yield few satisfactory insights to persons, places, events or ideas associated with the literary figure. In her essay "Ballads and Bandits," Barbara Hanawalt concludes: "Perhaps it would be better if a historical Robin Hood were never found. As Bruce Rosenberg concluded from his research on Custer and the epic of defeat, the true historical character at the base of the myth is inevitably disappointing."[1] It is, in fact, more productive to explore the literary ancestry for definitive clues to the genesis of Robin Hood's character as it appears in the poems and ballads of the later Middle Ages (1400–1600). Maurice Keen, in his volume *Outlaws of Medieval Legend,* initiates genealogical discussion of literary robbers, bandits, and rebels, and he notes that Robin Hood manifests lineal descent from the heroes of Anglo-Saxon England who were cast as exile figures in early sagas and romances.[2] Going a step further, it is possible to speculate that the Robin Hood of fifteenth and sixteenth-century works propagates the lineage of Old English exile characters of eighth and ninth-century Anglo-Saxon poetry in ways not previously examined. Robin Hood of this vintage evinces a spiritual and emotional isolation that is evocative of the Old English Wanderer, Seafarer and even of *Beowulf's* Grendel, who are all deprived of the material support and spiritual sustenance of their "dryhten" [lord] and "dryhtsele" [noble hall].

While there is often conflation of the terms "exile" and "outlaw" in literary and historical treatments of medieval texts and subjects, the two words do not signify identical status or experience in either legal or literary parlance from the eighth through the sixteenth centuries. Context-specific meanings and wider implications of the two concepts evolve and differentiate over time. Keen says that "Outlawry meant the putting of an individual outside the protection of the law of the land; and by that sentence the outlaw ... became an outcast from society."[3] Julius Goebel examined early applications of outlaw terminology in his volume *Felony and Misdemeanor: A Study in The History of English Criminal Procedure*, and posited that the Anglo-Saxon "utlah" [outlaw] conveys the distinction of being "out of the peace or out of the law." Goebel notes that post-conquest readers and writers in England understood outlawry as a description of flight from wrong doing rather than designation of specific criminal acts.[4] Timothy Jones writes about the pronouncement of outlawry in relation to the exploits of Earl Godwin suggesting that outlawry was "an expedient for a legal system lacking a centralized police force and facilities for imprisonment."[5] Timothy Lundrgren, writing on *Hereward The Wake*, notes that outlawry evolved over the centuries preceding and following the Norman Conquest in England from the domain of kinship groups to a prerogative exercised by the king over recalcitrant criminals. By the end of the eleventh century, being an outlaw carried with it the forfeiture of property and inheritance rights as well as loss of legal standing and protection. Outlaws could not be harbored by anyone; they could be killed outright without reprisal or payment of the common payment of the man price, the "wergeld." Moreover, outlaws were often excommunicated from the church as well as from the secular community.[6]

Medieval outlawry amounts to the loss of status and subsequent flight from familiar surroundings. As such, it parallels Old English portrayals of heroic exile on a descriptive level, a fact corroborated by Goebel, who traces outlawry as an institution to the Roman imposition of "exile," which entered England through the Germanic traditions of the Anglo-Saxons.[7] Gillian Spraggs brings the Roman outlaw, Felix Bulla, to light in this context. Bulla was active during the reign of Septimius Severus (r. 193–211 CE). Spraggs notes close parallels between the descriptions of Bulla rendered by Cassius Dio and the early accounts of Robin Hood. While Spraggs contends that there is no evidence of direct transmission of tales, the evidence points to a continuity of interest and a tendency to ennoble outcast figures from the earliest venues of western storytelling.[8] Thus, it is not surprising to find a large-scale conflation of outlawry with the literary exile convention. Lundgren suggests that such conflation occurred early in the tradition, and he observes that "the 'wineleas wrecca' [friendless exile] of the Old English elegies may have been indistinguishable in the popular imagination from the 'freondleas flyman'" [friendless outlaw] given the semantic complexity of outlawry at the time.[9] Roberta Kevelson alludes to this type of semantic fusion during the Middle Ages in her study of the language of relationships in *Inlaws/Outlaws*, and she notes that need for common frames of reference resulted in inventing equivalences between immediate appearances and past realities.[10] Kevelson concludes that "metaphorically, Robin Hood is equivalent not only with the concept of outlawry, but also with alienation, rebellion, and, in general, the appearance of something outside the predictable order of known reality."[11] For the medieval audience, the outsider equivalent points to the exile tradition of earlier English literature and makes contemporary merging of the terms "exile" and "outlaw" seem logical, when, in fact, they represent contingent, but distinct types and levels of alienation. In the accounts noted above, outlawry describes the physical reality of severance from society, while exile suggests the subtle interior side of that disconnection vested in emotional distress over being cut off.

Robin Hood of the early poems and ballads clearly fills the outlaw role as countless interpreters demonstrate, but his character also mirrors the image of the Old English exile as delineated by Stanley Greenfield in his landmark essay on the exile theme.[12] Among other points, Greenfield describes isolation or alien status and a sense of deprivation as significant markers of exile identification in Old English poetry. According to Greenfield's formulaic approach, alienation is defined by words like "mod cearig" [mind worn] and "werig" [discouraged], which convey subjective sides of the character's experience of exile.[13] Likewise, Greenfield says that the exile's sense of deprivation may extend beyond loss of material property to include disconnection from transcendent qualities denoted by phrases such as "dréame bedǽled" [joy deprived] and "duguðum bedǽled" [benefits deprived].[14] The Old English poems *The Wanderer*, *The Seafarer*, and *Beowulf* provide examples of this theory and offer a basis for identifying similar expressions of emotional alienation and loss in the Robin Hood poems.

The alien status of the Seafarer is announced early in the poem when the narrator calls himself lonely and friendless, and he complains about his lack of a patron:

> feasceaftig ferð nænig hleomæga
> frefran meahte.
> [No protector had I there who might have soothed my desolate spirit.][15]

Likewise, The figure of the Wanderer dubs himself "anhaga" [alone] and lordless, and he describes a plight similar to that of the Seafarer:

> Forþon wāt sē þe sceal wyn eal gedrēas.
> lēofes lārcwidum his winedryhtnes
> longe forþolian...
> [Now all joy has gone. He understands who long must do without the kind advice of his beloved lord].[16]

Robin Hood is similarly cast in the language of solitude typified in *A Gest of Robyn Hode* by his refrain that "no man abyde with me."[17] Robin is portrayed as one who hides, especially when he hunts:

> But alwey went good Robyn
> By halke and eke by hyll,   *hiding place*
> And alway slewe the kynges dere,
> And welt them at his wyll.¹⁸   *used*

Moreover, when he is alone and away from his band of men, he experiences "sorowe" and "mornyng." The first example is from the *Gest*, when Robin is in the service of the king:

> "Alas!" then sayd good Robyn,
> "Alas and well a woo!
> Yf I dwele lenger with the kynge,
> Sorowe wyll me sloo."¹⁹   *slay*

The second example is from *Robin Hood and the Monk*. Robin and Little John had an argument over a shooting contest; in a huff, Robin leaves his men:

> Then Robyn goes to Notyngham,
> Hym selfe mornyng allone,   *grieving*
> And Litull John to mery Scherwode,
> The pathes he knew ilkone.²⁰   *everyone*

Even more to the point is the corollary of Grendel from *Beowulf* where the "mǣre mearcstapa" [infamous marsh dweller] is a "wonsǣlī wer" [dark creature] who has been driven far from mankind for his crimes: "hē hine feor forwræc, / Metod for þȳ māne mancynne fram" [God drove him far from mankind for his evils deeds].²¹ Moreover, he is also described as an "atol āngengea" [dreaded loner].²² Like the Wanderer and the Seafarer, Grendel is a lordless creature who subsists on the fringe of society as a true outlaw. His concomitant exile status hinges on the fact, that although he stalks the treasure trove of Heorot and hears the music of the lyre, he cannot participate in the joys of the mead hall or receive gifts from lord Hrothgar:

> sincfāge sel   Heorot eardode,
> nō hē þone gifstōl   sweartum nihtum;–
> māþðum for Metode... grētan mōste,

[He dwelt in Heorot, the treasure-laden hall, in the dark nights; but he might not approach the gift-throne for fear of God...]²³

The fact that Grendel experiences distress at this life as he exists apart from others is clear from the early lines of the epic:

> Ðā se ellengǣst   earfoðlīce
> þrāge geþolode,   sē þe in þȳstrum bād...

[Then the mighty spirit painfully / endured distress, he that dwelt in darkness...]²⁴

Grendel acknowledges Hrothgar's presence and even his position of authority, and Hrothgar is certainly aware of Grendel's on-going threat to Heorot, but neither is able to deal directly or successfully with the other. At best, their relationship suggests a dysfunctional *dryhten-dryht-guma* (lord-retainer-man) dependency.

An interesting echo of Grendel's character and his exile experience occurs in the story of Hereward the Wake, which was delineated in the thirteenth-century *Gesta Herewardi*. Sources for this version of the Hereward story date from the twelfth century and recount events that took place shortly after the Norman Conquest of England. Hereward, who is frequently noted as a prototypical Robin Hood figure and daunting outlaw, is depicted as violent and vengeful in action against Norman invaders, scenes that recalls to an uncanny degree Gendel's mead-hall encounter with the Danes. Like the monstrous Grendel, Hereward appears as an unnaturally large and somewhat misshapen character who "was formidable in appearance ... [with] great strength in all his limbs."[25] He is distinguished by the fact that his right eye is "slightly different from the left," which contributes to his eccentric visage.[26] In tandem with his outlaw activities, Hereward's exile demeanor emerges early in the *Gesta* where he is cast as a lordless alien returning to his occupied homeland to exact revenge for a kinsman's death. He is the solitary outsider on the periphery of a wine-hall culture, and just as Grendel is incensed by the music and comradeship at Heorot that he cannot join, Hereward's anger also escalates at the "sound of harp and viol and the merriment of those applauding" as he approaches the Norman-French enclave.[27] The Normans in the text view Hereward as a runaway, and in keeping with the tradition of an exile who is deprived of both goods and pleasures, he emerges as one who "stole the gifts which were sent to the prince of our country."[28] Hereward-as-exile who steals gifts is similar to Grendel's activities and desires, for he threatens the "gift-throne" of Heorot. Just as Grendel raids Hrothgar's hall at night when the men are most vulnerable, Hereward's overwhelming success in laying "low fourteen of them together with their lord" is due in large part to his covert approach under cover of nightfall when the Normans are drunk or asleep and generally unprepared to defend themselves.[29] Such solitary and surreptitious moves become the trademark of the disconnected exile avenger and play out in Robin Hood's antics throughout the early poems.

While the Robin Hood poets may not replicate the Grendel/Hereward characterization or Greenfield's formulaic expression of exile to a word, the depiction of Robin's outsider status echoes the portrayal of the earlier exile figures. As Maurice Keen notes, "if Hereward was the lineal ancestor of Robin Hood, he was also the lineal descendent of the aristocratic heroes of Anglo-Saxon history."[30] Robin Hood's dysfunctional relationship with authority figures — the Sheriff of Nottingham, certain Bishops and officers of the church, and even the King himself — recalls Hereward's difficulties with the Norman-French overlords and resembles the Grendel-Hrothgar predicament on several levels. In the *Gest*, Robin is introduced as a "gode yeman" and "prude outlaw," and while he is surrounded by cohorts, he has no mutually beneficial relationship with an overlord or master as convention would dictate for an exemplary yeoman of the day.[31] Like the Wanderer, there is no liege lord to whom Robin pledges fealty or from whom he receives gifts. Like Grendel and Hereward, Robin is typically presented as a threat to the "gifstol" or seat of medieval bounty and authority. In the fifth fytte of the *Gest*, Robin gets the better of his most immediate superior — the Sheriff of Nottingham — in a shooting match. The central narrative of *Robin Hood and the Potter*, which may derive from an episode of the Hereward story by the same name, echoes not only this immediate source, but also presents a central scene reminiscent of Grendel's penetration of Heorot. Through cunning and deception, Robin gains access to the Sheriff's house, tampers with the Sheriff's wife, and lures the Sheriff out of town and into the woods where he plunders his belongings.

In the seventh and eight fyttes of the *Gest*, Robin meets the king himself in an initially hostile encounter. Once hostilities are resolved, Robin agrees to accompany the King to his court — more as hostage than a guest — with the following proviso:

> "But me lyke well your servyse,   *Unless; pleases me*
> "I come agayne full soone,
> And shote at the donne dere,   *brown*
> As I am wonte to done."[32]   *accustomed*

At length, Robin does long to return to the forest, and he predicts this:

> "Yf I dwele lenger with the king,
> Sorowe wyll me sloo."[33]   *slay*

Unexpectedly, it is during Robin Hood's sojourn at court with the King, his logical "dryhten," that his exile status emerges in force. In an ingenuous reversal of images, it is precisely the isolated forests and fenlands dreaded by other exiles that serve as home to Robin Hood, while the prospect of a visit to Nottingham in *Robin Hood and the Monk* distresses Robin and finds him "mornyng allone."[34] In a similar vein, he pines for his familiar forest haunts in the *Gest* declaring, "Me longeth sore to Bernysdale."[35] Like the Wanderer, the Seafarer, and Grendel, Robin Hood is one who necessarily lives apart from the mainstream of life for reasons that are not entirely clear or above board; like the earlier figures, Robin experiences distress in consequence of this necessity. Yet the environment of Robin Hood's life, and his attitude towards that environment, seems at odds with the resistance of Old English exiles to a place "þonne eall þisse worulde wela / wēste stondeð..." [when all of the wealth of this world lies wast][36] and the "iscealdne sæ" [ice-cold sea][37] of their exile pathways. The initial lines of *Robin Hood and the Monk* describe Robin Hood's woodland in glowing terms:

In somer, when the shawes be sheyne,	*woods are bright*
And leves be large and long,	
Hit is full mery in feyre foreste	*fair*
To here the foulys song,	*hear; birds'*
To se the dere draw to the dale,	*deer*
And leve the hilles hee,	*high*
And shadow hem in the leves grene,	*shelter themselves*
Under the grene wode tre.[38]	

The impression here is one of sweetness and light with emphasis on the bright leaves and bird songs of the woodland. With an abundance of deer for the taking, the Eden-like image is complete. The initial stanza of *Robin and the Potter* reads much the same:

In schomer, when the leves spryng,	*summer*
The bloschoms on every bowe,	*blossoms*
So merey doyt the berdys syng	*merry do*
Yn wodys merey now.[39]	*completely joyful*

When Robin does return to the woods after his sojourn with the king in the *Gest*, he listens appreciatively to the birds, and slays a "donne deer" to celebrate his homecoming. While this sounds idyllic on one level, it is well to remember that the Robin Hood poets often prove as wily as their hero: the setting in question is, in fact, the wild woods of medieval England, and the conventional understanding of such places almost always carries with it a subtext of danger. Despite the benign appearance of the environment, it is still an isolated location where trouble can brew and get quickly out of hand without the mitigating forces of law and order available in the towns.[40] Even Robin Hood and his own men occasionally get carried away with their rough-house games and wagers in the depths of the greenwood where anything goes by way of rambunctious behavior. In *Robin Hood and the Monk*, Little John and Robin, who are traversing the woods alone together, come to blows over a bet gone bad. There is no one else around to intervene, and Robin deals John a vicious whack on the head.[41]

Perhaps the strongest evidence in all of the Robin Hood poems of the contrast between the appearance and reality of the setting occurs in *Robin Hood and the Potter*. Robin, disguised as a Potter, lures the Sheriff away from his home, out of town, and into the wilds of the woodland, which is described thus:

And when he cam yn to the foreyst,
Under the leffes grene,
Berdys there sange on bowhes prest,   *Birds sang freely on boughs there*
Het was gret goy to se.⁴²   *great joy*

Soon, however, the mood changes as the Sheriff realizes the true identity of his host, and the serious predicament he faces. Robin's narrative sums up the situation:

"Here het ys merey to be," seyde Roben,   *To be here is merry*
"For a man that had hawt to spende;   *who had anything to spend*
Be mey horne ye schall awet   *By my horn you shall discover*
Yeff Roben Hode be here..."

"Y thanke God that ye be here;
Thereffore schall ye leffe yowre hors with hos,   *leave; us*
And all yowre hother gere."⁴³   *your other gear*

The Sheriff laments that he ever agreed to enter the forest. Indeed, he should have known better. For all of its apparent beauty and merriness, the forest is still the site of disorder and unpredictability. Its deceptive appearance renders it all the more dangerous to unsuspecting victims. In this respect, the greenwood *is* like the exile haunts of earlier English poetry. It is a place of isolation and danger, and while Robin embraces these qualities to his own purpose, they nonetheless cut him off from civilization and contribute to the sense of social deprivation that Robin, like other exiles, eventually expresses.

Isolation and the consequent deprivation of exile materialize in various ways for Robin Hood, with one of the most remarkable episodes occurring in the early poem *Robin Hood and Guy of Gisborne*. This poem, which probably dates from the fifteenth century, suggests strong links to the brutal figures of the Anglo-Saxon exile tradition.⁴⁴ Here, the initial predator, Guy, wears a horsehide in his quest to find and slay Robin Hood:

There were the ware of wight yeoman,   *they were aware; strong*
His body leaned to a tree.

A sword and a dagger he wore by his side,
Had beene many a mans bane,   *murderer*
And he was cladd in his capull-hyde,   *horse-hide*
Topp and tayle and mayne.⁴⁵

Stuart Kane notes that this costume "functions not at all as a type of disguise but rather as a marker for his identity." Kane further observes that this is a bestial identity of "a human who claims the traits of 'wildness.'"⁴⁶ Following Robin's brutal murder and decapitation of Guy that recalls the ritualistic blood-letting scenes of *Beowulf*, Robin appropriates the horsehide for himself along with the bestial identity that it signifies. There are overtones of the "wild man" figure here as described by Richard Bernheimer in his book, *Wild Men in the Middle Ages*. Bernheimer notes that in extreme circumstances humans are capable of losing the "unique metaphysical dignity of man" and of degenerating into unreasonable instinctive behavior to protect or prolong their own existence.[47] The horsehide indicates this degeneration as Robin Hood's identity blurs between human and non-human. Like Hereward, with his mismatched eyes and large limbs, or Grendel, with his ogre-like visage ("eotenas"),[48] the horsehide marks Robin as something both more and less than human: stronger but unrestrained in his exercise of strength. For it is no lighthearted prank or ruse that Robin plays with his adversary here; rather, it is a deadly game that is rendered all the more egregious by the similarity of the two figures. Guy, like Robin, is a forester, "a good archer"[49] and thus a metaphorical brother of the greenwood. In slaying, decapitating, and disfiguring Guy, Robin becomes a killer of his own kind. In this respect, Robin is much like Grendel, whom the *Beowulf* poet identifies as a member of "Cāines cynne" [Cain's race].[50] Subsequently, Grendel suffers exclusion from the human community and subsists on the margins of society. Following his cruel dispatch of Guy, Robin separates himself from the reasonable side of human nature with separation manifesting in the horse-hide of the now-deceased Guy. Bronislaw Geremek writes about just such a process of marginalization in the Middle Ages, and he observes that it "moved people outside social bonds, on their voluntary abandonment of those bonds."[51] Geremek further notes that "dress was the most frequent form of [social] 'distinction,'" indicating infamy or exclusion.[52] Thus, with his horse-hide in tow, Robin approximates a Grendel-like exclusion as an individual who is capable of crossing the line that separates acceptable human violence from bestial brutality. The terrified response of the Sheriff of Nottingham and his company to the revelation of Robin's identity at the end of the poem serves to point out this fact: even the most determined adversaries take flight and cut short the possibility of any further interaction.[53] While Robin's character seldom strikes such a violent pose in later poems, this early rendering in *Robin Hood and Guy of Gisborne* imparts a complex and even sinister dimension to Robin's image.

Exile deprivation for figures such as the Wanderer, the Seafarer, and even Grendel manifests itself in severance from the mead-hall society of Anglo-Saxon warriors commonly understood in terms of the Germanic *comitatus* tradition.[54] Grendel cannot join the revelers at Heorot, and the Wanderer cannot forget or replace the hall-joys of his former life:

> Gemon hē selesecgas and sincþege,
> hu hine on geoguðe his goldwine
> wenede tō wiste...

> [He remembered gifts of treasure, and hall-thanes, and
> how in youth, his Lord treated him to feasts...][55]

For Robin, it is not a land-lord or earthly gift-giver whom he seeks. Instead, he seeks to avoid the interference of temporal authority-figures. Nor is it the absence of friends or merry making that plagues him; he has plenty of both. But for Robin Hood, the real problem posed by his isolation is a spiritual one. He is cut off from religion and is deprived of the community of worshippers in a way and to a degree that parallels the severance of the earlier poetic exiles from "drygh-sele" [splendid hall] of the heroic *comitatus*. Alvin Lee maintains that in Old English poetry "the order of the dryht becomes, in fact, a major source of imaginative figures and organizing patterns."[56] He posits that this concept functions on multiple levels in Old English poetry denoting the gold hall of an Anglo-Saxon "dryhten" and his "dryht-guma," the angelic society of the heavenly "Dryhten," the Christian community on earth, or all three simultaneously through a mythical metaphorical connection.[57] Thus, much like the Old English characters, Robin Hood's exile status robs him of transcendent joys and solace, but in his case this deprivation occurs in the context of Christian faith.

Robin's piety and faithfulness receive at least a passing note in most of the early poems and ballads. Pollard observes that Robin Hood is portrayed throughout the poems as genuinely pious and devout, in contrast with contemporary churchmen who appear as greedy, avaricious, and hypocritical.[58] Even in the grisly tale of *Guy of Gisborne*, Robin invokes the aid of the Virgin Mary, and at the outset of the *Gest*, he is described as one who would—if he could—hear three masses every day and who "loved Oure dere lady."[59] Near the end of the same work, Robin claims to have built a chapel dedicated to Mary Magdalene to which he longs to return in pilgrim-fashion, "barefote and wolwarde" [with wool next to the skin].[60] But Robin's religious zeal is thwarted by his status in much the same way that earlier exiles are deprived of the joys of the mead-hall; although, it is well to remember that it is not so much a connection with the institutional church that Robin Hood seeks, but rather it is the opportunity to engage in simple acts of devotion. In fact, Robin voices grievance with a number of bishops and archbishops and with one abbot in particular in he *Gest*. Here, Robin comes off as generous, fair-minded, and heroic in comparison with the churchmen who are depicted as conniving and mercenary in their eagerness for cash and land. Moreover, in *Robin Hood and the Monk,* Robin takes issue with a member of a religious order over his exclusion from worship, and he makes this complaint:

> "Ye, on thyng greves me," seid Robyn,   *one*
> "And does my hert mych woo: *woe*

> That I may not no solem day
> To mas nor matyns goo. *Mass nor Matins*
>
> "Hit is a fourtnet and more," seid he, *It's been a fortnight*
> "Syn I my Savyour see; *Since I've been to Mass*
> To day wil I to Notyngham," seid Robyn,
> "With the myght of mylde Marye."⁶¹ *Virgin Mary*

Like Grendel, who cannot enter the hall or approach the lord of Heorot, and the Wanderer, who is denied access to his earthly lord, Robin Hood's exclusion from Mass and Matins denies him communion with his heavenly "Dryhten." It is this "lord-longing" or loss of spiritual communion that sets Robin apart from the run-of-the-mill outlaw, and it is what elevates him to a position of heroic exile in the early ballads and poems. Evidence of this longing on Robin's part appears somewhat unexpectedly near the end of *Robin Hood and Guy of Gisborne*. Here, Robin ostensibly attempts to perform an office of the church and plays the role of a priest as he momentarily wants to hear Little John's confession:

> "Stand abacke! stand abacke!" sayd Robin;
> "Why draw you mee soe neere?
> Itt was never the use in our countrye
> One's shrift another shold heere."⁶² *confession*

While this activity is partly an effort to distract bystanders, it indicates Robin's close affiliation with important tenets of the faith, and it suggests that rubrics of the church are on his mind at a crucial moment in the action. Above all, this effort to "shrift" his fellow outlaw may indicate Robin's awareness of his own need to realign himself with his Lord after his inhuman demeanor and inhumane treatment of Guy. Although there is not full atonement for his crimes or sins, Robin's gesture demonstrates recognition of the need for it, softens his bestial visage, and marks his desire for reconnection and spiritual communion. While he is no less a bandit for his devotion, Robin's insistent piety gives shape and purpose to his banditry throughout the poems. In the *Gest*, the outlaw sets out to "bete and bynde"⁶³ his clerical adversaries, and it is clear-cut revenge that he harbors towards the churchmen slain in *Robin Hood and the Monk*.

In sum, Robin Hood of the early ballads and poems manifests a hodgepodge of parallels and contradictions to the Old English exile tradition. He is one who seems merry, but remains unfulfilled; one who seems bent on material gain, but harbors a spiritual side; and he is one who dwells in a seemingly benign setting that nonetheless poses dangers and drawbacks evocative of earlier poetic exile. Of course, it is precisely this potential for complexity that renders Robin Hood capable of heroic stature. Like the Old English

Wanderer, Seafarer, and Grendel, Robin suffers markedly for his alienation and deprivation, and it is this capacity for suffering that is manifested in the transcendental side of the character that renders Robin Hood an obvious descendant of the heroes of Old English literature as well as a fitting model for the archetypal heroes of romance that populate the pages of English literature from King Arthur to Harry Potter.

Notes

1. Barbara A. Hanawalt, "Ballads and Bandits: Fourteenth-Century Outlaws and the Robin Hood Poems," in *Chaucer's England: Literature in Historical Context*, ed. Barbara A. Hanawalt. Medieval Studies at Minnesota 4 (Minneapolis: University of Minnesota Press, 1992), 154–175 at 171.
2. Keen, 21.
3. Keen, 9
4. Julius Goebel, *Felony and Misdemeanor: A Study in the History of English Criminal Procedure*, vol. 1 (New York: Commonwealth; London: Oxford University Press, 1937), 15.
5. Timothy S. Jones, ed. and trans., *The Outlawry of Earl Godwin*, in Ohlgren 2005, 3–27 at 4.
6. Timothy Lundgren, "Hereward and Outlawry in Fenland Culture: A Study of Local Narrative and Tradition in Medieval England" (PhD diss., Ohio State University, 1996), 15. For some recent scholarship on Hereward, see Elisabeth Van Houts, "Hereward and Flanders," *Anglo-Saxon England* 28 (1999): 201–23; Rolf H. Bremmer, Jr., "The *Gesta Herwardi*: Transforming an Anglo-Saxon into an Englishman," in *People and Texts. Relationships in Medieval Literature: Studies Presented to Erik Kooper*, ed. Thea Summerfield and Keith Busby. Costerus, n.s., 166 (Amsterdam: Rodopi, 2007), 29–42; and Paul Dalton, "The Outlaw Hereward 'the Wake': His Companions and Enemies," in *Outlaws in Medieval and Early Modern England: Crime, Government and Society, c. 1066–1600*, ed. John C. Appleby and Paul Dalton (Farnham: Ashgate Press, 2009), 7–36.
7. Goebel, *Felony and Misdemeanor*, 57.
8. Gillian Spraggs, "Section from the Roman History of Cassius Dio," *Outlaws and Highwaymen*, 2007, http://www.outlawsandhighwaymen.com//bulla.htm (accessed February 10, 2010).
9. Lundgren, "Hereward and Outlawry," 29.
10. Roberta Kevelson, *Inlaws/Outlaws, a Semiotics of Systemic Interaction: "Robin Hood" and the "King's Law"* (Bloomington: Indiana University Press, 1977), 6.
11. Kevelson, *Inlaws/Outlaws*, 78–78.
12. Stanley B. Greenfield, "The Formulaic Expression of the Theme of 'Exile' in Anglo-Saxon Poetry," *Speculum* 30, no. 2 (1955): 200–06.
13. Ibid., 201–02.
14. Ibid., 202.
15. Ida L. Gordon, ed., *The Seafarer*, rev. ed. (Exeter: University of Exeter Press, 1996), 36, lines 25–26.
16. Roy F. Leslie, ed., *The Wanderer*, rev. ed. (Exmouth: University of Exeter, 1985), 66, lines 36–38.
17. *A Gest of Robyn Hode*, in Knight and Ohlgren, 80–168 at 92, line 68; and 116, line 832.
18. Ibid., 136, lines 1461–64.
19. Ibid., 145, lines 1749–52.
20. *Robin Hood and The Monk*, in Knight and Ohlgren, 31–56 at 39, lines 62–66.

21. Fr. Klaeber, ed., *Beowulf and the Fight at Finnesburg*, 3rd ed. (Lexington: D.C. Heath, 1950), 5, lines 103, 105, 109–110.
22. Ibid., 7, line 165.
23. Ibid., 7, lines 166–69.
24. Ibid., 4, lines 86–87.
25. Michael Swanton, ed. and trans., *The Deeds of Hereward*, in Ohlgren 2005, 28–99 at 41.
26. Ibid., 41.
27. Ibid., 61.
28. Ibid., 61.
29. Ibid., 62.
30. Keen, 21.
31. Knight and Ohlgren, 90, lines 3, 5.
32. Ibid., 143, lines 1665–68.
33. Ibid., 145, lines 1751–52.
34. Ibid., 39, line 64.
35. Ibid., 146, line 1765.
36. Leslie, *The Wanderer*, 67, line 74.
37. Gordon, *The Seafarer*, 34, line 14.
38. Knight and Ohlgren, 37, lines 1–8.
39. *Robin Hood and the Potter*, in Knight and Ohlgren, 57–79 at 62, lines 1–4.
40. Catherine A. M. Clarke, *Literary Landscapes and the Idea of England, 700–1400* (Cambridge: D. S. Brewer, 2006), 36–37.
41. Knight and Ohlgren, 38, lines 55–62.
42. Ibid., 70, lines 246–49.
43. Ibid., 70, 71; lines 250–53, 277–79.
44. *Robin Hood and Guy of Gisborne*, in Knight and Ohlgren, 169–183 at 169.
45. Ibid., 174, lines 25–30.
46. Stuart Kane, "Horseplay: Robin Hood, Guy of Gisborne, and the Neg(oti)ation of the Bestial," in Hahn, 101–110 at 106.
47. Richard Bernheimer, *Wild Men in the Middle Ages* (Cambridge: Harvard University Press, 1952), 9.
48. Klaeber, *Beowulf*, 5, line 112.
49. Knight and Ohlgren, 176, line 94.
50. Klaeber, *Beowulf*, 5, line 107.
51. Bronislaw Geremek, "The Marginal Man," in *Medieval Callings*, ed. Jacques Le Goff, trans. Lydia G. Cochrane (Chicago: University of Chicago Press, 1990), 346–73 at 368.
52. Ibid., 370.
53. Knight and Ohlgren, 180, lines 227–30.
54. Frank M. Stenton, *Anglo-Saxon England* (Oxford: Clarendon Press, 1947), 299.
55. Leslie, *The Wanderer*, 66, lines 34–36.
56. Alvin A. Lee, *The Guest-Hall of Eden: Four Essays on The Design of Old English Poetry* (New Haven and London: Yale University Press, 1972), 13.
57. Ibid., 13.
58. A. J. Pollard, *Imagining Robin Hood: The Late Medieval Stories in Historical Context* (London: Routledge, 2004), 112–120.
59. Knight and Ohlgren, 91, lines 32, 37.
60. Ibid., 146, line 1767.
61. Ibid., 37–38, lines 21–28.
62. Ibid., 180, lines 215–18.
63. Ibid., 92, line.

8

Histories of Contexts: Form, Argument, and Ideology in *A Gest of Robyn Hode*

ALEXANDER L. KAUFMAN

The Robin Hood tradition is one that is ripe with contexts. From the earliest historical records, to the first literary mention of the mythical outlaw in William Langland's B-text of *Piers Plowman*, to his appearances in medieval historical literature and the chronicle tradition, and finally to poems and plays from the fifteenth century onward that bear his name, Robin Hood's popularity and cultural versatility was and remains quite astounding. The fellow certainly got around. The origins of Robin Hood the person and his original context are perhaps best left to those individuals who wish to search for that which is forever to be a quest. However, as Stephen Knight has demonstrated, an examination of the earliest contexts of the figure of Robin Hood — in the play-games, the bergerie Robin Hood and the French text *Robin et Marion*, and his possible hybridization into the individual outlaw robber of the greenwood with that ever-present hood — underscores the complex nature of the legend and demonstrates the care with which one must read the available source material.[1]

The crowning jewel of the early Robin Hood texts is *A Gest of Robyn Hode*. As a text that is so central to the development of the tradition, it has become — and rightly so — one of the dominant referents to Robin Hood, Little John, and the life of the greenwood outlaws. As with any literary text, the way in which one reads the work is highly individualized, and the *Gest* is no exception. Some readers focus their attention on the plot of the impoverished knight, Richard at the Lee; others have read the text as a witness to Robin Hood's unfortunate demise at the hands of the prioress at Kirklees Abbey; while still others see the text as a possible window into a long-lost series of Little John adventures. At the heart of this essay lies the experience of reading the *Gest* within and through a series of cultural and historical contexts.

In his published dissertation *The Gest of Robin Hood*, William Hill Clawson emphatically states that the early Robin Hood text *A Gest of Robyn Hode* is "one of the best examples in medieval literature of skillfully arranged and effectively phrased narrative ... a masterly narrative of a popular medieval hero, but also a contribution to the problem of epic origins and of the relation between ballad and epic."[2] A lengthy text at 1,824 lines, *A Gest of Robyn Hode* remains a well crafted, well constructed, and a well-contextualized piece of literature. It is a self-referential text, for the *Gest* relies not only on past histories of England and outlawry to maintain narrativity, the text and its author/compiler also rely and work closely with the text itself so as to maintain a strong narrative flow. As we will see, the *Gest* is a composite text that is complex in its narrativity and construction. To illustrate this point, I will be examining the structural form of the *Gest* by applying the concept of historical contextualization to the literary text so as to uncover within the narrative several layers of historical reality.

As a literary historian, Hayden White seeks to uncover the various notions of historical reality by examining the formal argument that the historian has laid down within the historical and literary texts. White says that "such an argument provides an explanation of what happens in the story by evoking principles of combination which serve as putative laws of historical explanation."[3] In any historical or literary-historical work, White theorizes that there are four distinct paradigms (a pattern, here related to concepts of knowledge) that account for the different ideas of historical reality: Formist, Mechanistic, Organicist, and Contextualist. Within any given text, one or more of these paradigms will be present, attempting to shape a historical reality, that is, a history that is not imagined or fleeting, but one that is actual and can be seen as taking place now in the present. The *Gest* is working within the Contextualist argument of historical reality, but in order to see how this is, we must first come to an understanding of what constitutes a Contextualist argument.

In any given historical text there are several different concepts, stories, facts, and people that inhabit and work within the framework of a historical narrative. It is the author — and in the case of the *Gest* the possibility of a compiler — who must sort through the historical information and organize it into a text. In Contextualism, events can be explained by being placed within the context of their occurrence. Why these events occurred can be explained by the revelation of the specific relationships they bore to other events, events that have occurred in their own historical space and time. White says that the Contextualist "insists that 'what happened' in the field can be accounted for by the specification of the functional interrelationships existing among the agents and agencies occupying the field at any given time."[4] A text that belongs to the genre of historical literature can therefore be seen as a collection of various elements, elements that can be isolated and examined for their own historical merit and reality, but also as a series of elements that move "in a wavelike motion," in which certain phrases, events, or culminations are considered to be intrinsically more significant to the text and the historical reality than others.[5] The narrative of *A Gest of Robyn Hode*, with its historical moments, moves in this "wavelike" manner; within the text there are certain narratival elements that are intrinsically more significant in accounting for the text's historical reality. My aim is to examine three main contexts that the narrator created so as to provide the reader (and listener) with a tale that is not only entertaining but which also blurs the lines of the historical for the sake of the entertainment value and possibly the moral and ideological concerns that are behind the tale. By contextualizing certain elements, the *Gest* becomes a text that holds within it an inherent ideological position of mercantile superiority that at the time of its creation the audience would have possibly supported.[6] The history of late-medieval England thus becomes a backdrop for the narrator who will shape historical reality as he sees fit so as to maintain a dominant mercantile ideology throughout the narrative. But the text is not just caught up in mercantile interests; indeed, the narrative still addresses issues of honesty, integrity, compassion for the community, and the abuse of the common people by those who are in positions of care and law.

In order to contextualize the historical reality of the text we must examine these textual crests that are prevalent throughout the work. The first of these textual crests to be discussed is the importance of the audience and oral tradition and its relationship to the narrator. As we will see, the narrator molded the story to fit a particular audience, and through the use of oratorical devices the narrator subversively implemented many ideological implications that he shared with his listeners.[7] The second context to be examined will be those instances throughout the text where the narrator places the reader into a context of mercantile behavior and culture. The author/compiler of the *Gest* has here constructed a historical reality within the poem that mirrors the shifting class structure in the fourteenth and fifteenth centuries. The third and final context to be examined will be the textual construction of the poem. The *Gest* author/compiler drew upon several other literary texts to construct the piece; moreover, he integrated into the text several historical allusions to Edward III (and possibly Edward IV) and the monarch's social and political practices. The technique of using ideas and concepts of earlier works was normal during the medieval period; furthermore, this reduplication of narratival themes and concepts was used to help get the underlying message(s) across in relation to the various contexts.

Oral Tradition and the Audience of the Gest

> Lythe and listin, gentilmen,   *Attend*
> That be of frebore blode;   *freeborn blood*
> I shall you tel of a gode yeman,
> His name was Robyn Hode.[8]

So begins *A Gest of Robyn Hode*. It is a wake-up call to the audience, ordering or encouraging them to keep silent and pay attention; it is a phrase that is repeated three more times in the text: lines 573, 1125, and 1265. More importantly, it is the first event within the text that can be placed within a specific context, that of an oral tradition. Each interjection by the narrator reminds the reader (and the audience) that *he* is the one who is in full control of the story.[9] And to place the orator into another context, we should turn to the language that is used as a means to identify and account for the historical reality. In his essay "Criticism in History," Fredric Jameson regards the rhetoric of oration as follows:

> Rhetoric is an older and essentially precapitalist mode of linguistic organization; it is a collective or class phenomenon in that it serves as a means of assimilating the speech of individuals to some suprapersonal oratorical paradigm, to some non-or preindividualistic standard of the *beau parler*, of high style and fine writing. A profound social value is here invested in spoken language, one that may be gauged by the primacy of such aristocratic forms as the sermon and the verse tragedy, the salon witticism and the poetic epistle.[10]

While certainly not written in a high style, nor considered "fine" writing, the rhetoric and language of the *Gest* does indeed serve a purpose.[11] Stephen Knight and Thomas Ohlgren comment: "The language is limited in vocabulary and range, and most striking of all, there are very few images or even descriptions of the whole poem. But what might seem uninspired and unimaginative from a Shakespearean viewpoint can also have a curious potency."[12] This potency lies in the constant repetition of phrases, such as the aforementioned "Lythe and listin, gentilmen," but also in the descriptions of the main characters. The sheriff is "proude" twenty-three times; the Knight, Richard at the Lee, is described as "gentyll" nineteen times; and Robin and his men are called "gode" some seventeen times.[13] The author, in his purposeful repetition of certain descriptive adjectives, brings us (the present-day reader) into the context of medieval customs and manners. That the sheriff is "proud" is not a positive marker of his character; on the contrary, it a personality trait rooted in the sin of pride. Medieval lives were constructed around the penitential cycle, and for the sheriff to be identified with a cardinal sin (and perhaps the most dangerous sin, a sin that can be viewed as a "gateway" sin) would not be lost on the medieval audience.[14] The impoverished knight is "gentle," a trait that the author holds to be beneficial and one he may wish his audience to adopt. The knight is also one person who was damaged (physically, emotionally, and monetarily) by the economic and cultural system.[15] Robin Hood and his men are of course (nominally) good, and their actions are often viewed in similar terms. This repetition of names, of phrases, and of descriptions by the author/compiler can therefore be placed in a historical context of ritualistic storytelling, a context where the orator is in full command of the history, of the past deeds of men and women, and of the message (i.e., ideology) that he wishes to express. Given the above three character types that are repeated throughout the *Gest*, one could say that the author was attempting to strengthen the character and moral fortitude of his audience. In examining Northrop Frye's theories of mythic criticism, Fredric Jameson believes that it is a "preindividualistic storytelling that seals the unity of the tribe, confirms their common past through the celebration of the heroic founders of culture itself, and unites their individual minds through a shared symbolism and a shared ritual."[16] The ritual of storytelling, therefore, serves to unite a common class through shared experiences, ideologies, and symbols.

While there appears to be an agreement among scholars that the audience of *A Gest of Robyn Hode* was probably a mixed listening/reading audience, it is still possible, and I believe necessary, to contextualize the major, or dominant audience, for this text.[17] The audience can be identified by the manner in which the narrator addresses them, but also by examining the ideology of Robin and his band. As mentioned before, the opening of the *Gest* (and subsequent fyttes) begins with the lines "Lyth and listin, gentilmen, / That be of frebore blode." Here, the *Gest*-poet is directly addressing his audience and is referring to hereditary freedom, which was a freedom that was a prerequisite for a guildsman who had "passed his apprenticeship" and therefore "qualified for citizenship and freedom of the City."[18] This context is, as Ohlgren notes, of particular ideological importance. The author is targeting the merchant class in England, which by this point in the later Middle Ages in England was a growing economic and social force that was beginning to influence the political hierarchy of the landed class.[19] The author of the text is therefore creating, shaping, and appropriating the economic ideology of the merchant class into a narrative of large societal implications. The author is cognizant of this growing mercantile class, and by his language and knowledge of mercantile practices he is seeking to create a text that will communicate with the mercantile audience, which is quite a bold move. This is the concept of appropriation; the author is creating a text where the outlaws of Sherwood and Barnesdale fulfill the need for a mercantile hero to replace the knightly hero of the aristocratic romances.[20] The author sees the merchant guildsman as the new hero and driving force for England, and the reader will witness Robin and his band of social outlaws adopt and appropriate many aristocratic customs.[21] The author has, in a sense, written "a history" of the economic and social change within England during the fourteenth century; however, while contextualizing this information within the story, the reader must be reminded that the *Gest* is a "constructed" story whose ideology is implicit.

In the *Gest*, the narrator is ever present; whether he is addressing the reader or showing his knowledge of mercantile practice, the reader never doubts that the voice of the narrator is always there and that he is the person in control of the story and its ideological and historical contexts. In the following excerpt, Hayden White examines how the amount of narrativity may influence the historical reality of a text:

> The amount of narrative will be greatest in accounts designed to tell a story, least in those intended to provide analysis of the events of which it treats. Where the aim in view is the telling of a story, the problem of narrativity turns on the issue of whether historical events can be truthfully represented as manifesting the structures and processes of events met with more commonly in certain kinds of "imaginative" discourses, that is, such fictions as the epic, the folk tale, myth, romance, tragedy, comedy, farce, and the like ... the story told in the narrative is a mimesis of the story lived in some region of historical reality, and insofar as it is an accurate imitation, it is to be considered a truthful account thereof.[22]

The *Gest* is considered "the most complex as well as the most important and lengthy (c. 13,900 words) item in the corpus of English outlaw literature,"[23] and the narrative that runs through the text can be seen as a truthful account of the historical reality of the shifting social and economic structures of the fourteenth century. The context that now must be examined is the author's attempt at contextualizing mercantile behavior and their imitations of courtly behavior. By doing so, the author is suggesting to the audience and the reader what historical reality (and therefore ideology) he wishes to present to the audience. Of course, we are dealing with a work of literature, and so one underlying question still nags: how can that audience or future audiences of the printed edition deem these accounts to be historically truthful or accurate?

Contextualizing Mercantile Behavior

In the first fytte, after hearing from Robin Hood that he must dine with another person or he will not dine at all, the narrator constructs his own history of Robin and his social practices:

A gode maner than had Robyn;	*custom*
In londe where that he were,	

> Every day or he wold dyne   *before*
> Thre messis wolde he here.   *masses; hear*
>
> The one in the worship of the Fader,
> And another of the Holy Gost,
> The thirde of Our dere Lady,   *Virgin Mary*
> That he loved allther moste.   *the most of all*
>
> Robyn loved Oure dere Lady:
> For dout of dydly synne,   *fear; of deadly sin*
> Wolde he never do compani harme
> That any woman was in.[24]

This historical construction of the social practice of not eating until a guest has arrived is an imitation of knightly behavior that the narrator constructs. It is clear that this is not an act of narration based solely on literary conventions; that is, the author is presenting the reader with this particular context of courtly behavior appropriated and initiated by a member of the yeoman class based not on imagination but rather based on real events. The narrator is speaking to an audience that would be familiar with the new guilds that are evolving, and these audience members may even be members of the new social class. The narrator would certainly be speaking to them of a history, of a set of ideological concepts of which they would be familiar and supportive. As Ohlgren notes, "The parallels between guild policies and practices and specific scenes in the *Gest* are compelling, offering convincing evidence that the poem was composed for an audience who would not only recognize the mercantile allusions but also appreciate the yeoman hero's proving himself superior to a member of the knightly class."[25] Robin, in the above scene, is seen as chivalric, of having a sense of honor and reverence towards God and in particular the Virgin Mary under the understanding of Christian beliefs. The narrator has contextualized for the audience the ideology that all guildsmen should follow.

Medieval guilds originally were formed to help those in their respective communities who needed assistance. This charitable nature of the early guilds was, by the 1400s, all but replaced by a culture of monetary and political power and control. Fifteenth-century London was a city ruled, some have argued, by an oligarchy of guild members.[26] And while that ideology can be read as mercantile, it should also be noted that Robin is very much at one with the knight. Robin understands from whence the knight fell and how to help him rediscover his self-worth. Robin is attempting to bridge the gap between classes, possibly for moralistic reasons (one of the text's deep messages) but also to add an additional plot element and character angle. This is most clearly seen when Robin Hood and his men wash their hands before eating their meal, an example of behavior associated with those people from upper yeomanry right up to the king, here presented by the narrator as a example to the audience of the new model of societal behavior that all guildsman *and* rising yeomen should follow.[27] But by placing this scene within the historical context of the later Middle Ages, we must still recognize that this is only one text with one narrator. It is the narrator who is in full command of the text, and it is the narrator who decides when and how to shape the historical records of the past so as to communicate then to a present audience. In examining the politics of narration, Hayden White dissects G.W.F. Hegel's "internal vital principle," which in essence states that "the content (or referent) of the specifically historical discourse was not the real story of what happened but the particular relation between a public present and a past that a state endowed with a constitution made possible."[28] For Hegel and White, historical reality and its ideological implications are not seen in events and doctrines that have taken place in a distant past, nor are they seen in the historical present; real history and real historical reality can be witnessed the in the narration of historical texts where past doctrines and their ideologies are seen in relation (or contexts) to one another. The true historical reality of the *Gest* is witnessed in those areas where past political, social, and economic ideologies and histories are seen in relation to present ones. The impact of the hand washing scene in the *Gest* is not comprehended by seeing the text as taking place in the present context, but rather the scene's social and historical impact is experienced when the past history of hand washing and its past social implications are brought forward to the narrator's present, and the yeoman class is seen appropriating the courtly ritual.

If the narration of past literary histories centered on courtly rituals and practices of the aristocracy, where the audience would agree that King Arthur and Gawain represented the dominant ideologies of the period, then the narration of the *Gest* contextualizes a new mercantile ideology that was becoming dominant in the late fourteenth century. Carnivalesque in nature and theme, this power shift is seen in the textual nuances and allusions that the author (sometimes) subtly imbeds throughout the text in wavelike motions of historical reality. These multiple narrative contexts create and represent a historical reality, a reality of which the audience of the text was a member of a new politically powerful class. As Jameson argues, "It is in detecting the traces of that uninterrupted narrative, in restoring to the surface of the text the repressed and buried reality of this fundamental of history, that the doctrine of a political unconscious finds its function and its necessity."[29] This reality that the author of the *Gest* buries, and which is most contextually important to the ideological implications of the historical reality of the text, is the practice of measuring, giving, and selling of liveries.[30] The audience is placed within the context of the drapery guilds, and Robin Hood and his men represent a new social order that is slowly controlling the economy (and replacing the once all-powerful and driving monetary force of the Church) and controlling the narrative. In the first fytte, Robin Hood orders Little John to measure out deeply dyed scarlet cloth for Richard at the Lee,[31] and we are told by the narrator that Little John became incensed:

> And at every handfull that he met   *measured*
> He leped footes three.   *added*

While this could be an act of guild rivalry or tradesmen intimidation, it is nonetheless just one of dozens of references to cloth and its use as social and political power.[32] The ultimate instance of political subversion found within the context of mercantile behavior occurs in fytte eight. The king has recognized Robin Hood and his men, and he asks the outlaw if he has any cloth to sell:

> "Haste thou ony grene cloth," sayd our kynge,
> "That thou wylte sell nowe to me?"
> "Ye, for God," sayd Robyn,
> "Thyrty yerdes and thre."[33]

As Ohlgren notes, "Although the text does not depict the actual sale, it does imply that a deal was made and coin exchanged for Lincoln green cloth."[34] The subject, once outlawed, has now become inlawed and recognized as fiscally legitimate.[35] By contextualizing this and the previous scenes relating to cloth guilds and their mercantile practices, the author has (through allusion and repetition) highlighted the new-found system of power that the mercantile class (and therefore the possible medieval reading/listening audience) has obtained. This new upward mobility by the guilds is represented by the narrative of the *Gest*, and the contextual waves of mercantile ideology that flow through the text represent a new, emerging social class in late fourteenth-century England.[36] Taken as such, it is sufficient to say that this narrative acts an instrument of ideology; the author has created a series of contextual constructs, which, examined as a whole or individually, drape the historical reality that is here presented as one of social and economic turnover. The author has consciously chosen to represent and construct a series of historical contexts, contexts that are tied to the narrator's own sense of audience and oration, existing and emerging social classes, and courtly and mercantile ideology. The narrative echoes words that were written five centuries into the future:

> The history of all hitherto existing society is the history of class struggle: freeman and slave, patrician and plebeian, lord and serf, guild-master and journeyman — in a word, oppressor and oppressed — stood in constant opposition to one another, carried on an uninterrupted, now hidden, now open fight, a fight that each time ended, either in a revolutionary reconstruction of society at large or in the common ruin of the contending classes.[37]

The narrativity of the *Gest* and its ideological contexts of subversion and appropriation as seen in the emergence of the political, physical, and mass power of the guild represents a constructed historical reality, a reality that is meant to represent an accurate example of the nature the class structure and struggle in the late fourteenth century.

Edward III and the Construction of A Gest of Robyn Hode

To contextualize *A Gest of Robyn Hode* further, there needs to be some discussion of the construction of the text. Of primary concern here are the various sources that were used in the *Gest's* composition and construction, and the problematic nature of maintaining a true sense of historical reality. The aim of the author of the *Gest*, I sense, is to construct and present this text as an example of real history while concurrently delivering a message (in a manner very much akin to the tradition of the sermon exemplum) that is cognizant of others who are less fortunate and respecting their status; nonetheless, it is virtually impossible for a reader (of this or any period) to view the text as such due to its multi-layered construction and highly literary qualities.

As noted earlier, there have been varying opinions as to the overall construction of the text. J. C. Holt has called it clumsy and artificial,[38] while in his dissertation Clawson noted that, "the compiler of the *Gest*, besides intimate knowledge of the Robin Hood ballads and a complete sympathy with them, was possessed of admirable skill. His poem is not a mere stringing together of ballads, but a complete re-handling and fusion of ballads and mediaeval tales a well, into a unified narrative."[39] The narrative can be broken down into what Francis James Child calls "a three-ply web,"[40] where the first section deals with Richard at the Lee, the impoverished knight who must borrow and then repay a loan Robin had given him, and Little John, who is to help the Knight and in the process wrecks havoc in the Sheriff's kitchen.[41] While Little John hopes the staff would act honorably and assist him in his mission, they instead follow through with churlish behavior and language to boot. In the second part, the Sheriff stages an archery game to trap the outlaws who instead kidnap and later kill, thus illustrating the sheriff's cunning and shrewd belief that the legal system is there to entrap, and not assist, others. The third ply deals with the "King and the Subject" recognition scene, where Robin Hood and his outlaws are pardoned, and Robin is invited to join the King's court. The king, acting in accordance to God's law, sees the righteousness and honor in Robin and thus does not view him as an outlaw who is guilty of poaching his deer. Within this three-ply web structure, several tales stand out from the overall narrative; yet within this text, there are constant textual reminders of historical reality, most notably in the repeated phrase, "our comly kynge."

The first node of the contextual nature of the text's structure is the beginning. As readers, we are not given any prior history of Robin Hood — his past deeds, his parentage and lineage, his personality, why he and his band are in the forest — nor are we given any prior history of Sir Richard at the Lee, the impoverished knight who wanders into the greenwood. Robin, like many outlaws, may have been given safe harbor by the local townspeople who often saw the good in people and chose to look beyond their societal transgressions. The narrator begins in the middle of things; we as readers have entered into a literary context whose past we are not privy to, yet it is the lessons to be learned from the situations that are important — as well as a good tale to keep our attention. Unlike other outlaw tales, such as *The Deeds of Hereward, The Acts and Deeds of Sir William Wallace*, or *Eustace the Monk*, where the narrator constructs a history of the outlaw, the narrator of the *Gest* expects his audience to know the material. He has possibly left out the material for the sake of time (at 465 stanzas, the *Gest* is lengthy Robin Hood text), or he simply did not know the past histories of the Robin Hood and so did not wish to place any more historically questionable facts in the epic. However, by leaving out this prior history, the narrator creates a story that is unlike *Hereward* or *Fouke le Fitz Waryn*, for the *Gest* does not read like a chronicle or an ancestral romance; rather, it reads like a series of events that are woven together to form a story. Hayden White argues:

> The chronicle, by contrast, often seems to wish to tell a story, aspires to narrativity, but typically fails to achieve it. More specifically, the chronicle usually is marked by a failure to achieve narrative closure. It does not so much conclude as it simply terminate. It starts out to tell a story but breaks off *in medias re*, in the chronicler's own present; it leaves things unresolved, or rather, it leaves them unresolved in a storylike way.[42]

A Gest of Robyn Hode does not read like a chronicle. The narrator connects the first part of the narrative together with a series of separate stories. The second fytte does not feature Robin at all, but is a continuation of the narrative line from the end of fytte one. Robin is lending the services of Little John to Richard:

"I shall the lende Litell John, my man,   *thee*
For he shalbe thy knave;   *servant*
In a yemans stede he may the stande,   *place; serve thee*
If thou greate nede have."

The Seconde Fytte

Now is the knight gone on his way:
This game hym thought full gode;

> Whanne he loked on Bernesdale
> He blessyd Robyn Hode.⁴³

It is a seamless transition. The narrator has subtly moved forward in the story's progress, and in the second fytte the Knight repays the loan to the monk of St. Mary's Abbey in York, and the Sheriff and Chief Justice attempt to raise money so as to take the land away from Richard. The subtlety of this section is striking; it is not as direct or confrontational as many of the anti-monastic sections of *Robin Hood and the Monk*, yet it succeeds in suggesting how avaricious the monasteries had become. Again, it must be noted that Robin Hood is absent, and that the location has moved out of the forest and into York and, a year later, at Wentbrydge.⁴⁴ This intertextual story is another contextual element of the narrative as a whole, but within the second fytte we also learn from the narrator of another key historical context that relates to the historical reality of the text. First, the Prior states that Richard is "ferre beyonde the see, / In Englonde ryght [cause]."⁴⁵ Later, Richard raises the four hundred pounds by acting as an arrayer for the crown, as he gathers together one-hundred archers.⁴⁶ This places, as some have argued, the Knight in France at the beginning of the Hundred Years' War serving the King of England.⁴⁷ This subtle context that the narrator uses as a foundation for the historical reality of the text serves as a skillful maneuver, true; but moreover, it adds an organic element of reality to the narrative.

It is important to underscore the differences between historical events and fictional events. In the *Gest*, the author uses a combination of real and imaginary places, people, and events to create and tell a story. While historians are concerned with events that can be assigned to specific time-space occasions and that are (or at one time were) in principle observable or perceivable, Hayden White has noted that imaginative writers — poets, novelists, playwrights — are concerned with both these events (the real events) and imagined, hypothetical, or invented ones.⁴⁸ This concept is important to understand, because in the *Gest* the narrator moves us from a context that contains a hypothetical reality that has real time-space historical elements (the Hundred Years' War, the Abbey at Saint Mary, the practice of arraying for the King), to the third fytte, where the narrator moves away from this historical context and to another context, one that appears to be from a different tale or ballad, and which therefore disrupts any sense of true historical reality.⁴⁹

The third fytte begins with the author in full command:

> Lyth and lystyn, gentilmen,
> All that nowe be here,
> Of Litell Johnn, that was the knightes man,   *servant*
> Goode myrth ye shall here.⁵⁰   *hear*

The narrator, it appears, is in full command of the text. He has chosen to insert into the narrative and historical frame a tale that feels and reads as if it has come from another source. This fytte, which may be labeled "Little John and the Sheriff," can be read as a tale all in its own. Once again, Robin is virtually absent, arriving at the very end of the fytte. The fytte is concerned with Little John adopting the alias of Reynolde Grenelefe. As Reynolde, Little John plays the part of the bad servant while the sheriff employs him. After a tussle with the kitchen staff, John tricks the sheriff into being captured by Robin. As Clawson argues, "the introduction, out of their proper consecutive order, of the adventures of Little John, reveals itself on analysis as an admirable artistic construction, and furnishes another striking piece of evidence of the skill of the compiler."[51] The author/compiler, it seems, was not caught up in producing a text to be read and seen as historical reality. The context of the third fytte of Little John's adventure, and the notion that it derived from an earlier tale or an entire cycle of Little John stories, seem probable. Like the opening of the *Gest*, the narrator does not provide any background on Little John, for it was most likely understood by the audience and deems unnecessary for inclusion in the text; moreover, the elaboration on Little John's or Robin Hood's backgrounds would be superfluous to the overall reason for telling the story. This seems rather important, that the author/compiler was very aware of his audience's knowledge of tales. By our expectations today, what was left unsaid in this text could be seen as a lapse of discipline on behalf of the narrator; however, by leaving out the history of Little John and folding his tale skillfully into the *Gest*, the narrator shows his social and cultural connection with his audience. The narrator here asks the audience to do something courageous: follow his lead and have faith in where the story takes you, for you may learn something in the end. If the audience is unable (or unwilling) to make that leap, they will still have an entertaining tale to keep them happy. In our society, this performer-audience connection is a rarity. Jameson comments that "what was hitherto a cultural institution — the storytelling situation itself, with its narrator and class public — now fades into the silence and the solitude of the individual writer, confronted with the absence of a reading public as with some form of the absence of God."[52] The modern novel, Jameson argues, is no longer a medium for a societal exchange of ideas, but rather a medium by which authors can forge individual sentences for the practice of style. Style, it seems, is not an issue for the *Gest*; if it were, fytte three would most likely be absent.

Because the *Gest* is a compilation of various stories from different sources, to contextualize them in a true historical time would be difficult.[53] However, Thomas Ohlgren identifies King Edward III (1327–77) as the person whom the narrator calls on several occasions "our comely king." The phrase "our comly king" has, as Ohlgren points out, "recently been discovered in the political poetry of Laurence Minot, who wrote eleven poems in Middle English commemorating English victories against the Scots and the French, between March 1333, the Battle of Halidon Hill, and the capture of the French town Guines in January 1352."[54] Yet the *Gest*, as we have seen, is a text with multiple contexts. The poet of the *Gest*, its compiler, and (if the text was performed) its speaker may have transferred the allusions from Edward III to Edward IV, for the latter was king, as Ohlgren notes, "during or shortly after the period 1461–83" when the *Gest* was composed.[55] W. M. Ormrod has also observed the significance of the "brode targe" [shield][56] that Edward takes out is in fact a reference to the king's privy seal, and that the "references in the *Gest* to the specific use of the privy seal in the letter summoning Robin to Nottingham carry certain messages about notions of privileged access to the king."[57] Our author's allusions to Edward III are mostly seen towards the end of the *Gest*, where Robin and the King meet in a "King and the Subject" story; in the final two fyttes the line "our comely king" is repeated six times. Works such as *King Edward and the Shepherd* and *King Edward and the Hermit*, both dated c. 1450, show that Edward III apparently made a habit of meeting his subjects in disguise, having a meal with them, listening to their complaints, and then pardoning and rewarding them for any poaching done on the King's land.[58] Thomas Hoccleve, in his *Regiment of Princes*, also alludes to this practice:

> O worthy Kyng benigne, Edward the laste,
> Thow haddist ofte in herte a drede impressid,
> Which that thyn humble goost ful sore agaste;   *frightened*
> And to knowe if thow cursid were or blessid,
> Among the peple ofte hastow thee dressid
> Into contree in symple array allone
> To heere what men seide of thy persone.[59]

Like these authors, the compiler of the *Gest* has taken these accounts of Edward III out of their historical context and placed them within a larger, more subjective literary context. Past scholars have also tried to place the character of the king in the *Gest* in his own proper historical context. Joseph Hunter states that the king is Edward II because he had a *valet de chambre* in 1324 by the name of Robin Hood of Wakefield.[60] Dobson and Taylor counter this argument by pointing out that, "there is no direct evidence whatsoever that he Wakefield Robin Hoods(s) of the early fourteenth century was ever an outlaw, or indeed a criminal at all."[61] Stephen Knight states that the reign of Edward IV (1461–83) is consistent with the *Gest,* due to a portrait depicting the King in the National Portrait Gallery as being very handsome and having a large head, fitting the two phrases "our comely king" (lines 353 and 365) and "grete above his cole" (line 372).[62] This historical context of Edward III's or Edward IV's reign within the *Gest* may in fact be secondary to the social and territorial context of London, where the *Gest* was printed and possibly written and compiled.

Moreover, this connection between Robin Hood and London may have yet more areas of shared interest: the destitute knight of the story, Sir Richard at the Lee, whom Robin and his band befriend, and the corpus of civic historical writings of late-medieval England that combine historical events with literary flourishes, and here I am thinking specifically of the London chronicles of the Fifteenth Century. John Bellamy argues that the knight in the *Gest* was one Richard de la Lee who became parson of Arksey in 1319.[63] However, it remains unclear just how old the *Gest* is, and since no extant manuscripts exist, the dating of the poem rests on the printings of the early texts and on historical allusions, the latter option always being somewhat dubious. What Bellamy did not consider is that the historical time as seen in the *Gest* may in fact be more closely related temporally to its early printed forms. The Sir Richard at the Lee in the *Gest* may in fact be Sir Richard Lee (d. 1472), who was a Grocer, the mayor of London in 1460 and 1470, and an alderman of the Queenhithe ward in London from 1452 until his death.[64] Richard Lee, along with other past and current London civic leaders, was knighted by Edward IV in 1471 for his honorable service in the Wars of the Roses "agaynst the bastard, and his crwell hooste," Henry VI.[65] This is not to say that Richard Lee was a Yorkist; Polydore Virgil recounts that in October 1470, after Edward IV and his brother Richard fled to Flanders, Richard Lee, along with the sheriffs of London, Robert Draper and Richard Gardener, "delyveryd king Henry owt of pryson" and "unto the chirche of St. Paule, the people on the right and left hand rejoysing with clapping of hands, and crying, God save king Henry."[66] None of the chronicles that describe Edward's French expeditions mentions Sir Richard Lee the mayor and alderman. However, with the mercantile allusions so prevalent in the *Gest* and other Robin Hood poems, it is not improbable to speculate that like the London chronicles, *A Gest of Robyn Hode* was written for a growing middle class who had sizable political and monetary powers, and whose contents were concerned not with the crown but with their own social and civic interests.[67]

The line between reality and fiction is a hazy one in the *Gest*, and the author has contextualized historical events and individuals so as to add a literal element to the story. It is here important to remember two of F. R. Ankersmit's theses on the Narrativist Philosophy of History: "1.0: Historical narratives are interpretations of the past ... 1.4: Narrative interpretations are not necessarily of a sequential nature; historical narratives are only contingently stories with a beginning, a middle, and an end."[68] *A Gest of Robyn Hode* is a story whose compiler contextualized certain textual elements, thus creating a text where the narrator, the audience, and certain "real" historical events all played important roles in the artistic production of the epic poem. While it is not "pure" history, the *Gest* is, nonetheless, an impressively woven set of tales that holds an inherent mercantile ideology within the narrative structure, and which draws upon other historical and literary sources to contextualize the narrative for the reader and audience. In the *Gest,* the narrator is the individual who has the power, through his expressed ideology and his style, to shape history. *A Gest of Robyn Hode* remains a text where the contexts that were created and implemented by the author/compiler remain a dominant force in uncovering and understanding the ideology of the text and its notions of historical representation.

NOTES

1. Stephen Knight, "Robin Hood: The Earliest Contexts," in *Images of Robin Hood: Medieval to Modern,* ed. Lois Potter and Joshua Calhoun (Newark: University of Delaware Press, 2008), 21–40.
2. William Hill Clawson, *The Gest of Robin Hood* (Toronto: University of Toronto Library, 1909), 1.
3. Hayden White, *Metahistory: The Historical Imagination in Nineteenth Century Europe* (Baltimore: Johns Hopkins University Press, 1973), 11. The seminal study on medieval historiography that embraces the "linguistic turn" is Gabrielle M. Spiegel's *The Past as Text: The Theory and Practice of Medieval Historiography* (Baltimore and London: Johns Hopkins University Press, 1997). The theorist who dominates Spiegel's work is Jacques Derrida, especially his early works *Of Grammatology, Writing and Difference,* and *Dissemination.* Spiegel comments that in examining medieval chronicles, she was "employing a technique of interpretation that was coming to the fore in literary study itself and that, in its largest sense, has been termed the 'linguistic turn.' The principle effect of the 'linguistic turn,' for historians, has been to alert us to the mediating force of language in the representation of the past, and thus help us to understand that there is no direct access to historical events or persons, so that all historical writing, whether medieval or modern, approaches the past via discourses of one sort or another," xvi–xvii.
4. White, *Metahistory,* 18.
5. Ibid., 19.
6. *A Gest of Robyn Hode* is a text that could also be read as a narrative that looks back at two older tales, *Robin Hood and the Monk* and *Robin Hood and the Potter,* and works through certain concepts initially introduced in those two (slightly) older works. See Ohlgren 2007, 26.
7. This is a technique that comedians, politicians, and many invited speakers frequently adopt: they often personalize their performance (or at the very least parts of it) to fit the attitude of their audience and the particular moment of hand. The Greek term *kairos* is here an apt one, for there appears to be a "timely" quality to the execution of the narrative.
8. Knight and Ohlgren, 80–168 at 90, lines 1–4.
9. There is much debated as to who the correct audience was for *A Gest of Robyn Hode.* See Holt, 109–159; Rodney H. Hilton, "The Origins of Robin Hood," *Past and Present* 14 (1958): 30–44; and Keen, xi–xxi. Hilton sees the poem as a creation intended for peasant yeomen who were unsatisfied with their economic situation, while Holt believes that the popularity of Robin Hood lies in its connection with the landed gentry, the northern aristocracy, and the household retainers. In the fist edition of Keen's book, the scholar agreed with Hilton, but in the introduction to his second and subsequent edition he recanted.
10. Fredric Jameson, "Criticism in History," in *Criticism: Major Statements,* ed. Charles

Kaplan and William Anderson, 3rd ed. (New York: St. Martin's Press, 1991), 574–94 at 578.

11. The language of the *Gest* could be related to the type of entertainment it is and where it may have been performed: at an open-air environment, such as a pub or tavern, a hall, or an outdoor festival. On the possible performative aspects of the *Gest* in a guildhall, see Dean A. Hoffman, "'I wyll be thy true servaunte / And trewely serve thee': Guildhall Minstrelsy in the *Gest of Robyn Hode*," *The Drama Review* 49, no. 2 (2005): 119–34; and Ohlgren 2007, 163–69.

12. Knight and Ohlgren, 8.

13. Knight and Ohlgren, 85.

14. The various entries for s.v., "prŏud" (adj) in the *MED* further illustrate the various ways one could interpret the sheriff's behavior: "1(a) Guilty of the sin of Pride; haughty, arrogant; also, obstinate, rebellious." and "4(a) Noble, excellent, splendid; (b) noble in bearing or appearance."

15. *MED*, s.v., "ǧentīl" (adj): "1(a) Of noble rank or birth, belonging to the gentry, noble;—often implying character or manners befitting one of gentle birth;—also used of Christ. 2(a) Having the character or manners prescribed by the ideals of chivalry or Christianity; noble, kind, gracious, etc.; (b) courteous, polite, well-bred, charming; graceful, beautiful, handsome."

16. Jameson, "Criticism in History," 582.

17. Knight and Ohlgren, 82.

18. Thomas H. Ohlgren, "The 'Marchaunt' of Sherwood: Mercantile Ideology in *A Gest of Robyn Hode*," in Hahn, 175–90 at 181.

19. We can begin to see the rise of this new middle class during the Black Death of 1349 and certainly after the Peasants Revolt of 1381, a revolt that started in part as a reaction against the Ordinance of Laborers Act of 1349 and the subsequent Statute of Laborers Act of 1351; both acts froze wages at pre-plague levels.

20. Ohlgren, "The 'Marchaunt' of Sherwood," 175–76.

21. As Ohlgren argues throughout his book, there is not just one *Gest* but several; therefore, much like the various versions of William Langland's *Piers Plowman*, there is not just one audience or ideology of the *Gest*. When reading the later versions of the *Gest*, for example William Copland's 1560 edition, it is important to recognize the interests of Protestant printers and readers; see Ohlgren 2007, 128–34.

22. Hayden White, *The Content of the Form: Narrative Discourse and Historical Representation* (Baltimore: Johns Hopkins University Press, 1987), 27.

23. Dobson and Taylor, 74.

24. Knight and Ohlgren, 91, lines 29–40.

25. Ohlgren, "The 'Marchaunt' of Sherwood,'" 178.

26. In particular, see Stephen H. Rigby, "Urban 'Oligarchy' in Late Medieval England," in *Towns and Townspeople in the Fifteenth Century*, ed. John A. F. Thomas (Gloucester: Alan Sutton, 1988), 62–86; and Sheila Lindenbaum, "Ceremony and Oligarchy: The London Midsummer Watch," in *City and Spectacle in Medieval Europe*, ed. Barbara A. Hanawalt and Kathryn L. Reason. Medieval Studies 6 (Minneapolis and London: University of Minnesota, 1994), 171–88. We should also keep in mind Chaucer's portrait of the five guildsmen in his *General Prologue* to *The Canterbury Tales*, for all five are more concerned about their outward appearance of wealth and power rather than any notion of charitable benevolence.

27. Knight and Ohlgren, 94, lines 125–28.

28. White, *The Content of the Form*, 29.

29. Fredric Jameson, *The Political Unconscious: Narrative as a Socially Symbolic Act* (Ithaca: Cornell University Press, 1981), 20.

30. See Ohlgren, "The 'Marchaunt' of Sherwood,'" 180–83, for a complete list of cloth and clothing references and guild terminology.

31. Knight and Ohlgren, 98–99, lines 277–96.

32. Ohlgren, "'Marchaunt' of Sherwood," 8.

33. Knight and Ohlgren, 143, lines 1669–72.

34. Thomas Ohlgren, "Edwardus redivivus in *A Gest of Robyn Hode*," *Journal of English and German Philology* 99, no. 1 (2000): 1–28 at 25.

35. See Michel Foucault, *The Order of Things: An Archaeology of the Human Sciences* (New

York: Vintage, 1970), 166–208. Here, Foucault examines the rise of mercantilism alongside the regulation of currency.

36. In a certain sense, here the text could also be seen as a warning to the guild members that they should not forget their original purpose: to provide care and support for those in need.

37. Karl Marx and Friedrich Engels, "The Communist Manifesto," in *Karl Marx: On Revolution*, ed. and trans. S. K. Padover (New York: McGraw-Hill, 1971), 81.

38. Holt, 17.

39. Clawson, *The Gest of Robin Hood*, 128.

40. Francis James Child, ed., *The English and Scottish Popular Ballads*, 5 vol. (New York: Dover, 1965), 3: 50.

41. The knight is a fine example of just how deep the corruption of power and religious sensibilities and the mismanagement of resources had affected once proud and virtuous members of the first estate.

42. White, *The Content of the Form*, 5.

43. Knight and Ohlgren, 100, lines 321–28.

44. Ibid., 100–08.

45. Ibid., 101, lines 353–54.

46. Ibid., 106, lines 517–32.

47. Ohlgren, "Edwardus redivivus," 5–6.

48. Hayden White, *Tropics of Discourse: Essays in Cultural Criticism* (Baltimore: Johns Hopkins University Press, 1978), 121.

49. As Clawson notes, stanzas 17–44 and 208–251 are similar in their word choice and usage and in their narrative progression, and he argues that this demonstrates how the narrator was skillful in his parallelism and construction of the text. See *The Gest of Robin Hood*, 9–15.

50. Knight and Ohlgren, 108, lines 573–76.

51. Clawson, *The Gest of Robin Hood*, 59.

52. Jameson, "Criticism in History," 597.

53. Knight and Ohlgren suggest that"[t]he only major source suggested for the *Gest* is the Robin Hood ballads themselves, and the scholars have often pointed out how the rescue of the knight from Nottingham is in many ways similar to *Robin Hood and the Monk*, how John tricks the sheriff much as Robin does in *Robin Hood and the Potter*, and the final stanzas relate to *The Death of Robin Hood* in some way," 82. Clawson, *The Gest of Robin* Hood, 25–43, believes that the story of Richard at the Lee was based on two "Miracle of the Virgin" tales: *The Merchant's Surety*, c. 1390, and Wynkyn de Worde's late fourteenth century printing of *The Myracles of Oure Lady*.

54. Ohlgren, "Edwardus redivivus," 4.

55. Ohlgren 2007, 148.

56. Knight and Ohlgren, 139, line 1537.

57. W. M. Ormrod, "Robin Hood and the Public Record: The Authority of Writing in the Medieval Outlaw Tradition," in *Medieval Cultural Studies: Essays in Honour of Stephen Knight*, ed. Ruth Evans, Helen Fulton, and David Matthews (Cardiff: University of Wales Press, 2006), 57–74 at 65.

58. Ohlgren, "Edwardus redivivus," 10. This practice could very well be a fictitious creation created by the king and his nobility to get over an ideology; indeed, a king should respect and encourage his people under the law of God first, then his own. For the text of *King Edward and the Shepherd*, see Walter Hoyt French and Charles Brockway Hale, ed., *Middle English Metrical Romances*, 2 vol. (New York: Russel and Russel, 1964), 2: 949–85. For *King Edward and the Hermit*, see Charles H. Hartshorne, ed., *Ancient Metrical Tales* (London: William Pickering, 1829), 293–315.

59. Thomas Hoccleve, *The Regiment of Princes*, ed. Charles R. Blyth. TEAMS Middle English Texts (Kalamazoo: Medieval Institute Publications, 1999), 114, lines 2556–62.

60. See Joseph Hunter, "The Great Hero of the Ancient Minstrelsy of England: Robin Hood, his Period, real Character, etc., Investigated," *Critical and Historical Tracts* 4 (London:

Smith, 1852), 28–38.
  61. Dobson and Taylor, 13.
  62. Knight 1994, 47–48.
  63. John Bellamy, *Robin Hood: An Historical Inquiry* (Bloomington: Indiana University Press, 1984), 73–109.
  64. See Ohlgren 2007, 169–72.
  65. John Bruce, ed., *The Historie of the Arrival of King Edward IV*, Camden Society, o.s., 1 (London: Royal Historical Society, 1838; repr. New York: AMS Press, 1968), 38 and 46.
  66. Polydore Virgil, *Three Books of Polydore Virgil's English History, Comprising the Reigns of Henry VI, Edward IV, and Richard III*, ed. Henry Ellis. Camden Society, o.s., 29 (London: Royal Historical Society, 1844; repr., New York: AMS Press, 1968), 133. For a brief description of Sir Richard Lee's career, see Sylvia L. Thrupp, *The Merchant Class of Medieval London* (Ann Arbor: The University of Michigan Press, 1948; repr. 1962), 353.
  67. For studies on the London Chronicles of the fifteenth century, see Charles Lethbridge Kingsford, *English Historical Literature in the Fifteenth Century* (1913; New York: Burt Franklin, repr. 1972), 70–112; Edward Donald Kennedy, *A Manual of the Writings in Middle English 1050–1500, Volume 8: Chronicles and Other Historical Writings* (New Haven: Archon, 1989), 2647–54; and Mary-Rose McLaren, *The London Chronicles of the Fifteenth Century: A Revolution in English Writing, With an Annotated Edition of Bradford, West Yorkshire Archives MS 32D86/42* (Cambridge: D. S. Brewer, 2002).
  68. F. R. Ankersmit, *History and Tropology: The Rise and Fall of Metaphor* (Berkeley: University of California Press, 1994), 33.

9

Popular Devotion and Prosperity Gospel in Early Robin Hood Tales

CRYSTAL KIRGISS

As one of the most endearing characters of English literary legends, Robin Hood is also one of the most enduring.[1] From the first recorded mention of him in various medieval texts to numerous Hollywood images of the 20th Century — a silent Douglas Fairbanks of the 1920s, a swashbuckling Errol Flynn of the 1930s, an animated sly fox of the early 1970s, an aged Sean Connery of the late 1970s, an American-English speaking Kevin Costner of the early 1990s, an equally British-English speaking Patrick Bergen of the same year, an off-color Cary Elwes of the mid 1990s, and many more — Robin Hood has persistently made himself known to a broad and popular audience, managing to morph his way into multiple identities, each of which serves its particular context uniquely. Those who grew up watching the contemporary cinematic versions of this green-clad hero would be hard-pressed if asked to identify his original setting and description. Far from the modern day displaced nobleman whose sole purpose in life is to rob the wicked rich to serve the pious poor during the reign of King Richard I, Robin Hood began his life as a frowned-upon delinquent who threatened the social, religious, and legal stability of his day. Ironically, this legendary hero, who was denounced extra-textually by pious religious leaders, was applauded inter-textually in early tales as a devout and devoted follower of the Virgin Mary and the sacred Mass. This study is an attempt to examine and ultimately refute these claims of the outlaw's pure devotion, for though Robin Hood does verbally proclaim his commitment to Our Lady, and though he seemingly forsakes his own personal interests in order to partake of regular and frequent attendance at Mass, a close reading of several early Robin Hood texts reveals that he in fact is devoted to the Virgin only insofar as it serves his own mostly financial purposes.

The early history of Robin Hood's literary and historical references has been well-documented in numerous scholarly publications. Almost all of these references have something to say about Robin Hood's religiosity, or lack thereof. One of the first is recorded by Walter Bower, a Scottish historian, in his continuation of John of Fordun's *Scotichronicon*, c. 1445:

> Then arose the famous murderer, Robert Hood, as well as Little John, together with their accomplices from among the disinherited, whom the foolish populace are so inordinately fond of celebrating both in tragedies and comedies, and about whom they are delighted to hear the jesters and minstrels sing above all other ballads. About whom also certain praiseworthy things are told, as appears in this — that when once in Barnsdale, avoiding the anger of the king and the threats of the prince, he was according to his custom most devoutly hearing Mass and had no wish on any account to interrupt the service — on a certain day, when he was hearing Mass, having been discovered in that very secluded place in the woods when the Mass was taking place by a certain sheriff (*viscount*) who had very often lain in wait for him previously, there came to him those who had found this out from their men to suggest that he should make every effort to flee. This, on account of his reverence for the sacrament in which he was then devoutly involved, he completely refused to do. But the rest of his men trembling through fear of death, Robert, trusting in the one so great whom he worshipped, with the few who then bravely remained with him, confronted his enemies and easily overcame them, and enriched by the spoils he took from them and their ransom, ever afterward singled out the servants of the church and the Masses to be held in greater respect, bearing in mind what is commonly said: "God harkens to him who hears Mass frequently."[2]

Some may point to this reference as proof of Robin's religious devotion and genuine Christian beliefs, but there are several interesting things to note in this regard. First, Robin is referred to as a "famous murderer" replete with accomplices, a role that would seem to contradict true Christian devotion. Second, he is "inordinately" adored and celebrated by the "foolish populace," a comment that seems to reflect either bitter jealousy (perhaps Bower wished he himself were inordinately adored and celebrated by the foolish populace?) or more likely to provide commentary on the ill-advised and misdirected devotion that foolish people have towards the likes of Robin Hood instead of Our Lord and Savior, Jesus Christ. Third, Robin Hood's faith is transformed within this short text from someone who is merely a devout hearer of the Mass to someone who, after being "enriched by the spoils he took from [his enemies] and their ransom," consciously committed to holding the "servants of the church and the Masses ... in greater respect." According to Bower's account, this change in devotional depth is not a result of "confront[ing] his enemies and easily overc[oming] them," something for which Robin perhaps should have thanked God, but rather is based primarily on the lucrative payoff of spoils and ransom. In this instance, Robin is more grateful for the monetary return God provides than for the preservation of his physical or spiritual well-being. As Bower so aptly points out to his listeners and readers, "God harkens to him who hears Mass frequently," or, as Singman translates it, "To him God gives ear who does often Mass hear."[3] This early account of Robin Hood sets a foundation for my theory that his religious devotion is based in large part on financial prosperity and gain. Fourth, this early text is clearly non-anti-clerical in tone. In other early Robin Hood tales and ballads, Robin's supposedly pure religion is often pitted against that of professional religious leaders, especially monks. But here, Robin goes so far as to hold "servants of the church ... in greater respect," a sentiment that would be contradicted in later texts. However, because these particular "servants of the church" are apparently connected to the service of the Mass, they are also connected to the proverbial payoff with which Bower concludes. That is, these "servants of the church" will be respected by Robin Hood insofar as they have a causal effect on God's harkening ear.

Those who are familiar with 21st Century proponents and adherents of what is commonly called the Prosperity Gospel (also referred to as Word of Faith or Name It and Claim It)[4] may find Robin's brand of religiosity, as recorded in Bower, familiar. According to this religious doctrine, God's deepest desire is for his children to be happy, healthy, financially comfortable, financially stable, and even financially prosperous. This is in direct opposition to the actual gospel of Christ, which reminds readers that those who follow Him risk ridicule, misunderstanding, rejection, opposition, and even possibly loss of worldly possessions as recorded in the collected sermons and saying of Jesus found in Matthew, Chapters 5 through 7, as well as other Biblical passages.

Direct references to Robin Hood's religious devotion are mentioned in two of the earliest ballads, *Robin Hood and the Monk* and *Robin Hood and the Potter*.[5] In *Monk*, Robin is identified as a "kynggis felon" (line 85), a known thief. The ballad opens with a description of the countryside, and Little John's declaration of happiness and contentment. It continues:

"Ye, on thyng greves me," seid Robyn,	*one*
"And does my hert mych woo:	*woe*
That I may not no solem day	
To mas nor matyns goo.	*Mass nor Matins*
"Hit is a fourtnet and more," seid he,	*It's been a fortnight*
"Syn I my Savyour see;	*Since I've been to Mass*
To day wil I to Notyngham," seid Robyn,	
"With the myght of mylde Marye."	*Virgin Mary*
Whan Robyn came to Notyngham,	
Sertenly withouten layn,	*Certainly; lie*

> He prayed to God and myld Mary
> To bryng hym out save again.   *safe*
>
> He gos in to Seynt Mary chirch,
> And knelyd down before the Rode;   *Cross*
> Alle that ever were the church within
> Beheld wel Robyn Hode.⁶

Neither God nor Mild Mary answers Robin Hood's request to "bring hym out save again." Instead, he is spotted by a previously robbed monk, identified to the sheriff, captured, and imprisoned. When Little John hears of Robin's situation, he says:

> "He has servyd Oure Lady many a day,
> And yet wil, securly;   *surely*
> Therfor I trust in hir specialy
> No wyckud death shal he dye.
>
> "Therfor be glad," seid Litul John,
> "And let this mournyng be;
> And I shal be the munkis gyde,   *take care of the monk*
> With the myght of mylde Mary…"⁷

After several murders, numerous lies, and multiple deceptions, Little John frees Robin from prison and says:

> "I have done the a gode turne for an ill,
> Quit me whan thou may."⁸   *repay*

There is no mention of thanks to God, nor to mild Mary, and Little John goes so far as to credit himself with the rescue, though he had earlier stated that it would only be with the "myght of mylde Mary" that his task would be successful. The religion of both Robin Hood and Little John seems selective; that is, when it suits their purposes, God and Mary be praised. When it does not, well then, Robin and John be praised.

Religion is also a topic in *Robin Hood and the Potter* where the audience is introduced as "god yemen, / comely, corteys, and god," (that is, fair, well-bred, and good), before Robin is described as

> On of the best that yever bare bowe,   *One; ever bore*
> Hes name was Roben Hode.
>
> Roben Hood was the yemans name,
> That was boyt corteys and fre;   *both courteous and generous*
> For the loffe of owre ladey,   *love of our lady (Virgin Mary)*
> All wemen werschepyd he.⁹   *honored*

After exchanging identities with a potter, Robin Hood departs for Nottingham to sell his newly acquired pots, but not without a warning from Little John regarding the sheriff. Robin replies:

"Thorow the helpe of Howr Ladey,	*With; Our Lady*
Felowhes, let me alone.	
Heyt war howte!" sayde Roben,	*Gee up!*
"To Notynggam well Y gon."¹⁰	*will I go*

Robin Hood then sets out on what he hopes will be a prosperous and successful venture, a venture that is certainly less than pious and Christian in that he intentionally undercuts fellow merchants in his attempts to goad the sheriff. Robin also makes advances towards the sheriff's wife,¹¹ an ironic twist on the early ballad line, "For the loffe of our ladey, All wemen wersheypd he." Worshipped, indeed.

The pottys that were worthe pens feyffe,	*five pence*
He solde tham for pens thre;	
Preveley sayde man and weyffe,	*Privately; woman*
"Ywnder potter schall never the."¹²	*Yonder; prosper*

The townspeople recognize that Robin Hood-as-potter would never prosper by selling his pots for less-than-market value, but in the early Robin Hood ballads and plays the outlaw never prospered, so far as we know, by selling things for fair market value, or by putting in a hard day's work for that matter, unless that hard day of work included shooting and eating the king's deer. In this particular situation, he prospers by getting close access to the sheriff (and in the process, hurting the business of his fellow potters), by luring the sheriff into the forest under false pretences, and then by stealing the sheriff's horse and riding gear. After a long day of "work," Robin is more prosperous, and because he did not harm any women in the process (one wonders whether Robin gave any thought as to how his actions might have affected the wives of the potters who were essentially out of work during Robin's stunt), he feels justified in calling himself a "trow Cerstyn man," that is, a "true Christian man."¹³

A Gest of Robyn Hode also includes references to Robin's religious beliefs and behaviors:

A gode maner than had Robyn;	*custom*
In londe where that he were,	
Every day or he wold dyne	*before*
Thre messis wolde he here.	*masses, hear*
The one in the worship of the Fader,	
And another of the Holy Gost,	
The thirde of Our dere Lady,	*Virgin Mary*
That he loved allther moste.	*the most of all*
Robyn loved Oure dere Lady:	
For dout of dydly synne,	*fear; of deadly sin*
Wolde he never do compani harme	
That any woman was in.¹⁴	

These opening lines reflect a parallel religious devotion to that mentioned in *Robin Hood and the Potter*; because he is devoted to the Virgin Mary, Robin will never harm a woman. One might be justified in supposing that the reason Robin is explicitly devoted to the Virgin Mary rather than Jesus Christ is because then, for the love of Our Dear Savior, he would be required to do no harm to any man or any company of men, which would in effect put Robin Hood out of business.

Robin Hood's devotion to, and reliance on, the Virgin Mary over and above that of Jesus Christ is made abundantly clear when he encounters an impoverished knight who is in need of 400 pounds that he plans to use in order to repay a debt and reclaim his land. While Robin considers whether or not to loan the knight the required funds, the following exchange takes place:

> "Hast thou any frende," sayde Robyn,
> "Thy borowe that would be?"   *security (guarantee)*
> "I have none," than sayde the knyght,
> "But God that dyed on tree."   *Except; the Cross*
>
> "Do away thy japis," than sayde Robyn,   *jokes*
> "Thereof wol I right non;
> Wenest thou I wolde have God to borowe,   *Think you*
> Peter, Poule, or Johnn?
>
> "Nay, by Hym that me made,
> And shope both sonne and mone,   *created*
> Fynde me a better borowe," sayde Robyn,   *security*
> Or money getest thou none."
>
> "I have none other," sayde the knight,
> "The sothe for to say,
> But yf yt be Our dere Lady;   *Unless*
> She fayled me never or thys day."   *failed; before*
>
> "By dere worthy God," sayde Robyn,
> "To seche all Englonde thorowe,
> Yet fonde I never to my pay   *pleasure*
> A moche better borowe."[15]   *security*

Robin's disgust with the knight's suggestion that Jesus Christ would provide sufficient security for a loan (ironic, since the major doctrine of Christianity is that Christ willingly paid a debt that he did not owe in order to save humanity from a debt that it could not pay), and his correlating acceptance of Mary as the best of all loan guarantees are reflective of popular religious beliefs during the later Middle Ages.[16] Throughout this era, the justice of God and Christ became more and more separated from the mercy of Mary. St. Anselm refers to Christ as "judge of the world" and Mary as "reconciler of the world."[17] He also writes of her that "it is incredible that you should not have mercy on the miserable men who implore you." One of Anselm's English disciples, Eadmer, a Benedictine monk, wrote the following words:

> Sometimes salvation is quicker if we remember Mary's name than if we invoke the name of the Lord Jesus ... Her Son is the Lord and Judge of all men, discerning the merits of the individuals, hence he does not at once answer anyone who invokes him, but does it only after just judgment. But if the name of his Mother be invoked, her merits intercede so that he is answered even if the merits of him who invokes her do not deserve it.[18]

Hilda Graef makes the following observation about how such doctrinal teachings affected popular belief in the middle ages:

> So we have here the naïve idea that it takes Christ some time to weigh the pros and cons of a case, whereas if we turn to his mother he no longer judges but only considers her merits and grants a man's prayer at once — a view which became quite common and explains why, in the Middle Ages and after, prayer to Mary so often almost superseded prayer to Christ in popular devotion.[19]

This explains Robin's exclusive devotion to Mary, as well as his exclusive acceptance of her as the loan guarantee. Not only did it reflect the popular religious practice of his day, but it also uniquely fit his situation and lifestyle as an outlaw, thief, and deceiver. If he had accepted the knight's original offer of Jesus Christ as security for a loan, Robin Hood would have run the risk of being judged in both motive and action by Christ, and subsequently the outlaw would have been found lacking in genuine religious piety, a finding that may have weakened his chances for repayment. In popular religious belief of the Middle Ages, the general populace had a felt need for a mediator between themselves and Christ, in the same way that Christ served as a mediator between themselves and God.[20] This role was filled by Mary, "more powerful than the saints and less awful than God; as His mother she had a quite peculiar influence with Christ."[21] Robin Hood reflects this popular belief to some extent, but as will be discussed, he ultimately turns it on its head and makes it more about money and prosperity than anything else. Sometime between 1435 and 1440, Johann Herolt, a Dominican friar in the convent at Nuremberg, wrote *The Miracles of the Blessed Virgin Mary*, and these following remarks that discuss the role of Mary in regards to those who transgress are significant:

> Although the Virgin was ever gracious to chivalry and to great bishops of the church, it was the common people that she loved the best, poor clerks, humble monks and nuns (the lower ranks of the ecclesiastical hierarchy) and simple laymen, jonglcurs and thieves and poor mothers of erring sons ... most strange to modern minds appears the Virgin's predilection for the disreputable.... The moral to be drawn from some of her miracles does not seem a very lofty one, laying, as it does, so much stress on purely verbal exercises, the recital of the Angelic Salutation outweighing a lifetime of ill-doing.[22]

This description of Marian devotion seems to have been written with Robin Hood in mind, for not only does the outlaw deliver verbal platitudes to the Virgin, but he also is the recipient of what some believe is his own personal Miracle of the Virgin,[23] an event that I believe is more aptly viewed as a Miracle of Robin, and that reflects the prosperity gospel referred to earlier.

The conditions for Robin Hood's loan to the impoverished knight are that the funds must be repaid within one year. Twelve months later, Little John and Robin have the following exchange:

> "Go we to dyner," sayde Littell Johnn;
> Robyn Hode sayde, "Nay,
> For I drede Our Lady be wroth with me,   *angry*
> For she sent me nat my pay."
>
> "Have no doute, maister," sayde Litell Johnn,
> "Yet is nat the sonne at rest;
> For I dare say, and savely swere,   *safely*
> The knight is true and truste."[24]

This, then, is the extent of Robin's confidence in Mary. The good outlaw, who so quickly pays lip service to Our Lady, is filled with doubt when faith is most required. Little John, on the other hand, reassures him that the day is not yet done, and so there is time to wait for repayment. But Robin, in his impatience, or perhaps lack of trust, takes matters into his own hands and sends Little John, Much, and William Scarlock (i. e., Will Scarlett) into town to fetch a guest and bring him back to the greenwood. His men bring back a Benedictine monk who, it turns out, is in possession of 800 pounds. Upon this discovery, Little John says to Robin:

> "Our Lady hath doubled your cast."   *doubled your throw (the knight's loan)*
> "I make myn avowe to God," sayd Robyn,
> Monke, what tolde I the?
> Our Lady is the trewest woman
> That ever yet founde I me."[25]

Robin once again pays verbal homage to the Virgin, but in fact, if he had truly believed in her power as both Mother of God and guarantee of the knight's loan, he would have waited either for the knight's return or for Mary's direct intercession. This is popular devotion *a la* Robin Hood, a devotion that is one of two things: practiced only when convenient, or contrived to fit the situation. So is this unexpected discovery of 800 pounds a miracle of the Virgin, or is it only a fortunately profitable score by Robin Hood and his men?

There are numerous recorded miracles of the Virgin from the Middle Ages.[26] Of these, many feature robbers or thieves that resemble Robin Hood in some respects. In Herolt's collection, Miracle V begins:

> There was once a very great robber, a most wicked man.... Yet he had this good in him that he scrupulously fasted on bread and water during the vigil of the Blessed Mary; and, when he went out to rob he used to salute her with such devotion as he could, asking her not to allow him to die in mortal sin.[27]

Miracle XLV says:

> There was a certain great robber who had never done any good, except that he had fasted on Saturday in honour of the Blessed Virgin and kept one mass to her, that she might convert him before his death.[28]

From Miracle L:

> There was a certain man who was religious in name only, but, wherever true religion was concerned, hardhearted and careless. He was, however, in the habit of praying to the Blessed Virgin and saying once every day a hundred "Hail, Mary's."[29]

And from Miracle XCVI:

> ... there is a wood frequented by a very notorious robber, by whom many people were plundered, who were slain if they attempted to defend themselves and could not.
> Having, however, one day met a monk of the Order of Preachers and hoping he possessed and carried with him money, the robber said: "Unless you follow me willingly I shall kill you."[30]

In response to the monk's question about his life, the robber says: "...going on to manhood, I engaged in brigandage, in which I was so successful that to-day I am the head and master of all the brigands in this province."[31] The monk encourages the robber to seek salvation for his soul by following a few simple steps: "Fast one day a week in honour of Mary the holy Mother of God and do no hurt to any one on that day." The robber agrees, and adds that on that day he "will rob no man and harm no woman."[32]

Though there is no definitive proof that the Robin Hood legends found their source in the immensely popular miracle tales of that era, Evelyn Underhill points out "it was among the people that the Mary-legends prospered and to the people that they were primarily addressed ... they were a part of the texture of the common life.... In England, where devotion to Our Lady has always flourished, her miracles were well known and greatly loved."[33] Underhill also notes that the legends were retold in various and numerous ways, with the particular details of each, such as characters and locale, changed to suit specific venues. Certainly, if the miracle legends were well-known to the English populace, then that same populace would have likely recognized certain elements of them in the Robin Hood ballads and tales.

The miracle known as "The Merchant's Surety" or "The Christian's Surety"[34] bears certain narratival similarities to the plot line in the *Gest* that concerns the knight's loan, most especially in the rejection of Christ as a loan guarantee, the acceptance of Mary as loan guarantee, a one-year repayment limit, and a last-minute appearance of the funds. In "The Merchant's Surety," the money arrives via the sea in a trunk because the borrower, who is unable to make the trip himself, is determined to hold up his end of the bargain. He entrusts the money to the Virgin, believing that she will deliver it to the lender on time, which she does. In the *Gest*, Robin the lender has less faith than the borrower of the miracle tale, and he essentially creates his own miracle when he robs 800 pounds from the monks. Had he really trusted the Virgin's power and faithfulness, he would have waited for the knight to appear with the money he owed. The knight, in fact, arrives in time with the required repayment, evidence that he at least trusted Mary enough to get him where he needed to be, on time.

To his credit, Robin gives to the knight 400 of the 800 pounds that he stole from the monks — or, as Robin would have it, that Mary delivered to him via the monks. Still, at the end of the day, Robin is 400 pounds richer than before, without having put in even ten minutes of hard work. Little John comments thus when he first lays eyes on the monks, and before he delivers them to the greenwood:

> Then bespake Lytell Johan,
> To Much he gan say,
> "I dare lay my lyfe to wedde,   *as a pledge*
> The monkes have brought our pay."[35]

At this point in the ballad, Little John does not know how much money the monks are carrying, so his use of the phrase "our pay" is more likely a reference to the living wages that Robin Hood and his men regularly took from others, rather than to the repayment of the loan.

Of all the recorded miracles of the Virgin, only "The Merchant's Surety" involves a monetary loan like that which is found in the *Gest*. In fact, "The Merchant's Surety" is a tale that has a double miracle. The first involves the return of the money within the allotted one-year deadline. The second, and probably the more important of the two since it not only closes the tale but also underscores the importance of the Christian faith for medieval readers, is the conversion of the Jewish lender to the Christian faith. The pseudo miracle in the *Gest* is focused solely on monetary repayment, which is an ironic twist on the corpus of miracle legends; those tend to focus on physical healings, rescues from dangerous situations, deathbed confessions, spiritual conversions, preservation of corpses, and admission into heaven. Indeed, most are opposed to unwarranted prosperity.

Whether or not the knight episode in the *Gest* reflects an actual miracle, it almost certainly would have reminded its listeners of certain details in "The Merchant's Surety" and would have introduced to readers the possibility of the miraculous. Miraculous or not, the episode leaves no doubt that Robin's devotion to Mary is tied to her role as guarantor of prosperity. As long as Mary delivered, Robin worshipped. When she failed to deliver, Robin took matters into his own hands but still gave credit to the Virgin, quite probably to protect his future prosperity at the Virgin's hands.

How do we explain the origin and meaning of this ironic intersection between piety and profit in the *Gest*? One answer is provided by Thomas Ohlgren's study of the mercantile elements in the poem. In brief, Ohlgren locates about a dozen parallels between guild policies and practices and scenes and themes in the poem.[36] Others have also recognized the relationship between piety and profit that existed in guilds. Eamon Duffy notes that many local parishes were paired with guilds that not only provided a needed service, such as maintaining fabric or ornaments within the church, but also were a source of significant funding.[37] The piety/profit combination has also been commented on by those in the social sciences who take as their starting point the fact that craft guilds were the site of both "occupational and religious endeavors."[38]

All of this leaves us with the original question: was Robin Hood religious, or merely ritualistic? Was he devoted, or merely superstitious? Was he a Christian, or merely a follower of the cult of the Virgin Mary when it was convenient? Within a Christological and evangelical[39] framework, Robin Hood's religion was predominantly outward. While no one can judge a man's heart, a man's actions ought to reflect the condition of his heart. Were Robin's devotion more than merely surface, he would have lived his life in pursuit of holiness, obedience, and complete surrender to "Hym that dyde on tre." He would have loaned 400 pounds to the knight with no demand for surety. He would have kept his hands off the sheriff's wife. He would have found legal and legitimate ways to provide for the poor. And he would have made his money by putting in a full day of honest hard work rather than stealing it from monks and sheriffs, even if said monks and sheriffs were less-than-righteous themselves.

Even within a more liberal social gospel mentality, it would be difficult to defend Robin's piety. He never went hungry in order to feed someone else. He never gave up his own livery in order to clothe someone else. He never put himself in peril in order to help the helpless. The well-known phrase commonly associated with Robin Hood, "steal from the rich, give to the poor," is only half true. Stealing from the rich was certainly part and parcel of Robin's *modus operandi*, but evidence that he stole from the rich in order to give to the poor is notably lacking in the early texts. Errol Flynn and Kevin Costner may have operated under this premise, but certainly the early Robin Hood did not.

It seems evident that devotion to the Virgin Mary was, for Robin Hood, a comfortable form of outward religion that had major payoffs. It did not require more of him than to attend mass whenever possible and to never harm a company of women. This was a small price to pay for the protection and profit offered by his "dere lady." In fact, I would posit that profit was the bottom line — pun intended — for Robin. If the Virgin had not delivered even one time on her promise of protection and surety, then Robin would have found a different object of veneration, which is exactly what happened after Protestantism had found a firm foothold in England and when the Virgin Mary was no longer in vogue. Maid Marian became his object of devotion, replacing the Virgin Mary permanently and completely. Whether the payoff for this devotion was as lucrative as that of his previous devotion is something only Robin Hood himself can say.

Suffice it to say that Robin Hood's religion was one whose purpose he willingly served as long as it served his purposes in return; his devotion to Mary was willingly given as long as her devotion to him was given in return; his attendance at Mass was faithful and frequent as long as the Virgin's attendance to him was faithful and frequent in return. All of this seems to point to wise maneuvering and savvy superstition rather than true piety and genuine devotion, or at least to a paradoxical combination of the two. Certainly in the early Robin Hood tales we can find an accurate reflection of what was the current popular religious expression of the times for at least part of the populace. Let us recall what the historian Walter Bower wrote many centuries ago regarding Robin's religion: "For he heeded what they say: 'To him God gives ear who does often Mass hear.'"[40]

Notes

1. I would like to thank David Hepworth for his helpful comments on an early draft of this paper, Ann W. Astell for her every-insightful comments regarding early Marian doctrines, and Thomas Ohlgren for his careful vetting and scholarly guidance of this study. This paper was presented in an earlier form at the 2009 Medieval Congress. I would like to thank Stephen Knight, Lorraine Kochanske Stock, and Alan T. Gaylord for their helpful comments and feedback.

2. "The Chroniclers' Robin Hood," in Knight and Ohlgren, 21–29 at 26.

3. Jeffrey L. Singman, *Robin Hood: The Shaping of the Legend* (Westport, CT: Greenwood Press, 1998), 13.

4. The most widely known adherent and teacher of this doctrine is Joel Osteen, pastor of a mega-church in Texas that meets in what used to be the Houston Rockets' coliseum.

5. *Robin Hood and the Monk*, in Knight and Ohlgren, 31–56; *Robin Hood and the Potter*, in Knight and Ohlgren, 57–79.

6. Knight and Ohlgren, 37–38, lines 21–28; 39, lines 67–74.
7. Ibid., 41, lines 133–40.
8. Ibid., 46, lines 305–6.
9. Ibid., 62, lines 7–12.
10. Ibid., 65, lines 109–12.
11. There is no agreement on the extent of Robin's advances towards the sheriff's wife, but the language is reminiscent of that used by knights who bid farewell to their lady after a night of trysting. For a discussion on this episode, see Ohlgren 2007, 85–91.
12. Ibid., 66, lines 137–40.
13. Ibid., 67, line 175.
14. *A Gest of Robyn Hode*, in Knight and Ohlgren, 80–168 at 91, lines 29–40.
15. Ibid., 97–98, lines 245–64.
16 For more complete discussions of popular piety and Mary devotion in the later middle ages, see, among others, the following studies: Hilda C. Graef, *Mary: A History of Doctrine and Devotion* (New York: Sheed and Ward, 1963–1965); John Raymond Shinners, ed., *Medieval Popular Religion 1000–1500: A Reader* (Peterborough: Broadview Press, 2007); Eamon Duffy, *The Stripping of the Altars: Traditional Religion in England, c. 1400–1580* (New Haven: Yale University Press, 1992); and Keith Thomas, *Religion and the Decline of Magic* (New York: Scribner, 1971).
17. Quoted in Graef, *Mary*, 212.
18. Quoted in Graef, *Mary*, 216.
19. Graef, *Mary*, 216.
20. See the Introduction of Johann Herolt, *Miracles of the Blessed Virgin Mary*, ed. and trans. C. C. Swinton Bland (New York: Harcourt, Brace, & Co., 1928).
21. Herolt, xiii.
22. Herolt, xxii–xx.
23. This theory has been put forth by, among others, Stephen Knight and Thomas Ohlgren. See Knight 2003, 22–23; and Ohlgren 2007, 152–54 and 185–86.
24. Knight and Ohlgren, 116, lines 821–28.
25. Ibid., 121, lines 992–96.
26. In addition to Johannes Herolt, mentioned previously, see also Beverly Boyd, ed., *The Middle English Miracles of the Virgin* (San Marino: Huntington Library, 1964); Peter Whiteford, ed., *The Myracles of Oure Lady: Ed. from Wynkyn de Worde's Edition*. Middle English Texts 23 (Heidelberg: Carl Winter, 1990); Gonzalo de Berceo, *Miracles of Our Lady*, trans. Richard Terry Mount and Annette Grant Cash (Lexington: University of Kentucky Press, 1997); Evelyn Underhill, ed. and trans., *The Miracles of Our Lady Saint Mary; Brought Out of Divers Tongues and Newly Set Forth in English* (New York: E. P. Dutton, 1906); Ruth Wilson Tryon, "Miracles of Our Lady in Middle English Verse," *PMLA* 38, no. 2 (1923): 308–388; Marcus Graham Bull, *The Miracles of Our Lady of Rocamadour: Analysis and Translation* (Woodbridge: Boydell Press, 1999); and Carol M. Schuler, "The Seven Sorrow of the Virgin: Popular Culture and Cultic Imagery in Pre-Reformation Europe," *Simiolus: Netherlands Quarterly for the History of Art* 21, no. 1/2 (1992): 5–28. For a Freudian analysis of why males are attracted to the cult of the Virgin, see Ralph W. Hood, Jr., Ronald J. Morris, and P. J. Watson, "Male Commitment to the Cult of the Virgin Mary and the Passion of Christ as a Function of Early Maternal Bonding," *International Journal of the Psychology of Religion* 1, no. 4 (1991): 221–31.
27. Herolt, *Miracles*, 22–23.
28. Ibid., 71.
29. Ibid., 76.
30. Ibid., 126.
31. Ibid., 127.
32. Ibid., 127.
33. Underhill, *Miracles of Our Lady*, xiv–xv.
34. This miracle appears in several Middle English manuscripts and early printed books, and for a discussion of them see Tryon, *Miracles of Our Lady*, 340–41, 363–65; and Whiteford, *Myracles of Oure Lady*, 106–7, 117–18.

35. Knight and Ohlgren, 117, lines 853–56.

36. Ohlgren 2007, 154–69. For example, the emphasis on good yeomanry, recruitment of members, giving of liveries, training of new apprentices, selling of cloth, feasting, money-lending, and patronage of the Virgin Mary. These, and other parallels, lead Ohlgren to conclude that the poem was commissioned in the mid-to-late fifteenth century by one of the major London guilds for recitation at an annual election dinner or mayoral inauguration. The presence of numerous references to cloth and cloth-making strongly suggests to him that one of the three major cloth guilds — the Drapers, the Mercers, and the Clothworkers — was responsible for creating the poem as it presently exists.

37. Duffy, *Stripping of the Altars*, 140–46.

38. See Gary Richardson, "Craft Guilds and Christianity in Late-Medieval England: A Rational-Choice Analysis," *Rationality and Society* 17, no. 2 (2005): 139–189 at 140. Richardson ultimately concludes that the link between spiritual and occupational ends "helped [the guilds] overcome the free rider problems that hindered both," 174. This conclusion that does not negate my hypothesis that Robin Hood's piety was less than genuine.

39. "Evangelical" is here used in its Reformation sense, when it referred to those who believed in the authority of scripture and salvation by grace through faith alone. Though "Protestant" had this meaning on the continent, "evangelical" was the word of choice in England. See Doreen M. Rosman, *The Evolution of the English Churches 1500–2000* (Cambridge: Cambridge University Press, 2003), 35.

40. Knight and Ohlgren, 26.

10

The Late Medieval Robin Hood Ballads: Radical Economics Revisited

KIMBERLY A. MACUARE THOMPSON

If you were to ask someone in the twenty-first century about the economic significance of Robin Hood, you could be sure of receiving a fairly standard response. Robin Hood would certainly be described as a thief, but he would probably also be painted more flatteringly as a dispossessed nobleman who stole only from the corrupt religious and aristocratic orders to aid the oppressed poor classes of thirteenth-century England.[1] Indeed, Robin's redistributive brand of economic justice has become his key trait, providing the link to all types of modern "good-hearted bandits," from Jesse James to Bonnie and Clyde.[2] In fact, this idea of stealing from the rich to give to the poor is so ubiquitous in modern culture that "Robin Hood" has evolved from being just a descriptor for like people (i.e. other just criminals) or organizations and functions metaphorically across a whole spectrum of consumer brands and advertising, signaling positive savings for our own oppressed masses of contemporary shoppers.[3] However, this popular conception of Robin Hood as a disguised noble who offers the wealth of the well-to-do to those who lack liquidity is simply not accurate or helpful when studying the medieval Robin Hood ballads and fragments. In fact, what must stand out to a reader of these ballads is that Robin and his men are not noble in terms of their birth or their actions, as they are a group of yeomen criminals ready and able to rob anyone who passes through the forest and keep the money for themselves.

It would be a mistake, however, to believe that this contradiction between the medieval and the modern versions of Robin Hood signals that the economic radicalism lies on the modern side of the divide. It simply means that we must look at the ballads in a more complex way, tracing the tales' movements of money and financial references to unearth the medieval Robin's economic politics. Such an investigation must begin with the fact that in each of the medieval texts, Robin disguises himself as a different person, taking on the clothing and mannerisms of the other in order to move through the forest and town undetected on various missions. What is fascinating about these moments, however, is that disguises are supposed to function to disguise identity and should therefore be seamless representations of the chosen figure. In the case of the medieval Robin Hood ballads, however, the disguises are always interrupted, broken, or imperfect, serving to draw attention to the performance instead of conceal it.

In addition to being imperfect, Robin's disguises are also consistent in their imperfection. That is, all the disguises fail in exactly the same way. Whether Robin is disguised as a bounty hunter, a potter, an aristocrat, a merchant, a usurer, or a servant, he always reveals himself by his flawed replication of economic behaviors and attitudes. For example, as a potter, he sells pots poorly at the wrong prices; likewise, as a bounty hunter, he refuses the payment for his capture. Moreover, as if to highlight these flawed performances, other characters notice and comment upon these failures, suggesting that the heart of each of these identities is in the economic performance itself. Robin Hood has the dress and accoutrements of each identity, but it is only in his flawed financial moves that he reveals that he is not what he seems to be.

In what I term the economic interpellation of the subject,[4] I would like to argue that at various times in the early ballads, Robin takes on another identity for the intended purpose of interrogating both the construction and also the boundaries of the individual subject positions that are occupied. That is, the Robin Hood ballads are interested both in the social critique of the various medieval estates and, more broadly, in the process by which all subjects increasingly understood themselves to be constructed by their economic activity.[5] Elsewhere, I have examined how the characterization of Robin Hood in the poem *Robin Hood and the Potter* as a bad potter in disguise in not necessarily a commentary on greedy merchants, but rather one could read that text as an examination on the limitations of definitional categories, such as merchants.[6] I would here like to expand this examination of the late-medieval representation of economic forces in the Robin Hood ballads. Specifically, in the texts *Robin Hood and Guy of Gisborne*, *A Gest of Robyn Hode*, and *Robin Hood and the Monk*, a number of the characters disguise themselves so as to attempt to "pass" into and within a world that exists outside of their greenwood world. As I suggested above, these performative disguises often fail and do so during textual moments that concern economic activity.[7]

If we read these bad performances as failed "economic passing," it seems worthwhile to look not just at what Robin and his men are passing as but also at their original identity positions, positions that I argue allow for a special site for the interrogation of subjectivity. The primary category that Robin and his men occupy is that of the outlaw or criminal, and as Hilary Kahn has argued that "crime is determined within the same cultural and historical webs that identify selves and others," the outlaws often serve to delineate borders between acceptable versus non-acceptable, normal versus aberrant, us versus them.[8] In sum, criminals are often viewed as natural transgressors who, by their actions, subvert normal social systems, including justice, public order, and the market.

One of Robin's most obvious transgressive acts is theft of money and goods, an activity that clearly upsets the normal social order. Mike Presdee argues that "the theft of private property itself presupposes the existence of the social and economic organization of private property along with the cultural practices that support it. As such, theft is an act which challenges the social and economic organization of life and its culture."[9] Theft is not just disruptive on the personal level of the individual robbed, but more significantly it is an act that calls into question the cultural logic of the economic system itself. Theft can be economically disruptive in other ways as well "since the thief may value a stolen item at an amount below its owner's valuation, resources may move to lower-valued uses when items are stolen."[10] That is, in addition to the initial act of disregarding ownership, the thief can add insult to injury through a "misuse" of the acquired goods, something we will explore in detail in the ballad of *Robin Hood and the Potter*.

In addition to disrupting systems of order, one of the most important functions of the band's outlawry is to illuminate the way existing dominant power structures create criminality. In effect, "the criminalisation process then is that cultural process whereby those with power come to define and shape dominant forms of social life and give them specific meanings."[11] In the case of Robin Hood, this point seems especially relevant in regard to his status as a poacher.[12] Medieval poaching, or even wood-gathering, was criminal precisely because the elites claimed both the forest and everything within it as their own, leaving any other activity as illegitimate and unlawful. In part, this was clearly economic, as the forest served as a clear and valuable source of revenue. As Humphries and Greenberg argue, "Exploiting classes will ... define as illegal, and try to punish, actions that threaten its interests. For example, it may seek to eliminate forms of appropriation of wealth that are inconsistent with the mode of production in question by defining them as theft and attaching penal sanctions to those who 'steal.'"[13] Another more complex part of the equation involves the ways in which hunting helped define aristocratic identity.[14] In addition to the clearly differentiated hunting practices performed by different classes, there were various statutes limiting the privileges of the masses so that, theoretically at least, hunting was maintained as their preserve. Therefore, Robin's poaching and its criminalization within the world of the ballads reveals a central site of conflict and focuses attention on the way dominant powers structure lawful and unlawful activity to maintain their economic and class privileges.

To the extent that poaching was defined as a crime by the elite, the ballads also enlist it as a form of resistance on the part of the outlaw in literal and metaphorical senses. By poaching, they upset the literal spatial boundaries that should keep them in place, the economic boundaries that try to limit others' access to valuable forest resources, and identity boundaries that try to delimit exactly who can take part in the activity. According to Jeffrey L. Singman, poaching, among other illegal activities, means that:

> Within the world of Robin Hood, individuals and behavior normally objectified and marginalized by external social structures are subjectified and centralized.... The inhabitants of Robin Hood's world can violate the hierarchical order by adopting social roles other than their own, and can even reverse normal societal relationships; they may steal form the rich or poach the king's deer; they may use violence at will. Normally objectified, marginalized, and dominated, they become central and dominant.[15]

Rather than being content to maintain their marginal place in the criminalized world of the other, Robin and his men bring their dangerous bodies literally into the authorized spaces of the dominant groups and metaphorically into the bodies of those individuals whose identities they occupy through disguise.

All of Robin's criminal activities only make sense within this complex interlacing social context. While some argue that "a distinctive feature of the Robin Hood poems is the mysterious separateness of the outlaw realm," I would suggest that it is Robin's very embeddedness in the system which allows him to subvert it.[16] First, the forest is not a cultural dead space, but "a hive of economic activity and a center of legislation and rules."[17] This is true both on the official and outlaw levels. Certainly, the "authorized" forest has a complex and strict code of law attached to it, as well as a sophisticated system of resource extraction. However, the outlaw forest also has rules and codes, such as who can and cannot be molested, and when people are robbed and when they get to keep their money; moreover, forests hold a seemingly inexhaustible supply of natural resources and human quarry to sustain the criminals' economic activity. That these two systems intersect and overlap is clear in the ballads, and Robin is the more dangerous and disruptive character for both his involvement in and refutation of various social and economic practices.

The last point that I would like to make in connection with the concept of an outlaw identity is that it is not only subversive because it definitively opposes dominant views or because it offers a merely differently defined identity space. Rather, to be a criminal, in a sense, involves entering an undefined state, where the very indeterminacy of the identity claimed allows considerable disruptive potential. Brian Reynolds, writing of early modern ideas of crime, defines criminality as a type of transversal territory or space where potentially unlimited ways of being are opened up. He writes:

> To reiterate, people occupy transversal territory when they defy or surpass the conceptual boundaries of their prescribed subjective addresses, opening themselves, as it were, to subjective awareness outside the self that is currently principal. Transversal territory invites people to deviate from the hierarchizing assemblages — whether vertical or horizontal — of any organizational social structure.[18]

Again, they are invited to deviate but not in set ways. Rather, Robin's outlawry "expands subjective territory through entrance into a disorganized, possibly unlimited, space by means of processual movement through performances of iconoclasm, impropriety, immorality, criminality, and insanity."[19]

While they certainly draw much liminal power from their criminal status, the band's designation as a group of yeomen may be more important still to interpreting the social critique of the ballads. As many Robin Hood scholars have realized, one of the key cruxes in the tradition is the term "yeoman."[20] Robin Hood and his men are clearly and insistently identified as "yeman" through all of the medieval ballads. As Maurice Keen writes, "Robin Hood's status is differentiated, explicitly and emphatically, from that of knighthood and gentility. Their [the medieval ballads'] Robin is always a yeoman: his 'good yeomanry' is indeed a recurrent theme."[21] However, the ballads' very insistence, emphatic and repeated, draws attention to the term and begs the question of what a yeoman is and what good yeomanry means in the texts.

If one turns to the definition of yeoman in medieval society, there is a dazzling array of concomitant and conflicting meanings. One of the most common definitions of yeoman is offered by Stephen Knight:

> Essentially, the term indicates a free man who is not a bound serf. He may own land or run a business, but he is usually a skilled worker of some kind. Although he may develop a good income, the yeoman is essentially linked to the lower orders of society; he is not inherently a member of the gentry, those landowners of substance who fought on horseback and to some degree aspired to the elaborate chivalric culture outlined in medieval romances like those about King Arthur.[22]

While this definition certainly encompasses many of late medieval England's yeomen, there are still more ways to define the term. The *MED* records a yeoman could be

> (a) free-born male attendant in a royal or noble household holding a rank above that of groom and page but below that of squire, a household official; an attendant or assistant to someone of higher rank, a retainer

(b) a subordinate officer in a specific department of a royal or noble household, ranking below a sergeant and above a groom; also, as a prefix to the titles of various officers of the household

(c) a subordinate military officer; an officer in charge of cannon for a town

(d) a hired laborer; also, a member of a ship's crew, seaman

(e) as a term of disparagement: an underling, inferior[23]

In the Middle Ages there was also the "yeoman of the forest," who was charged with guarding the forests and chases of medieval England. Given this varied list, perhaps the most striking feature, then, is the term's drastic instability.

The instability of the yeoman designation provides subversive potential in the ballads in two clear ways. First, the very insistence on an identity that is in key ways a non-identity suggests the desire to flout categorization and move freely across diverse social terrain. Rather than choose one meaning, such as yeoman of the forest or yeoman as class status, the ballads instead flit from meaning to meaning, ultimately suggesting that they cannot be encompassed in one category. Dobson and Taylor are on the right track when they suggest that, "it is self-evident that the late medieval audience for the ballads of Robin Hood was being consistently asked to identify with a hero who was neither a knight nor a peasant or 'husbonde' but something in between."[24] In fact, I would argue that Robin's "in betweenness" is precisely the point in choosing to reiterate his yeoman status. The yeomen's disruptive potential may also have been of some concern to the late medieval subject, as with a growing economic power, they began to exercise more political power, sometimes in dangerous ways.[25] While there are various uprisings that involve the yeoman class, we might briefly mention Jack Cade's Rebellion in 1450. If we are to judge from the pardon rolls drawn up afterwards, this uprising involved significant numbers of yeomen. Their part was so important that a prevailing view of the conflict posits that "the rebellion of 1450 ... illustrates vividly that there was a social group below that of the aristocracy and the gentry who could figure in an important way in political life."[26] I would add that, given the fear and unrest generated by the rebellion, it also proved that this group could be potentially disorderly.[27]

The second and perhaps more important move achieved by claiming yeoman status is the ability to queer other social identities through performance. That is, Robin, or sometimes Little John, as a yeoman, with all of that term's attendant instability and disorder, takes on other seemingly more stable identities, such as potter, knight, and bounty hunter. In doing so, his very presence in their skin raises immediate questions about the security of these identities as well. This type of destabilization must seem even more important given that the Black Death and Peasants' Revolt of the fourteenth century led to stiffening of boundaries and hierarchy in the fifteenth century.[28] With this framework of disorderly identity politics, we can turn to the ballads for their specific critiques of medieval social and economic ideologies.

Economic Borders and Imperfect Crossings

Robin Hood and Guy of Gisborne[29] begins inauspiciously enough for a medieval poem with a traditional invocation of spring:

> When shawes beene sheene and shradds full fayre,
> And leeves both large and longe,
> Itt is merry, walking in the fayre forrest,
> To heare the small birds singe.[30]

However, in a turn that would make Chaucer envious, the ballad quickly substitutes traditional musings on love with the dark dreams of Robin Hood, whose "sweaven," or dream, foreshadows his mortal encounter with Guy of Gisborne, the bounty hunter and requisite villain of this piece. This initial dissidence is carried throughout the poem through a series of jarring juxtapositions, most notably Robin's turn as Guy the bounty hunter, a role play that allows him to critique his new position within a system that defines subjects through economic markers.

In the initial meeting — between Sir Guy, a bounty hunter who has been dispatched to take care of the outlaw, and Robin Hood — the poet immediately establishes the centrality of economics to the ballad through its careful linguistic play. He writes:

> How these two yeomen together they mett,
> Under the leaves of lyne,   *lime (trees in general)*
> To see what marchandise they made   *business*
> Even at that same time.[31]

The use of the word "merchandise," or business, here highlights the mercantile interest Guy has in finding Robin and receiving his commission from the sheriff. However, Robin quickly displaces this central exchange, suggesting to Guy, "'Let us some other pastime find, / Good fellow, I thee pray.'"[32] Instead, the two make a series of alternative exchanges. First, they exchange shots in a contest of archery; then, they exchange blows after Guy learns Robin's true identity; and finally, and most importantly, they exchange clothes, with Robin taking up the dead Guy's distinctive horse-hide costume.[33]

Robin carefully frames his stealing of Guy's garments in the literal language of exchange, saying, "If thou have had the worse stroakes at my hand, / Thou shalt have the better cloathe."[34] Of course, clothes are never merely garments in the medieval milieu but carefully controlled markers of the social self. In taking on Guy's clothes, Robin also takes on Guy's identity, an assumption that is clearly successful on the level of the physical, as Robin enters easily into the sheriff's camp. As if to further emphasize the point that identity is what is truly at stake:

> Robin pulled forth an Irish kniffe,
> And nicked Sir Guy in the face,
> That hee was never on a woman borne
> Cold tell who Sir Guye was.[35]   *Could*

Robin mutilates Sir Guy, effectively obliterating any trace of him.

In addition to taking Guy's identity away from him, Robin then assumes it for himself by putting on Guy's horse-hide, a move which Claire Sponsler describes as Robin literally slipping into Guy's skin.[36] Other critics, too, identify this moment with a change in self. Stuart Kane argues "where the animal skin served as a marker of Guy's identity, for Robin it functions as a disguise, that which obscures identity, and allows him to approach Barnesdale. It is also a grotesque costume which allows him to cross the borders between man and animal, and outlaw and agent of authority."[37] While I agree that the assumption of Guy's identity allows a type of border-crossing, I would argue that it is an imperfect crossing. Rather, Robin is Guy with a difference, a difference which works to undermine the very ground upon which Guy's own identity was based.

With Robin in Guy's place, the ballad quickly moves to its real stakes, the refutation of economically defined identity. Of course, as a bounty hunter, Sir Guy is inextricably bound up with economics, as he trades in bodies for money. Upon meeting the still unidentified Robin, Guy speaks longingly of Robin Hood, saying, "'I had rather meet with him upon a day, / Then forty pound of golde.'"[38] The irony here is that Guy's implied choice of meeting Robin Hood or receiving money is a false one; for him, the two episodes would be elided into the same result given his profession. This is made clear not only by the sheriff's offer of forty pounds here, but also in the closely related play, *Robyn Hod and the Shryff off Notyngham*, where we see the actual negotiation for payment take place. The Sheriff says, "I wyll the gyffe golde and fee / This beheste thou holde me,"[39] thus making the body = money equation clear to the reader.

Thus, when Robin/Guy approaches the sheriff, who believes that his quarry is safely dead, he is immediately offered his payment for having killed Robin Hood. The sheriff says, "'Come hither, thou good Sir Guy, / Aske of mee what thou wilt have.'"[40] Rather than accept the payment, the new Guy refuses: "'Ile none of thy gold,' sayes Robin Hood."[41] Rather, he says, "'Let me goe strike the knave; / This is all the reward I aske.'"[42] Robin replaces his cash reward with a non-monetary payment. Claire Sponsler argues that Robin's conversion move is an attempt to ultimately move bodies out of the system of commodities, which is the economic logic of bounty-hunting.[43] While I agree that there is a systemic critique here, I also believe that the critique may have less to do with Little John's body figured as a commodity and more to do with "Guy's" identity being linked to finance, an important distinction.

In essence, by refusing cash compensation, Robin offers a poor performance of a bounty hunter, a fact that is emphasized by the sheriff:

> "Thou art a madman," said the shiriffe,
> "Thou sholdest have had a knights fee; *fief (land-holding)*
> Seeing thy asking bee soe badd,
> Well granted it shall be."[44]

Guy, through refusing the bounty, is not only negating his current identity as a bounty hunter, but he is also rejecting the "knight's fee," which would transform his status to that of a knight through yet another economic maneuver. The sheriff clearly thinks madness might be the only explanation for a move so out of character for the bounty hunter and outside of what he sees as a sensible economic system. However, it is to critique this very system that Robin gives his bad performance. He refuses the identity proffered by the sheriff, an identity based in and constructed by economic possessions and roles.

Writing of Robin's performances, Christine Chism argues that "at every stage Robin Hood both opposes his enemies and mimics them."[45] I would like to shift the emphasis slightly and suggest that he actually opposes enemies, and here I would interpret enemy broadly to include not only the textual enemies but the extra-textual institutions being critiqued, *by* mimicking them. That is, performance is not a companion to opposition here but the mode. This opposition through possession of another's identity plays into what Stuart Kane sees as "the obsessive focus of the narrator on the poem's bodies and the co-extensive difficulty of defining and regulating them."[46] Robin's assumption of Guy's identity plays havoc with society's attempts to order its subjects, especially with regard to defining them by their economic activities and gestures.

Gifts, Loans, and Mortgaging Knighthood

Before discussing Robin's own performances in *A Gest of Robyn Hode*, I would like to first turn to the ways in which the category of performance, specifically economic performance, is foregrounded in the text by the character of Sir Richard, an impoverished knight. When we first meet Sir Richard, he is hardly recognizable as a knight, a fact which the narrator draws attention to again and again through a detailed description and discussion of his appearance and possessions. Sir Richard enters the story in ignominious fashion:

> All dreri was his semblaunce,   *sad; appearance*
> And lytell was his pryde;
> His one fote in the styrop stode,   *stirrup*
> That othere wavyd beside.
>
> His hode hanged in his iyn two;   *hood; eyes*
> He rode in symple aray,   *array (clothing)*
> A soriar man than he was one   *sadder*
> Rode never in somer day.⁴⁷

As we can clearly see, Richard is far from the picture of a prosperous knight. He is described as being poorly dressed, almost slovenly with his hood hanging over his face. Perhaps more unforgivably, he is not even mounted correctly on his horse but carelessly placed, with one foot dragging. After arriving in the outlaw's camp, Robin and his followers find that Sir Richard not only fails in appearance but also in wealth, as his coffers contain a poor 10 shillings.

Robin quickly connects the knight's appearance and lack of funds with his identity. He notes:

> "Moche wonder thinketh me   *Much; it seems to me*
> Thy clothynge is so thin."⁴⁸   *threadbare*

Then, he moves immediately to questioning Richard's knighthood based on these visual cues. Robin asserts:

> "I trowe thou warte made a knyght of force, *by compulsion*
> Or ellys of yemanry."⁴⁹   *else*

Barring that, he suggests that the knight has done something wrong, such as being guilty of usury, lechery, or poor household management.⁵⁰ Robin cannot accept this knight as normal because he too clearly violates the performative norms of his status in appearance, array, and finances, norms that we have seen continuously repeated and reinforced in romances, such as *Sir Amadace* and *Octavian*.

Sir Richard defends his knightly status, insisting that his ancestors have been knights for over a hundred years. However, rather than moving the portrait of the knight away from the financial, Sir Richard's comments cement ideas about the ways in which identity and economics are intertwined. He reveals that he has lost his money because he had to defend his son from a homicide charge after a tournament. While he is not poor for the same reasons as Sir Amadace, a parallel which must assert itself given the focus here on chivalry and economics, his story has striking parallels in that they are both bankrupted in the pursuits key to knightly identity, Amadace with largesse and the knight through his son's exercise of prowess. Also like Amadace, we learn that the knight has mortgaged his lands to rescue himself financially, but here we see the darker side of the mortgage, as his creditor, the abbot of St. Mary's, actively works to keep him from regaining his lands.

When asked if he has any friends to help him out in his time of need, Sir Richard responds:

> "Syr, never one wol me knowe:
> While I was ryche ynowe at home
> Great boste than wolde they blowe.   *boast; spread*
> "And nowe they renne away fro me..."[51]   *run*

Again, as in the tale of *Amadace*, we see the ways in which money functions to both create and destroy social identities. With his money, Sir Richard is a respected knight, confidently ensconced in his social world and accepted as a knight by his peers. However, denied his funds, he becomes an outcast, avoided by his former companions and difficult to situate as a knight even by the sympathetic Robin.

The important gestures that go into the creation and sustenance of an economic identity are detailed as Robin and his men literally and figuratively aid Sir Richard in regaining his lost place. Sir Richard regains the exact amount of his lost knightly income in the form of a loan from Robin. Then, starting with Little John, the knight's appearance is altered so that he will look more like a knight, beginning with a new rich array.[52] After this, each of Robin's men shouts out other necessary objects for a knight — a horse, a new saddle, a palfrey, new boots, and a pair of shining spurs — until Richard is just right. This is a striking scene as we get to see knighthood, defined as the acquisition of requisite objects, basically constructed before our eyes.

Robin adds the last piece to the perfect chivalric figure, a yeoman to serve the knight loyally:

> "It were greate shame," sayde Robyn,
> "A knight alone to ryde,
> Withoute squyre, yoman, or page,
> To walke by his syde."[53]

Again, as in *Sir Amadace*, the idea of shame is connected to the performance of identity. Robin's suggestion that Sir Richard needs a man, as well as all of the other objects of knighthood, is connected to the desire to avoid shame — that devastating rupture of identity — and present a seamless performance of one's class role.

That this performance ultimately succeeds is clear when Sir Richard returns a year later to repay Robin's generous loan. In place of the disheveled knight falling from the saddle, Richard arrives in splendor, with a rich array, a coffer full of money, one hundred men to accompany him, and a hundred bows and arrows burnished with silver to offer Robin as a gift. While the episode with Sir Richard suggests some provocative connections between identity and economics, as well as exposing the constructedness of knightly identity, this episode is markedly different from Robin's own performances. Sir Richard is, in fact, a knight, one with a hundred years of precedence, when he performs his role. He is, in an important sense, "becoming" what he is. When Robin takes on different identities, however, he is very decidedly becoming something that he is not, a fact exacerbated by his own amorphous position as a yeoman. This is why I must disagree with Claire Sponsler when she asserts that Robin "has draped himself with the cross-dresser's liminal powers."[54] I think that the power comes not just from the act of cross-dressing itself but from who is doing the cross-dressing.

The text makes this clear when Robin gives his own knightly performance. The beginning of *A Gest of Robyn Hode* works very hard to set up Robin in a gentlemanly fashion, and he performs a wide variety of appropriately chivalric behaviors. In the opening description of Robin, we are told:

> Robyn was a prude outlaw,   *proud*
> Whyles he walked on grounde:
> So curteyse an outlawe as he was one
> Was nevere non founde.[55]

Robin's courtesy, a familiar aspect of the aristocratic romance hero, is the first thing mentioned by the author. As Stephen Knight argues, "the words 'prude' and 'curteyse' seem to construct Robin as a more lordly figure than the usual yeoman."[56] His courtesy is augmented by other behaviors more typical to the knightly classes. Like Arthur, that chivalric figure par excellence, he insists that he will not eat a bite until he has seen "'som bolde baron, / Or som uncouth gest [strange visitor].'"[57] His feast, when he deigns to eat is one that could grace the best of aristocratic houses with bread, wine, deer, swans, pheasants, and every type of delicacy.[58] Robin also insists on other gentle behaviors, such as washing before dinner.[59] As with the other ballads, all of the elements are in place for Robin to offer the perfect performance and pass as a knight.

However, Robin is far from the perfect storybook knight, specifically when it comes down to economic concerns, here his display of chivalric largesse. After Robin's elaborate dinner, Sir Richard responds in typical knightly fashion to his gracious host:

> "Gramarcy, sir," sayde he,   *Grant mercy, thank you*
> "Such a dinere had I nat

> Of all these wekys thre. *weeks*
> "If I come ageyne, Robyn,
> Here by thys contré,
> As gode a dyner I shall the make *thee*
> As that thou haest made to me."⁶⁰

Richard views the dinner as a gift, and he offers the possibility of a future dinner as a return gift to Robin. By offering this present to Robin, Sir Richard accepts him as an equal, assuming a shared status and sense of value.

It is at this moment, however, that Robin's chivalric performance is abruptly ruptured by his aggressive resumption of his yeoman identity. Rejecting Sir Richard's suggestion, Robin changes the terms of the offer:

> "Gramarcy, knyght," sayde Robyn,
> "My dyner whan that I it have;
> I was never so gredy, bi dere worthy God, *hungry*
> My dyner for to crave.
>
> "But pay or ye wende," sayde Robyn; *before you go*
> "Me thynketh it is gode ryght; *It seems to me*
> It was never the maner, by dere worthi God, *custom*
> A yoman to pay for a knyght."⁶¹

Robin suggests that the transaction be a purely financial one, where the knight makes immediate cash payment for the dinner—not a future equal gift exchange. As in *Sir Amadace*, this demand places the gift economy at risk, as "at the moment of giving the giver cannot demand an explicit quid pro quo if he or she does not wish to endanger the efficacy of the entire transaction."⁶² However, putting the transaction in danger is exactly what Robin wants to do, drawing attention to the ways in which these financial gestures create and sustain interpersonal relationships.

Robin bases his recourse to the payment on his social ideas, where it would be inappropriate for him, as a yeoman, to be the host of the knight in some type of equal relationship. He rejects Sir Richard's assumption that they share a status or notion of value and aggressively asserts his difference. That this difference is a question of identity seems clear both from Robin's insistence on identifying himself as a "yeoman," as opposed to Sir Richard's "knight," and by his determined misinterpretation of what Richard is offering. Specifically, Richard tries to place their relationship on the terrain of gift exchange with an undefined waiting period until he will be able to offer a return "gift" dinner. In lines 141–44 above, Robin, however, purposefully misunderstands Richard. Here, Robin purposefully misinterprets the graciousness of the knight's offer. He, instead, insists that he will only offer thanks when he actually receives something and suggests that his anticipation of a future dinner would indicate avarice rather than the positive fellowship Richard extends.

Robin is actively asserting his difference, suggesting that he shares neither a language nor a mindset with Richard.

One way to read this would be to simply see mercantile values as infecting largesse, perhaps offering a critique of the chivalric class and its ruse of sustaining a gift economy. However, this is complicated by the fact that Robin quickly resumes his previous role as soon as he realizes the knight has no money. Now, Robin is determined to aid the knight with a much needed loan. Once again adopting a quasi-royal persona, Robin says:

> "Come nowe furth, Litell Johnn.
> And go to my tresouré,
> And bringe me foure hundered pound,
> And loke well tolde it be."⁶³   *counted*

Before we can become too comfortable with this resumption of royal airs, however, the performance is again undermined by Robin's anxious waiting for repayment and his insistence on the contractual nature of the transaction. No gift, this is a business loan complete with terms of payment and guarantors.⁶⁴

At the end of this episode, Robin quickly moves back to chivalric generosity and allows Richard to keep his £400 loan because he insists that he has already received payment, given that he has stolen from the very abbey holding Sir Richard's mortgage. If this is not sufficient largesse, Robin then gives him an additional £400 as a gift. However, once again, Robin's actions do not wholly conform to chivalric norms. As stolen goods, the money is never, in effect, his to give. Additionally, he offers the second sum immediately after Sir Richard offers him the bows and arrows as a gift, a violation, albeit it a small one, of the waiting period usually involved in gift transactions as opposed to commercial transactions.

And so the poem goes on, constantly constructing and undermining categories of identity, playing with Robin's various performances, never seeming to definitively rest in one area. This incessant and insistent play seems to suggest even more than the other ballads that we have seen that neither mercantile nor chivalric values is the sole target but rather the ways in which Robin's performance of "knighthood" is consistently ruptured by economic failure, as his largesse is tainted by contract and his gifts by payments, showcasing the spectacular instability of identity positions supposedly fixed in and by financial gestures.

Retaining Bad Servants

Finally, I would like to take a look at two examples of "bad servants" from *Robin Hood and the Monk*⁶⁵ and from *A Gest of Robyn Hode*, both of which offer more explicit commentary on the yeoman status claimed by Robin and his men. As suggested in the introduction to this chapter, the term "yeoman" had a complex set of associations for a late medieval audience. It could variously refer to a rank of service (valet), a stage in the career of a young man on his way to becoming a squire, a social category between husbandmen and gentlemen, countrymen akin to the same status as artisans and tradesmen in urban life, freedom of blood and tenure, those of questionable birth and tenant status, and a burgeoning class in the fifteenth century that was created by both upward and downward social mobility.[66] From this dizzying list, I want to focus on just two differing ideas of yeomanry that are present in these two ballads: yeoman as servant and yeoman as class status.

In *Robin Hood and the Monk*, Little John is forced to take on the role of the king's yeoman in order to rescue Robin Hood from prison. By performing as the king's yeoman, John places himself in an ambiguous position that tests loyalties, questions the basis for service relationships, and complicates the category of yeoman. From the king's point of view, John is a yeoman in the strict sense of his own paid servant. He emphasizes these formal economic links with these words:

> "I made hem yemen of the crowne,   *them*
> And gaf hem fee with my hond..."[67]   *money*

For him, this monetary exchange should cement John's status as his servant and guarantee loyalty. It seems clear that both here and in the "Little John and the Sheriff" episode from the *Gest* (discussed later in this chapter) that there is a critique of one of the key characteristics of bastard feudalism, the often more temporary "fee for service" relationship between a lord and his retainers rather than the earlier and more long-lasting bonds of land.[68] In this scheme, John highlights the tenuous nature of such bonds by treating his relationship to the king as purely functional. After the king is no longer useful, Little John throws off his role as king's yeoman in favor of the less formal but more tenacious bond he has to Robin, highlighting the emptiness of the purely monetary connection.[69]

This scene is made more powerful given the fact that Robin has alienated John at the beginning of the tale by treating him poorly and trying to cheat him out of money won in a bet. His choice to return to Robin's band and his explicit desire to have Robin as his master circumvents key notions of late medieval paid service, while it affirms the bonds between the two men as fellow yeomen. Similar to the sheriff's reaction to Guy in *Robin Hood and Guy of Gisborne*, the king in *Robin Hood and the Monk* notes in almost disbelief:

> "He is trew to his maister," seid oure kyng;
> "I sey, be swete Seynt John,

> He lovys better Robyn Hode
> Then he dose us ychon."[70]   *Than; each of us*

John's love for Robin, contrary to logical self-interest, stymies the king, but it suggests to the reader the existence of enduring and meaningful connections in the outlaw realm, a realm that does not depend on the cash nexus for bonds.

This difficulty in comprehension is made clear as the king continues with the theme, trying to explain away John's actions. He notes the obligation of Robin to John:

> "Robyn Hode is ever bond to hym,
> Bothe in strete and stalle;
> Speke no more of this mater," seid oure kyng,
> "But John has begyled us alle."[71]

This relationship between Robin and John certainly seems like the yeoman/lord relationship that the king believed he had obtained with his payment to John. However, the reader sees that it is a more complex mixture that is not completely reducible to either the servant role or shared class status and one adamantly not tied to cash payment. Again, ironically, the poor performance, here as the king's yeoman, serves to highlight the complexity of identity categories, as Little John outdoes the expectations for servant loyalty by being a bad servant to the king.

Similar themes about servant loyalty and the cash nexus also appear in the third part of the *Gest* commonly known as "Little John and the Sheriff." Here, Little John becomes the sheriff's yeoman, once again emphasizing the sense of yeoman as a servant. When the sheriff comes upon Little John in the woods, he is at once struck by his prowess and soon offers him "twenty marks to thy fee" if he will become his man.[72] To further cement the official (and material) nature of this relationship, the sheriff also gives Little John a good horse, and they even go through all of the official motions of asking the permission of John's current master, Sir Richard.

Little John very clearly sets out with the intention of performing badly and offers the only overt statement about these bad performances in any of the ballads. He says, "'I shall be the worst servaunt to hym / That ever yet had he.'"[73] Little John does not have to wait long for opportunity to present itself. One day, having overslept and been left behind by the sheriff and his other men, John wakes up hungry and demands food. A combination of his laxity in arriving so late and his belligerent attitude make the keeper of the pantry reluctant to indulge him. Little John then beats the man viciously, grabs the keys, and helps himself to the contents of the pantry. The cook observes this behavior and declares this to Little John:

> "I make myn avowe to God," saide the coke,
> "Thou arte a shrewde hynde   *cursed servant*
> In ani hous for to dwel,
> For to aske thus to dyne."[74]

He very clearly connects what John has done to being outside of the acceptable behavior for a servant. John has violated the rules governing the master/servant relationship. Rather than stopping John, however, this exchange merely gives John an opening to further his insurrection by trying to lure the cook away from the sheriff's service into Robin's band. Importantly, when Little John tells the cook the terms of Robin's service, they are very similar to those of the sheriff: livery twice yearly and twenty marks.[75] This similarity suggests that it is something beyond economics which ultimately motivates the men. Abandoning their master, the two renegade servants rob the sheriff of all of his goods and more than £300 in cash and run off to rejoin Robin and his men.

Given the grotesque nature of Little John's badness, A. J. Pollard interprets this particular scene in this manner:

> In fact it can be read as a parody of the *Book of Nurture*, in which a masterless young man is instructed in all the arts of service and finer points of etiquette so that he can enter and prosper in household service. Little John, masquerading as a masterless man, turns the sheriff's household upside down. Where the conventional book of courtesy celebrates service, this rejects it.[76]

However, rather than service in general (remember, they are eager to enter Robin's service), it seems that a different point is being made, one which interrogates the role of money in the retention of servants and, more broadly, the use of money to construct social roles and bonds.

As with the episode discussed above in *Robin Hood and the Monk*, the clear point being made is that money does not make the master. John and the cook, by preferring Robin's service, are using criteria other than monetary, criteria which fall out of the understanding of the dominant view of service. A later episode in the *Gest* further illustrates this difference. After Little John is injured, he begs to be killed rather than captured. However, Robin rejects this:

> "I wolde not that," sayd Robyn,
> "Johan, that thou were slawe,   *slain*
> For all the golde in mery Englonde,
> Though it lay now on a rawe."[77]   *in a row*

Robin, too, rejects money in favor of their shared bond. This episode of "Little John and the Sheriff" offers another one of the small performative moments in the ballads. After arriving in the woods with all of the sheriff's stolen goods and his cook, Little John decides to push the game even further. He seeks the sheriff out where he is hunting and invites him to chase after a bigger prize, a "ryght fayre harte."[78] Pollard suggests that this scene is a "mockery of aristocratic hunting 'par force' (chase by mounted huntsmen)."[79] I would agree, and I would also suggest that, given the important economic and self-definition issues tied to hunting for aristocratic or gentle subjects, this fake hunt highlights the ways Robin and his band co-opt and thus oppose these identities, exposing their constructedness.

Robin, while usually enjoying the position of master, also gets his turn at performing service at the end of the *Gest*. After he goes to the king's court, the emphasis shifts to his spending money as a man of the king. According to the poem, he spent more than one hundred pounds in a little over a year:

> In every place where Robyn came
> Ever more he layde downe,   *paid down*
> Both for knyghtes and for squyres,
> To gete hym grete renowne.[80]

We learn here that Robin's renown is now connected to his ability to spend, a not uncommon occurrence in court life. However, as this is Robin Hood and not a typical courtier, he quickly grows discontented.

His discontent importantly climaxes one day as he sees young men shooting and despairs. He says, "'Alas!' than sayd good Robyn, / 'My welthe is went away.'"[81] However, rather than lamenting the loss of his money, the next line makes it clear that his "wealth" is something else, yet another move to reject definition by economic values and reclaim other status markers. Robin says:

> "Somtyme I was an archere good,
> A styffe and eke a stronge;   *hardy*
> I was comted the best archere   *reckoned*
> That was in mery Englonde."[82]

Here he rejects money as the basis for gaining "renowne," and thus identity within the world of the court, and returns to his woodland roots, where he was defined for his skill as an archer.

He rejects a court logic that says "that the very essence of being is having; that if one has nothing, one is nothing."[83] As Robin lies and escapes the king's service, he is playing on the same identity points as the other "service" episodes studied here, but he is also making a bigger statement about the overall project that we have seen throughout all of these bad performances — the constant interrogation and exposure of the economic processes and gestures constructing available subject positions in late medieval England.

Robin Hood Performances and "Economic Trouble"

I would like to conclude with a comparison of two Robin Hood "performances," one medieval and the other early modern, both of which return our attention to what I defined as the distinctive characteristics of the medieval figure at the outset of this chapter. In a legal record from the King's Bench Rolls of 1441,[84] a riotous outbreak is recorded, in which a group of yeomen and laborers in Norfolk blocked the highway, threatening to murder Sir Geoffrey Harsyk and fiercely singing "'We arn Robynhodesmen, war, war, war.'"[85] In this record, the yeomen dissidents are said to actively seize the outlaw identity and directly link it to both violence, through their cries of beware, and revolt, because of their threats to a member of the gentry and their waylaying of passersby. Merely seventy years later, we find an account of a very different performance of Robin Hood. In the chronicle of Edward Hall, we find a description of an aristocratic game involving King Henry VIII and his men:

> His grace, therles of Essex, Wilshire, and other noble menne, to the nombre of twelve, came Sodainly in a morning, into the Quenes Chambere, al appareled in shorte cotes, of Kentishe Kendal, with hodes on their heddes and hosen of the same, every one of them, his bowes and Arowes, and a sword and a bucklar, like out lawes, or Robyn Hodes men, whereof the Quene, The Ladies, and al other there, were abashed aswell for the straunge sight, and also for their Sodain coming, and after certain daunces and pastime made, thei departed.[86]

Here we see the adoption of Robin Hood's persona as part of an erotic courtly pastime, where the outlaw disguise simply adds spice to routine aristocratic behaviors.

Much of the difference between these two descriptions is related to a shift in the depiction of the outlaw figure from the medieval period to the early modern period, where most of our modern notions of the outlaw originate. In our modern milieu, the name of Robin Hood is synonymous with a certain brand of justice, particularly an economic justice based on a redistributive model favoring the poor of society at the expense of the wealthy. We acknowledge that Robin engages in rather unorthodox financial behavior as a thief, but this potentially threatening behavior is ameliorated by the fact that his ultimate interests are not in pocketing the wealth but in achieving a more humane social balance. In addition, his gentrification opens him up to rapprochement with dominant interests, as can be seen in the courtly games above.

Of course, the Robin to whom these facts apply is a modern creation, and if we return to the origins of the criminal hero in the medieval textual evidence, a very different picture emerges. I think the ways in which the medieval Robin

Hood we have seen in these pages could lend himself to expressions of rebellion and discontent like that of the Norfolk rioters has been made abundantly clear. Like these yeomen, Robin implicitly chants "war, war, war" as he flouts convention and questions established economic practices. In contrast, the Robin of Henry VIII's time, a figure who has been recuperated as a dispossessed noble, could never elicit such discomfiting sensations. A dispossessed thirteenth-century aristocrat fighting for justice is in many ways a less socially radical figure than a yeoman who is more concerned with destabilizing the system rather than righting it. To the extent that we let only the "medievalized" modern view of Robin Hood dominate our cultural memory, we risk losing the radical socioeconomic work of these texts and the figure of the outlaw himself.

Indeed, Robin Hood is an important figure in light of this research as a whole, as his cultural work is to show up the problems and anxieties generated by new economic systems of thought that threatened to reduce identity to purely financial terms. This cultural work echoes that of many of the earlier texts in this analysis, texts deeply interested in the determination of value, the concept of class status, and the connections between wealth and identity. For example, *Sir Amadace*, a text which fails to make sense as a chivalric text under traditional models because of its overt and insistent economic emphases, takes on new importance when seen as an exploration of gentry fears about the inter-relationships of class status, inborn distinction, and economic solvency. The *Octavian* romances, too, rather than being a hodgepodge set of romances, mark the struggles surrounding the creation of what we today understand as mercantile identity. The various versions of the Alexius legend in Middle English grapple with the centrality of poverty to religious identity, an increasing concern in a period that had to deal with the harsh realities of increasing real poverty as well as the deployment of the language of poverty in attacks on the wealthy medieval Church.

The medieval Robin Hood ballads, then, can be viewed not simply as comic or parodic texts, but as a series of social commentaries that can talk back to these other texts in important and provocative ways. Robin's various class cross-dressings or performances interrogate the interpellation of knights, merchants, and yeomen as economic subjects. When he takes on the figure of the courtly gentleman and refuses to maintain the appropriate façade of financial disinterest, we need to think back to the romances of *Sir Amadace* and Northern *Octavian*, which articulate the straight version of this scenario, suggesting that this behavior is innate to nobility. Robin's queering of this scenario has the potential to respond to these texts, showing up not only the constructedness of these identities, but also their severe limitations. Likewise, when Robin takes on the role of the potter, we should remember *Octavian's*

Clement, both in his turn as vilified bourgeois and in his socially mobile fantasy of butcher to knight. Again, Robin's refusal to play the economic game and to answer the call of his own economic interpellation points to the emptiness of both scenarios for Clement. In effect, these Robin Hood tales cause trouble, in Judith Butler's sense, and a particularly important kind because they refuse to stand still and allow for easy assumptions about identity to take hold.[87] Instead, they constantly throw fixed categories into doubt and offer complex mixes of behavior which gesture to the ways in which medieval subjects were attempting to negotiate new subject positions in the transitional era of the late medieval period.

NOTES

1. This description is common of modern depictions of the outlaw, from Pyle's classic *The Merry Adventures of Robin Hood* to Kevin Costner's *Robin Hood: Prince of Thieves*.
2. The latest film addition, Ridley Scott and Russell Crowe's 2010 *Robin Hood*, portrays Robin as a crusader against corruption, although he is, interestingly, not a nobleman in the back-story of the film but a simple archer.
3. In addition to the namesake Robin Hood flour brand and Robinhood kitchen accessories line, the outlaw figure has appeared in a variety of advertising for other products and stores to signal great savings. One of the most interesting and ironic of these is an advertisement for Wal-Mart, where their yellow-dot figure is wearing a Robin Hood costume and shooting at the price-point signs throughout the store, supposedly lowering them in favor of the consumer. It is a delicious irony, of course, that the store has become more famous from stealing from the poor, in the form of their employees and shoppers, to line the pockets of the rich rather than vice versa.
4. Here, I am working off of Althusser's model of ideology, in which a subject is hailed and responds by recognizing itself to be the subject indicated in the greeting, thus taking up his or her place in the social order. In the case of economic interpellation, the subject is constituted by its recognition and acceptance of a set of financial behaviors and attitudes as the norm. Robin, by his refusal answer the hail correctly, exposes the relations of the individual to his material conditions and opens the way for the social and economic critique offered by the ballads.
5. In my dissertation, I explore the relationship between the profound economic changes of the late medieval period and shifting models of subjectivity. I argue that often-noted economic transformations, such as the expansion of the money economy, the commercialization of English society, and the general increase in personal wealth, had consequences far beyond the marketplace. Indeed, such changes had a significant impact on how people imagined themselves and others to be defined, causing a shift from societal models of birth and function to paradigms emphasizing economic activity and income. Increasingly, I suggest, being was related to having. See Kimberly A. Thompson, "Money and the Man: Economics and Identity in Late Medieval English Literature" (PhD diss., The Ohio State University, 2007).
6. Kimberly A. Thompson, "The Late Medieval Robin Hood: Good Yeomanry and Bad Performances," in *Images of Robin Hood: Medieval to Modern*, ed. Lois Potter and Joshua Calhoun (Newark: University of Delaware Press, 2000), 102–10.
7. For essays that examine the performative quality of characters within the Robin Hood poems, see Christine Chism, "Robin Hood: Thinking Globally, Acting Locally in the Fifteenth-century Ballads," in *The Letter of the Law: Legal Practice and Literary Production in Medieval England*, ed. Emily Steiner and Candace Barrington (Ithaca: Cornell University Press, 2002),

12–39; and Claire Sponsler, *Drama and Resistance: Bodies, Goods, and Theatricality in Late Medieval England*. Medieval Cultures 10 (Minneapolis: University of Minnesota Press, 1997), especially Chapter 2, "Counterfeit in Their Array: Cross-Dressing in Robin Hood Performances," 24–49.

8. Hilary A. Kahn, "Traversing the Q'eqchi' Imaginary: The Conjecture of Crime in Livingston, Guatemala," in *Crime's Power: Anthropologists and the Ethnographies of Crime*, ed. Philip C. Parnell and Stephanie C. Kane (New York: Palgrave Macmillan, 2003), 33–54 at 34.

9. Mike Presdee, *Cultural Criminology and the Carnival of Crime* (London: Routledge, 2000), 18.

10. Antony W. Dnes, "The Economics of Crime," in *The Economic Dimensions of Crime*, ed. Nigel G. Fielding, Alan Clarke, and Robert Witt (New York: St. Martin's Press, 2000), 70–81 at 71.

11. Presdee, *Cultural Criminology*, 17.

12. For deer poaching, see Jean Birrell, "Peasant Deer Poachers in the Medieval Forest," in *Progress and Problems in Medieval England*, eds. Richard Britnell and John Hatcher (Cambridge: Cambridge University Press, 1996), 68–88 and Barbara Hanawalt, "Men's Games, King's Deer: Poaching in Medieval England," *Journal of Medieval and Renaissance Studies* 18 (1988): 175–193.

13. Drew Humphries and David Greenberg, "The Dialectics of Crime Control," in *Crime and Capitalism: Readings in Marxist Criminology*, ed. David Greenberg, exp. ed. (Philadelphia: Temple University Press, 1993), 463–508 at 467. For commentary on the medieval forest laws, see Roland Bechmann, *Trees and Man: The Forest in the Middle Ages*, trans. Katharyn Dunham (New York: Paragon House, 1990), especially Chapter 10; and Charles R. Young, *The Royal Forests of Medieval England* (Philadelphia: University of Pennsylvania Press, 1979).

14. For the relationship between hunting practices and identity, see Matt Cartmill, *A View to Death in the Morning: Hunting and Nature throughout History* (Cambridge: Harvard University Press, 1993), 60–75.

15. Jeffrey L. Singman, *Robin Hood: The Shaping of a Legend* (Westport, CT: Greenwood Press, 1998), 150–51.

16. Douglas Gray, "The Robin Hood Poems," in Knight 1999, 3–37 at 35.

17. Helen Phillips, "Forest, Town, and Road: The Significance of Places and Names in Some Robin Hood Texts," in Hahn, 197–214 at 209.

18. Bryan Randolph Reynolds, *Becoming Criminal: Transversal Performance and Cultural Dissidence in Early Modern England* (Baltimore: Johns Hopkins University Press, 2002), 19.

19. Ibid., 20.

20. See especially A.J. Pollard, *Imagining Robin Hood: The Late Medieval Stories in Historical Context* (New York: Routledge, 2004), who devotes an entire chapter of his study to the explication of the word "yeoman" in its various socio-historical contexts, 29–56.

21. Keen, xvi-xvii.

22. Knight 2003, 2.

23. *MED*, s.v. "yēman."

24. Dobson and Taylor, 34.

25. In one of the famous references to Robin Hood, a sermon writer castigates the public for interest in these tales, but at least one critic suggests that his yeoman status might have made the reference more than just the same old critique. Indeed, "in a sermon concerned to present a picture of an harmonious society, Robin Hood is a particularly apt exemplar of precisely what was to be avoided; in the fifteenth century he generally appears to have connoted a yeoman marauder, someone with whom the anti-social and even criminally disposed might be inclined to identify. Class strife and rebellion are a notable energy source in tales attached to him," Alan J. Fletcher, *Preaching, Politics and Poetry in Late-Medieval England* (Dublin: Four Courts Press, 1998), 153–54.

26. I. M. W. Harvey, *Jack Cade's Rebellion of 1450* (Oxford: Clarendon Press, 1991), 185. For other examinations of the parallels that exist between Cade's Rebellion and the Robin Hood tradition, see Alexander L. Kaufman, *The Historical Literature of the Jack Cade Rebellion* (Farnham:

Ashgate Publishing, 2009), 175–94; and Pollard, *Imagining Robin Hood*, 176–80; and A. J. Pollard, "Political Ideology in the Early Stories of Robin Hood," in *Outlaws in Medieval and Early Modern England: Crime, Government and Society, c. 1066–1600*, ed. John C. Appleby and Paul Dalton (Farnham: Ashgate Press, 2009), 111–28 at 118–22.

27. I would like to thank Kellie Robertson for the suggestion to investigate yeoman connections to the Jack Cade Rebellion.

28. Christine Carpenter, *Locality and Polity: A Study of Warwickshire Landed Society, 1401–1499* (Cambridge: Cambridge University Press, 1992), 44–45.

29. The only extant copy of the ballad "Robin Hood and Guy of Gisborne" exists in a manuscript much later than those of our other medieval ballads, a seventeenth-century manuscript owned by Thomas Percy, who later published it in his 1765 *Reliques*. However, it is generally accepted that the tale is much older, both because of its archaic language and its having a witness in the late medieval play fragment *Robyn Hod and the Shryff off Notyngham*, which dates from 1475.

30. *Robin Hood and Guy of Gisborne*, in Knight and Ohlgren, 169–83 at 173, lines 1–4. Line 1 can best be translated as follows: "When woods are bright and branches full fair ..."

31. Ibid., 176, lines 87–90.

32. Ibid., 176, lines 105–06.

33. This costume, described in the text as a "capull-hyde, / Topp and tayle and mayne," is one of the oddest parts of the poem, 174, lines 29–30. It has been described as a ritual costume by Knight and Ohlgren in their edition of the ballad, 168. Guy's attire is also discussed by Stuart Kane in "Horseplay: Robin Hood, Guy of Gisborne, and the Neg(oti)ation of the Bestial," in Hahn, 101–10. I would suggest that we should pay attention to the animal nature of the costume, a marker of the animal/human divide, one often suggestive of identity issues and boundaries.

34. Knight and Ohlgren, 178, lines 173–74.

35. Ibid., 178, lines 167–70.

36. Sponsler, *Drama and Resistance*, 25.

37. Kane, "Horseplay," 110.

38. Knight and Ohlgren, 176, lines 101–2.

39. *Robyn Hode and the Shryff off Notyngham*, in Knight and Ohlgren, 269–80 at 276, lines 2–4.

40. Knight and Ohlgren, 179, lines 195–96.

41. Ibid., 179, line 197.

42. Ibid., 179, line 200–1.

43. Sponsler, *Drama and Resistance*, 32–33.

44. Knight and Ohlgren, 179, lines 203–6.

45. Chism, "Robin Hood," 18

46. Kane, "Horseplay," 102

47. *A Gest of Robyn Hode*, in Knight and Ohlgren, 80–168 at 92–93, lines 85–92.

48. Ibid., 95, lines 175–76.

49. Ibid., 95, lines 179–80.

50. Ibid., 95, lines 181–84.

51. Ibid., 97, lines 234–37.

52. This scene where Sir Richard is outfitted also contains one of the many small moments of performance, which exist side-by-side with the more extended cross-dressing episodes. Here, Little John is sent by Robin to measure out cloth for the knight. There are several details that suggest that Robin is being framed in this vignette as a merchant and Little John as his apprentice. Little John cuts the cloth with a much too generous hand, assuring that the knight will receive a "Robin Hood's pennyworth." While the standard interpretation of this scene is to view it as comic, when viewed along with the other episodes, it seems clear that once again Little John's bad performance points to issues of identity.

53. Knight and Ohlgren, 100, lines 317–20.

54. Sponsler, *Drama and Resistance*, 31

55. Knight and Ohlgren, 90, lines 5–8.

56. Knight 2003, 27
57. Knight and Ohlgren, 90, lines 23–24.
58. Ibid., 94, lines 127–32. Here, again, we might usefully think back to Sir Amadace's feast as a performance of identity. However, Robin's feast does have a criminal aspect because of the presence of venison, indicating the specter of his illegal poaching of the king's deer.
59. Ibid., 90, lines 125–26.
60. Ibid., 94, lines 134–40
61. Ibid., 94, lines 141–48.
62. Valentin Groebner, *Liquid Assets, Dangerous Gifts: Presents and Politics at the End of the Middle Ages*, trans. Pamela E. Selwyn (Philadelphia: University of Pennsylvania Press, 2002), 1.
63. Knight and Ohlgren 98, lines 265–68.
64. Interestingly, given all of the complex religious critique in this particular text, the guarantor for this loan is Robin's beloved Virgin Mary.
65. Regarding the manuscript that contains *Robin Hood and the Monk*, Cambridge University Library MS Ff.5.48, Douglas Gray notes: "This book is an interesting miscellany, which contains religious and didactic matter (directions to parish priests, lamentations of the Virgin Mary, etc.) as well as a series of secular poems, which include *King Edward and the Shepherd*, a comic story of a king (probably Edward III) disguised as a merchant, who meets a very independent shepherd, who (it turns out) has been driven to poaching because of the depredations of the king's men, the burlesque *Tournament of Tottenham*, and *The Tale of the Basyn*, a bawdy and fantastic story of an enchanted basin," in "The Robin Hood Poems." See also Ohlgren 2007, 28–67.
66. R. L. Almond and A. J. Pollard, "The Yeomanry of Robin Hood and Social Terminology in Fifteenth-Century England," *Past and Present* 170 (2001): 52–77 at 52–53.
67. *Robin Hood and the Monk*, in Knight and Ohlgren, 31–56 at 47, lines 339–40.
68. For studies on bastard feudalism, see these two classic K. B. McFarlane essays: "Parliament and 'Bastard Feudalism,'" *Transactions of the Royal Historical Society*, 4th Series, 26 (1944): 53–79; and "'Bastard Feudalism,'" *Bulletin of the Institute of Historical Research* 20 (1945): 161–80. See also, J. G. Bellamy, *Bastard Feudalism and the Law* (Portland: Areopagitica Press, 1989); and Michael A. Hicks, *Bastard Feudalism* (London: Longman, 1995).
69. Of course, this is not to say that bastard feudalism **was** a purely monetary connection, but I believe that this quality is being exaggerated for effect in the financial logic of the ballads.
70. Knight and Ohlgren, 48, lines 347–50.
71. Ibid., 48, lines 351–54.
72. Ibid., 109, line 600.
73. Ibid., 109, lines 615–16.
74. Ibid., 110, lines 653–56.
75. Ibid., 111, lines 679–82.
76. Pollard, *Imagining Robin Hood*, 172.
77. Knight and Ohlgren, 128, lines 1221–24.
78. Ibid., 113, line 737.
79. Pollard, *Imagining Robin Hood*, 50–51.
80. Knight and Ohlgren, 145, lines 1733–36.
81. Ibid., 145, lines 1743–44.
82. Ibid., 145, lines 1745–48.
83. Erich Fromm, *To Have or to Be?* (New York: Harper & Row; repr., New York: Continuum, 2007), 13.
84. Legal records yield several other interesting anecdotes about medieval Robin Hood "performances," such as this interesting one: "At Tutbury, Staffordshire, in 1439 the court records complain that one Piers Venables, of Aston, gentleman, gadered and assembled unto hym many misdoers ... and, in maner of insurrection, wente into the wodes in that contre, like as it hadde be Robyn Hode and his meyne," Knight 2003, 6. Also, in 1497, Roger Marshall from Westbury in Staffordshire (not far from Piers Venables's Tutbury) was hauled before the powerful Star

Chamber on charges of leading a "riotous assembly" to the town of Willenhall under the name of Robin Hood," ibid., 8.

85. Ibid., 8. Perhaps not unimportantly, Knight identifies these men as laborers, but A. J. Pollard, in discussing the same record, clearly identifies them as yeomen and laborers, *Imagining Robin Hood*, 109–110. This is significant because Robin and his men are insistently identified with the term yeoman in the medieval ballads, and many scholars, including me, locate an important interpretive crux in the usage and meaning of yeoman.

86. Knight 2003, 46.

87. It is this insistence on the idea of troubling identities rather than inverting them that keeps me from following the various Bakhtin influenced critiques, such as Gray, "The Robin Hood Poems," 19-ff.

11

"Where Shall We Rob?": Fantasies of Justice in the Early Robin Hood Ballads

MARK LEAHY

One of the most enduring controversies surrounding the Robin Hood legend centers on the possible audiences and rhetorical functions of the early ballads in medieval English society. In the last century, the discussion seems to have been split along the standard lines of high and low culture: was Robin a product of peasant unrest, an avenger of the common man; or was he a creation of the upper crust, a figure who could only have been imagined by educated minds, and whose value was in delighting the wealthy and mollifying the rabble with carnivalesque release? There is merit, I think, in either of these arguments, and more recently several scholars have effectively attempted to reconcile the two. But while these arguments serve as intriguing provocations to examine how the Robin Hood legend could have originated, and provide early examples of the instability of high/low cultural distinctions, I want to look at what role the legend (particularly as it is articulated the early Robin Hood ballads) might play beyond these simple cultural binaries, and how the sense of justice and fantasy that we associate with the legend cannot be separated from the ideological apparatuses of the period in which it was conceived.

Critical Images of Robin Hood

One of the earliest critics to challenge the traditional image of Robin Hood as a people's hero was J. C. Holt, who in his article "The Origins and Audience of the Ballads of Robin Hood" was responding to R. H. Hilton's assertion that the "earliest versions of the Robin Hood legend were 'a by product of the agrarian social struggle' over rents, services and social status which culminated, after a century and a half, in the rising of 1381."[1] If Robin Hood was a popular figure who arose from popular unrest, then it seemed reasonable that the ballads would reflect this attitude. However, Holt finds "no evidence that the ballads were concerned to any significant degree with the agrarian discontents of the thirteenth and fourteenth centuries," even claiming (rather spectacularly) that he does not "consider that the ballads expressed exclusive class interests, attitudes or ambitions."[2] Of the most iconic expression of the Robin Hood legends' notion of justice — that Robin robs from the rich to give to the poor — Holt finds that it is all but absent in the early ballads: "This view of Robin is chiefly derived from Martin Parker's *True Tale of Robin Hood* of 1632" in which Robin's acts of redistribution are "made to illustrate his Christian charity rather than any deliberately conceived social policy."[3]

The value of Holt's argument is not, I think, found in any specific claim that he makes or refutes. In fact, one of these claims, that the Robin Hood ballads are "fundamentally ... not class literature,"[4] seems to contradict his assertion that they represent rather the concerns of the upper, knightly classes. However, Holt does go a great way towards complicating what seemed for so long to be a rather natural assumption: that the Robin Hood legend is wholly a product of popular unrest, whose sole appeal is to an exploited peasantry. To the contrary, he finds that the opening lines of *A Gest of Robyn Hode* are aimed at a markedly more privileged audience:

> Lythe and listin gentilmen   *Attend*
> That be of frebore blode[5]   *freeborn blood*

The words "gentle" and "free-born" have special significance in this context, being descriptors exclusive to privileged citizens. Later, we will see how Thomas Ohlgren will use these lines to further tease out the specific class ideology of the ballads. But suffice it to say, Holt's complication had the potential to controvert the most fundamental ideas about one of the most beloved and popular cultural heroes in the English language.

That the gentry and the nobility (Henry VIII not least of whom)[6] obviously found something in the Robin Hood legend that they, his ostensible targets, could enjoy implies that there is something more complex about Robin's roles in medieval culture than one might assume. That there was, indeed, a "mixed audience," as Holt and others assert, points to a seemingly contradictory collection of cultural appeals encoded into the Robin Hood figure that force him, as a "good outlaw," to challenge and uphold the laws and values of medieval England. In this reading, I will attempt not to reconcile these contradictions but to look at how they serve to create a peculiar ideological fantasy in which Robin Hood excels in remedying injustices, while ensuring that the conditions under which those injustices took place remain relatively stable.

Maurice Keen, siding with Hilton, at first disagreed with Holt's identification of Robin Hood as a "hero of the gentry."[7] Keen examined the social conditions of the medieval peasantry and found that "[t]he ballads in fact mirror accurately the attitudes and the grievances of the socially oppressed."[8] Of Robin's seemingly troublesome identification with the knightly class and performance of knightly courtesies, Keen makes a startling cultural observation: "Medieval social thought accepted the idea of a stratified society: indeed, it is doubtful if it could have contemplated any other."[9] However, Keen brushes away the striking question of what was even *conceivable* to the medieval mind, finding that the "dominant theme appears ... to be rather the righting of wrong done and the downfall of those who control the law by bribery and abuse of office."[10] It seems to me that these two observations are in fact bound in one another, where there exists not only the lack of an ability to effectively draw a new system of justice in which the formation of the kind of fantasy of justice is molded, but also the audacious "righting of wrong done" that Robin Hood represents. Furthermore, I will draw on the works of Slavoj Žižek, where he demonstrates how this fantasy of justice is not only necessitated by this desire for justice, but that it also "constitutes our desire, provides its coordinates; that is, it literally 'teaches us how to desire.'"[11] In this way, the Robin Hood ballads are not simply expressions of medieval desire for justice in a time when abuse by the upper class was more than rampant, but they are codified; that is, they represent in large part how justice could be conceived in such a world.

It is worth noting here that Maurice Keen would later, rather humbly, reverse his position and bring his thinking much more in line with the evidence presented by J. C. Holt: the original audience of the ballads was not "rural peasantry," and was rather more privileged, but this did not end the matter of the ballads' rhetorical appeal.[12] However, the seemingly settled debate between Keen and Holt only prompted later scholars such as Peter Stallybrass, Richard Tardif, and Joseph Nagy to explore how divergent configurations of audience and purpose in the legend allow us to see Robin Hood as a far more complex and politically interested character than almost any other "folk" hero, before or since.

To reconcile Robin Hood's probable audience with his seeming hostility toward its members, Joseph Nagy attempts to construct a "liminal" reading of Robin, who is "not so much a figure outside society as one who exists *between* culture and nature, and several other pairs of opposed categories as well,"[13] among which are "man and animal, culture and nature, knight and yeoman, even man and woman."[14] Robin's identity is thus fluid, and it is in this fluidity, this ability to play both sides of essential binaries, that he succeeds in evading the law and aiding the downtrodden. Of the many paradoxes this reading incorporates, the most central one occurs while Robin is "a master of disguise and deception, ironically [he] is very concerned about exposing falsehood and finding out the truth."[15] More than a simple irony, I would argue that this assessment points toward the larger problem that a gentry-oriented Robin produces; in essence, if Robin is not a people's hero who exemplifies a popular ideal of social justice in an unjust society, from where do his values arise? How does Robin distinguish between his own deceptions and the falsehoods he punishes? Nagy answers the question this way:

> The world of the outlaw is peripheral to society. Yet it is to an extent a mirror for society, for the world of Robin Hood is based on essential social values such as truth, loyalty, honesty, reciprocity, and religiosity; the outlaw's adventures are a context for the reaffirmation of these values, which seem in the ballads to be barely operative in the society proper.[16]

This account is problematic on several levels, not the least of which is his reliance, like Keen, on "essential social values." More importantly, or rather, as a consequence of this reliance, Nagy's argument neglects the deeper ideological dilemma presented by Holt's original rearticulation of Robin as an outlaw hero who was constructed for privileged audiences, which Nagy sees as merely confirming Robin's "anomalous nature."[17] In this way, Nagy is far too willing to leave Robin's contradictions catalogued but unexamined, applying the term "liminal" to any aspect of the ballads that resists his interpretation.

An example of where this strategy fails to satisfy even the mildest scrutiny is Nagy's explanation for one of the more prickly inconsistencies in Robin's character—his tender relationship with the king. As we will see later, Keen also struggles to explain how Robin, an enemy to corrupt authority, can maintain a robust love for his king. Nagy, however, does not struggle long with this question. For him, the king, like Robin Hood, is a liminal figure, "a social figure intimately associated with nature,"[18] and thus the two must be "either very good friends or mortal enemies." That the case is, for Robin at least, always the former, does not trouble Nagy, because paradoxes abound and are to be abided as such.

Finding Robin likewise vexed by paradox, Peter Stallybrass attempts to describe the character's rhetorical construction, relying on Mikhail Bakhtin and Julia Kristeva to read the legend as a carnivalesque formation.[19] For Bakhtin, Kristeva, and Stallybrass, the carnivalesque refers to a temporary, authorized inversion of everyday social, religious, and political hierarchies, allowing those under the rule of these hierarchical structures a chance to relieve tensions and (again, temporarily) criticize those in power. This has the effect of both exposing the arbitrary nature of power, and of reaffirming "local norms of domestic hierarchy"[20] because the carnival generally ends at some point, and its participants return to their everyday lives, complacent until the next carnival. Also, by allowing or "licensing" the carnival, the state maintains its control (or appears to) even in these ostensibly anarchic bubbles.

More concerned with the later ballads and plays, which featured so prominently in medieval May game ceremonies, Stallybrass still finds that a "[c]arnivalesque discourse permeates even the earliest ballads."[21] This discourse operates not through fence-straddling liminality, as in Nagy's interpretation, but instead through rhetorical inversions of the dominant social order such as trading "fast for feast" or the profaning of the sacred.[22] Stallybrass's Robin Hood is a rhetorically transgressive figure, whose function was, at least at first, to critique unjust practices such as enclosure laws, "to legitimate popular justice against the official ideology and legal apparatus."[23] In Stallybrass's reading, it is only after the Robin Hood of the ballads becomes a star of the May games that the state begins to "patronize May-games and village sports as a means of social control."[24] However, Stallybrass does not consider that the features of Robin that he sees being appropriated by the privileged to enforce their ideological control over the poor may have already been appropriated by the participants of the May games from ballads whose original audience were privileged, and whose original purpose, as Holt points out, may not have been to critique social injustices at all. It may seem perverse to add further complication to an already well-formed account of the "tug-of-war" of which Robin Hood has been the object, which Stallybrass certainly provides, but for me this reaffirms the depth to which Holt has exposed a most fundamental, baffling contradiction within the legend and literary genealogy of Robin Hood.

Stallybrass's reading has many fascinating implications and begins to account for how the ballads could have become such a schizophrenic affair, but he ultimately leaves us in the same kind of untroubled paradox as Nagy's reading, this one in which Robin represents a kind of "licensed misrule." Stallybrass is not so much alarmed by the ramifications of hegemonic appropriations (or re-appropriations) of the legend because they are a matter of course in the carnivalesque model. Moreover, he does not address the idea that the ballads (or the later plays) may have been constructed from material already in ideological accord with a privileged elite, and that even their most popular reconfigurations may still serve to legitimize the ideologies and corrupt political structures they seem to oppose. Richard Tardif, not content to abandon Robin in this kind of limbo, looks to the specific historical era of the ballads' propagation (dismissing the troublesome matter of origins) and finds that the locus of contradiction in the ballads is not Robin but the surrounding social order itself.²⁵ Robin, for Tardif, is a man of his time, reflecting the upheaval, hypocrisy and frustration of an "embryonic" professional class.

Taking another look at the controversy stirred by Holt, Tardif finds the matter far from settled.²⁶ Where Hilton and Holt fall short is in assuming that the class composition of the ballads is strictly rural or "manorial," while Tardif identifies their actual settings as predominantly urban. When not actually in town, Robin inhabits the greenwood, which for Tardif is hardly a rural setting: on the one hand because it rejects rural "social restrictions," and on the other because it is always located adjacent to urban locations, always "at the edge of the town."²⁷

What Tardif discovers is not paradoxical at all but instead is a strikingly unified Robin whose gestures and transgressions are wholly determined by the schismatic economic and cultural conditions of the fourteenth and fifteenth centuries. Indeed, the fluidity of the word "yeoman," which in the ballads is applied equally to Robin, his men, merchants, farmers, craftsmen, and even the entire town of Nottingham,²⁸ provides Tardif with a key insight into the ideological threats Robin embodies, namely class instability and social mobility:

> The single most significant event to generate the mobility of serving-men and undermine their structural links with the established order was of course the plague of 1348. The resultant shortage of labor gave workers such bargaining power they were able to demand higher wages or shift where such wages were available, giving rise to a substantial movement of the peasantry from farms to the towns, where they sought unskilled crafts and menial occupations.²⁹

These conditions led the English parliament and King Edward III to institute the 1349 Ordinance of Laborers, later reinforced by the 1351 Statute of Laborers, which governed such things as wages (which were not allowed to exceed pre-plague levels), profit margins, and retirement age. These statutes clearly favored in several instances those who did the hiring, and Tardif sees the resultant frustration of newly organized craftsmen as a central concern in the ballads, which catalogue the collusion of religious, political, and financial organizations in corrupt practices. What Tardif ignores is that this sense of frustration is not simply a high/low class opposition, but it is a result of a newly privileged class running afoul of the entrenched power structures of another privileged class.

Where he may also overstate his case is in reading Robin Hood and his band as a "realization of the rupture in social organization initiated by the development of journeyman fraternities."³⁰ To say that the Robin Hood ballads are an allegory for the devaluation of medieval craftsmen is a far more troubling position than to say that organizations of such craftsmen were the audience for these works. The lack of clear historical referents in the ballads (the Ordinance of Labourers, for example, is never mentioned or alluded to) and the missing narratival pieces on which Tardif remarks, makes this kind of intentional conjecture unverifiable. However, Tardif's claim that Robin Hood's band was structured *like* a guild, and that the ballads employ the language of mercantile rhetoric, are ideas that Thomas Ohlgren will revisit rather persuasively, while looking much more closely at the ideological apparatuses present within the ballads.

Each of these readings, by attempting a unified account of the disparate rhetorical threads in the earliest articulations of the legend, helps us answer the fundamental question first implied by J. C. Holt in 1960: namely, why is a character who openly opposes the wealthy and the privileged constructed as a hero for and by the very people he is portrayed as opposing? The historical, rhetorical, and literary strategies we have seen all have necessary limitations in addressing this question, but it is in the very things they leave out, the parts of Robin they do not touch, that we may perhaps begin to see him not as a paradox or a recognizable historical figure, but as an expression of the desires and ideologies of a particularly privileged people at a particular time that has been continually refigured around that privileged class's desire for justice in an unjust world — or, rather, as I argue, the desire for justice *and* an unjust world. Whatever the interpretation, and all of those that I have discussed here have merit, I think another look at the ballads can help us understand how we construct justice through the figure of Robin Hood, while incorporating what we now believe about the conditions and people through which they were constructed.

Robin Hood and Jouissance

One of the most interesting features of the Robin Hood ballads is how they continually locate justice not as simply legal, religious, or economic concerns (areas where justice is easily perverted toward whatever end agents empowered by those forces desire), but as an act of enjoyment, or *jouissance* for Robin and his men. *Jouissance* may be translated simply as "enjoyment," but can be further defined as the "largely unconscious enjoyment one derives from habits, attitudes, beliefs, and activities."[31] *Jouissance*, while it may be ideologically motivated, is not understood in ideological terms, and it is in this seemingly simple enjoyment that ideologies mask their motives. Justice in the ballads then is a matter of satisfying a particular sense of outrage at contemporary abuses of power and differing contemporary mores which, as Keen points out, belong to a society that only values or cannot but conceive of a stratified, inherently unjust society. Robin Hood is someone in whom certain privileged notions of justice and moral rectitude can find expression, even exhilaration. I say exhilaration because the righting of wrongs is not simply a moral calculation; that is why justice is hard to pin down as a matter of law or philosophy. Justice, it seems, in the ballads, follows a more poetic logic, a playing on the emotional responses of medieval English subjects following the Norman Conquest and subsequent centuries of ethnic class oppression. A rather dramatic example of this is the full four stanzas devoted at the end of *Robin Hood and Guy of Gisborne* to Little John's execution of the fleeing, beaten Sheriff (of Barnesdale, in this instance), in which the final stanza particularly delights in drawing out the moment:

> But he cold neither soe fast goe,   *could*
> Nor away soe fast runn,
> But Litle John, with an arrow broade,
> Did cleave his heart in twinn.³²   *twain*

This is a rather satisfying end to a tale in which John is arrested and held at the sheriff's mercy and tied fast to a tree for thirty-odd stanzas. And it is in this kind of quite enjoyable revenge on state officials that the ballads always seem to find their resolution. What is interesting about *Guy of Gisborne* is that Little John was not strictly innocent. He encountered the sheriff while he chased after several of his fellows and quickly slays one of the sheriff's men, but to say that he was arrested without cause would be to read quite a deal more into the narrative than exists on the page. The justice of this moment, then, is not that of an oppressed, imprisoned John against a corrupt sheriff, but rather of one competing, empowered organization (Robin's) with another (the sheriff's), and a satisfying turning of the tables by one's own "band."

We do, however, find moments of privileged corruption, but they are always particular, never systemic. In the *Gest* when the Sheriff of Nottingham complains to the king that Robin and Sir Richard at the Lee are in collusion, King Edward declares that he himself will capture the two. Sir Richard is put into custody, but Robin quickly rescues him and kills the Sheriff. Later, when Robin clearly has King Edward at his mercy in the greenwood, Robin instead challenges the king to an archery contest, and he and Sir Richard pledge their loyalty to the king. Never is it suggested that the extent of the king's power was what allowed the Sheriff, whom the king empowered, to enact his injustices. It suffices that the king is mildly scolded and the Sheriff is dead, and that Robin, in both these cases, seems quite satisfied with the outcome. Robin's concern seems to be in finding his own satisfaction in instances of unfairness, not in preventing their recurrence. That Robin appeals to both the oppressed and the privileged (whom we may view as either being oppressors or simply the less oppressed) has as much (if not more) to do with his adventurousness and success as with his politics, but this does not mean that adventure and politics are separate affairs in the ballads.

Thomas Ohlgren makes the most convincing assessment of Robin Hood's ideological underpinnings in the ballads, for in particular he finds that in the *Gest* there are signs of Robin's strong affiliation with and employment of mercantile rhetoric. He agrees largely with Tardif in locating the audience of the plays as urban, professional organizations, and he notes how those organization become associated metaphorically with criminal bands; however, he finds Tardif's account of the presence of chivalric and knightly values (what Tardif refers to as "ideology lag") to be specifically lacking.[33] For Ohlgren, there is a discursive process at work in the construction of Robin himself, a re-imagining of the standard knightly hero for a mercantile audience, which accounts for the conflicted nature of Robin as a heroic outlaw and locates the specific ideological motives that drive such a conflicted construction. In order to invent a Robin Hood, one had to appeal not only to recognizable tropes in hero mythology, tropes ideologically aligned with the landed classes, but also with new ideas about privileged economic justice (property laws, not essential social values) that would appeal to a burgeoning professional class. This was not simply a balancing act: whereas "[m]ost chivalric romances either ignore mercantile matters completely ... or treat them in a condescending or contemptuous manner," the Robin Hood ballads display a privileging of elite merchant concerns, employ key terms that merchant guilds would have recognized and appreciated, and even describe Robin's men in much the same way a merchant guild was organized.[34] Robin was a merchant-class hero.

Among the tell-tale signs are the aforementioned use of the words "gentle" and "free-born," which would have held special meaning for merchants, as they "delineat[ed] both the senior officers of the fraternity — the master and the four wardens, the bailiff, the clerk, the chaplains, and the assistants."[35] Furthermore, this articulation of the Robin Hood legend mirrors a wholesale shift in medieval society, one not of peasant revolt or noble anxiety, but "the rise of the merchant class in London to positions of power and influence,"[36] which Tardif refuses to acknowledge directly, preferring to ignore the growing empowerment of that class in order to reclaim Robin as a hero of the underprivileged. Ohlgren instead reads this sense of entitlement as the heart of the ballads' ideological construction.

The mercantile rise to power was marked by a provisional loyalty to the king, predicated not on blood relation, or economic or martial dependence, but on the understanding that the government would protect discreet business practices and secure monopolies for the guilds. "The merchant elite was strongly loyal to the monarchy," Ohlgren tells us, "as long as their business interests were not compromised."[37] It is in these cultural conditions that the Robin Hood ballads were constructed and manipulated, and it is these same conditions under which the ballads' sense of justice ultimately operates. The ballads never directly identify a general condition of oppression, only specific instances, specific oppressors with whom Robin must deal. This appears to fit the attitudes of a mercantile class who would not be concerned with the overall social condition under which they operated, as long as those conditions continued to favor their economic and entrepreneurial freedom. Maurice Keen points to this willingness in the ballads to accept the prevailing social structures:

> It is strange to find in the guardians of the law the villains in a poetic cycle whose undercurrent theme is the triumph of justice. Yet it is consistently so.... It is significant, therefore, that the ballad makers are always careful to particularize the abuse which these men have made of their position.... They are not hated because of the law they administer, but because their administration of it is corrupt.[38]

This pervasive specificity places blame on the shoulders of individuals, not with the systems and ideologies that put them in the position to abuse their stations in the first place. In fact, in most instances, Robin reveres his king and country, as in the *Gest,* when Robin says, "I love no man in all the worlde / So well as I do my kynge."[39] Robin, then, is not a revolutionary; he has nothing with which to replace the existing order. In fact, without the inconsistencies and injustices of the prevailing social hierarchies, it is arguable that there would be no need of a Robin Hood. More than this, as we have seen, Robin displays a remarkable deference to gentry, to women (out of his religious devotion to the Virgin Mary), and to the yeoman class, which would have included "honest" merchants but not those who gave a bad name to their professions (a potentially successful marketing strategy). He appears in the ballads and later plays as a rather comfortable leader and loyal subject, courteous (in the sense that he often behaves like a knight, granting boons), and pious. He does not transgress social boundaries (save that he is an outlaw) or taboos; in fact, the designation "good outlaw" implies that there are some moral lines that he adamantly will not cross. For instance, we are told in the *Gest* that he would "never do compani harme / That any woman was in,"[40] and later Robin admonishes his men:

"But loke ye do no husbonde harme, That tilleth with his ploughe.	*small farmer*
"No more ye shall no gode yeman That walketh by grene wode shawe,	*thicket*
Ne no knyght ne no squyer That wol be a gode felawe."[41]	*companion*

Whereas Robin Hood does not provide a complete program for justice, he may provide an effective *fantasy* of justice. Fantasy, for Slavoj Žižek, operates in very specific ways to obscure "the true horror of a situation."[42] Žižek works with Lacanian psychoanalysis, postmodern theory, and popular culture to construct several insightful accounts of the way fantasy and desire structure and make comprehensible everyday lived experiences.

Robin Hood and the Fantasy of Outlaw Justice

Slavoj Žižek disagrees with the Marxist notion that fantasy somehow keeps us from seeing the objective truth of reality — the Marxist example being so-called "commodity fetishism," the idea that we are fooled into believing that "the concrete content of a commodity (its use-value) is an expression of its abstract universality (its exchange value)," that can exist separate from social relations.[43] Žižek inverts the roles of reality and fantasy: "What they [Marxists] overlook, what they misrecognize, is not the reality but the illusion which is structuring their reality, their real social activity."[44] We overlook these "ideological fantasies" (act as if we are not aware of them), and allow ourselves to use them to structure our social relations. We do not want to see the "hard reality" of our situations, and so we employ fantasies that allow us to interact on an everyday level (money and commodities have value) so that we can maintain normative social relations. If we viewed economy as groups of sophisticated primates trading valueless shiny rocks back and forth, it may become less attractive to sustain the practice. It is not that this idea does not occur to the stockbroker: it is simply that the stockboker and his or her coworkers and clients have a healthy fantasy of value and profit to structure their social reality.

Just as the stockbroker can use the illusion of accruing value to make his or her business practices worthwhile, and an airline can produce an in-flight safety manual to provide a palatable fantasy to replace our own morbid midair uncertainty, so too may the Robin Hood legends provide the "gentrifying of a catastrophe," as Žižek puts it.[45] Simple obfuscation is, however, not the entirety of the function of fantasy. Fantasy structures our reality through the construction of desires, and several of the phantasmic "features" Žižek describes as being at work in this operation may help illuminate many of the paradoxes in our current discussion of the Robin Hood legend.

The first of these is the aforementioned role of fantasy in not only expressing our desires, but also in creating them, that "fantasy mediates between the formal symbolic structure and the positivity of objects we encounter in reality."[46] Žižek elaborates:

To put it in somewhat simplified terms: fantasy does not mean that when I desire a strawberry cake and cannot get it in reality, I fantasize about eating it; the problem is rather: *how do I know that I desire a strawberry cake in the first place?* This is what fantasy tells me.[47]

In much the same way, the Robin Hood ballads provide a fantasy of redress for a system that often did not provide clear means for it. In the *Gest*, when Sir Richard at the Lee explains to Robin his precarious financial and legal situation that stems from his son's indiscretions, he makes no mention of how, barring an act of heroism, he will ever see his son again, or how he will keep from being wholly dispossessed by the cruel Abbot, Monk, and Justice to whom he finds himself legally indebted. To say that the system itself is at fault is beyond him for the same reasons we have already discussed. What remains is a smoldering sense of wrong being done with no larger cause or solution. Robin's response, to give Sir Richard not only means to repay his debt, but also to trick his tormenters, not only satisfies this sense of wrong, it also provides the wronged party with a map of appropriate redress, namely to see the knight's property restored and the wicked outwitted. Notice that, unlike more modern narratives, a rewriting of easily perverted laws or systemic change is not included in the recipe for this particular strawberry cake.

Secondly, fantasy for Žižek includes an "impossible gaze," an ideology that the fantasy necessarily supports that obviates other ideologies. "Apropos of the phantasmic scene," Žižek explains, "the question to be asked is thus always: for which gaze is it staged? Which narrative is it destined to support?"[48] For our purposes, the work of Thomas Ohlgren in identifying the key features of mercantile ideology allows us to see how the Robin Hood ballads, which were written and staged for merchants and explicitly and implicitly referencing their trades, make alternate forms of political redress seem impossible. Žižek uses the example of Mother Theresa, for he says that "in so far as she suggests to the poor and terminally ill that they should seek salvation in their very suffering, Mother Theresa deters them from probing into the causes of their predicament — from politicizing their situation."[49] The Robin Hood ballads must necessarily support the idea that the system in which Robin operates is impossible to combat, except through means that do not upset the ideological order that allows the system to continue. Robin's repeated demonstrations of religious and political fealty, his concern for monetary recompense, and his precise choice of targets, all maintain a sense of ideological order in his lawlessness. But by characterizing outlawry this way, nothing truly "outside" of the prevailing political order, nothing truly transgressive, is ever allowed. Again, there can be no revolution, only the specific attack of specific, corrupt personages.

Finally, Žižek describes how "unwritten rules" play a role in how fantasy manages desire. Robin's kind of justice is never explicitly laid out, but as I said before, it belongs to a more poetic order, a pleasurable outwitting of power. These unwritten laws both point out the failings of the prevailing ideology, while they also encourage the idea that redress may only be had through phantasmic means. Again, Žižek:

> Or — to put it another way — the paradoxical role of unwritten rules is that, with regard to the explicit, public Law, they are simultaneously *transgressive* (they violate explicit social rules) *and more coercive* (they are additional rules which restrain the field of choice by prohibiting the possibility allowed for — guaranteed even — by the public Law).[50]

Robin Hood not only undermines the idea of alternative forms of social justice, his methods also argue against the possibility of any legal solution within his own system, that only an outlaw can compete against a corrupt sheriff, not appeals to higher officials or the courts (such as they were). This ensures that the corrupt practices of privileged elites and clerics cannot ever be legally contested because only by going outside the law can we provide the kind of poetic justice that satisfies the Robin Hood fantasy.

Žižek offers another succinct explanation of how the minor revolts and wrong-righting of the Robin Hood ballads actually work to maintain the authority of the King and the upper classes:

> In the dialectic of Master and servant, the servant (mis)perceives the Master as amassing *jouissance*, and gets back (steals from the Master) little crumbs of *jouissance*; these small pleasures (the awareness that he can also manipulate the Master), silently tolerated by the Master, not only fail to present any threat to the Master but, in fact, constitute the 'libidinal bribery' which maintains the servant's servitude. In short, the satisfaction that he is able to dupe the Master is precisely what guarantees the servant's servitude toward him.[51]

So we can see that while Robin may live outside of society, poaching the king's deer and staying always just beyond the Sheriff's reach, as a cultural production he always remains safely within the society he poaches from, and his values are still indicative of that society's ideological framework. Furthermore, as reflective of a particular class's anxieties and frustrations, Robin Hood makes specific claims about the shape and feel of justice — and its possibility — which serve to structure the larger society towards that privileged class's benefit. That Americans, in particular, have had such an intense love affair with Robin may have less to do with our ideas about "essential social justice" and more to do with our privileged, mercantile roots, and our continuing insistence on monetary recompense as justice and economic freedom for a privileged few. Robin provides no real remedy to the grave injustices he encounters, only a fantasy that allows for a temporary satisfaction and enjoyment — the *jouissance* of a corrupt official caught red-handed. In this way, his kind of justice, the possibility of monetary relief, the undermining of local authority, and the trickery and frustration (but not overthrow) of tyrants, contributes greatly to the medieval (and modern) sense of justice, as much or more so that the betterment of social conditions or the fairness of laws.

All of this is not to say that Robin Hood is merely counterproductive to effective social change, but as a hero of a specific time and place, he cannot but reflect and reinforce the dominant, situated ideological possibilities of his culture. The product of such a culture is an ideology whose interests are not the outlaw's or the peasant's or the knight's, but the burgeoning merchant class, a section of society whose sense of justice is far more concerned with monetary compensation and privileged freedom of movement than it is with progressive social practices. As fantasy, Robin stands between this injustice and any possible remedy, a source of *jouissance*, but his successes can never represent real gains; rather, they are simply happy fantasies of how good justice can feel, even if we can never have it.

Notes

1. J.C. Holt, "The Origins and Audience of the Ballads of Robin Hood," *Past and Present* 18 (1960): 89–110 at 89.
2. Ibid., 90.
3. Ibid., 91.
4. J.C. Holt, "Robin Hood: Some Comments," *Past and Present* 19 (1961): 16–18 at 17.
5. *A Gest of Robyn Hode*, in Knight and Ohlgren, 80–168 at 90, lines 1–2.
6. There are several telling accounts of Henry VIII's affection for the Robin Hood legend. W. E. Simeone tells us that "no less a person than Henry the VIII delighted to have his courtiers dress as merry Robin Hood and his yeoman," in "The May Games and the Robin Hood Legend," *The Journal of American Folklore* 64 (1951): 265–274 at 270–1. Robin then invites the king into the forest to "see how the outlaws live," demonstrating that the concept of "slumming" is not a modern invention. Thomas Ohlgren cites Edward Hall's 1515 chronicles and tells us that "the young Henry VIII loved dressing up as Robin Hood," and even went so far as to stage mock attacks on his queen, in Ohlgren 2007, 186.
7. Maurice Keen, "Robin Hood — Peasant or Gentleman?" *Past and Present* 19 (1961): 7–15 at 7.
8. Ibid. 14.
9. Ibid. 7.
10. Ibid., 7.
11. Slavoj Žižek, *The Plague of Fantasies* (New York: Verso, 1997), 7.
12. Keen, xii–xxxi. Most notably, Keen admits in the updated introduction, "Reconsidering the position, I am therefore no longer inclined to claim an exclusively popular appeal for the Robin Hood ballads, and am much more attracted by Professor Holt's suggestion that one of the focal centers for the dissemination of Robin's legend was the gentleman's household," xxiv.
13. Joseph Kalaky Nagy, "The Paradoxes of Robin Hood," *Folklore* 91, no. 2 (1980): 198–210 at 198.
14. Ibid., 203.
15. Ibid., 204.
16. Ibid., 206.

17. Ibid., 200.
18. Ibid., 202.
19. Peter Stallybrass, "'Drunk with the cup of liberty': Robin Hood, the Carnivalesque, and the Rhetoric of Violence in Early Modern England," in Knight 1999, 297–328.
20. Ibid., 303.
21. Ibid., 299.
22. Ibid., 298.
23. Ibid., 303.
24. Ibid., 315.
25. Richard Tardif, "The 'Mistery' of Robin Hood: A New Social Context for the Texts," in Knight 1999, 345–361.
26. Tardif actually characterizes his argument as a "complete rejection of Holt's thesis," ibid., 347. But it is important to note that he uses Holt's controversy, as I do, as a kind of instigation. I would go further and say that Tardif does not "completely" disagree with Holt in that he similarly finds the audience of the ballads to be a more complicated affair than simple popular unrest, even if he identifies significantly different demographic explanations for those complications.
27. Ibid., 347.
28. Ibid., 349.
29. Ibid. 349.
30. Ibid., 361.
31. Thomas Rickert, *Acts of Enjoyment: Rhetoric, Žižek, and the Return of the Subject* (Pittsburgh: University of Pittsburgh Press, 2007), 3.
32. *Robin Hood and Guy of Gisborne*, in Knight and Ohlgren, 169–183 at 180, lines 231–34.
33. Ohlgren 2007, 134–5.
34. Ibid., 143.
35. Ibid., 165.
36. Ibid., 143.
37. Ibid. 143.
38. Keen, 149–50.
39. Knight and Ohlgren, 139, lines 1541–42.
40. Ibid., 91, lines 39–40.
41. Ibid., 91, lines 51–56.
42. Slavoj Žižek, *The Sublime Object of Ideology* (New York: Verso, 1989), 7.
43. Ibid., 31.
44. Ibid., 32.
45. Žižek, *Plague of Fantasies*, 6.
46. Ibid., 7.
47. Ibid., 7.
48. Ibid., 16.
49. Ibid., 18.
50. Ibid., 28–9.
51. Ibid., 34.

12

"All the yemandry that ys here": *Mankind* and Robin Hood

MICHELLE M. BUTLER

Mankind can be dated with atypical but welcome precision. As Donald C. Baker has shown, the "rede reyallys" mentioned in *Mankind* first appeared in 1464; however, the "angel" gold coin, first used in 1469, is not referred to within the play. From these facts Baker argues "it is quite inconceivable that, considering the profuse allusions to current coin found in *Mankind*, a reference to, or a pun upon, the name of the angel would not have appeared in the play if the coin had indeed been current at the time of its composition," and he concludes that *Mankind* was almost certainly written during the period 1464–69.[1] Outlaw legends had been widespread for much of the Middle Ages, but in the fifteenth century the Robin Hood legend in particular was increasingly enjoying popularity, especially in performance-based entertainment. As Stephen Knight and Thomas Ohlgren have put it:

> Notwithstanding his important role in ballads and prose fiction, Robin Hood would have been best known in communities throughout fifteenth- and sixteenth-century Britain as the subject of a wide range of theatrical and quasi-theatrical entertainments. Most took the form of ceremonial games, dances, pageants, processions, and other mimetic events of popular culture of which we only get a fleeting glance in surviving civic and ecclesiastical records. Revels featuring the legendary outlaw appear to have surged in growth towards the close of the fifteenth century and remained popular from the royal court to the rural village green throughout the following century. Indeed, it is not exaggerating to say that Robin Hood plays and games were *the* most popular form of secular dramatic entertainment in provincial England for most of the sixteenth century.[2]

The popularity of the Robin Hood legend in the form of play-games as well as ballads invites us to consider it alongside extant fifteenth-century drama. When we do so, intriguing parallels emerge. Perhaps the most striking appears in *Mankind*. The presentation and characteristics of Mischief and the three Worldlings (New Guise, Nowadays, and Nought) in *Mankind* are highly reminiscent of the outlaw legends, particularly Robin Hood.[3] They should not be understood, I believe, to *be* Robin Hood and his men, but rather to evoke the legend, and in doing so, enter into a longstanding societal conversation about the spiritual and moral dimensions of outlaw tales. While I will be focusing here on the parallels between the Robin Hood legend and *Mankind*, there are some parallels with other outlaw legends as well, which is unsurprising given the interconnectedness of the legends themselves. The parallels between Mischief and the Worldlings and Robin Hood and his men are by far the most numerous. This may be because of the Robin Hood legend's widespread popularity; however, the legend was not as popular in East Anglia, from where *Mankind* derives, as in other parts. It may also have to do with Robin Hood's presence as a figure in drama. These are worthwhile and intriguing issues, but it is beyond the scope of this paper to attempt to discover and demonstrate why *Mankind*'s devils parallel the characters of Robin Hood legend more strongly than other outlaw legends. I focus here instead on showing that this parallel exists and the significance of it.

As is well known, the Robin Hood legend was widespread long before the fifteenth century. References to Robin Hood can be found as early as the thirteenth century.[4] Fourteenth-century evidence — most notably, of course, the famous first literary reference found in the B-Text of William Langland's *Piers Plowman*—attests to the ongoing popularity of the legend.[5] Indeed, the Appendix of "References of Robin Hood up to 1600" in Stephen Knight's *Robin Hood: A Complete Study of the English Outlaw* provides ample evidence of the pervasive nature of the legend from the thirteenth century onwards. "Robin Hood" appears in place names, surnames, and pseudonyms; he is referred to in literary works, chronicles, and sermons; and there is considerable evidence of his stature as a proverbial figure.[6] Robin Hood "rymes" were clearly circulating, although no texts survive until the fifteenth century. As popular as the ballads were, however, by the fifteenth century Robin Hood was almost certainly even better known, as Knight and Ohlgren point out above, through play-games. The Records of Early English Drama (REED) project, which has collected an astonishing number of references to Robin Hood dramatic activity, has brought to light the early history of Robin Hood plays, games, ales, and other such medieval and early modern performances.[7] Unfortunately, even fewer texts of these entertainments survive than of the early ballads. But from such sources as we have, we can and have derived a picture of how Robin Hood and his men were understood in the fifteenth century. As we will see below, in *Mankind* Mischief and the Worldlings exhibit many of those same characteristics.

First, the number and names, with their attendant implication of character traits, of Mischief and the Worldlings evoke Robin Hood and his men. Mischief, like Robin Hood, is surrounded by a core of three loyal henchmen. In the play-games, the three are Little John, Friar Tuck, and Maid Marian.[8] Little John is, of course, associated with Robin Hood from the earliest references, while Friar Tuck and Maid Marian are perhaps stand-alone figures with their own stories who became incorporated in the Robin Hood legend.[9] By the first years of the sixteenth century, and most likely earlier as well, Robin Hood and his followers, particularly Friar Tuck and Maid Marian, participate in dancing in the play-games, among other activities.[10] Mischief's followers, New Guise, Nowadays, and Nought, also dance:

> NEW GYSE. Ande how, mynstrellys, pley þe comyn trace!
>   Ley on wyth þi ballys tyll hys bely breste!
> NOUGHT. I putt case I breke my neke: how than?
> NEW GYSE. I gyff no force, by Sent Tanne!
> NOWADAYS. Leppe about lyuely! þou art a wyght man.
>   Lett ws be mery wyll we be here!
> NOUGHT. Xall I breke my neke to schew yow sporte?
> NOWADAYS. Therfor euer be ware of þi reporte.
> NOUGHT. I beshrew ye all! Her ys a schrewde sorte.
>   Haue þeratt þen wyth a mery chere![11]

The dancing strongly implied by their dialogue is explicitly stated in the stage direction that immediately follows these lines: "Her þei daunce." Stage directions are rare, and hence noteworthy, in medieval drama. This dancing is important enough to merit considerable attention in the dialogue itself, and the author is at apparent pains to ensure that it is included in the performance, providing a stage direction to underscore its presence.

Moreover, attention is drawn to this dancing because it occurs as part of the Worldlings' first appearance in the play. New Guise, Nowadays, and Nought enter the action of the play either accompanied by minstrels or playing music themselves, and they dance. This procession likely looked and sounded very much like the processions involved with the Robin Hood play-games. David Wiles provides many examples of Robin Hood's entourage in the play-games dancing, with the music of minstrels.[12] The Worldlings' dancing has typically been understood to indicate their frivolity, yet the seeming harmlessness of their fun-seeking lifestyle later is shown to have been concealing their true nature; that is, a personality and temperament that is evil rather than merely entertaining. While this is certainly true, their dancing is also a characteristic that they share with the figures of the Robin Hood play-games.

In the early ballads, Robin Hood's three dedicated followers are Little John, Will Scarlet, and Much, and *Mankind*'s Worldlings parallel this triad as well.[13] New Guise and Nowadays are named to skewer fashion and those who follow fashion, but their behaviors suggest their kinship with Robin's men. New Guise, like Little John, is the second-in-command and leads the Worldlings when Mischief is absent. Nowadays is an accomplished sneak thief, as Robin Hood's man Will Scarlet's original name, "Scarlock" or "Scathelock," implies of him.[14] The name of the third Worldling, "Nought," provides a clever contrast with the name of the third of Robin's henchmen, "Much." Here also, the evidence is allusive rather than definitive; the name "Nought" has multiple likely meanings and provides several opportunities for punning on those various possibilities throughout the play, but a referent to the Robin Hood legend seems likely as well. Similarly, the name given to the leader of the Worldlings, "Mischief," is particularly appropriate for evoking Robin Hood. Like Robin Hood, Mischief is the leader of the band. "Mischief," of course, is a much stronger word in the fifteenth century, meaning something more like "deliberate harm" rather than "harmless prank."[15] Given the trickster elements of Robin Hood in the early ballads, it seems plausible that this character's name is meant to bring him to mind.

The physicality of Mischief and the Worldlings also parallels the Robin Hood play-games and ballads. Along with play-games that consisted largely of processional dancing, frequently with a fundraising element,[16] there were play-games that centered on enacted combat.[17] The little manuscript evidence of the plays themselves bears this out. The sole surviving scrap of a fifteenth-century play-game, *Robyn Hod and the Shryff off Notyngham*, consists essentially of brief lines of dialogue motivating various contests and fights. The play has two scenes. In the first scene, the Sheriff of Nottingham hires the Knight to capture Robin Hood, who then finds him and participates in a variety of physical contests with him: archery, stone-throwing, axle-throwing, wrestling, and finally sword-fighting. *Hamlet* it is not, but as Wiles has observed, "Combat always made for a popular spectator sport."[18] It is almost certainly the case that the scant lines of dialogue that survive for this first part of the play — only twenty-one lines as written in the manuscript — would have manifested as a satisfying twenty minutes or so of entertainment.[19] The second scene is likewise action-oriented; Robin Hood has been imprisoned and is rescued by his men, which unsurprisingly involves a considerable amount of fighting, including Friar Tuck personally attacking the Sheriff.[20]

The stories of the early ballads also tend to focus around physical action. As has long been recognized, the plot of *Robyn Hod and the Shryff off Notyngham* has much in common with that of *Robin Hood and Guy of Gisborne*, including physical contests between the two that result in a sword fight, ending in the death of Robin's attacker and Robin's disguising himself as him; the ballad concludes with the death of the Sheriff of Nottingham, killed by Little

John rather than Robin.[21] In the ballads, Robin always fights but he doesn't always win. In *Robin Hood and the Potter*, he fights but loses to the Potter; Robin does, however, win an archery contest later in the same ballad.[22] In *Robin Hood and the Monk*, Robin loses an archery match with Little John and is captured in Nottingham; meanwhile Little John and Much fight and dispatch the monk, as well as his page, who betrayed Robin's presence to the Sheriff, then lead a rescue of Robin. The evidence of both play-games and ballads is that in the fifteenth and sixteenth centuries, one of the core elements of Robin Hood entertainment is the action.

It is thus suggestive how many physical altercations Mischief and the Worldlings become involved with in *Mankind*. As the Worldlings first come into the play, as seen in the lines cited above, New Guise is apparently forcing Nought to dance; Nought protests that he might get hurt, but New Guise does not care, insisting that Nought dance for their amusement. The Worldlings thus enter the play not merely dancing, but dancing with an element of fighting; indeed, New Guise instructs the minstrels to whip Nought until he performs: "Ande how, mynstrellys, pley þe comyn trace! / Ley on wyth þi ballys tyll hys bely breste!"[23] Not long after, the three aggressively "invite" Mercy to dance with them. When Mercy refuses, New Guise threatens him: "Yf ȝe wyll, ser, my brother wyll make yow to prawnce,"[24] while Nought warns him that the dancing can get painful: "ȝe, ser, wyll ȝe do well / Trace not wyth þem, be my cownsell / For I haue tracyed sumwhat to fell."[25] The Worldlings dance, but their dancing contains a noteworthy element of physical violence and physical danger.

Physical violence figures prominently elsewhere in the play as well. The Worldlings attempt to persuade Mankind to abandon his work, join them, and to become involved in a physical confrontation with Mankind when he refuses. As frequently happens to Robin Hood and his men, the Worldlings are beaten by their opponent. Using his spade, Mankind fights the Worldlings and drives them away. Even allowing for comic exaggeration of their injuries, the results seem noteworthy. Nowadays has taken a blow to the head, New Guise fears that the hit to his groin will make him useless to his wife, and Nought cries that his arm hurts so badly he is unable to move it.[26] Their beating is revisited shortly, when Mankind leaves and Mischief returns. Mischief and the Worldlings go through the litany of their injuries, drawing our attention again to the fight and its effects.

Moreover, Mischief and the Worldlings' presence in the play ends in violence, with the near-hanging of New Guise. Having successfully tempted Mankind to leave his work and his wife to follow them, the Worldlings remind Mankind of how far he has fallen, suggesting that his best course of action would be to kill himself. Nowadays holds the tree while New Guise demonstrates how Mankind should go about hanging himself, when Mercy returns with a whip and chases them away.[27] Indeed, it is often argued that the level of physical action in the play indicates that the work must originally have been performed by professional actors and that it was part of the repertoire of any early troupe of traveling players. Indeed, the coordination of the fight sequences, with their real inherent danger, would require the skills of full-time actors rather than community players. Perhaps. But this line of reasoning certainly points to the intensity of the physical altercations within the play, a level that brings to mind contemporary Robin Hood entertainments, which also focus so notably on fighting.

Other core characteristics of the Worldlings closely parallel the Robin Hood legend. In the early ballads, boldness and cleverness are defining elements of Robin Hood, and, to a lesser extent, of his men as well. In *Robin Hood and the Monk*, Robin boldly goes to Nottingham to attend Mass, ignoring Much's advice to take twelve of his yeomen, and goes accompanied only by Little John; indeed, when he quarrels with Little John, he goes on alone.[28] In this same ballad, having killed the monk, Little John (accompanied by Much) takes the letters that the monk was carrying to the king, and he blandly says that the monk "dyed after [along] the way" when the king asks about him.[29] The narrative describes Little John here as "full bolde," which seems a fair assessment.[30] Little John's boldness continues with his rescue of Robin Hood from the Sheriff of Nottingham's jail. In *Robin Hood and the Potter*, Robin boldly sets out to encounter the potter; however, Little John has warned him that the potter gave him a memorable thumping.[31] In the same ballad, Robin continues his boldness by disguising himself as the potter and going to Nottingham, where he wins the Sheriff's archery tournament and in fact flirts with the Sheriff's wife.[32] Similarly, in *Robin Hood and Guy of Gisbourne*, after Robin kills Guy, exchanges clothes with him, cuts off Guy's head and disfigures it beyond recognition, and audaciously goes to the Sheriff with the head to claim the reward for killing Robin Hood, the outlaw finds Little John captured there. Robin rescues him right out from under the Sheriff's nose with yet another ploy.[33] Indeed, in addition to their participation in violent confrontations, the boldness of Robin Hood and his men are one of their central features in the ballads.

The boldness and cleverness of Mischief and the Worldlings call to mind those same elements of the Robin Hood figures. Mischief cheekily interrupts Mercy's opening speech and argues with him, cleverly showing how chaff has even more uses than corn.[34] We see this from Mischief as well in his handling of the Worldlings' injuries after their battle with Mankind. He tells them he can solve their problems easily — by chopping off the damaged body parts.[35] Not surprisingly, the Worldlings reject this solution, and they hastily decide that they will be okay after all. Mischief is thus able to both cleverly harass his subordinates by threatening to amputate some bits of their bodies that they would just as soon keep, and also trick them into revealing that their injuries were not as dire as they were pretending. New Guise, Nowadays, and Nought similarly exhibit boldness; although, much of their audacious behavior manifests verbally. They harass Mercy, as cited above, "inviting" him to dance with them and threatening him if he does not, but there is no indication in the text that they actually attempt to physically assault Mercy. However, they continue to harass him verbally, in shockingly bold terms, involving scatological and sexual humor, which includes a joke involving both oral sex and also the pope, surely an instance of great audacity.[36] Likewise, although they are involved in a physical confrontation with Mankind, they are beaten by him; their successful harassment of Mankind is boldly offensive verbal taunts.[37] Arguably, the Worldlings' most audacious move, though, is inviting the audience to sing the "Christmas Song" with them, a song whose lyrics can shock even our jaded modern ears[38]:

> NEW GYSE and NOWADAYS. Yt ys wretyn wyth a coll...
> NOUGHT. He þat schytyth wyth hys hoyll...
> NOUGHT. But he wyppe hys ars clen...
> NOUGHT. On hys breche yt xall be sen.[39]

Whereupon, the direction is for all three to sing six times "Hoylyke!" [hole-like (pun on holy)].[40] The boldness and cleverness of Mischief and the Worldlings, although often manifesting in words rather than action, is just as striking and definitive as that of the Robin Hood figures, and thus a further connection between them can be shown.

In addition, the Worldlings evoke another crucial element of Robin Hood — social status. Robin Hood is a yeoman, more or less persuasively according to the particular text, in the surviving fifteenth-century ballads. In *Robin Hood and Guy of Gisbourne*, for instance, Robin and Guy are both referred to as yeomen when they encounter one another ("How these two yeomen together they mett"[41]) and again as they begin to fight ("To see how together these yeomen went"[42]). In *Robin Hood and the Monk*, Robin is likewise explicitly called a yeoman, and this time he is grouped with Little John in the referent ("Thus shet thei forth, these yemen too"[43]). In *A Gest of Robyn Hode*, Robin is called a "gode yeman" on more than one occasion[44] (whether his behavior is consistent with that is a different consideration). Perhaps most intriguingly, for the purposes of considering the Robin Hood legend and *Mankind* as contemporary entertainments, is *Robin Hood and the Potter*. In this ballad, not only is Robin, as above, called a yeoman,[45] but the audience is as well:

> Herkens, god yeman   *Listen*
> Comley, corteys, and god,   *Fair, well-bred, and good*
> On of the best that yever bare bowe,   *One; ever bore*
> Hes name was Roben Hode.[46]

The ballad ends by returning to this point:

> God haffe mersey on Roben Hodys solle,   *soul*
> And saffe all god yemanrey![47]

I am aware of the complexity involved in attempting to determine what "yeomanry" meant in the fifteenth century[48] and the composition of the audience of Robin Hood ballads and games.[49] These are important and worthy concerns, but for the purposes of this study, it is suggestive simply to note how the Worldlings in *Mankind* make the same appeal.

The Worldlings' thievery likewise suggests Robin Hood and his men. Theft is, of course, a crucial component of the Robin Hood legend, albeit as the legend developed, attempts were made to make this element more palatable. As early as the *Gest*, Robin Hood is provided with rationales to justify his stealing. For example, he robs only those who lie to him about how much money they actually have, such as the monk who claimed to be carrying "no more but twenty marke" but his traveling chest turned out to contain "[e]yght hundred pounde and more."[50] Indeed, the *Gest* is at some pains to present Robin's stealing as justified, suggesting that in other manifestations, Robin Hood had no such compunctions. Like Robin Hood's gang, the Worldlings steal, and indeed steal from the Church. Titivillus sends his underlings off with explicit instructions to thieve,[51] and we see the results of their work when they return; among this recitation is Nowaday's report:

> I haue laburryde all þis nyght; wen xall we go dyn?
> A chyrche her besyde xall pay for ale, brede, and wyn.
> Lo, here ys stoff wyll serue.[52]

Nowadays has robbed a church to finance the Worldlings' debauched lifestyle, much as Robin Hood's thievery would have appeared to the unsympathetic.

Similarly, both the Worldlings and Robin Hood are willing to kill to accomplish their goals. Robin Hood's men cold-bloodedly dispatch both a monk and his page in *Robin Hood and the Monk*; later in the same ballad, Little John kills a jailer.[53] In *Robin Hood and Guy of Gisbourne*, Robin Hood personally takes care of Guy of Gisbourne, while Little John kills the Sheriff of Nottingham.[54] In the extant snippet of the fifteenth-century play-game, *Robyn Hod and the Shryff off Notyngham*, Robin kills the knight, who, hired by the Sheriff, had come to capture him, then decapitates him and disguises himself as the knight, actions similar to *Robin Hood and Guy of Gisbourne*, as has long been recognized.[55] Even in the *Gest*, which is seemingly at pains to present Robin as positively as possible, Robin kills the Sheriff of Nottingham, hitting him first with an arrow and then cutting off his head.[56] Of course, it is quite likely that the original audience of the legend were not troubled by this characteristic; indeed, they perhaps saw it as an indication of his strength and power, and thus a reason to admire Robin rather than condemn him. But it must be admitted as well that Robin and his men's willingness to kill their enemies also allows for fairly easy critique of the legend for those inclined to do so, as we shall see below.

In *Mankind*, Mischief and the Worldlings are likewise killers as well as robbers. Most intriguingly, Mischief, like Little John, has killed a jailer:

> MYSCHEFF. Here cummyth a man of armys! Why stonde ȝe so styll?
> Of murder and manslawter I haue my bely-fyll.
> NOWADAYS. What, Myscheff, haue ȝe ben in presun? And yt
>   be yowr wyll,
> Me semyth ȝe haue scoryde a peyr of fetters.
> MYSCHEFF. I was chenyde by þe armys: lo, I haue þem here.
> The chenys I brast asundyr and kyllyde þe jaylere…[57]

The play draws attention to this killing, having Mischief return bragging of it ("Of murder and manslawter I haue my bely-fyll"), then luridly telling the story of what he did in detail ("The chenys I brast asundyr and kyllyde þe jaylere…"). Like Robin Hood and his men, Mischief and the Worldlings are outlaws, willing to fight and kill the authorities.

Indeed, the Worldlings' induction of Mankind into their gang likewise parallels the Robin Hood legend. New Guise makes Mankind promise to "goo robbe, stell, and kyll, as fast as ye may gon."[58] Mischief similarly exhorts Mankind:

> ȝe must haue be yowr syde a longe da pacem,
> As trew men ryde be þe wey for to onbrace þem,
> Take þer monay, kytt þer throtys, thus ouerface þem.[59]

Mankind responds to both, "I wyll, ser."[60] If he were to follow through on those promises, he could have fit well into Robin Hood's gang. Moreover, Mankind's entry into the Worldlings' group follows the same arc as is typical of new members of Robin Hood's. Mankind first defeats, then joins, the Worldlings, the same course of action followed in the Robin Hood legend for new members, such as in *Robin Hood and the Potter*.

A final element of *Mankind* that connects the Worldlings with contemporary manifestations of Robin Hood is their gathering of money. In the play-games, Robin Hood and his men would collect money; indeed, it is arguably *the* central purpose of much play-game activity. Alexandra F. Johnston has pointed to "five distinct elements" of Robin Hood play-games that can reliably be ascertained from the surviving records, largely churchwardens' accounts: "rhyming, playmaking, 'gathering,' archery, and morris dancing."[61] "Gathering"—that is, collecting money—is an expected, important, and definitive element of Robin Hood during the fifteenth and sixteenth centuries. As John Wasson has observed based upon his research as the REED editor for Devon, "the chief function of Robin Hood and Little John was to collect money for the parish..."[62] But it seems clear as well that the money-collecting tactics were intimately connected to other elements of the Robin Hood legend; that is, the gathering had the flavor of a mock-robbery. The play-games' Robin Hood provides important funds through, as Johnston has described it, "the custom of accosting neighbors (and even strangers) and demanding money for the support of the parish."[63]

In *Mankind*, Mischief and the Worldlings likewise collect money, and they do so through equally dubious methods. Mischief has summoned Titivillus, a higher ranking devil, but he demands payment to bring him out into view. The Worldlings pass this demand along to the audience:

> NEU GYSE. 3e, go þi wey! We xall gaþer mony onto,
> Ellys þer xall no many hym se.
> Now gostly to owr purpos, worschypfull souerence,
> We intende to gather mony, yf yt plesse yowr neclygence,
> For a man wyth a hede þat ys of grett omnipotens.[64]

In other words, the Worldlings threaten that they will not bring on Titivillus until they have collected enough money. It is almost certainly the case, of course, that the money collected by the Worldlings had a legitimate, real-life purpose as well, perhaps to pay the actors, as is often assumed. But the means used to secure these funds are highly problematic: the audience pays to see the devil. The money-collecting itself and the extortive fundraising tactics used strongly recall the Robin Hood play-games. Indeed, it is striking that the Worldlings twice call their money-collecting "gathering," the same word most commonly used to describe the fundraising tactics of Robin Hood's men as well.

The presentation and characterization of Mischief and the Worldlings in *Mankind* thus shows considerable parallels with the Robin Hood legend. The structure of their band evokes Robin Hood's men in both their ballad and play-game compositions through their names and their functions within the group. Their dancing-cum-fighting parallels one of the most common characteristics of the Robin Hood play-games, while the Worldlings' actual fighting evokes Robin Hood and his men in both the ballads and the play-games. Like Robin Hood and his men, the Worldlings do not win every altercation but end up recruiting their defeater. The cleverness and boldness of the Worldlings parallels the Robin Hood legend as well, as does their social status. A key element of Robin Hood in the ballads is, of course, his thievery, and this characteristic is seen in the Worldlings as well. Alone, any one of the similarities pointed to here between Mischief and the Worldlings in *Mankind* and Robin Hood and his men would not itself be sufficient to suggest a connection to the Robin Hood legend. Taken together, however, the evidence indicates that substantial parallels exist. Mischief and the Worldlings are not Robin Hood and his men — indeed, Robin Hood is not even mentioned in the play — nor are they merely "disguised" versions of these characters. Rather, Mischief and the Worldlings have the characteristics of outlaws because they are, among other things, outlaws. If I am correct in this suggestion, the implications are considerable.

First, we need to revisit the meaning of the money-gathering in *Mankind*. This is often pointed to as evidence of early "professional" theatrical activity and/or evidence of production by traveling players. However, if the event parallels the gatherings of the Robin Hood play-games, such a conclusion may not be appropriate. It is important to remember that we do not know from the play itself what the gathered money is *actually for*—within the play, all we know is that the Worldlings demand money or else they will not bring on Titivillus. What happens after the performance — whether the money is used to pay the performers, for instance — is conjectural. Reasonable conjecture, certainly. But if instead the gathering is part of a systematic series of allusions to contemporary Robin Hood ballads and play-games in order to establish Mischief and the Worldlings as outlaw figures, we should be hesitant about using this as evidence of early professional theatrical activity.

Mankind's allusion to the Robin Hood legend may also point towards a strategy for making the play's purposes work more successfully for a modern audience. *Mankind* seems clearly designed to have the audience be entertained by and attracted to Mischief and the Worldlings. They then gradually reveal their wickedness and show the audience the initial lure but ultimate unsavory-ness of evil. Putting them in Robin Hood-like costumes might help a modern audience make this connection more easily. Robin Hood and his men are, for modern audiences, generally positive characters, so if the Worldlings' costumes could call them to mind without implying that they *are* Robin Hood and his gang, the positive connotation of Robin Hood could carry over to the Worldlings, putting the audience into the intended frame of mind towards them.

Most importantly, though, *Mankind*'s presentation of Mischief and the Worldlings as outlaw figures, by giving them substantive and numerous characteristics that parallel the Robin Hood legend, indicates that the play is participating in an ongoing societal conversation about the spiritual and moral dimensions of outlaws. As is well known among scholars of outlaw literature, there has been considerable discussion of the role and impact of Robin Hood in medieval culture. Some have argued, like Peter Stallybrass, that Robin Hood is a transgressive force provides an area of "licensed misrule" for the enactment of subversive impulses, with all the inherent actual danger that such condoned but (sort of) contained challenges to the social order necessarily carry with them.[65] This understanding of Robin Hood's societal position has been influential; Paul Whitfield White characterizes current scholarship is largely in agreement on this point, for he states that "the fabled outlaw's critically perceived reputation as a transgressive, carnivalesque hero and implacable enemy of the church."[66] White then seeks to "question, or at least modify" this reputation by bringing attention to the "well-developed (though scarcely recognized) medieval tradition of the *holy* Robin Hood."[67] White's corrective is well-advised, and one suspects that his conclusion points us towards a more realistic assessment of the matter:

> I hope I have advanced the scholarship of Tudor parish revels a little further in this essay by showing that Robin Hood revels and other guild-sponsored entertainments supported the pious and orthodox values of both the guilds themselves and the surrounding parish community. Having said that, it is perhaps best to think of a figure like Robin Hood as mediating between the sacred and profane interests of holy day ceremonial. On the one hand, he is the quintessential lord of misrule, the perfect spring festival symbol of liberty, adventure, and transgression; on the other, his devotion to the Virgin and his commitment to the Mass represent the higher values that the revels are designed to support through pious giving.[68]

In other words, we find evidence of Robin Hood as a transgressive figure because, at some times and in some places, this *is* a role he plays, but we find examples as well of Robin Hood in fully orthodox pursuits, presumably merrily reinscribing the status quo. It seems sensible, as White suggests, that we must reconcile ourselves to the apparent reality that Robin Hood appears in both roles, seemingly contradictory as they are.

Moreover, this dual position of Robin Hood in the late Middle Ages and the Early Modern period seems to occur at least in part because the famous outlaw's societal role is continually under construction and discussion during this time. We know that Robin Hood was both extremely popular in both ballad and play-games but also that criticism of the figure was not uncommon. The view of Robin Hood as a thief and murderer with few if any redeeming qualities is typical of much contemporary clerical opinion of the legend. As David Wiles explains, "[t]he educated classes, from the time of Langland onwards, had little sympathy for popular manifestations of the Robin Hood cult."[69] As is widely known, clerical disapproval of Robin Hood is not hard to find. In his *Continuation* of John of Fordun's *Scotichronican* (c. 1440), for instance, Walter Bower says that

> Then arose the famous murderer, Robert Hood, as well as Little John, together with their accomplices from among the disinherited, whom the foolish populace are so inordinately fond of celebrating both in tragedies and comedies, and about whom they are delighted to hear the jesters and minstrels sing above all other ballads.[70]

To be fair, later in the same passage Bower says that "certain praiseworthy things"[71] are also said about Robin Hood, chief of which is his custom of hearing Mass frequently. Bower's attempt at evenhandedness, however, is perhaps not as persuasive as it might at first seem. He couches his assessment of Robin Hood as a "famous murderer" as a statement, but Robin Hood's custom as hearing Mass as less-reliable rumor, something that "is told" about Robin Hood. Moreover, Bower chooses to open his discussion of Robin Hood with his overall and unambiguous assessment of Robin Hood as a "famous murderer" whom the "foolish populace ... so inordinately" celebrate, an assessment that does not appear to be altered by his admission that "certain praiseworthy things are told" as well about Robin Hood.

Nor were concerns about Robin Hood exclusively clerical. David Wiles cites, for example, a 1497 instance of the "blurring of the distinction between a game and a criminal act,"[72] in which the man playing Robin Hood was accused of using his followers to beat people from the town of Walsall, but he claims that they were simply gathering money like they were supposed to do. The atmosphere of the gatherings, Wiles says, was likely similar to that which resulted in the following complaint in the fourteenth century about the tactics of a mock Abbot and his followers who were likewise collecting money:

> They held them against their will until they had exhorted from them certain sums of money in lieu of a "sacrifice." And although they appear to attempt this under veil and colour of a game — or rather, a mockery — yet it is undoubtedly theft inasmuch as money is taken from the unwilling, and by force too.[73]

Alexandra F. Johnston likewise points to this example in discussing the concern of local, secular authorities that Robin Hood games could get out of hand.[74] Paul White is certainly correct in reminding us that the view of Robin Hood by the clerical authorities was not as unambiguously negative as has sometimes been asserted, but it is also undeniable that both clerical and secular criticism of the play-games existed, both in spiritual concerns about Robin Hood as a role model and also in pragmatic worries in regard to the attendant celebrations becoming uncontrolled.

But the societal effects of Robin Hood are not the only area of discussion in contemporary considerations of the legend. There is also significant concern for the spiritual and moral implications of the Robin Hood legend in particular and of the popularity of outlaw figures generally. Moreover, this conversation is long-standing, dating back at least to the fourteenth century, and, most likely, earlier. As is well-known, the famous reference in *Piers Plowman* to Robin Hood that was mentioned at the beginning of this essay clearly presents Robin Hood as a distraction from more important, holy pursuits.[75] However, it is less well recognized that *Piers Plowman* elsewhere provides more implicit commentary on outlaws. In Passus VI, Piers Plowman guides the repentant crowd in the work that is proper for each group to do. Some, with Piers, till the earth to grow food; the women are instructed to sew and spin; and the knight is told to guard the workers "[f]ro wastours and fro wikked men that this world destruyeth."[76] "Wastours," as the Passus continues, are a particular threat to the well-being of the community, and indeed cause trouble, scorning Piers' injunction to work for their living and instead threatening to steal whatever they want despite Piers, until finally Piers summons Hunger to bring them to heel. But as this line hints, the rest of the Passus clarifies, and the *MED* confirms, "wastours" are not simply those who carelessly misuse ("waste") resources but those who steal them without having participated in producing them — i.e., outlaws and thieves. As the *MED* indicates, "wastour" is largely a synonym for "thief"; it cites, for instance, the 1331 Statutes Realm: "Diverses roberies, homicides, & felonies ont este faitz einz ces heures par gentz qi sont appellez Roberdesmen, Wastours, & Draghlacche."[77] Nor, of course, was such banditry entirely fictitious. In her "Ballads and Bandits: Fourteenth-Century Outlaws and the Robin Hood Poems," Barbara Hanawalt discusses the potential paradox of the popularity of the Robin Hood legend when outlaws were both real and less scrupulous about their victims then their fictional counterparts; unlike Robin Hood, real outlaws robbed peasants, women, and servants.[78] Hanawalt considers how and why Robin Hood differs from such outlaws in ways that allow for the popularity of the legend. What is noteworthy, however, from my perspective, is how *Piers Plowman* demonstrates the breadth and depth of discussion about outlaws, encompassing the social and spiritual implications of both legendary and real outlaws, and that this wide consideration of outlaws is in place at least a century before *Mankind*.

This consideration of the social and spiritual effects of outlaws, both real and legendary, is of course complicated by the fact that the line between real and legendary outlaws is rather fuzzy. Many of the most famous medieval outlaws, among them Hereward the Wake, Fulke Fitz Waryn, and Eustache the Monk, have at their core a historical person. We also know that in the wake of the popularity of such legends, real-life figures tended to posit their grievances in the language of the legends, such as the well-known example from 1441 of the Norfolk mob singing "We are Robynhodesmen, war, war, war."[79] It is also, of course, well-known that *Piers Plowman* itself was appropriated by the 1381 Peasants' Revolt as justification for their demands, and that Langland revised his poem in response. The volatile century that followed the Black Death included profound social and spiritual reevaluations, among them the role of Robin Hood and other outlaw legends.

By the time of *Mankind*, then, this consideration and reconsideration of the role of outlaws was long-standing. In the early fifteenth century, *Dives and Pauper*, as *Piers Plowman* had done, cites Robin Hood as a distraction from more important, holy concerns, expressing disapproval of those who "gon to þe tauerne þan to holy chirche, leuer to heryn a tale or song of Robyn Hood or of som rubaudye þan to heryn messe or matynys or onyþing of Goddis seruise or ony word of God."[80] In his introduction to his translation of *Eustache the Monk*, Thomas E. Kelly suggests that some outlaw tales may actually be intended as negative examples rather than positive or neutral ones. Citing the work of Keith Busby, Kelly discusses how Busby has argued that Eustache the Monk's unsavory exploits suggest a hitherto unrecognized outlaw motif, the Bad Outlaw, in contrast to the Good Outlaw.[81] Even more interesting is *The Hermit and the Outlaw*.[82] Roughly contemporary with *Mankind*, this text is an exemplum in which the spiritual condition of the Outlaw is very much the focus. The Outlaw, "who frequented the wild wood in order to rob and kill men," on a Good Friday has a realization of his sinfulness, repents, and is saved (causing something of a spiritual crisis in his brother, the hermit, who has lived a holy life and feels put out that his badly-behaved brother gets saved so easily).[83] It seems clear that there was an ongoing conversation about the spiritual implications of outlaws, both real and legendary, and one strand of that discussion typically posited them as morally problematic.

Mankind, I would suggest, is adding its voice to this discussion. The parallels between the Worldlings and the Robin Hood legend are too numerous and too precise to be accidental; rather, they evoke the legend and in doing so, both participate in and draw upon a discussion that had been ongoing at least since the time of *Piers Plowman* about the spiritual implications of outlaws.[84] The spiritual position of outlaws just as intense a concern as the social role of outlaws, specifically because outlaws did not have merely a fictional existence. *Mankind* makes these parallels, giving the Worldlings outlaw characteristics, at a time in which the memory of another peasant uprising was still fresh. As with the 1381 Peasants' Uprising, Jack Cade's popular revolt was easy for contemporary authorities to dismiss as brigands and outlaws; indeed, their 1450 "Proclamation of Grievances" is at some pains to claim that they are not common thieves or outlaws, calling themselves "the pore commyns of Ingelond," commons of England" and Henry VI's "trewe comyns," and saying that "[w]e wyll that it be knone we wyll not robbe, ne reve [plunder], ne stelle, but that thes defautes be amendyd, and then we wyll go home."85 What it meant to be an outlaw — and particularly what the spiritual and moral status of an outlaw was — would naturally be of considerable importance when anyone who disagreed with the authorities would be painted as such.

Thanks to the work of White and Stallybrass, among many others, our understanding of the role of Robin Hood and other outlaws as a force in medieval and early modern society has deepened considerably in recent years. We have only recently begun to give similar attention to a complementary area of concern, one that was most likely just as important, if not more so, to the original audience of these legends: the spiritual dimensions and implications of the popularity of outlaw legends. White's corrective that Robin Hood often occupied a positive, socially-sanctioned role begins to point us in that direction; indeed, in such cases, Robin Hood's acceptable spiritual condition as a devotee of the Virgin Mary tended to be emphasized. However, it seems clear that the spiritual condition of outlaws, both real and legendary, was by itself a subject for considerable concern and discussion. One strongly suspects that the underlying question in such a discussion is this query: what is the appropriate, Christian response to injustice? Outlaw legends are clearly full of concerns about responding to injustice, and the society which birthed them must then grapple with whether the responses such stories contain, satisfying as they are, are consistent with Christian morality. Answers to such questions varied then, as indeed they vary now.

But it should not be surprising to find *Mankind*, a text that is deeply concerned both with how we save our souls and also even more so with how we live once we have been saved. Moreover, it is a texts that engages the question of the spiritual condition of outlaws, and it participates in a specific discussion, which is itself part of a wider conversation, about the role of outlaws generally in medieval and early modern society. In truth, one suspects that *Mankind* is engaging in and responding to a wider discussion on the causes, nature, and ramifications of injustice. Indeed, *Mankind*'s strategy of stepping into and drawing upon this ongoing conversation about the spiritual position of outlaws fits particularly well with its dramatic structure. As an allegory, *Mankind* makes maximum use of the flexibility of that genre, operating on several levels of meaning simultaneously. *Mankind* used to be thought of as a "degraded example of a morality" play, but recent scholarship has revealed the misunderstanding and prejudice that led to that assessment, and have instead shown the care and complexity with which the play is constructed.86 It is now well-understood that *Mankind* instructs the audience both by providing the example of representative figure of humanity, whose fall into sin and repentance the audience learns from by watching, but also by taking the audience through that process themselves. That is, the play lures the audience themselves into sin and then reveals their need for repentance. Indeed, the play ends with Mercy's call to the audience to repent. *Mankind*'s incorporation of the conversation about the spiritual condition of outlaws into its characterization of the Worldlings is thus impressive but not surprising. Moreover, this discourse operates simultaneously on two levels. First, it warns the audience against the temptations of the world, the flesh, and the devil, generally. And second, it also provides its stance on the ongoing consideration of outlaws' spiritual condition.[87] *Mankind*, it seems clear, presents Mischief and the Worldlings with outlaw characteristics in part to suggest that outlaws are similarly bad spiritual examples, no matter how attractive they seem.

But *Mankind*'s concern is never solely about the spiritual conditions of its characters; the true focus of the play is on the audience's spiritual condition. The character Mankind exists to guide the audience onto the right spiritual path, but the purpose of the play is to affect the audience's spiritual growth. *Mankind* begins with Mercy's exhortation to the audience to remember their Savior, and the play ends with his invitation to them to accept salvation:

> Now for hys lowe þat for vs receywyd hys humanite,
> Serge ȝour condicyons wyth dew examinacion.
> Thynke and remembyr þe world ys but a wanite,
> As yt ys prowyd daly by diuerse transmutacyon.
>
> Mankend ys wrechyd, he hath sufficyent prowe.
> Therefore God grant ȝow all per suam misericordiam
> Þat ye may be pleyferys wyth þe angellys abowe
> And hawe to ȝour porcyon vitam eternam. Amen![88]

Mankind's continuing and overriding concern with its audience's spirituality suggests another element to its referencing of the ongoing discussions of the spiritual implications of outlaws. The audience's spiritual health, attending as they are to the outlaw-like Worldlings, is also at stake. This ongoing conversation about the spiritual condition of outlaws seems likely to be part of a wider discussion of morally acceptable responses to injustice, and *Mankind* is deeply concerned about this aspect. The Worldlings mock Mankind for working hard for so little effect, and Titivillus' frustrating of Mankind's attempts to dig his soil and plant his crop opens Mankind up to his further temptations. Mankind's unjust poverty is intimately connected to his spiritual health. But even more important is the audience's spiritual condition. *Mankind* steps into a longstanding discussion about the spiritual implications of outlaws; just as significant, it acknowledges the importance of this conversation and provides a gentle reminder that *the* most crucial element of the discussion was ultimately the spiritual impact of outlaws on those real people who read their stories, sympathized with their struggles, and perhaps wondered if they should follow their example.

Notes

1. Donald C. Baker, "The Date of *Mankind*," *Philological Quarterly* 42, no. 4 (1963): 90–91.
2. Knight and Ohlgren, 269.
3. See Keen, especially 1–8.
4. Knight 1994, 262.
5. William Langland, *The Vision of Piers Plowman: A Critical Edition of the B-Text Based on the Trinity College Cambridge MS B. 15. 17*, ed. A. V. C. Schmidt, 2nd ed. (London: Dent, 1995), Passus V, 82, lines 395–97. In Passus V, Will encounters the Seven Deadly Sins. William Langland's allegorical representation of Sloth is a priest who does not know his "Lord's Prayer." He does, however, know the popular verses about Robin Hood:

I kan noght parfitly my *Paternoster* as the preest syngeth,	*do not know properly*
But I kan rymes of Robyn Hood and Randolf Erl of Chestre,	*about*
Ac neither of Oure Lord ne of Oure Lady the leeste that evere was maked	*composed*

6. Knight 1994, 262–88.
7. See John Marshall, "Gathering in the Name of the Outlaw: REED and Robin Hood," in *REED in Review: Essays in Celebration of the First Twenty-Five Years*, ed. Audrey Douglass and Sally-Beth MacLean (Toronto: University of Toronto Press, 2006), 65–84.
8. See David Wiles, "Robin Hood as Summer Lord," in Knight 1999, 77–98 at 83; also his *The Early Plays of Robin Hood* (Cambridge: D. S. Brewer, 1981), 4, 13, 20, and 26.
9. Wiles, *Early Plays*, 20–26.
10. Ibid., 23.
11. All references to *Mankind* are from Mark Eccles, ed., *The Macro Plays: The Castle of Perseverance, Wisdom, Mankind*. EETS, o.s., 262 (London: Oxford University Press, 1969), 156, lines 72–81. *trace*, "music for a song"; *Sent Tanne*, "St. Anne"; *wyght*, "nimble"; *Xall*, "shall"; *beschrew*, "curse."
12. See, for instance, Wiles, *Early Plays*, 6, 20–30.
13. See for example *Robin Hood and the Monk*, in Knight and Ohlgren, 31–56 at 49 n. 13.
14. Ibid., 49 n. 13.
15. See *MED*, s.v. "mischēf." For example, n. 1a(a): "Misfortune, affliction, trouble; a grievous situation, distressing state of affairs; problem, plight; consequence or effect of sin; also, misery, unhappiness, suffering."
16. Wiles, *Early Plays*, 31.
17. Ibid., 31–42.
18. Ibid., 32.
19. *Robyn Hod and the Shryff off Notyngham*, in Knight and Ohlgren, 269–80.
20. The Robin Hood plays that survive from the sixteenth century, *Robin Hood and the Friar* and *Robin Hood and the Potter* also demonstrate a focus upon combat entertainment. In the first, Robin Hood and Friar Tuck meet and fight before becoming friends; in the second, Robin Hood fights a potter. See texts of these plays in Knight and Ohlgren, 281–95.
21. *Robin Hood and Guy of Gisborne*, in Knight and Ohlgren, 169–83.
22. *Robin Hood and the Potter*, in Knight and Ohlgren, 57–79.
23. Eccles, *Mankind*, 156, lines 72–73.
24. Ibid., 157, line 91.
25. Ibid., 157, lines 94–96.
26. Ibid., 166, lines 381–91.

27. Ibid., 180, lines 800–10.
28. Knight and Ohlgren, 37–39, lines 21–64.
29. Ibid., 44, line 226.
30. Ibid., 44, line 216.
31. Ibid., 62–63, lines 13–32.
32. Ibid., 67–69, lines 169–218; and 70, lines 238–40.
33. Knight and Olhgren, 178–80, lines 159–220.
34. Eccles, *Mankind*, 155–56, lines 45–71.
35. Ibid, 168, lines 429–447.
36. Ibid., 158–58, lines 129–61.
37. Ibid., 165–66, lines 345–75.
38. Indeed, early twentieth-century sensibilities found the song so shocking that it was omitted from the first printed editions: John Matthew Manly, ed., *Specimens of the Pre-Shakespearean Drama* (Boston: Ginn, 1897); and Joseph Quincy Adams, ed., *Chief Pre-Shakespearean Dramas: A Selection of Plays Illustrating the History of the English Drama from Its Origin Down to Shakespeare* (Boston: Houghton Mifflin, 1924). Adams substitutes ellipses after the first line of the song with this footnote: "The song is unprintable," 311.
39. Eccles, *Mankind*, 165, lines 335–41. *hoyll*, "anus." I have omitted only the repetition of the lines, which is presumably intended to represent the audience joining in.
40. Ibid., 165, line 343.
41. Knight and Ohlgren, 176, line 87.
42. Ibid., 177, line 145.
43. Ibid., 38, line 47.
44. Ibid., 90, line 3.
45. Ibid., 62, lines 9 and 13, for instance.
46. Ibid., 62, lines 5–8.
47. Ibid., 72, lines 322–23.
48. See, for instance, A. J. Pollard, *Imagining Robin Hood: The Late-Medieval Stories in Historical Context* (New York: Routledge, 2004), 29–56; and Ohlgren 2007, 135–39.
49. See, for instance, J. C. Holt, "The Origin and Audience of the Ballads of Robin Hood," *Past and Present* 18 (1960): 89–110; and Knight 1994, 50–51.
50. Knight and Ohlgren, 121, lines 983 and 988.
51. Eccles, *Mankind*, 170, line 502.
52. Ibid., 174, lines 632–34. *stoff*, "furnishings."
53. In Knight and Ohlgren, 43, lines 187–90; and 45, lines 275–78.
54. Ibid., 178, lines 161–62; and 180, lines 231–34.
55. Ibid., 277, lines 23–24.
56. Ibid., 134, lines 1389–92.
57. Eccles, *Mankind*, 174–75, lines 638–43. Indeed, Mischief's speech continues with his revelation that he proceeded to sexually abuse the jailer's wife.
58. Ibid., 177, line 708.
59. Ibid., 177, lines 714–16. *da pacem*, "weapon"; *onbrace*, "carve up, take apart"; *ouerface*, "overcome."
60. Ibid., 177, lines 709 and 717.
61. Alexandra F. Johnson, "The Robin Hood of the Records," in *Playing Robin Hood: The Legend as Performance in Five Centuries*, ed. Lois Potter (Newark: University of Delaware Press, 1998), 27–44 at 29.
62. John M. Wasson, ed., *Devon*. Records of Early English Drama (Toronto: University of Toronto Press, 1986), xxv.
63. Johnston, "Robin Hood of the Records," 38.
64. Eccles, *Mankind*, 168, lines 457–61. *gostly*, "devoutly"
65. Peter Stallybrass, "'Drunk with the cup of liberty': Robin Hood, the Carnivalesque, and the Rhetoric of Violence in Early Modern England," in Knight 1999, 297–327.
66. Paul Whitfield White, "Holy Robin Hood! Carnival, Parish Guilds, and the Outlaw

Tradition," in *Tudor Drama Before Shakespeare, 1485–1590: New Directions for Research, Criticism, and Pedagogy*, ed. Lloyd Edward Kermode, Jason Scott-Warren, and Martine van Elk (New York: Palgrave, 2004), 67–89 at 67.

67. Ibid., 67.
68. Ibid., 83.
69. Wiles, *Early Plays*, 53.
70. Knight and Ohlgren, 21–29 at 26. See also Knight 1994, 33–36.
71. Knight and Ohlgren, 26.
72. Wiles, *Early Plays*, 15.
73. Quoted in Wiles, *Early Plays*, 15.
74. Johnson, "Robin Hood of the Records," 38.
75. See note 5 above.
76. Langland, *Piers Plowman*, 96, lines 28–29.
77. *MED*, s.v. "wāstóur," n. 1.(b).
78. Barbara A. Hanawalt, "Ballads and Bandits: Fourteenth-Century Outlaws and the Robin Hood Poems," in *Chaucer's England: Literature in Historical Context*, ed. Barbara A. Hanawalt. Medieval Studies at Minnesota 4 (Minneapolis: University of Minnesota Press, 1992), 154–75 at 164–65.
79. Knight and Ohlgren, 26. Knight 1994, 265.
80. Priscilla Heath Barnum, ed., *Dives and Pauper*. EETS, o.s., 275 (London: Oxford University Press, 1976), 189, lines 38–41.
81. Thomas E. Kelly, *Eustache the Monk*, in Ohlgren 2005, 100–50 at 103–4.
82. For an edition, see Richard Firth Green, "*The Hermit and the Outlaw*: An Edition," in *Interstices: Studies in Middle English and Anglo-Latin Texts in Honor of A. G. Rigg*, ed. Richard Firth Green and Linne R. Mooney (Toronto: University of Toronto Press, 2004), 137–66. For a translation, see Alexander L. Kaufman, ed. and trans., *The Hermit and the Outlaw*, in Ohlgren 2005, 338–55. For an examination of the similarities between the outlaw and Robin Hood, see Richard Firth Green, "The Hermit and the Outlaw: New Evidence for Robin Hood's Death?" in Phillips 2005, 51–59.
83. Kaufman, *Hermit*, 347.
84. Indeed, this discussion almost certainly existed, in one form or another, much earlier as well.
85. James Gairdner, ed., *Three Fifteenth-Century Chronicles*. Camden Society, n.s., 28 (Westminster: Nichols and Sons, 1880), 94–99. For an examination of the influence that the Robin Hood tradition had on the Jack Cade Rebellion, see Alexander L. Kaufman, *The Historical Literature of the Jack Cade Rebellion* (Farnham: Ashgate Press, 2009), 175–94.
86. Anne Brannen, "A Century of *Mankind*: How a Very Bad Play Became Good," *Medieval Perspectives* 40, no. 2 (2000): 11–20 at 12.
87. As in *Piers Plowman*, the outlaws are negative examples. Indeed, one wonders if *Mankind* intends a stronger allusion to the type of spiritual iconography seen in *Piers Plowman*. Like the earlier work, *Mankind* contrasts the "wastours" with a hard-working plowman trying to till the earth and grow his crop. It is, of course, well-known that the figure of the plowman is an iconic figure of spiritual perfection, and one would be reasonable to speculate that *Mankind* means to reference that tradition as well, but such a consideration would be beyond the scope of the current study.
88. Eccles, *Mankind*, 184, lines 907–914. *Serge*, "examine"; *wanite*, "vanity"; *prowe*, "evidence from exerience"; *per suam misericordiam*, "through His pity"; *pleyferys*, "companions in joy"; *porcyon vitam eternam*, "portion forever."

Bibliography

Manuscripts

Kew, National Archives, A JUST 1 1098.

Primary Works

Adams, John Quincy, ed. *Chief Pre-Shakespearean Dramas: A Selection of Plays Illustrating the History of the English Drama from Its Origin Down to Shakespeare*. Boston: Houghton Mifflin, 1924.

Barnum, Priscilla Heath, ed. *Dives and Pauper*. EETS, o.s., 275. London: Oxford University Press, 1976.

Borrow, George Henry. *Wild Wales*. Edited by Clement King Shorter. Vol. 13 of *Works of George Borrow*. New York: AMS Press, 1967.

Boyd, Beverly. ed. *The Middle English Miracles of the Virgin*. San Marino: Huntington Library, 1964.

Brandin, Louis. ed. *Fouke Fitz Warin, Roman du XIVe Siècle*. Les Classimques Français du Moyen Âge 63. Paris: H. Champion, 1930.

Brie, Friedrich W. D., ed. *The Brut or The Chronicles of England*. EETS, o.s., 131 and 136. London: Kegan Paul and Oxford University Press, 1906, 1908; repr., Woodbridge and Rochester: Boydell and Brewer, 2000.

Bruce, John, ed. *The Historie of the Arrival of King Edward IV*. Camden Society, o.s., 1. London: Royal Historical Society, 1838; repr. New York: AMS Press, 1968.

Bull, Marcus Graham, ed. and trans. *The Miracles of Our Lady of Rocamadour: Analysis and Translation*. Woodbridge: Boydell Press, 1999.

Burgess, Glyn, ed. and trans. *Two Medieval Outlaws: Eustace the Monk and Fouke Fitz Waryn*. Cambridge: D. S. Brewer, 2009.

Calendar of the Close Rolls of Henry III. 14 vols. London: Public Record Office, 1902–38.

Calendar of the Patent Rolls of the Reign of Henry III. 6 vols. London: H. M. S. O., 1901–13.

Cawley, A. C., and J. J. Anderson, eds. *Sir Gawain and the Green Knight, Pearl, Cleanness, Patience*. London: Everyman-Dent, 1996.

Chaucer, Geoffrey. *The Riverside Chaucer*. Edited by Larry D. Benson. 3rd ed. Boston: Houghton, 1987.

Child, Francis James, ed. *The English and Scottish Popular Ballads*. 5 vols. New York: Dover, 1965.

Conlon, Denis Joseph, ed. *Li Romans de Witasse Le Moine: Roman du treizième siècle. Édité daprès le manuscrit, Fonds Français 1553, de la Bibliothèque Nationale, Paris*. University of North Carolina Studies in Romance Languages and Literatures 126. Chapel Hill: University of North Carolina Press, 1972.

de Berceo, Gonzalo. *Miracles of Our Lady*. Translated by Richard Terry Mount and Annette Grant Cash. Lexington: University of Kentucky Press, 1997.

Dobson, R. B., and J. Taylor, eds. *Rymes of Robin Hood: An Introduction to the English Outlaw*. London: Alan Sutton, 1989.

Eccles, Mark, ed. *The Macro Plays: The Castle of Perseverance, Wisdom, Mankind*. EETS, o.s., 262. London: Oxford University Press, 1969.

Ewert, Alfred, ed. *Gui de Warewic: Roman du XIIIe Siècle*. 2 vols. Les Classiques Français du Moyen Âge, 74–75. Paris: É. Champion, 1932–33.

Ferrante, Joan M., trans. *Guillaume d'Orange: Four Twelfth-Century Epics*. New York: Columbia University Press, 1974.

French, Walter Hoyt, and Charles Brockway Hale, ed. *Middle English Metrical Romances.* 2 vols. New York: Russel and Russel, 1964.

Gairdner, James, ed. *Three Fifteenth-Century Chronicles.* Camden Society, n.s., 28. Westminster: Nichols and Sons, 1880.

Gordon, Ida L., ed. *The Seafarer.* Rev. ed. Exeter: University of Exeter Press, 1996.

Green, Richard Firth, ed. "*The Hermit and the Outlaw*: An Edition." In *Interstices: Studies in Middle English and Anglo-Latin Texts in Honor of A. G. Rigg*, edited by Richard Firth Green and Linne R. Mooney, 137–66. Toronto: University of Toronto Press, 2004.

Hall, G. D. G., ed. and trans. *The Treatise on the Laws and Customs of the Realm of England Commonly Called Glanvill.* Oxford: Clarendon Press, 1993.

Hanna, Ralph, III, ed. *The Awntyrs off Arthure at the Terne Wathelyn: An Edition Based on Bodleian Library MS. Douce 324.* Manchester: Manchester University Press, 1974.

Hardy, Thomas Duffy, ed. *Rotuli chartarum in Turri Londinensi.* London: Public Record Commission, 1837.

Hartshorne, Charles H., ed. *Ancient Metrical Tales.* London: William Pickering, 1829.

Hathaway, E. J., P. T. Ricketts, C. A. Robson, and A. D. Wilshere, eds. *Fouke le Fitz Waryn.* Anglo-Norman Text Society, 26–28. Bristol: Basil Blackwell, 1975.

Henry de Bracton. *On the Laws and Customs of England.* Edited by George E. Woodbine. Translated by Samuel E. Thorne, 4 vols. Cambridge: Harvard University Press, 1968–77.

Herolt, Johann. *Miracles of the Blessed Virgin Mary.* Edited and translated by C. C. Swinton Bland. New York: Harcourt, Brace, 1928.

Hoccleve, Thomas. *The Regiment of Princes.* Edited by Charles R. Blyth. TEAMS Middle English Texts. Kalamazoo: Medieval Institute Publications, 1999.

Hunnisett, R. F., ed. *Bedfordshire Coroners' Rolls.* Publications of the Bedfordshire Historical Society 41. Streatly, UK: Bedfordshire Historical Record Society, 1960.

Jones, Timothy S., ed. and trans. *The Outlawry of Earl Godwin.* In Ohlgren 2005, 3–27.

Kaufman, Alexander L., ed. and trans. *The Hermit and the Outlaw.* In Ohlgren 2005, 338–55.

Kelly, Thomas E., ed. and trans. *Fouke fitz Waryn.* In Ohlgren 2005, 165–247.

Kemp-Welch, Alice, trans. *The History of Fulk Fitz-Warine Englished by Alice Kemp-Welch with an Introduction by L. Brandin Ph.D.* London: Moring, 1904.

Klaeber, Fr., ed. *Beowulf and the Fight at Finnesburg.* 3rd ed. Lexington: D.C. Heath, 1950.

Knight, Stephen, ed. and trans. *The Tale of Gamelyn.* In Ohlgren 2005, 264–89.

_____. and Thomas Ohlgren, eds. *Robin Hood and Other Outlaw Tales.* TEAMS Middle English Texts. Kalamazoo: Medieval Institute Publications, 2000.

Langland, William. *The Vision of Piers Plowman: A Critical Edition of the B-Text Based on the Trinity College Cambridge MS B. 15. 17.* Edited by A. V. C. Schmidt. 2nd ed. London: Dent, 1995.

Leland, John. *Joannis Lelandi Antiquarii De Rebus Britannicis Collectanea.* Edited by Thomas Hearne. 6 vols. London: Benjamin White, 1774; repr. Farnborough: Gregg International Publishers, 1970.

Leslie, Roy F., ed. *The Wanderer.* Rev. ed. Exmouth: University of Exeter, 1985.

Manly, John Matthew, ed. *Specimens of the Pre-Shakespearean Drama.* Boston: Ginn, 1897.

Marx, Karl, and Friedrich Engels. "The Communist Manifesto." In *Karl Marx: On Revolution.* Edited and translated by S. K. Padover. New York: McGraw-Hill, 1971.

Matthew Paris. *Matthæi Parisiensis, Monachi Sancti Albani, Chronica Majora.* Edited by Henry Richards Luard. 7 vols. London: Longman, 1872–1883.

_____. *Matthew Paris's English History. From the Year 1235 to 1273.* Translated by J. A. Giles. 3 vols. London: H. G. Bohn, 1852–1854.

Ohlgren, Thomas H., ed. and trans. *A Gest of Robyn Hode.* In Ohlgren 2005, 356–96.

_____. *Medieval Outlaws: Twelve Tales in Modern English Translation.* Rev. ed. West Lafayette: Parlor Press, 2005.

Pollack, Frederick, and Frederick William Maitland, eds. *The History of English Law Before the Time of Edward I.* 2nd ed. 2 vols. Cambridge: Cambridge University Press, 1968.

Prichard, Thomas Jeffrey Llewelyn. *The Comical Adventures of Twm Shon Catty (Thomas*

Jones, Esq.), Commonly Known as the Welsh Robin Hood. Wakefield: William Nicholson and Sons, 1886.

Ralph of Coggeshall. *Radulphi de Coggeshall Chronicon Anglicanum, De Expugnatione Terrae Sanctae Libellus, Thomas Agnellus De Morte et Sepultra Henrici Regis Angliae Junioris, Gesta Fulconis Filii Warini, Excerpta ex Otiis Inperialibus Gervasii Tileburiensis.* Edited by Josephus Stevenson. Rolls Series 66. London: Longman, 1875.

Revard, Carter, ed. and trans. *The Outlaw's Song of Trailbaston.* In Ohlgren 2005, 151–64.

Ritson, Joseph. *Robin Hood: A Collection of All the Ancient Poems, Songs and Ballads, Now Extant, Relative to That Celebrated English Outlaw.* London: John C. Nimmo, 1885.

Robbins, Rossell Hope, ed. *Secular Lyrics of the XIVth and XVth Centuries.* 2nd ed. Oxford: Clarendon Press, 1954.

Russell, John. *The Boke of Nurture Folowyng Englondis Gise,* in *The Babees Book.* Edited by F. J. Furnivall, EETS, o.s., 32. London: N. Trübner, 1868.

Sharpe, Reginald, ed. and trans. *Calendar of Letter-Books of the City of London: Letter Book K.* London: John Edward Francis, 1911.

Shinners, John Raymond, ed. *Medieval Popular Religion 1000–1500: A Reader.* Peterborough: Broadview Press, 2007.

Shirley, Walter Waddington, ed. *Royal and Other Historical Letters Illustrative of the Reign of Henry III.* 2 vols. London: Longman, Green, Longman, and Roberts, 1862–66.

Spraggs, Gillian. "Section From The Roman History of Cassius Dio." In *Outlaws and Highwaymen,* 2007, http://www.outlawsandhighwaymen.com//bulla.htm.

Smith, A. H., ed. *The Place Names of the North Riding of Yorkshire.* English Place-Name Society 5. Cambridge: Cambridge University Press, 1928.

——. *The Place Names of the East Riding of Yorkshire.* English Place-Name Society 14. Cambridge: Cambridge University Press, 1937.

——. *The Place Names of the West Riding of Yorkshire.* 8 vols. English Place-Name Society 30–37. Cambridge: Cambridge University Press, 1961–63.

Stenton, Doris Mary Parsons, ed. *Pleas Before the King or His Justices, 1198–1202.* 4 vols. Publications of the Selden Society, 67–68, 83–84. London: Quaritch, 1952–67.

Stubbs, William, and H. W. Carless Davis, eds. *Select Charters and Other Illustrations of English Constitutional History.* 9th ed. Oxford, Clarendon Press: 1913.

Swanton, Michael, ed. and trans. *The Deeds of Hereward.* In Ohlgren 2005, 28–99.

Thomas, A. H., and I. D. Thornley, eds. *The Great Chronicle of London.* London: George W. Jones, 1939; repr. Gloucester: Alan Sutton, 1983.

Thomas de Monmouth. *The Life and Miracles of St. William of Norwich.* Translated by Augustus Jessopp and Montague Rhodes James. Cambridge: Cambridge University Press, 1896.

Underhill, Evelyn, ed. and trans. *The Miracles of Our Lady Saint Mary; Brought Out of Divers Tongues and Newly Set Forth in English.* New York: E. P. Dutton, 1906.

Virgil, Polydore. *Three Books of Polydore Virgil's English History, Comprising the Reigns of Henry VI, Edward IV, and Richard III.* Edited by Henry Ellis. Camden Society, o.s., 29. London: Royal Historical Society, 1844; repr., New York: AMS Press, 1968.

Wasson, John M., ed. *Devon.* Records of Early English Drama. Toronto: University of Toronto Press, 1986.

Whiteford, Peter, ed. *The Myracles of Oure Lady: Ed. from Wynkyn de Worde's Edition.* Middle English Texts 23. Heidelberg: Carl Winter, 1990.

William of Newburgh. *Historia Reum Anglicarum,* in *Chronicles of the Reigns of Stephen, Henry II and Richard I.* Edited by Richard Howlett. 4 vols. Rolls Series 82. London: Longman, 1884–89.

Wright, Thomas, ed. and trans. *The History of Fulk Fitz Warine, an Outlawed Baron in the Reign of King John, Edited from a Manuscript Preserved in the British Museum, with an English Translation and Explanatory and Illustrative Notes.* London: Printed for the Warton, Club, 1855.

——. *Political Poems and Songs Relating to English History Composed During the Period from the Accession of Edward III to That of Richard III.* 2 vols. Rolls Series 14. Longman: London, 1859–61.

Secondary Works

Abulafia, Anna Sapir. *Christians and Jews in the Twelfth-Century Renaissance.* London: Routledge, 1995.

———. "The Intellectual and Spiritual Quest for Christ and Central Medieval Persecution of Jews." In *Religious Violence Between Christians and Jews: Medieval Roots, Modern Perspectives*, edited by Anna Sapir Abulafia, 61–85. New York: Palgrave, 2002.

Adler, Michael. *The Jews of Medieval England.* London: Jewish Historical Society of England, 1939.

Alexander, Philip S. "Madam Eglentyne, Geoffrey Chaucer and the Problem of Medieval Anti-Semitism." *Bulletin of the John Rylands Library of Manchester* 74 (1992): 109–20.

Almond, R. L., and A. J. Pollard. "The Yeomanry of Robin Hood and Social Terminology in Fifteenth-Century England." *Past and Present* 170 (2001): 52–77.

Anderson, George Kumler. *The Legend of the Wandering Jew.* Providence: Brown University Press, 1965.

Ankersmit, F. R. *History and Tropology: The Rise and Fall of Metaphor.* Berkeley: University of California Press, 1994.

Baker, Donald C. "The Date of *Mankind.*" *Philological Quarterly* 42, no. 4 (1963): 90–91.

Bale, Anthony P. "Fictions of Judaism in England Before 1290." In *Jews in Medieval Britain: Historical, Literary and Archaeological Perspectives*, edited by Patricia Skinner, 129–44. Woodbridge: The Boydell Press, 2003.

———. "'House Devil, Town Saint': Anti-Semitism and Hagiography in Medieval Suffolk." In *Chaucer and the Jews: Sources, Contexts, Meanings*, edited by Sheila Delany, 185–210. New York: Routledge, 2002.

Baraz, Daniel. *Medieval Cruelty: Changing Perceptions, Late Antiquity to the Early Modern Period.* Ithaca: Cornell University Press, 2003.

Barczewski, Stephanie L. *Myth and National Identity in Nineteenth-Century Britain: The Legends of King Arthur and Robin Hood.* New York: Oxford University Press, 2000.

Barnard, John. "Keat's 'Robin Hood,' John Hamilton Reynolds, and the 'Old Poets.'" In Knight 1999, 123–140.

Bayless, Martha. "The Story of the Fallen Jew and the Iconography of Jewish Unbelief." *Viator* 34 (2003): 142–56.

Beattie, J. M. "The Royal Pardon and Criminal Procedure in Early Modern England." *Historical Papers* 22, no. 1 (1987): 9–22.

Bellamy, J. G. *Bastard Feudalism and the Law.* Portland: Areopagitica Press, 1989.

———. *Crime and Public Order in England in the Later Middle Ages.* London: Routledge & Kegan Paul, 1973.

———. *The Criminal Trial in Later Medieval England: Felony Before the Courts from Edward I to the Sixteenth Century.* Toronto: University of Toronto Press, 1998.

———. *The Law of Treason in England in the Later Middle Ages.* London: Cambridge University Press, 1970.

———. *Robin Hood: An Historical Inquiry.* Bloomington: Indiana University Press, 1984.

Bechmann, Roland. *Trees and Man: The Forest in the Middle Ages.* Translated by Katharyn Dunham. New York: Paragon House, 1990.

Benecke, Ingrid. *Der gute Outlaw. Studien zu einem literarischen Typus im 13. Und 14. Jahrhundert. Studien zur englischen Philologie*, n.s., 17. Tübingen: Niemeyer, 1973.

Benin, Stephen. "Matthew Paris and the Jews." In *Proceedings of the Tenth World Congress of Jewish Studies, Jerusalem, August 16–24, 1989*, edited by David Assaf, vol. 2, bk. 2, 61–68. 4 vols. in 7. Jerusalem: World Union of Jewish Studies 1990.

Bernheimer, Richard. *Wild Men in the Middle Ages.* Cambridge: Harvard University Press, 1952.

Birrell, Jean. "Peasant Deer Poachers in the Medieval Forest." In *Progress and Problems in Medieval England*, edited by Richard Britnell and John Hatcher, 68–88. Cambridge: Cambridge University Press, 1996.

Bouchard, Constance Brittain. *"Strong of Body, Brave and Noble": Chivalry and Society in Medieval France.* Ithaca: Cornell University Press, 1998.

Bowers, R. H. "'Foleuyles Lawes' (*Piers Plowman*, C.XXII. 247)." *Notes and Queries*, n.s., 8 (1961): 327–28.

Brand, Paul. "Jews and the Law in England, 1275–90." *English Historical Review* 115, no. 464 (2000): 1138–58.

Brandin, Louis. "Nouvelles Recherches sur

Fouke Fitz Waryn." *Romania* 55 (1929): 17–44.

Brannen, Anne. "A Century of *Mankind*: How a Very Bad Play Became Good." *Medieval Perspectives* 40, no. 2 (2000): 11–20.

Breizmann, Natalia. "*Beowulf* as Romance: Literary Interpretation as Quest." *MLN* 113, no. 5 (1998): 1022–35.

Bremmer, Rolf H., Jr. "The *Gesta Herwardi*: Transforming an Anglo-Saxon into an Englishman." In *People and Texts. Relationships in Medieval Literature: Studies Presented to Erik Kooper*, edited by Thea Summerfield and Keith Busby, 29–42. Costerus, n.s., 166. Amsterdam: Rodopi, 2007.

Burgess, Glyn S. "Fouke Fitz Waryn III and King John: Good Outlaw and Bad King." In Phillips 2008, 73–98.

———. "'I kan rymes of Robyn Hood, and Randolf Erl of Chestre.'" In "*De sens rassis*": *Essays in Honor of Rupert T. Pickens*, edited by Keith Busby, Bernard Guidot, and Logan E. Whalen, 51–84. Amsterdam: Rodopi, 2005.

———. "Women in the *Fouke le Fitz Waryn*." In *Por le soie amisté*, edited by Keith Busby and Catherine M. Jones, 75–93. Etudes de Langue et Litterature Francaises 183. Amsterdam: Rodopi, 2000.

Burr, David. "The Antichrist and the Jews in Four Thirteenth-century Apocalypse Commentaries." In *Friars and Jews in the Middle Ages and Renaissance*, edited by Steven J. McMichael and Susan E. Myers, 23–38. The Medieval Franciscans 2. Leiden: Brill, 2004.

Butler, Marilyn. "The Good Old Times: Maid Marian." In Knight 1999, 141–53.

Calin, William. *The French Tradition and the Literature of Medieval England*. Toronto: University of Toronto Press, 1994.

Carpenter, Christine. *Locality and Polity: A Study of Warwickshire Landed Society, 1401–1499*. Cambridge: Cambridge University Press, 1992.

Cartmill, Matt. *A View to Death in the Morning: Hunting and Nature Throughout History*. Cambridge: Harvard University Press, 1993.

The Catholic Encyclopedia. 15 vols. New York: Robert Appleton Co., 1907–12.

Caviness, Madeline H. "Artistic Integration in Gothic Buildings: A Post-Modern Construct?" In *Artistic Integration in Gothic Buildings*, edited by Chieffo Raguin, Kathryn Brush, and Peter Draper , 248–61. Toronto: University of Toronto Press, 1995.

Chadwick, Dorothy. *Social Life in the Days of Piers Plowman*. Cambridge: Cambridge University Press, 1922.

Chazan, Robert. *Daggers of Faith: Thirteenth-Century Christian Missionizing and Jewish Response*. Berkeley: University of California Press, 1989.

———. *Fashioning Jewish Identity in Medieval Western Christendom*. Cambridge: Cambridge University Press, 2004.

———. *The Jews of Medieval Western Christendom, 1000–1500*. Cambridge: Cambridge University Press, 2006.

Chism, Christine. "Robin Hood: Thinking Globally, Acting Locally in the Fifteenth-century Ballads." In *The Letter of the Law: Legal Practice and Literary Production in Medieval England*, edited by Emily Steiner and Candace Barrington, 12–39. Ithaca: Cornell University Press, 2002.

Clarke, Catherine A. M. *Literary Landscapes and the Idea of England, 700–1400*. Cambridge: D. S. Brewer, 2006.

Clawson, William Hill. *The Gest of Robin Hood*. Toronto: University of Toronto Library, 1909.

Cohen, Jeffrey J. "The Flow of Blood in Medieval Norwich." *Speculum* 79, no. 1 (2004): 26–65.

———. *The Friars and the Jews: The Evolution of Medieval Anti-Judaism*. Ithaca: Cornell University Press, 1982.

Coupland, Reginald. *Welsh and Scottish Nationalism: A Study*. London: Collins, 1954.

Crane, Susan Dannenbaum. "Anglo-Norman Romances of English Heroes: 'Ancestral Romance'?" *Romance Philology* 35, no. 4 (1982): 601–8.

———. "The Writing Lesson of 1381." In *Chaucer's England: Literature in Historical Context*, edited by Barbara A. Hanawalt, 201–21. Medieval Studies at Minnesota 4. Minneapolis: University of Minnesota Press, 1992.

Dahood, Roger. "English Historical Narratives of Jewish Child-Murder, Chaucer's *Prioress's Tale*, and the Date of Chaucer's Unknown Source." *Studies in the Age of Chaucer* 31 (2009): 125–40.

———. "The Punishment of the Jews, Hugh of Lincoln, and the Question of Satire in the *Prioress' Tale*." *Viator* 36 (2005): 465–491.

Dalton, Paul. "The Outlaw Hereward 'the Wake': His Companions and Enemies." In *Outlaws in Medieval and Early Modern England: Crime, Government and Society, c. 1066–1600*, edited by John C. Appleby and Paul Dalton, 7–36. Farnham: Ashgate Press, 2009.

Davis, John J. *Biblical Numerology*. Grand Rapids: Baker Book House, 1977.

Despres, Denise L. "Immaculate Flesh and the Social Body: Mary and the Jews." *Jewish History* 12, no. 1 (1998): 47–69.

Dnes, Antony W. "The Economics of Crime." In *The Economic Dimensions of Crime*, edited by Nigel G. Fielding, Alan Clarke, and Robert Witt, 70–81. New York: St. Martin's Press, 2000.

Duffy, Eamon. *The Stripping of the Altars: Traditional Religion in England, c. 1400–1580*. New Haven: Yale University Press, 1992.

Edwards, John. "The Church and the Jews in Medieval England." In *Jews in Medieval Britain: Historical, Literary and Archaeological Perspectives*, edited by Patricia Skinner, 85–95. Woodbridge: The Boydell Press, 2003.

Elias, Norbert. *The Civilizing Process: The History of Manners*. Translated by Edmund Jephcott. Oxford: Blackwell, 1978.

Evans, Gwynfor. *Wales: A History*. New York: Barnes and Noble Books, 1996.

Field, Rosalind. "From *Gui* to *Guy*: The Fashioning of a Popular Romance." In *Guy of Warwick: Icon and Ancestor*, edited by Alison Wiggins and Rosalind Field, 44–60. Studies in Medieval Romance 4. Cambridge: D. S. Brewer, 2007.

Fleischman, Suzanne. "On the Representation of History and Fiction in the Middle Ages." *History and Theory* 22, no. 2 (1983): 278–310.

Fletcher, Alan J. *Preaching, Politics and Poetry in Late-Medieval England*. Dublin: Four Courts Press, 1998.

Fletcher, J. Kyrle. "*Western Mail*, August 22, 1921." In *Tregaron: Historical and Antiquarian*, edited by D. C. Rees, 104–5. Llandyssul: J. D. Lewis & Sons, Gomerian Press, 1936.

Foucault, Michel. *The Order of Things: An Archaeology of the Human Sciences*. New York: Vintage, 1970.

Fradenburg, Louise O. "Criticism, Anti-Semitism, and the *Prioress's Tale*." *Exemplaria* 1 (1989): 69–115.

Francis, Elizabeth A. "The Background to *Fulk FitzWarin*." In *Studies in Medieval French, Presented to Alfred Ewert in Honour of His Seventieth Birthday*, 322–27. Oxford: Clarendon Press, 1961.

Frank, Robert Worth, Jr. "Miracles of the Virgin, Medieval Anti-Semitism, and the 'Prioress's Tale.'" In *The Wisdom of Poetry: Essays in Early English Literature in Honor of Morton W. Bloomfield*, edited by Larry D. Benson and Siegfried Wenzel, 177–88. Kalamazoo: Medieval Institute Publications, 1982.

Fromm, Erich. *To Have or to Be?* New York: Harper & Row; repr., New York: Continuum, 2007.

Gager, John G. *The Origins of Anti-Semitism: Attitudes Toward Judaism in Pagan and Christian Antiquity*. New York: Oxford University Press, 1983.

Geiger, Julia. "The Trial of a Duchess: Heresy in Fifteenth-Century England and the Case of Eleanor Cobham." Masters Paper. Ohio State University, February 2007.

Geremek, Bronislaw. "The Marginal Man." In *Medieval Callings*, edited Jacques Le Goff, translated by Lydia G. Cochrane, 346–73. Chicago: University of Chicago Press, 1990.

Given, James Buchanan. *Society and Homicide in Thirteenth-Century England*. Stanford: Stanford University Press, 1977.

Goebel, Julius. *Felony and Misdemeanor: A Study in the History of English Criminal Procedure*. Vol. 1. New York: Commonwealth; London: Oxford University Press, 1937.

Graef, Hilda C., *Mary: A History of Doctrine and Devotion*. New York: Sheed and Ward, 1963–1965.

Gransden, Antonia. *Historical Writing in England: C. 550 to C. 1307*. Ithaca: Cornell University Press, 1974; repr. London: Routledge, 1996.

Gray, Douglas. "The Robin Hood Poems." In Knight 1999, 3–37.

Greatrex, Joan. "Monastic Charity for Jewish Converts: The Requisition of Corrodies by Henry III." *Studies in Church History* 29 (1992): 133–43.

Green, Richard Firth. "The Hermit and the Outlaw: New Evidence for Robin Hood's Death?" In Phillips 2005, 51–59.

———. John Ball's Letters: Literary History and Historical Literature." In *Chaucer's England: Literature in Historical Context*, edited by Barbara A. Hanawalt, 176–200. Medieval Studies at Minnesota 4. Minneapolis: University of Minnesota Press, 1992.

———. "Violence in the Early Robin Hood Poems." In *"A Great Effusion of Blood?" Interpreting Medieval Violence*, edited by Mark D. Meyerson, Daniel Thiery, and Oren Falk, 268–86. Toronto: University of Toronto Press, 2004.

Green, Thomas Andrew. *Verdict According to Conscience: Perspectives on the English Criminal Trial Jury, 1200–1800*. Chicago: University of Chicago Press, 1985.

Greenfield, Stanley B. "The Formulaic Expression of the Theme of 'Exile' in Anglo-Saxon Poetry." *Speculum* 30, no. 2 (1955): 200–06.

Groebner, Valentin. *Liquid Assets, Dangerous Gifts: Presents and Politics at the End of the Middle Ages*. Translated by Pamela E. Selwyn. Philadelphia: University of Pennsylvania Press, 2002.

Griffiths, Ralph A. "The Trial of Eleanor Cobham: An Episode in the Fall of Duke Humphrey of Gloucester." *Bulletin of the John Rylands Library*, 51 (1968): 381–399.

Hahn, Thomas, ed. *Robin Hood in Popular Culture: Violence, Transgression, and Justice*. Cambridge: D. S. Brewer, 2000.

Hames, Harvey J. "The Limits of Conversion: Ritual Murder and the Virgin Mary in the Account of Adam of Bristol." *Journal of Medieval History* 33 (2007): 43–59.

Hanawalt, Barbara A. "Ballads and Bandits: Fourteenth-Century Outlaws and the Robin Hood Poems." In *Chaucer's England: Literature in Historical Context*, edited by Barbara A. Hanawalt, 154–75. Medieval Studies at Minnesota 4. Minneapolis: University of Minnesota Press, 1992.

———. *Crime and Conflict in English Communities, 1300–1348*. Cambridge: Harvard University Press, 1979.

———. "The Female Felon in Fourteenth-Century England." *Viator* 5 (1974): 253–268.

———. "Men's Games, King's Deer: Poaching in Medieval England." *Journal of Medieval and Renaissance Studies* 18 (1988): 175–193.

———. (Weston). "The Peasant Family and Crime in England." *The Journal of British Studies* 13, no. 2 (1974): 1–18.

———. "Peasant Resistance to Royal and Seignorial Impositions." In *Social Unrest in the Late Middle Ages*, edited by Francis X. Newman, 23–47. Medieval and Renaissance Texts and Studies 39. Binghamton, NY: Center for Medieval and Early Renaissance Texts and Studies, 1986.

———. "Women Before the Law: Females as Felons and Prey in Fourteenth-Century England." In *Women and the Law: The Social Historical Perspective*, edited by D. Kelly Weisberg, 1: 165–95. 2 vols. Cambridge, MA: Schenkman, 1982.

Harding, Alan. *England in the Thirteenth Century*. Cambridge: Cambridge University Press, 1993.

Hasan-Rokem, Gail, and Alan Dundes, eds. *The Wandering Jew: Essays in the Interpretation of a Christian Legend*. Bloomington: Indiana University Press, 1986.

Harvey, I. M. W. *Jack Cade's Rebellion of 1450*. Oxford: Clarendon Press, 1991.

Hicks, Michael A. *Bastard Feudalism*. London: Longman, 1995.

Hillaby, Joe. "The Ritual Child Murder Accusation: Its Dissemination and Harold of Gloucester." *Jewish Historical Studies* 34 (1996): 69–109.

Hilton, Rodney H. "The Origins of Robin Hood." *Past and Present* 14 (1958): 30–44.

Hobsbawm, Eric. *Bandits*. New York: Delacorte Press, 1969.

Hoffman, Dean A. "'I wyll be thy true servaunte / And trewely serve thee': Guildhall Minstrelsy in the *Gest of Robyn Hode*." *The Drama Review* 49, no. 2 (2005): 119–34.

Holmes, Urban T. "The Adventures of Fouke Fitz Warin." In *Medium Aevum Romanicum: Festschrift für Hans Rheinfelder*, edited by Heinrich Bihler and Alfred Noyer-Weidner, 176–85. Munich: Max Hueber, 1963.

Holt, J. C. "The Origin and Audience of the Ballads of Robin Hood." *Past and Present* 18 (1960): 89–110.

———. *Robin Hood*. Rev. ed. London: Thames and Hudson, 1989.

———. "Robin Hood: Some Comments." *Past and Present* 19 (1961). 16–18.

Hood, Ralph W. Jr., Ronald J. Morris, and P. J. Watson, "Male Commitment to the Cult of the Virgin Mary and the Passion of Christ as a Function of Early Maternal

Bonding." *International Journal of the Psychology of Religion* 1, no. 4 (1991): 221–31.

Hsia, R. Po-chia. *The Myth of Ritual Murder: Jews and Magic in Reformation Germany.* New Haven: Yale University Press, 1988.

Humphries, Drew, and David Greenberg. "The Dialectics of Crime Control." In *Crime and Capitalism: Readings in Marxist Criminology*, edited by David Greenberg, 463–508. Exp. ed. Philadelphia: Temple University Press, 1993.

Hunter, Joseph. "The Great Hero of the Ancient Minstrelsy of England: Robin Hood, His Period, Real Character, etc., Investigated." *Critical and Historical Tracts* 4. London: Smith, 1852.

Hyams, Paul. "The Jewish Minority in Medieval England, 1066–1290." *Journal of Jewish Studies* 25, no. 2 (1974): 270–93.

Jacobs, Joseph. "Little St. Hugh of Lincoln." In *Jewish Ideals and Other Essays*, edited by Joseph Jacobs, 192–224. London: D. Nutt, 1896.

Jameson, Frederic. "Criticism in History." In *Criticism: Major Statements*, edited by Charles Kaplan and William Anderson, 574–94. 3rd ed. New York: St. Martin's Press, 1991.

———. *The Political Unconscious: Narrative as a Socially Symbolic Act.* Ithaca: Cornell University Press, 1981.

Johnson, Alexandra F. "The Robin Hood of the Records." In *Playing Robin Hood: The Legend as Performance in Five Centuries*, edited by Lois Potter, 27–44. Newark: University of Delaware Press, 1998.

Johnson, Willis. "Textual Sources for the Study of Jewish Currency Crimes in Thirteenth-Century England." *British Numismatic Journal, Including the Proceedings of the British Numismatic Society* 66 (1996–1997): 21–32.

Jones, Timothy. "Geoffrey of Monmouth, Fouke le Fitz Waryn, and National Mythology." *Studies in Philology* 91, no. 3 (1994): 233–49.

Justice, Stephen. *Writing and Rebellion: England in 1381.* Berkeley: University of California Press, 1994.

Kahn, Hilary A. "Traversing the Q'eqchi' Imaginary: The Conjecture of Crime in Livingston, Guatemala." In *Crime's Power: Anthropologists and the Ethnographies of Crime*, edited by Philip C. Parnell and Stephanie C. Kane, 33–54. New York: Palgrave Macmillan, 2003.

Kane, Stuart. "Horseplay: Robin Hood, Guy of Gisborne, and the Neg(oti)ation of the Bestial." In Hahn, 101–110.

Kaufman, Alexander L. *The Historical Literature of the Jack Cade Rebellion.* Farnham: Ashgate Press, 2009.

Keen, Maurice. *The Outlaws of Medieval Legend.* Rev. ed. London and New York: Routledge, 2000.

———. "Robin Hood — Peasant or Gentleman?" *Past and Present* 19 (1961): 7–15.

Kennedy, Edward Donald. *A Manual of the Writings in Middle English 1050–1500, Volume 8: Chronicles and Other Historical Writings.* New Haven: Archon, 1989.

Kennedy, Marjorie J. O. "Resourceful Villeins: The Cellarer Family of Wawne in Holderness." *Yorkshire Archaeological Journal* 48 (1976): 107–117.

Kevelson, Roberta. *Inlaws/Outlaws, a Semiotics of Systemic Interaction: "Robin Hood" and the "King's Law.*" Bloomington: Indiana University Press, 1977.

Kingsford, Charles Lethbridge. *English Historical Literature in the Fifteenth Century.* New York: Burt Franklin, 1913; repr. 1972.

Knight, Stephen, ed. *Robin Hood: An Anthology of Scholarship and Criticism.* Cambridge: D. S. Brewer, 1999.

———. *Robin Hood: A Complete Study of the English Outlaw.* Oxford: Blackwell, 1994.

———. "Robin Hood: The Earliest Contexts." In *Images of Robin Hood: Medieval to Modern*, edited by Lois Potter and Joshua Calhoun, 21–40. Newark: University of Delaware Press, 2008.

———. *Robin Hood: A Mythic Biography.* Ithaca: Cornell University Press, 2003.

———. "The Social Function of the Middle English Romances." In *Medieval Literature: Criticism, Ideology, & History*, edited by David Aers, 99–122. New York: St. Martin's Press, 1986.

Langmuir, Gavin I. "Hsia, *The Myth of Ritual Murder.*" Review of *The Myth of Ritual Murder: Jews and Magic in Reformation Germany*, by R. Po-chia Hsia. *Jewish Quarterly Review* 82, no. 3/4 (1992): 538–540.

———. "The Jews and the Archives of Angevin England: Reflections on Medieval Anti-Semitism." *Traditio* 19 (1963): 183–244.

———. *Toward a Definition of Antisemitism.*

Berkeley: University of California Press, 1990.
Lee, Alvin A. *The Guest-Hall of Eden: Four Essays on the Design of Old English Poetry.* New Haven and London: Yale University Press, 1972.
Legge, M. Dominica. *Anglo-Norman Literature and Its Background.* Oxford: Clarendon Press, 1963.
Leschnitzer, Adolf S. "Reflections on Medieval Anti-Judaism, 5: The Wandering Jew. The Alienation of the Jewish Image in Christian Consciousness." *Viator* 2 (1971): 391–96.
Lewis, Suzanne. "*Tractatus Adversus Judaeos* in the Gulbenkian Apocalypse." *Art Bulletin* 68, no. 4 (1986): 543–66.
Lindenbaum, Sheila. "Ceremony and Oligarchy: The London Midsummer Watch." In *City and Spectacle in Medieval Europe*, edited by Barbara A. Hanawalt and Kathryn L. Reason, 171–86. Medieval Studies 6. Minneapolis and London: University of Minnesota, 1994.
Lundgren, Timothy. "Hereward and Outlawry in Fenland Culture: A Study of Local Narrative and Tradition in Medieval England." PhD diss., Ohio State University, 1996.
Luxford, Julian M. "An English Chronicle Entry on Robin Hood." *Journal of Medieval History* 35, no. 1 (2009): 70–76.
Marshall, John. "Gathering in the Name of the Outlaw: REED and Robin Hood." In *REED in Review: Essays in Celebration of the First Twenty-Five Years*, edited by Audrey Douglass and Sally-Beth MacLean, 65–84. Toronto: University of Toronto Press, 2006.
Mauss, Marcel. *A General Theory of Magic.* Translated by Robert Brain. London: Routledge and K. Paul, 1972.
McCall, Andrew. *The Medieval Underworld.* 2nd ed. Stroud: Sutton Publishing, 2004.
McCulloh, John. "Jewish Ritual Murder: William of Norwich, Thomas of Monmouth and the Early Dissemination of the Myth." *Speculum* 72, no. 3 (1997): 698–740.
McFarlane, K. B. "'Bastard Feudalism.'" *Bulletin of the Institute of Historical Research* 20 (1945): 161–80.
———. "Parliament and 'Bastard Feudalism.'" *Transactions of the Royal Historical Society*, 4th Series, 26 (1944): 53–79.
McLaren, Mary-Rose. *The London Chronicles of the Fifteenth Century: A Revolution in English Writing, With an Annotated Edition of Bradford, West Yorkshire Archives MS 32D86/42.* Cambridge: D. S. Brewer, 2002.
Meisel, Janet. *Barons of the Welsh Frontier: The Corbet, Pantulf, and Fitz Warin Families, 1066–1272.* Lincoln: University of Nebraska Press, 1980.
Menache, Sophia. "Faith, Myth and Politics: The Stereotype of the Jews and Their Expulsion from England and France." *Jewish Quarterly Review* 75, no. 4 (1985): 351–74.
———. "Matthew Paris's Attitudes Toward Anglo-Jewry." *Journal of Medieval History* 23, no. 2 (1997): 139–62.
Middle English Dictionary. Part of the *Middle English Compendium.* Ann Arbor: The University of Michigan, 2001. http://quod.lib.umich.edu/m/med/. Accessed January 17, 2010.
Moore, R. I. *The Formation of a Persecuting Society: Power and Deviance in Western Europe, 950–1250.* New York: B. Blackwell, 1987.
Morgan, Gerald. "The First Anglo-Welsh Novel." *The Anglo-Welsh Review* 17, no. 39 (1968): 114–22.
Morris, Jan. *The Matter of Wales: Epic Views of a Small Country.* New York: Oxford University Press, 1984.
Nagy, Joseph Kalaky. "The Paradoxes of Robin Hood." *Folklore* 91, no. 2 (1980): 198–210.
Ocker, Christopher. "Ritual Murder and the Subjectivity of Christ: A Choice in Medieval Christianity." *Harvard Theological Review* 91, no. 2 (1998): 153–92.
Ohlgren, Thomas H. "Edwardus redivivus in *A Gest of Robyn Hode.*" *Journal of English and German Philology* 99, no. 1 (2000): 1–28.
———. "The 'Marchaunt' of Sherwood: Mercantile Ideology in *A Gest of Robyn Hode.*" In Hahn, 175–90.
———. *Robin Hood: The Early Poems, 1465–1560: Texts, Contexts, and Ideology.* Newark: University of Delaware Press, 2007.
Ormrod, W. M. "Robin Hood and the Public Record: The Authority of Writing in the Medieval Outlaw Tradition." In *Medieval Cultural Studies: Essays in Honour of Stephen Knight*, edited by Ruth Evans, Helen Fulton, and David Matthews, 57–74. Cardiff: University of Wales Press, 2006.

Osborn, Marijane. "The Real Fulk Fitzwarine's Mythical Monster Fights." In *Words and Works: Studies in Medieval English Language and Literature in Honour of Fred C. Robinson*, edited by Peter S. Baker and Nicholas Howe, 271–92. Toronto: University of Toronto Press, 1998.

Painter, Sidney. *The Reign of King John*. Baltimore: Johns Hopkins University Press, 1949.

———. "The Sources of *Fouke Fitz Warin*." *MLN* 50, no. 1 (1935): 13–15.

Pensom, Roger. "Inside and Outside: Fact and Fiction in *Fouke le Fitz Waryn*." *Medium Aevum* 63, no. 1 (1994): 53–60.

Phillips, Helen, ed. *Bandit Territories: British Outlaw Traditions*. Cardiff: University of Wales Press, 2008.

———. "Forest, Town, and Road: The Significance of Places and Names in Some Robin Hood Texts." In Hahn, 197–214.

———, (ed). *Robin Hood: Medieval and Post-Medieval*. Dublin: Four Courts Press, 2005.

———. "Scott and the Outlaws." In Phillips 2008, 119–42.

Pollard, A. J. *Imagining Robin Hood: The Late-Medieval Stories in Historical Context*. New York: Routledge, 2004.

———. "Political Ideology in the Early Stories of Robin Hood." In *Outlaws in Medieval and Early Modern England: Crime, Government and Society, c. 1066–1600*, edited by John C. Appleby and Paul Dalton, 111–28. Farnham: Ashgate Press, 2009.

Presdee, Mike. *Cultural Criminology and the Carnival of Crime*. London: Routledge, 2000.

Price, Adrian. "Welsh Bandits." In Phillips 2008, 58–72.

Price, Merrall Llewelyn. "Sadism and Sentimentality: Absorbing Antisemitism in Chaucer's Prioress." *Chaucer Review* 43, no. 2 (2008): 197–214.

Price, Paul. "Confessions of a Godless Killer: Guy of Warwick and Comprehensive Entertainment." In *Medieval Insular Romance: Translation and Innovation*, edited by Judith Weiss, Jennifer Fellows, and Morgan Dickson, 93–110. Cambridge: D. S. Brewer, 2000.

Prideaux, W. F. "Who Was Robin Hood?" *Notes and Queries*, 7th Series, 2 (1886): 421–24.

Rees. D. C., ed. *Tregaron: Historical and Antiquarian*. Llandyssul: J. D. Lewis & Sons, Gomerian Press, 1936.

Renn, Derek A. "'Chastel de Dynan': The First Phases of Ludlow." In *Castles in Wales and the Marches: Essays in Honour of D. J. Cathcaret King*, edited by John R. Kenyon and Richard Avent, 55–73. Cardiff: University of Wales Press, 1987.

Revard, Carter. "Scribe and Provenance." In *Studies in the Harley Manuscript: The Scribes, Contents, and Social Contexts of British Library MS Harley 2253*, edited by Susanna Fein, 21–109. Kalamazoo: Medieval Institute Publications, 2000.

Reynolds, Bryan Randolph. *Becoming Criminal: Transversal Performance and Cultural Dissidence in Early Modern England*. Baltimore: Johns Hopkins University Press, 2002.

Richardson, Gary. "Craft Guilds and Christianity in Late-Medieval England: A Rational-Choice Analysis." *Rationality and Society* 17, no. 2 (2005): 139–189.

Rickert, Thomas. *Acts of Enjoyment: Rhetoric, Žižek, and the Return of the Subject*. Pittsburgh: University of Pittsburg Press, 2007.

Rigby, Stephen H. "Urban 'Oligarchy' in Late Medieval England." In *Towns and Townspeople in the Fifteenth Century*, edited by John A. F. Thomas, 62–86. Gloucester: Alan Sutton, 1988.

Rock, Catherine A. "Forsworn and Foredone: Arcite as Oath-Breaker in the *Knight's Tale*." *Chaucer Review* 40, no. 4 (2006): 417–33.

Rokeah, Zefira Entin. "Money and the Hangman in Late Thirteenth-century England: Jews, Christians and Coinage Offences Alleged and Real (Part I)." *Jewish Historical Studies* 31 (1988–1990): 83–109.

———. "Money and the Hangman in Late Thirteenth-century England: Jews, Christians and Coinage Offences Alleged and Real (Part II)." *Jewish Historical Studies* 32 (1990–1992): 159–218.

Rosman, Doreen M. *The Evolution of the English Churches 1500–2000*. Cambridge: Cambridge University Press, 2003.

Ross, David J. A. "Where did Payn Peverell defeat the Devil?" In *Studies in Medieval French Language and Literature: Presented to Brian Woledge in Honour of His 80th Birthday*, edited by Sally Burch North, 135–44. Publications Romanes et Françaises 180. Geneva: Droz, 1988, 135–44.

Roth, Cecil. *A History of the Jews in England.* 3rd ed. Oxford: Clarendon Press, 1964.

Scala, Elizabeth. *Absent Narratives, Manuscript Textuality, and Literary Structure in Late Medieval England.* New York: Palgrave Macmillan, 2002.

Schuler, Carol M. "The Seven Sorrow of the Virgin: Popular Culture and Cultic Imagery in Pre-Reformation Europe." *Simiolus: Netherlands Quarterly for the History of Art* 21, no. 1/2 (1992): 5–28.

Simeone, W. E. "The May Games and the Robin Hood Legend." *The Journal of American Folklore* 64 (1951): 265–274.

Sims, Richard J. "Secondary Offenders? English Women and Crime, c. 1220–1348." In *Victims or Viragos?*, edited by Christine Meek and Catherine Lawless, 69–88. Studies in Medieval and Early Modern Women 4. Dublin: Four Courts Press, 2005.

Singman, Jeffrey L. *Robin Hood: The Shaping of the Legend.* Westport, CT: Greenwood Press, 1998.

Spearing, A. C. "Central and Displaced Sovereignty in Three Medieval Poems." *The Review of English Studies*, n.s., 33, no. 131 (1982): 247–61.

Spiegel, Gabrielle M. *The Past as Text: The Theory and Practice of Medieval Historiography.* Baltimore and London: Johns Hopkins University Press, 1997.

Sponsler, Claire. *Drama and Resistance: Bodies, Goods, and Theatricality in Late Medieval England.* Medieval Cultures 10. Minneapolis: University of Minnesota Press, 1997.

Stacey, Robert C. "The Conversion of the Jews to Christianity in Thirteenth-Century England." *Speculum* 67, no. 2 (1992): 263–83.

———. "Crusades, Martyrdoms and the Jews of Norman England, 1096–1190." In *Juden und Christen zur Zeit der Kreuzzüge*, edited by Alfred Haverkemp, 233–51. Vorträge und Forschungen 47. Sigmaringen: Jan Thorbecke Verlag, 1999.

———. "The English Jews under Henry III." In *Jews in Medieval Britain: Historical, Literary and Archaeological Perspectives*, edited by Patricia Skinner, 41–54. Woodbridge: The Boydell Press, 2003.

———. "Jews and Christians in Twelfth-Century England: Some Dynamics of a Changing Relationship." In *Jews and Christians in Twelfth-Century Europe*, edited by Michael Signer and John van Engen, 340–54. Notre Dame: University of Notre Dame Press, 2001.

Stallybrass, Peter. "'Drunk with the cup of liberty': Robin Hood, the Carnivalesque, and the Rhetoric of Violence in Early Modern England." In Knight 1999, 297–327.

Stenton, Frank M. *Anglo-Saxon England.* Oxford: Clarendon Press, 1947.

Stephens, Meic, comp. and ed. *The New Companion to the Literature of Wales.* Cardiff: University of Wales Press, 1998.

Stone, Carole. "Anti-Semitism in the Miracle Tales of the Virgin." *Medieval Encounters* 5, no. 3 (1999): 364–374.

Stow, Kenneth. *Alienated Minority: The Jews of Medieval Latin Europe.* Cambridge: Harvard University Press, 1992.

Summerson, H. R. T. "The Structure of Law Enforcement in Thirteenth Century England." *The American Journal of Legal History* 23, no. 4 (1979): 313–27.

Suppe, Frederick C. *Military Institutions on the Welsh Marches: Shropshire, A. D. 1066–1300.* Studies in Celtic History 14. Woodbridge: Boydell Press, 1994.

Tardif, Richard. "The 'Mistery' of Robin Hood: A New Social Context for the Texts." In Knight 1999, 345–361.

Thomas, Keith. *Religion and the Decline of Magic.* New York: Scribner, 1971.

Thompson, Kimberly A. "The Late Medieval Robin Hood: Good Yeomanry and Bad Performances." In *Images of Robin Hood: Medieval to Modern*, edited by Lois Potter and Joshua Calhoun, 102–10. Newark: University of Delaware Press, 2000).

———. "Money and the Man: Economics and Identity in Late Medieval English Literature." Ph.D. diss., The Ohio State University, 2007.

Thrupp, Sylvia L. *The Merchant Class of Medieval London.* Ann Arbor: The University of Michigan Press, 1948; repr. 1962.

Trachtenberg, Joshua. *Jewish Magic and Superstition: A Study in Folk Religion.* Philadelphia: Behrman's Jewish Book House, 1939.

Tryon, Ruth Wilson. "Miracles of Our Lady in Middle English Verse." *PMLA* 38, no. 2 (1923): 308–388.

Turner, Ralph V. *Magna Carta: Through the Ages.* Harlow: Longman, 2003.

Van Houts, Elisabeth. "Hereward and Flanders." *Anglo-Saxon England* 28 (1999): 201–23.

Veldhoen, Bart. "Psychology and the Middle English Romances: Preliminaries to Readings of *Sir Gawain and the Green Knight, Sir Orfeo*, and *Sir Launfal*." In *Companion to Middle English Romance*, edited by Henk Aertsen and Alasdair A. MacDonald, 101–28. Amsterdam: VU University Press, 1990.

Vickers, K. H. *Humphrey, Duke of Gloucester: A Biography*. London: Archibald Constable and Company, 1907.

Walker, Garthine. *Crime, Gender, and Social Order in Early Modern England*. Cambridge: Cambridge University Press, 2003.

Ward, H. L. D., and J. A. Herbert. *Catalogue of Romances in the Department of Manuscripts in the British Museum*. 3 vols. London: Trustees of the British Museum, 1883.

Watt, J. A. "The Jews, the Law and the Church: The Concept of Jewish Serfdom in Thirteenth-Century England." In *The Church and Sovereignty c. 590–1918: Essays in Honour of Michael Wilks*, edited by Diana Wood, 153–72. Oxford: B. Blackwell, 1991.

White, Hayden. *The Content of the Form: Narrative Discourse and Historical Representation*. Baltimore: Johns Hopkins University Press, 1987.

———. *Metahistory: The Historical Imagination in Nineteenth Century Europe*. Baltimore: Johns Hopkins University Press, 1973.

———. *Tropics of Discourse: Essays in Cultural Criticism*. Baltimore: Johns Hopkins University Press, 1978.

White, Paul Whitfield. "Holy Robin Hood! Carnival, Parish Guilds, and the Outlaw Tradition." In *Tudor Drama Before Shakespeare, 1485–1590: New Directions for Research, Criticism, and Pedagogy*, edited by Lloyd Edward Kermode, Jason Scott-Warren, and Martine van Elk, 67–89. New York: Palgrave, 2004.

Wiles, David. *The Early Plays of Robin Hood*. Cambridge: D. S. Brewer, 1981.

———. "Robin Hood as Summer Lord." In Knight 1999, 77–98.

Williams, Gwyn A. *Medieval London: From Commune to Capital*. London: Athlone Press, 1963.

Williams, Robert. *Enwogion Cymru: A Biographical Dictionary of Eminent Welshmen*. Llandovery: William Rees, 1852.

Wolffe, Bertram. *Henry VI*. 2nd ed. New Haven: Yale University Press, 2001.

Wolfthal, Diane. "The Wandering Jew: Some Medieval and Renaissance Depictions." In *A Tribute to Lotte Brand Philip*, edited by William W. Clark, et al., 217–27. New York: Abaris Press, 1985.

Young, Charles R. *The Royal Forests of Medieval England*. Philadelphia: University of Pennsylvania Press, 1979.

Yuval, Israel Jacob. "Jewish Messianic Expectations Towards 1240 and Christian Reactions." In *Toward the Millennium: Messianic Expectations from the Bible to Waco*, edited by Peter Schäfer and Mark R. Cohen, 105–21. Leiden: Brill, 1998.

———. *Two Nations in Your Womb: Perceptions of Jews and Christians in Late Antiquity and the Middle Ages*. Berkeley: University of California Press, 2006.

Žižek, Slavoj. *The Plague of Fantasies*. New York: Verso, 1997.

———. *The Sublime Object of Ideology*. New York: Verso, 1989.

About the Contributors

Kathryn Bedford is a doctoral student in the Department of History at Durham University. Her research interests include the transformation of historical individuals into literary characters, and medieval popular perceptions of the past.

Jennifer Brewer has a B.A. in history and classics from McMaster University, and an M.A. in medieval history from the University of Toronto's Centre for Medieval Studies in 1998. She is writing her doctoral dissertation, "Bearing the Wolf's Head: Outlawry in Yorkshire 1280–1305," while working as an adult education teacher for the Toronto District School Board.

Michelle M. Butler specializes in the study of audience address in medieval and Renaissance English drama. She has also directed and produced performances of medieval and early modern drama, such as *Mankind*, *The Knight of the Burning Pestle*, and *The Second Shepherds' Play*.

Antha Cotten-Spreckelmeyer holds a Ph.D. in English from the University of Kansas, where she is associate director of the Humanities and Western Civilization Program. She teaches and researches in Old and Middle English literature and world literature of the Middle Ages.

Mica Dawn Gould is an assistant professor of English at Grambling State University. She is a specialist in Middle English language and literature. Her research and teaching interests include Welsh literature, medieval romance, and history of the English language.

Barbara A. Hanawalt is the George III Professor of British History, emerita, of Ohio State University. She has published *Crime and Conflict in English Communities, 1300–1348*; *The Ties That Bound: Peasant Families in Medieval England*; *Growing Up in Medieval London: The Experience of Childhood in History*; *"Of Good and Ill Repute": Gender and Social Control in Medieval England*; and *The Wealth of Wives: Women, Law, and the Economy in Late Medieval London*. She is writing a book on civic ceremonial in medieval London.

Alexander L. Kaufman is an associate professor of English at Auburn University at Montgomery. He regularly teaches classes on medieval outlaws, Arthuriana, Chaucer, and history of the English language. He is the author of *The Historical Literature of the Jack Cade Rebellion*.

Crystal Kirgiss is a Ph.D. candidate at Purdue University. Her research interests include Middle English romances, literary representations of youth in the Middle Ages, and contemporary young adult fantasy fiction. She is the founder of the C. S. Lewis Society at Purdue.

Mark Leahy is a Ph.D. candidate at Purdue University, where he teaches writing and literature. He specializes in nineteenth-century blackface minstrelsy and humor studies. He lives in Lafayette, Indiana.

Kate McGrath earned her Ph.D. in history from Emory University in 2007 and is an assistant professor at Central Connecticut State University. Her research interests focus on the study of the rhetoric of anger and emotions in ecclesiastical histories in England from the eleventh to the thirteenth century. She participated in the 2010 NEH summer institute "Representations of the 'Other': Jews in Medieval Christendom."

Catherine A. Rock is an assistant professor of English at Stark State College. She is co-chair of the Ohio Medieval Colloquium. She is the author of "Forsworn and Fordone: Arcite as Oath-Breaker in the *Knight's Tale*," in *Chaucer Review*, 2006. She is particularly interested in Middle English and Anglo-Norman romance, Chaucer, and the Ludlow Scribe of MS Harley 2253.

Kimberly A. Macuare Thompson is the English Department chair at Colegio Internacional de Carabobo in Venezuela. She earned her Ph.D. in English from Ohio State University in 2007. Her research centers on the intersection of economic and literary discourses in medieval culture, especially in medieval romance. She has published on Robin Hood and is writing a book tentatively titled *Money and the Man: Economics and Identity in Late Medieval English Romance*.

Index

Aaij, Michel ix
Abraham the Jew 15
Abulafia, Anna Sapir 15
Act of Union (1536) 116, 123
The Acts and Deeds of Sir William Wallace 156
Adam Bell, Clim of the Clough, and William of Cloudesley 4, 114
Agincourt 57
Agnes (daughter of Searle) 33, 37
Agnes of Ferlington (wife of Aylmer) 31, 37, 39
Ahasuerus 21
Alice (daughter of Bylla) 38
Alice (daughter of Tassard) 38
Alice (wife of Henry) 34; *see also* Henry (son of Matilda)
Alice of Demild 34
Aliscans 90
Alveston 89
American Revolution 119
Ankersmit, F. R. 160
Ansterford 37
Antioch 73
Antwerp 5
Archbishop of Canterbury 81
Arcite 70–71
Arthur, King 69–70, 86, 144, 153, 190
Athelstan, King 73
Aunflor of Orkney (king) 79
The Awntyrs off Arthure 69–71
Aylmer of Ferlington 31, 37

Baker, Donald C. 219
Bakhtin, Mikhail 207
Ball, John 50, 56
Banks, Sir Joseph 120
Baraz, Daniel 13
Barbary 78, 82, 91, 101
Barbary, King of 83

Barczewski, Stephane 119
Barnesdale 211
Barrons' Revolt (1212–15) 105
Barrons' Revolt (1263–65) 52, 110
Bashall Eaves 33–34, 37, 39
Battle of Halidon Hill 159
Bayless, Martha 14–15
Beaufort, Cardinal 57–59
Bedford, Duke of 57
Bellamy, John 160
Benecke, Ingrid 75
Beowulf 6, 133, 135–37, 140
Bergen, Patrick 165
Bernheimer, Richard 141
Bevis of Hampton 84, 109
Bishop of Carlisle 20
Bishop Oliver of Lincoln 16
Black Death 184
Blauncheville 74–75
Boberon, Agnes 35–36
Boberon, Thomas 35
Bocerthur, John 31
Bodleian Library 58
Boke of Nurture (Russell) 50–51
Bolingbroke, Roger 58–60
Bonnie and Clyde 179
Boroughbridge 32
Borrow, George 117, 121, 125–27
Boulmer 31, 35–36
Boulogne 111
Bower, Walter 166–67, 176, 230–31
Brabant, Duke of 57
Bramham 34
Brandin, Louis 68, 80, 88–90, 98
Brecon 116
Breizmann, Natalia 80
Brunesford 34
Buchanan, James Given 37
Burgess, Glyn 75, 81–82, 99, 110
Burton-on-Trent 12

253

Busby, Keith 233
Butler, Judith 199

Cain 21
Calin, William 72
Call, Richard 5
Calvinist Methodist denomination 118
Camelot 71
Canterbury Tales (Chaucer) 2, 12, 70
Carmarthen Jack 123
Carthage, Duke of 79, 82–83, 90, 101
Cassio Dio 134
Cecilia of Kirk Bramwith 32, 36, 40 *see also* Richard of Kirk Bramwith
Cellarer, Adam 55
Cellarer, John 55–56
Cellarer, Richard 55
Cellarer, Thomas 55
Cellarer, William 56
Cellarer family 55–56, 62
Chaucer, Geoffrey 2, 185; *Canterbury Tales* 2, 12, 70; *Knight's Tale* 69–71; *Prioress' Tale* 2, 12
Child, Francis James 155
Chism, Christine 187
Christ 12–13, 16, 18, 20–21, 166–67, 170–71, 235
"The Christian's Surety" 173–75
Christ's Church (London) 60
Chronica Majora (Paris) 11–27
Clawson, William Hill 147, 155
Clement 198–99
Cobham, Eleanor 3, 46, 50–51, 56–62
Colebrant 73
The Comical Adventures of Twm Shon Catty (Prichard) 4, 114–130
Connery, Sean 165
Copin (Jew of Lincoln) 14, 16
Copland, William 5
Corineus 83
Cornhill (London) 62
Costner, Kevin 165, 175
Council of the Clergy and Barons 17
Count Jonas 73
Count of Bologne 87
Coupland, Sir Reginald 121
Crane, Susan 54, 81, 84–85
Crassus 19

David ap Madog ap Howel Moethau 115
Deacon, W. F. ("The Welsh Rob Roy") 117, 120
de Bracton, Henry 29; *see also Legibus et Consuetudinibus Angliae*

de Bracy, Audulf 77
de Brubyl, Pieres 77–78, 80–81, 85
de Burgh, Hubert 102
de Caus, Mahaud (Matilda) 81, 90, 100, 109
de Cornwall, Richard 53
de Dammartin, Renaud (count of Boulogne) 111
de Dynan Joce 74, 90
The Deeds of Hereward (*Gesta Herewardi*) 86, 134, 137, 156
de France, Marie 107
de la Bruere, Marioun 82, 87–88
de la Grene, Matilda 31
de la Lee, Richard 160
del Ferry, Cristancia 33, 37–38
del Ferry, William 33, 37
de Lyls, Ernalt 77, 82, 88
Demild, Alice 36
de Monte de Russie, Mador 101, 106
de Montfort, Simon 52–54
Denise (mother of Ralph son of Geoffrey) 49
Denning, Sybil 31, 36
de Powys, Morys 75, 100–102
de Rapaigne, Johan (John) 77, 100, 105–106
de Troyes, Chrétien 107
de Orleton, Adam (bishop of Hereford and Worcester) 99, 110
Devereux, Lady 126
Devereux, Sir George 4, 114, 126
The Devil 107
Devon 228
de Wincle, John 17
Dives and Pauper 233
Dobson, R. B. 184
Dr. Faustus 87
Domesday Book 55
Don Quixote 90
Doncaster 37
Draper, Robert 160
Duchess of Cartage 83
Duffy, Eamon 175
Dwnn, Lewys 115
Dynan 74, 77, 79, 82

Eadmer 171
East Anglia 220
Edward I 4
Edward II 110, 159
Edward III 55–56, 58, 148, 158–60, 209
Edward IV 148, 159–60
Elias, Norbert 47, 51, 62

Elizabeth I 4, 112, 116
Elwes, Cary 165
Emily 70–71
Emma of Salfordthure 34, 36; *see also* Matilda of Salfordthure
Engels, Friedrich 154
Ergmur, Robert 35
Eton Socon 49
Eustache the Monk 3, 87, 105–107, 232–33
Eustache the Monk (*Li Romans de Witasse le Moine*) 86–87, 97, 105–7, 156, 233
Evans, Gwynfor 123

Fairbanks, Douglas 165
Federles, Agnes 36
Federles, William 36
Felice 72
Felix Bulla 134
Field, Rosalind 73
Fielding, Henry 124
Flanders 160
Fletcher, J. Kyrle 114–15, 117
Floria (wife of Abraham the Jew) 15
Flynn, Errol 165, 175
Folville gang 102
Fouke le Fitz Waryn 3–4, 67–113, 156
France 52, 101, 105, 111
Francis, Elizabeth A. 89–90
French Revolution 119
Friar Tuck 221
Frye, Northrop 150

Galeron, Sir 70
Galt, Alice 34
Galt, Radulf 34
Gamelyn 86
Gardener, Richard 160
Gawain 70–72, 85, 153
Geoffrey of Monmouth 76
Geomagog 75–76, 83
Geremek, Bronislaw 141
Germany 73
A Gest of Robyn Hode 5–6, 86, 135–36, 138, 142, 146–64, 169–70, 172, 174–75, 180, 187–95, 205, 211–13, 215, 225–27
Gilling 31–32, 38
Godwin, Earl 134
Goebel, Julius 134
Gog and Magog 75–76
Graef, Hilda 171
Grammar (Rhys) 116
Graspacre-Hall 125
Green, Richard Firth ix, 56, 68
Green Chapel 71–72

Green Knight 71–72
Greenberg, David 181
Greenfield, Stanley 135, 137
Greenwich (London) 62
Grendel 133, 136–38, 141, 143
Grunne, Jordan 28
Grunne, Juliana (wife) 28, 37
Grunne, Juliana (daughter) 28–29, 31
Grunne, William 28
Guenevere 69–70
Gui de Warewic 72–74, 109
Guines 159
Guy of Gisborne 140–41, 185–87, 224–26
Gwenny Cadwagan 124

Hahn, Thomas ix
Halifax 37
Hall, Edward 197
Hanawalt, Barbara A. 30, 32, 38, 40, 47, 133, 232
Hanse 52
Harewood 33
Harry Potter 144
Harsyk, Sir Geoffrey 197
Harty, Kevin J. ix
Hathaway, E. J. 68, 87, 89, 98, 110
Havelok the Dane 8
Hawyse (mother of Fouke III) 103
Hebrew 13–14
Hegel, G. W. F. 153
Henry II 74, 84, 89, 104
Henry III 12, 16–21, 52–53, 85, 109
Henry IV 56
Henry V 57
Henry VI 57–59, 233
Henry VIII 116, 197–98, 205
Henry (son of Matilda) 33–34; *see also* Alice (wife of Henry); Isabella (daughter of Henry)
Heorot 137–38, 141
Hepworth, David ix
Heralt 72–73
Hereford 89
Hereward the Wake 1, 6, 86, 137–38, 141, 232
The Hermit and the Outlaw 233
Herolt, Johann 171–73
Hilton, R. H. 204–9
History of Cardiganshire 117
History of William Marshall 97
Hobbe the Robber 50
Hobsbawm, Eric 2
Hoccleve, Thomas 159

Holderness 55
Holmes, Urban T. 84
Holt, J. C. 155, 204–10
Home, John (Hunne) 58
Homer 120
Honeydon 49
"How the Goof Wijf Tauȝte Hir Douȝtir" 60
Hrothgar 136–37
Humphrey of Gloucester, Duke 3, 46, 50–51, 56–59
Humphries, Drew 181
Hundred Years' War 157
Hunter, Joseph 159

Idonea of Malebures 35
Inco Evans 125, 126
The Inn-Keeper's Album 117
Innocent III (pope) 20
Ireland 76
Isabella (daughter of Henry) 33–34, 37, 39; *see also* Henry (son of Matilda)
Isabella (queen) 110
Isle of Man 60
Isorie (sister of King Messobryn) 82
Italy 52
Ivanhoe (Scott) 119

Jack Cade's Rebellion 184, 233
Jacobs, Joseph 12
Jacqueline (countess of Hainault and Holland) 57–58
James, Jesse 179
Jameson, Fredric 149–150, 153, 158
Jesus Christ *see* Christ
Jews 11–27, 53
Joan of Navarre 58
John (king) 67, 74–81, 83–85, 87, 97, 100, 103–110
John of Ferlington 31
John of Lexington 16
John of Nemle 32
John, Thomas *see* Twm Siôn Cati
Johnson, W. 18
Johnston, Alexandra F. 7, 227–28, 231
Jonas of Powys 89
Jones, Catherine 115
Jones, Joan 115, 121
Jones, Theophilus 117
Jones, Timothy 110, 134
Jones, Thomas *see* Twm Siôn Cati
Jourdain, Margery (the "Witch of Eye") 58, 59
Judaism 14–15

Juliana of Donham 38; *see also* Robert of Donham
Jurnin 18
Justice, Stephen 54

Kahn, Hilary 181
Kane, Stuart 140, 186–87
Keen, Maurice 1–2, 86–87, 105, 108–9, 133–34, 137, 183, 206–7, 210, 213
Kelly, Thomas E. 87, 233
Kemp-Welch, Alice 90
Kent 57
Kevelson, Roberta 134–35
Kiggelay, Agnes 35–36
"King and the Subject" 155, 159
King Edward and the Hermit 159
King Edward and the Shepherd 159
King's Head (London) 58
Kirklees Abbey 146
Knight, Stephen ix, 5, 80, 119, 146, 159, 183, 190, 219, 220
Knight's Tale (Chaucer) 69–71
Kristeva, Julia 207

La Plesaunce 58
"The Lament of the Countess of Gloucester" 58, 60–62
Langland, William 50
Langmuir, Gavin I. 12, 16
le Barkerm Richard 37
le Cupere, Richard 37
le Despenser, Hugh 53
Lee, Alvin 142
Lee, Sir Richard (mayor of London) 160
le Fitz Waryn, Fouke (Fouke II) 104
le Fitz Waryn, Fouke (Fouke III) 1, 67–113, 232; "Amys del Boys" (alias) 78; "Maryn le Perdu de Fraunce" (alias) 78
le Fitz Waryn, Fouke (Fouke IV) 68, 84–85
le Fitz Waryn, Fouke (Fouke V) 84–85
le Fitz Waryn, Fouke (Fouke VI) 89–90
le Fullar, Annabella 37–38
le Fullar, John 37
le Fullar, William 37
Legge, M. Dominica 73–74, 82–83, 90
Legibus et Consuetudinibus Angliae (de Bracton) 29–30, 35–37
Leland, John 67–69, 88, 90–91, 98, 108, 110
Lewes 109
Lincoln 11–27
Lincoln Cathedral 16
Lincoln Tower 17, 19

Lincolnshire 6
Little John 136, 139, 143, 146, 154–58, 168, 172, 174, 184, 187, 193–96, 211, 221–27; "Reynolde Grenelefe" (alias) 158
Little St. Hugh of Lincoln 11–14
Llandovery Fair 127
Llywelyn (prince) 101, 104
London 5, 13, 46, 51, 53–54, 56, 62, 117, 152, 212; *see also* London Bridge; Christ's Church; Cornhill; Greenwich; King's Head; St. Michael in Cornhill; St. Paul's Cathedral; Tower of London; Westminster
London Bridge 53
London chronicles 160
Louis IX 18
Ludlow 3, 67
Ludlow scribe/poet 68, 85, 89, 91, 98
Lundgren, Timothy 134
Luxford, Julian M. 4–5
Lydgate, John 58

Mador 105
Magna Carta 52, 75, 80
Maid Marian 87, 176, 221
Maid Marian (Peacock) 119
Mankind 7
manuscripts: Cambridge University Library MS E.e.4.35 5; Cambridge University Library MS Ff.5.48 5; Cardiff City Library, Tonn MS 116; Eaton College MS 213 4; Kew, National Archives JUST 1 1089 3, 28–44; London, British Library MS Harley 2253 67, 68, 85; London, British Library MS Royal 12.C.XII 67–68, 88–89
Marmaduke Graspacre 125
Marshall John 7
Marx, Karl 154
Mary, Virgin 6, 15, 152, 165–78, 213, 234
Mass 143, 165–67, 231
Matheson, Lister M. 5
Matilda of Brite 31
Matilda of Salfordthure 34; *see also* Emma of Salfordthure
Matthew Paris 2, 11–27
May games 7, 208
Meaux, abbey of 55
Mcisel, Janet 99, 103
Menache, Sophia 19
"The Merchant's Surety" 173–75
Mercy 223–25, 235
Merlin 76
Merthyr Rising (1831) 118

Messobryn, King 82; *see also* Isorie (sister of King Messobryn)
Middleton 31
Minot, Laurence 159
Mischief 7, 219–38
Morgan, Gerald 116–17, 118, 123
Morley 31, 37
Morris Greeg (Grug) 124
Morris, Jan 128
Mortimer, Roger 110
Mother Theresa 215
Much the Miller's Son 172, 221–23

Nagy, Joseph 206–8
Napoleon Bonaparte 118
Newton, Sir Isaac 120
Norfolk 197–98, 232
Norman Conquest 74, 134, 137, 211
Normandy 103
Norwich 18
Nottingham 209, 223–24

Octavian 188, 198
Ohlgren, Thomas H. ix, 5, 149–50, 152, 154, 158–59, 175, 205, 210, 212–13, 215, 219
Old Norse–Old Icelandic Sagas 108
Ordinance of Laborers (1349) 209
Orkney 101
Ormrod, W. M. 159
Osborn, Marijane 81
Osgoldcross 31
Otun de Pavie, Duke 73
The Outlaw's Song of Trailbaston 85

Painter, Sidney 80, 85, 98, 102
Palamon 70–71
Paris, Matthew 2, 11–27
Parker, Martin 205
Passelewe, Simon 17
Paston, Margery 5
Peasants' Revolt of 1381 52–54, 184, 205, 233
Pensom, Roger 77, 108
Peverel, Payn 75–76, 83, 104
Peverel, William 89
Philip Augustus (king of France) 77–78, 90, 101, 103
Philip of Burgundy, Duke 57
Philip of Reading 20
Philip (son of Roger Golde) 49–50
Phillips, Helen ix
Piers Plowman (Langland) 48, 50, 87, 146, 220, 231–32

Pikehead, William 33, 37
Pilkington, Gilbert 5
Pollard, A. J. 195–96
Pontefract 31, 35
Pontius Pilate 13
Pope, Alexander 120
Potter, Lois ix, 7
Powell, Justice 127
Presdee, Mike 181
Price, Sir John 115
Prichard, Rhys 121
Prideaux, W. F. 84, 88
Prioress' Tale (Chaucer) 2, 12
Prosperity Gospel 165–78
Protestantism 176
Pynson, Richard 5

Ralph of Coggeshall 105
Ralph son of Geoffrey 49
Randolf Earl of Chester 87
Rasur, Agnes 32, 35–36
Records of Early English Drama (REED) 7, 220, 228
Rees, D. C. 115
Regiment of Princes (Hoccleve) 159
Reinbrun 72
Reynolds, Brian 183
Rhys, Sion Dafydd 116, 121
Richard I 3, 30, 75, 100, 165
Richard II 54
Richard at the Lee, Sir 146, 149, 154–57, 160, 170, 187–92, 194, 211, 215
Richard of Cornwall 19
Richard of Kirk Bramwith 32, 40; see also Cecilia of Kirk Bramwith
Richard son of Gervase 37
Ricketts, P. T. 68
Rider, John 35
Risden, Edward L. ix
Ritson, Joseph 119
Robert, Earl of Cornwall 17
Robert of Donham 38
Robert of Ergmur 32
Robert of Leathly 33, 37
Robert son of Inette 33
Robin et Marion 146
Robin Hood 3–5, 45–51, 56, 67, 87, 103, 119–20, 127–128, 131–238
Robin Hood and Guy of Gisborne 140–41, 143, 180, 185–87, 193, 211, 222, 224–26
Robin Hood and the Monk 5, 136, 138–39, 142–43, 157, 167–68, 180, 192–95, 223–26
Robin Hood and the Potter 5, 138–40, 167–70, 180–81, 223–27

Robin Hood of Wakefield 159
"Robin Hood: To a Friend" (Keats) 119
Robson, C. A. 68
Robyn Hod and the Shryff off Notyngham 186, 222, 226
Roger of Powys 89
Roger of Wendover 105
Rondulf of Cestre 76
Rosenberg, Bruce 133
Ross, David 108
Round Table 69–70
Rudde, Agnes 33, 37, 39
Rudde, Radulf 33, 37
Russell, John 50

Sabbath 14
St. Albans 11
St. Anselm 170–71
St. Augustine 19–20
St. Benedict 13
St. Clement's Day 17
St. Mary's Abbey (York) 157
St. Michael in Cornhill (London) 60
St. Paul 14
St. Paul's Cathedral (London) 53, 59–60
St. Peter and Paul Festival 12
St. William of Norwich 17–18
Saracen King 101–2, 107
Scala, Elizabeth 71
Seacroft 28
The Seafarer 6, 133, 135, 138–39, 143–44
Septimius Severus 134
Sheriff of Nottingham 103, 138–41, 149, 158, 211, 216, 222–24, 227
Short Metrical Chronicle 89
Shropshire 68, 97–98, 100, 108
Simon of Eastwick 28
Singman, Jeffrey L. 167, 182
Sir Amadace 188–89, 191, 198
Sir Gawain and the Green Knight 69, 71–72, 85–86
Skyrack 28, 33
Spain 101, 108
Spearing, A. C. 70
Sponsler, Claire 187, 190
Spraggs, Gillian 134
Squire Graspacre 123–25
Stacey, Robert C. 20
Staincliffe 33
Stallybrass, Peter 206–8, 230, 234
Stanley Abbey 102
Statute of Laborers (1351) 55, 209
Statute of Winchester (1285) 50
Stephen (king) 17

Stephenson, G. 89–90
Stevenson, Josephus 81
Steybain, Thomas 33, 37
Stoke, Margery 31, 36
Strafforth 34–35
Sweden 101

The Tale of Gamelyn 4, 86, 114
Tardiff, Richard 206, 208–10, 212
Taylor, J. 184
Thames River 53
Theseus 70–71
Thomas Siôn Dafydd *see* Twm Siôn Cati
Titivillus 226, 228–29, 235
"Tomshone Catty's Tricks" (Ross) 117
Tower of London 53
Treaty of Troyes (1429) 57
Tregaron 115, 125
Trenekyrtle, Emma 31–32
Trunfield 31
Twm Siôn Cati (Thomas Jones, Thomas John, Thomas Siôn Dafydd) 4, 114–130

Underhill, Evelyn 173
Upper Claro 33–34, 37

Virgil, Polydore 160
Virgin Mary *see* Mary, Virgin

Wale, John 37
Wale, Matilda 37
Wales 4, 67–130
Walsall 231
Walter, Matilda 103
Walter, Theobald 103
The Wanderer 6, 133, 135, 138–39, 141–44
Wandering Jew 20–21

Wars of the Roses 160
Waryn, Garin 88
Wasson, John M. 228
Watt 126
Waverley 12
Welsh Marches 97, 102
Wentbridge 157
Westminster Abbey 59
Westminster (London) 53, 60
White, Edward 5
White, Hayden 147, 151, 153, 156–57
White, Paul Whitfield 230–31, 234
Whitsuntide 7
Whittington 74, 97, 100–2
Wigun, Richard 103
Wiles, David 221, 230–31
Will Scarlett *see* William Scarlock
William I 6, 74–75, 76, 104
William of Barton 35
William of High Ercall 103
William of Newburgh 102
William of Ryther 28
William of Roxton 49
Williams, Karen ix
William Scarlock (Will Scarlett) 172, 221–22
Wilshere, C. A. 68
The Worldlings (New Guise, Nowadays, and Nought) 7, 219–38
Wright, Thomas 68, 84, 98
Wykes, Thomas 53
Wynn, Sir John 117, 121, 124

York 5, 157
Yorkshire 3, 28–44

Žižek, Slavoj 7, 206, 214–16

www.ingramcontent.com/pod-product-compliance
Ingram Content Group UK Ltd.
Pitfield, Milton Keynes, MK11 3LW, UK
UKHW041932140426
5217IPUK00014B/437